D1165543

# THE GARDENS OF THE BRITISH WORKING CLASS

# MARGARET WILLES
# THE GARDENS OF
# ❧ THE BRITISH ❧
# WORKING CLASS

YALE UNIVERSITY PRESS
NEW HAVEN AND LONDON

Published with acknowledgement to the Marc Fitch Fund.

For information about this and other Yale University Press publications, please contact:
U.S. Office: sales.press@yale.edu    www.yalebooks.com
Europe Office: sales@yaleup.co.uk    www.yalebooks.co.uk

Set in Adobe Caslon Pro by IDSUK (DataConnection) Ltd
Printed in Great Britain by TJ International Ltd, Padstow, Cornwall

Library of Congress Cataloging-in-Publication Data

Willes, Margaret.
   The gardens of the British working class / Margaret Willes.
      pages cm
   Includes bibliographical references and index.
   ISBN 978-0-300-18784-7 (alk. paper)
1. Gardens—Great Britain—History. 2. Gardening—Great Britain—History.
3. Working class—Dwellings—Great Britain—History. I. Title.
SB451.36.G7W54 2014
635—dc23
                                                          2013041145

A catalogue record for this book is available from the British Library.

10 9 8 7 6 5 4 3 2 1

# Contents

# Introduction

WHILE WRITING THIS book, I have talked to many people about the areas of my research. Often the response has been 'Do you mean allotments?' I do mean allotments, but much else besides, which I hope will surprise and perhaps change perceptions.

Our image of rural working-class gardens, for instance, has been coloured by the writers and artists of the nineteenth century. In the Regency period, Mary Russell Mitford published a series of sketches of her village, Three Mile Cross in Berkshire. She described her own 'flower-yard' in romantic terms: 'the walls, old and weather-stained, covered with hollyhocks, roses, honey-suckles, and a great apricot tree' and 'full of common flowers, tulips, pinks, larkspurs, peonies, stocks and carnations, with an arbour of privet, not unlike a sentry-box, where one lives in a delicious green light, and looks out over the gayest of all gay flower beds'.[1]

This charming depiction elicited a furious outburst in verse from Tom Hood, beginning 'Our village, that's to say, not Miss Mitford's village, but our village of Bullock's Smithy'. He went on to paint a very different picture:

That's the Doctor's with a green door, where garden pots in the window is seen;
A weakly monthly rose that don't blow, and a dead geranium, and a teaplant with five black leaves and one green.
As for hollyhocks at the cottage doors, and honeysuckles and jasmines, you may go and whistle;
But the Tailor's front garden grows two cabbages, a dock, a ha'porth of penny-royal, two dandelions, and a thistle![2]

The debate continues today, with some writers maintaining that the gardens of agricultural labourers in the nineteenth century were entirely given over to the practical cultivation of vegetables and herbs, and possibly fruit, but no flowers. In Chapter 5, I look at both sides of the argument, using the first-hand accounts of working-class gardeners, including Flora Thompson, whose memories of her childhood in an impoverished community in north Oxfordshire at the end of the century, distilled in *From Lark Rise to Candleford*, have become a classic.

For Victorian urban gardens, it is Charles Dickens who very much sets the scene, colouring them in grim hues. In *Bleak House*, he describes the brickmakers' hovels in St Albans in Hertfordshire, with their 'miserable little gardens before the doors growing nothing but stagnant pools'.[3] The house where Pancks lodged in north London in *Little Dorrit* has a tiny front garden 'where a few of the dustiest leaves hung their dismal heads and led a life of choking'.[4] Up to the 1960s, Britain's cities had indeed been increasingly choked by pollution, which has set generations of gardeners of all classes and situations a severe challenge, but one that has been met with amazing fortitude, determination and often passion. In Chapter 4, I describe the florists – often craftsmen and industrial workers – who bred beautiful flowers in their tiny backyards and on the windowsills of their workshops. In Chapters 6 and 8, I look at floricultural societies founded by working-class gardeners in some of the poorest parts of London, and the fruit and flower shows that proliferated from the middle of the nineteenth century.

The story does not, however, begin in the nineteenth century, but goes back much further, to Tudor times. As the term 'working class' was not used until the 1790s, with the swift development of industrialisation, it is not so easy to categorise these earlier gardeners. The sixteenth-century commentator William Harrison tried to do so, but got confused and fell back onto the capacious phrase, 'the lower orders'. In country areas, they were husbandmen, combining horticulture in their gardens or yards with cultivating strips in common fields and keeping some animals. We get rare glimpses of their lives from writers such as Thomas Tusser and contemporary records. In addition, I have used in Chapter 1 the invaluable resource of the recreated gardens at the Weald and Downland Open Air Museum in Singleton, Sussex. The museum has drawn on careful research in the layout of the gardens and to ensure that the correct varieties of plants are cultivated. For the sixteenth and seventeenth centuries, for example, the museum has looked to the United States for the vegetables that were taken to the New

World by early settlers, but died out in their home country. Although the subject of horticultural history can be beset by lack of information, here the experts have an advantage over other fields of history, as they are using living plants in their recreations. I have drawn not only on the Weald and Downland Museum, but other museums for the later chapters, including miners' gardens at Beamish in County Durham, and a nineteenth-century squatters' cottage at Ironbridge in Shropshire.

Thomas Tusser not only looked at the role of the husbandman in the sixteenth century, but also at the gardening activities of the housewife. He stands out as a pioneer: women gardeners were often passed over in silence by writers, and only really began to emerge from the shadows in the nineteenth century – indeed one twentieth-century commentator expressed surprise at the proportion of women gardeners he discovered in his research. Yet women have made a vital contribution – literally so, for they cultivated plants for the kitchen and for the medicine chest, hence Tom Hood's reference to 'a ha'porth of penny-royal' in his poem. It was such a useful herb that even the smallest garden would make room for it. As one herbalist explained, ''Tis used to provoke the Courses, and to help Delivery. 'Tis good for Coughs, for the Gripes, the Stone, Jaundice and Dropsie. A spoonful of the juice given to Children, is an excellent remedy for the Chin-cough [whooping cough] . . . The fresh Herb wrap'd in a Cloth, and laid in a Bed, drives away Fleas; but it must be renewed once a week.'[5]

Women as medicinal gardeners are described in Chapter 2 and Chapter 13, a reminder that a visit to a doctor and professional advice was for centuries beyond the pocket of most poor households. Only with the establishment of the National Health Service in 1948 did this situation change, although herbs and plants still play an important role in medicines. Women were also employed as members of the gardening establishments of large households, and so feature in Chapters 3 and 7 where I look at gardeners who earned their wages from horticulture. Here, women were employed not only as weeders but in a whole range of other jobs that were nevertheless always lowly.

For their male colleagues, however, gardening could provide a career ladder which brought prosperity and status to some. None rose so high as Joseph Paxton, whose career is reflected in the title of Chapter 7, 'Climbing the Wall', but it has to be remembered that he was the son of an agricultural labourer. Many other working gardeners came from a similar background, learning their trade 'on the job', including experience in nurseries and market gardens.

Some became jobbing gardeners, working for a number of employers. One such man provides the earliest 'voice' of an ordinary gardener. Leonard Wheatcroft, who wrote an autobiography in the second half of the seventeenth century, was a tailor from Ashover in Derbyshire, who also composed poetry alongside his planting of orchards. Two centuries pass before more voices are heard: I have been able to use four diaries from the Victorian period. John Donaldson, from Banff in Scotland, kept a diary as an apprentice gardener charting the very beginning of his career. This personal document went with him when he emigrated to America. William Cresswell's diary, found in a second-hand book market, has helped English Heritage to restore the garden buildings at Audley End in Essex, and recreate the lives of the gardeners there in the 1870s. The diary of Joseph Turrill of Garsington, kept on the pages of two rent books between 1863 and 1867, describes his life as an Oxfordshire market gardener. The pocket diary of Charles Snow, an Oxford stonemason, was rescued by the oral historian Raphael Samuel. Despite its fragile state, and the brevity of the notes, it gives a glimpse of the daily life of a keen gardener in his squatter village at Headington Quarry in the 1880s.

Sometimes the voices can be difficult to decipher. When William Jolly quotes the botanist linen weaver, John Duncan, in his biography, the strong Scottish accent obscures what he is saying, although it also takes the reader back to nineteenth-century rural Aberdeenshire. The same happens with the Cockney, Parky, so named after Victoria Park, which was a very important public garden for the inspiration and education of working-class gardeners in east London. The London accent Charles Dickens gave to Sam Weller in *Pickwick Papers* is echoed by the line 'Oh! it really is a wery pretty garden' in the song 'If It Wasn't for the 'Ouses In-Between' that was a hit in the music halls in the 1890s. Clearer tones then take over with invaluable oral history projects, such as Paul Thompson's 'Family Life and Work Experience before 1918'. This survey, conducted in the 1960s and early 1970s for Essex University, captured the memories of men – and at last, women are heard too – brought up in villages, towns and cities in the years leading up to the First World War.

The value of these first-hand accounts is that they express the thoughts and opinions of people who are rarely named, let alone heard. I have come to see garden history in Britain as rather like an iceberg. This may seem a peculiarly inappropriate analogy, given that ice fields are horticultural deserts, but studies have concentrated on the magnificent, whether as landscapes or as resplendent plantings, and on the owners, the rich and the famous. The gardens of 'ordinary gardeners' are submerged below the water line. The author of an essay on gardening as a recreation pointed out:

> Little has been written about the history of popular gardening in Britain. Historians of the garden have been dazzled by the rare and the beautiful. Whole forests have been felled to feed the appetite for books describing the history and appearance of the handful of prestigious gardens attached predominantly to the nation's stately homes. Our authors guide us lovingly around the parterres, knot gardens, grottoes, lawns and terraces of Chatsworth, Stourhead, Bodnant, Hampton and Hidcote.[6]

Ironically, Hidcote Manor Garden in Gloucestershire does have a place in a book about working-class gardeners, along with that other great twentieth-century garden, Sissinghurst Castle in Kent. Ideas for the layout of some of the compartments of these gardens were inspired by the little plots of cottagers as shown in Chapter 10. Cottagers, moreover, had over the centuries successfully bred old favourites in ideal conditions, acting as a kind of 'gene pool' for plants and flowers that became greatly sought after in the later nineteenth century.

As far back as the seventeenth century, there was a recognition that gardening was a recreation of all levels of society. John Worlidge celebrated this in his *Systema Horti-culturae*, published in 1677:

> Neither is there a noble or pleasant seat in England, but hath its gardens for pleasure and delight; scarce an ingenious citizen that by his confinement to a shop, being denied the priviledge of having a real garden, but hath his boxes, pots, or other receptacles for flowers, plants, &c ... there is scarce a cottage in most of the southern parts of England but hath its proportionable garden, so great a delight do most of men take in it; that they may not only please themselves with the view of the flowers, herbs and trees, as they grow, but furnish them-selves and their neighbours upon extraordinary occasions, as nuptials, feasts, and funerals, with the proper products of their gardens.[7]

This interesting observation is an early manifestation of the concept that England (later Britain) is a nation of gardeners. It also reflects the idea of gardening as a communal activity, a theme that runs right through this book and holds good today, when the distinctions between class have become blurred, as well as a source of fascination to commentators.

I mentioned earlier that gardening, especially for the poorer members of society, has always required fortitude and determination. That the working classes *did* garden to some extent runs counter to logic. The two vital factors are space and time, both of which were severely curtailed for a social class which rarely owned the land they lived on, and had to work long hours to put food on the table. For agricultural labourers it must have been at times a thankless occupation after a long day in the fields. Allotments were sometimes located a considerable distance from their homes, and were of variable soil quality. For miners and factory workers, on the other hand, it could be quite the reverse, a relief after their day's work in confined and noisy surroundings. At times in people's lives, even today with so many aids, gardening is just not feasible, for example for those with young children, or in old age. And some people are simply not interested or have other preoccupations. An old story goes that you could tell a member of the Communist Party by the state of their garden.

Horticulture requires not only physical effort, but aptitude, observation and experience. Generations of families learnt their gardening through

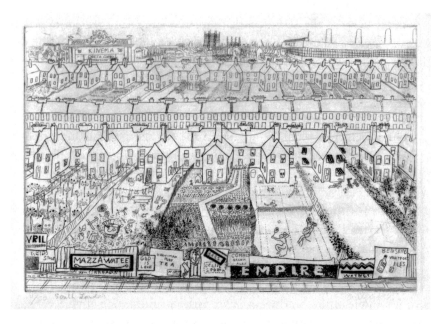

1 An etching by Anthony Gross, showing suburban back gardens in South London in the 1930s. Not every garden is a horticultural paradise.

being taught by their parents and grandparents, and by remembering basic rules through ballads and sayings rather than books, as described in Chapters 2 and 13. They could also learn by observation, by looking at other people's gardens and public parks, as shown in Chapter 8, and by reading the newspapers and magazines that proliferated in the nineteenth century. In the twentieth century many families acquired gardens for the first time with the building of estates across the country. For these novice gardeners books and magazines were invaluable, along with the new media of radio and television, as charted in the final chapters.

If we are indeed a nation of gardeners, then it is important to celebrate the unsung heroes over the centuries, to find their voices and to present the history of all of us. One branch of my ancestors were agricultural labourers from Whittlesea (now Whittlesey), Isle of Ely. Sometime in the 1860s, the Hart family moved down to Hornchurch in Essex with their farm bailiff, presumably in search of a better life, working in a market garden with good access to London. Writing this book has brought me to realise how very difficult their lives must have been for them to have made such a move. I also hope that my rather modest horticultural skills are evidence of what I have inherited from them.

CHAPTER I

# Finer Points of Husbandry

In March 1609 plague struck the village of Upton-by-Southwell near Newark in Nottinghamshire. Upton was by all accounts a typical agricultural community of the period, and the plague, sadly, was an intermittent threat.[1] What is unusual, however, is that the churchwardens' books for the period have survived. As a result, we get a rare glimpse of the inhabitants of the village, and the kind of gardening and husbandry in which they were involved.[2]

Upton, with a population of about 300 to support, was unenclosed at this time, with five great fields, three of which were cultivated in a yearly rotation of wheat, barley and fallow. Strips belonging to the villagers were marked out by stones and pegs. The meadows were used for winter feeding and summer pasture for the villagers' animals. Waste and woodland provided fuel and turf for roofs. A village bull was bought annually from Newark, and the old one was either killed or sold on to avoid inbreeding. A common plough was probably used for ceremonial on Plough Monday and for villagers who could not afford one of their own. The churchwardens undertook the administration of poor relief to residents, drawing on the rates as laid down in the 1601 Poor Law. Some of these monies were derived from beastgate, a charge on the right to graze on the common pasture – twopence per head of cattle, threepence for a score of sheep.

One of the poorest households in Upton was that of a cottager, William Beacocke, scourer of drains and dykes. Sanitation for the village was provided by the Common Issue, an open drain that ran through the main street, into which refuse was poured from all the households. Beacocke lived in a two-roomed cottage with his wife and four children. One room served as the hall, with a table for food and trestles for dressing hemp which was then spun and woven. There is no mention of a bedstead in the records, so the family probably slept on straw paliasses, though they did have pillows and pillow bere cloths. Beacocke was landless, meaning he did not hold strips in the common fields, but had a yard adjoining his cottage, with a 'hovel-house' (sty), a heap of manure, hens, sows and three pigs. In the March outbreak he and his whole family, apart from his wife, died in an epidemic that killed nearly one-third of the population of Upton. Beacocke's possessions at his death were valued at a total of £3 9s 2d.

Another victim of the plague was Gabriel Birch, whose estate in the same valuation was put at £19, more than five times that of Beacocke. Birch held two small strips in the open fields, twenty sheep in common pasture, a heifer, and a sow and two pigs in his yard. He leased his house, which had a store chamber over the parlour, and through his common rights was not entirely dependent on his wages. A third household was that of a husbandman, Thomas Cullen, who died in 1628. His house was much bigger than those of Birch and Beacocke, consisting of ten rooms, three of which were set aside to store grain and food. He probably also had a live-in labourer. He is known as 'Goodman' Cullen in the records, a sign that he was not a tenant farmer, was able to buy his own property and perhaps enclose his strips: in good times, he could become a yeoman farmer. No mention is made of what land he had attached to his house, but his inventory mentions a 'stocke of bees' valued at five shillings. Cullen served at one time as a churchwarden, so may have been able to read and write. As the editor of the records notes, he would have been limited in his travel, perhaps journeying as far as Nottingham.

Although the resources of the three men are very different, they all had land adjoining their dwellings, where they could keep their domestic animals, for husbandry and gardening were inextricably intertwined at this time. The term 'yard' now has a connotation of limited space in Britain, but in North America can still mean a substantial garden. In other records gardens were also known as garths or closes. In 1589 Elizabeth I issued an act requiring new cottages to have at least four acres of land attached. This legislation was primarily intended to restrict the growth of inferior houses that were springing up on the outskirts of London, but it does give an indication of the amount of land considered as adequate to sustain a household. However big the area of the yards of Upton, they would have been used to grow vegetables and fruit, and Cullen's bees needed flowers. The honey taken from the hives would be used for sweetening food and in brewing. Beacocke's meagre possessions included a 'fracket', a leather bottle used for carrying beer while working in the fields, so his yard may have included barley as he had no strips in the common fields. The most educated member of the village community was the vicar. His income was partly derived from tithes, a penny levied on every garden in the village, along with one-tenth of all hay, poultry, eggs, pigs and fruit trees.

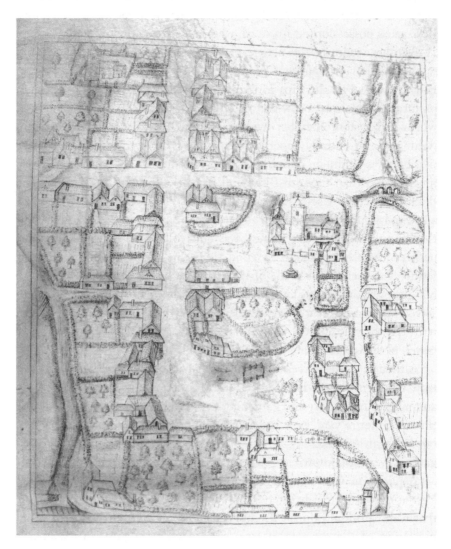

2  A bird's-eye view of Wilton in Wiltshire from a survey of Lord Pembroke's estates made about 1565. Although Wilton was officially a town, its population was similar to many villages, providing a rare image of the gardens of rural communities in Elizabethan England. Vegetable plots, orchards, hedges and fences, including a pound for stray animals, have been depicted.

A bird's-eye drawing of Wilton in Wiltshire contained in a survey of the estates of Lord Pembroke in south-west England, made around the year 1565, gives an idea of what Upton might have looked like. Because a market was held in Wilton, it had the status of a town, but its population was similar to that of villages like Upton. The cottages and houses in Wilton all have their gardens with vegetable plots, orchards, thorn hedges and courtyards for keeping their animals.[3]

When William Harrison wrote his *Description of England*, published in 1577, he devoted one of his chapters to explaining the nation's social hierarchy. 'Of Degrees of People in the Commonwealth of England' starts confidently: 'We in England divide our people commonly into four parts, as gentlemen, citizens or burgesses, yeomen and artificers or labourers'. The villagers at Upton would have fitted into the third and fourth categories, with the wonderful catch-all phrase of 'the lower orders'. The term 'working class' was not coined until the end of the eighteenth century, with the coming of the Industrial Revolution. But even within his chapter Harrison began to waver, noting that yeomen were usually farmers, or 'at leastwise artificers'. Shortly after he ranked all artificers among the fourth and last sort.[4] Craftsmen he found really difficult to categorise, while farmers could be wealthy men, or just owners of smallholdings like Gabriel Birch and Thomas Cullen.

William Harrison had an unusually broad experience of the society of Tudor England. Born the son of a London citizen, probably a merchant venturer, he gained a good education before becoming chaplain to Henry Brooke, Lord Cobham. His patron set him up with a living at Radwinter in Essex, a rural parish, albeit relatively close to London and therefore catering for its markets. Harrison was interested in gardens, and his patron had one of the most famous, at Cobham in Kent. Harrison cultivated his own in Essex, which he described as more than 300 feet in length, containing over 300 plants, 'no one of them being common or usually to be had'.[5]

Harrison tells us relatively little about the gardens of the lower orders. The main thrust of his argument was that things had gone downhill with the civil strife of the fifteenth century, and had only recently been rescued by the arrival of the Tudors on the English throne. Thus he writes:

Such herbs, fruits, and roots also as grow yearly out of the ground of seed have been very plentiful in this, in the time of the first Edward and after his days; but in the process of time they grew also to be neglected, so that from Henry the Fourth till the latter end of Henry the Seventh and beginning of Henry the Eighth there was little or no use of them in England, but they remained either unknown or supposed as food more meet for hogs and savage beasts to feed upon than mankind.

Harrison was delighted to report that with the good times of the sixteenth century, these foodstuffs – 'melons, pompions [pumpkins], gourds, cucumbers, radishes, skirrets [species of water parsnips], parsnips, carrots, cabbages, navews [rape], turnips and all kinds of salad herbs' – were being cultivated again by 'the poor commons'.[6]

Even this brief foray into the vegetables and salads on dinner tables of all levels of society is an exception to most accounts of gardening in England at this period. German travellers arriving in the kingdom in the 1590s, for instance, extolled the wonders of the gardens of the Queen and of the circle that surrounded her. So in order to catch a glimpse of what the gardens of 'ordinary' people might be like, it is necessary to turn to books of husbandry which also covered horticulture. Sir John Fitzherbert's *Boke of Husbandry*, first published in 1533, was based upon classical traditions of writing on estate management, aimed at landowners, although it does contain glimpses of more modest households. Much more pertinent to the common people – both men and women – were the books written by Thomas Tusser. Like William Harrison, Tusser was well educated and had an aristocratic patron, William Paget, but the political upheavals that took place in England in the reign of Edward VI caused him to leave Paget's household and embark on a farming career in Suffolk.

His first manual of husbandry, *A Hundreth Good Pointes of Husbandrie*, first appeared in 1557. This was developed and enlarged five years later, with the addition of 'a hundred good poyntes of huswifery', and further expanded in 1573 as *Five Hundred Pointes of Good Husbandrie, United to as many of Good Huswifery*. Tusser's books were popular and long-lasting, going through eighteen editions between 1557 and 1599, with more appearing in the seventeenth century. Indeed, a copy of 'prime Tusser' is mentioned by the poet John Clare as being part of a cottager's tiny library in the early nineteenth century.

Tusser's books are arranged as a calendar, helping the husbandman through the various months of the year. In his 1573 edition, he shifted the start of the year from August to September as that would be the point when changes of tenure occurred, on 26 September, the feast of St Michael:

At Mihelmas lightly new fermer comes in,
new husbandrie forceth him new to begin.[7]

His books are printed in blackletter, or Gothic, which we would find
difficult to read compared to Roman, but apparently the opposite pertained
in sixteenth-century England. They are written in simple verse, a style that
Sir Walter Scott pointed out was comparable with the old English
proverb, where the rhyme and alliteration made it easier for even the
unlettered to remember the information offered. It is not easy to assess the
level of literacy in Tudor England, but it has been estimated that one-third
of the population in London could neither read nor write, with a higher
proportion in the countryside, and the figures were always higher for
women. Even if they were able to read, comparatively few 'ordinary
gardeners' could have afforded Tusser's books, but they are invaluable in
giving us a glimpse of their way of life.

Tusser is principally concerned with agriculture, ploughing, threshing,
and the care of animals, but interwoven with this is his advice on
gardening, particularly for women. This is a significant departure for,
although women of every level of society below the aristocracy had clearly
been cultivating their gardens for centuries, there is little recognition
of this in books and accounts. Moreover, the role of women gardeners
continued to be largely overlooked in the future, William Lawson's
*Country Housewife's Garden*, published in 1626, being a rare exception.
Tusser, then, could be regarded as a pioneer of feminism. In his 1562
edition of *A Hundreth Good Pointes* he provides 'a digression from
husbandrie: to a point or two of huswifrie':

> Now here I think nedeful, a pawse for to make;
> to treate of some paines, a good huswife must take.
> For huswifes must husbande, as wel as the man:
> or farewel thy husbandrie, do what thou can.
>
> In Marche, and in Aprill, fxrom morning to night:
> in sowing and setting, good huswives delight.
> To have in their gardein, or some other plot:
> to trim up their house, and to furnish their pot.
>
> Have millons [melons] at Mihelmas, parsneps in lent:
> in June, buttred beans, saveth fish to be spent.

With those, and good pottage inough having than:
thou winnest the heart of thy laboring man.[8]

He sets the housewife to work in September, encouraging her:

Wife into thy garden and set me a plot
with strawberry rootes, of the best to be got:
Such growing abroad, among thornes in the wood
wel chosen and picked proove excellent good.[9]

Tusser then advises her to plant gooseberries, raspberries and roses. He often mentions a combination of 'respis' (raspberries) with roses, echoing their planting at Lyveden New Bield in Northamptonshire by Sir Thomas Tresham in the 1590s. Tresham was a notable and determined Catholic recusant, and is thought to have chosen the combination – red and white flowers, thorns and prickles – as a symbol of Christ's Passion, so Tusser may be harking back to a pre-Reformation custom.

The keeping of bees is included in Tusser's points. He addresses his advice on beekeeping to a 'good conie', or rabbit, a term of endearment for a woman. In September he advises:

Now burn up [smoke out] the bees that ye mind for to drive,
at Midsomer drive them and save them alive:
Place hives in good ayer, set southly and warme,
and take in due season wax, honie and swarme.[10]

William Harrison explains in his description of England how mead was made from honey. He also describes, with a singular lack of enthusiasm, 'swish-swash', a drink 'made also in Essex and divers other places with honeycombs and water, which the homely country wives, putting some pepper and a little other spice among, call mead'.[11]

Tusser instructs his beekeepers to:

Set hive on a plank (not too low by the ground)
Where herbe with the flowers may compas it round:
And bourdes to defend it from north and north-east
From showers and rubbish, from vermin and beast.[12]

Beehives, often known as skeps, were woven from wicker into an inverted basket that could be placed on a flat surface. To protect the wicker from

3 Alfred Watkins photograph taken in the 1880s of bee skeps at Upton Mill in Herefordshire. These are the last known wicker skeps, the traditional beehives that had prevailed for centuries. Hackles of straw would cover each skep, but the one on the right has disintegrated, showing the weaving of the wicker.

damp, an overcoat of straw, known as a hackle, could be added. To encourage the bees, blossom from fruit trees was recommended, along with violet, and herbs such as thyme, marjoram and rosemary.

In November he instructs that the garden should be properly dug over, composted using refuse from the privies and covered with leafmould. The following month he recommends protecting plants from frost, including covering strawberries with straw. The bees too should be protected, given water and a dish of rosemary branches put in the hive. A list of fruit trees and soft fruit to be planted or moved is provided.

But it is in March that he encourages the gardener really to get going, with lists of seeds and herbs for the kitchen, for salads and sauces, to strew in the house, and for window boxes and pots. These cover a wide range of the traditional herbs such as parsley, thyme and rosemary, and also flowers. Thus marigolds, primroses and violets are grown for use in the kitchen. Lavender, roses, violets and daisies are recommended for strewing around and sweetening the house. Window boxes and pots can include columbines, daffodils, eglantine roses, carnations, hollyhocks, snapdragons, pansies and lilies. These lists give us an idea of what the country gardens contained, including some colour and scent. He also specifies root vegetables to boil or to cook in butter.

Echoing Harrison's list, he includes beans, carrots, cabbages, gourds, pompions (pumpkins), parsnips, runcevall (large) peas and turnips.

His advice for the garden dies down during the late spring and summer months, when attention has to be focused on tasks in the fields. But in August he counsels the provident gardener that seeds must be saved, and reminds us that this was a communal life, where shops and suppliers were available only to those with contacts in the larger towns and cities, above all, London:

> Good huswifes in sommer will save their owne seedes
> Against the next yeere, as occasion needs.
> One seede for another, to make an exchange
> With fellowlie neighbourhood seemeth not strange.[13]

An idea of what the gardens of a Tudor or early Stuart agricultural community might have looked like is provided by the Weald and Downland Open Air Museum at Singleton in Sussex. Using Tusser's books, along with other sixteenth-century texts, a garden has been recreated for Bayleaf Farmstead, a yeoman farmer's house dating from the 1540s.[14] Three houses are from the Stuart period: Pendean Farmhouse, a yeoman farmer's house; Walderton, a village house; and Poplar Cottage, a landless labourer's dwelling (Plates I–IV). Although these houses are from southern England, and thus built of different materials from the Upton-by-Southwell dwellings, their gardens would have been similar in style and content. The plot that 'Goodman' Cullen might have had around his ten-roomed farmhouse can be brought to life by looking at the gardens of Bayleaf and Pendean.

Gardens such as these were the province of the woman of the house, while her husband looked after the cultivation of the fields. For the earlier garden at Bayleaf, the fencing is provided by hazel, for the later at Pendean, a quickset hedge with layering of hawthorn and some elder. Most of the area is laid out as beds, narrow enough to reach across, with paths at least a foot wide, and some wider for access with barrows and baskets. Crops like peas and beans would have been cultivated in the fields, leaving the garden for root vegetables like onions, leeks, skirrets and carrots, and leaf vegetables such as beet, collards or worts. Edible weeds, like fat hen, sow thistle and Good King Henry (also known as poor man's asparagus), could be grown between the sown crops to serve as living mulch. All these plants, including the weeds, would provide the basis for pottage, the daily diet of most country dwellers.

As Tusser reminds us, the country housewife would also grow 'gruiting' herbs for flavouring ale, such as yarrow, alecost and germander, and strewing herbs such as tansy and wormwood, which would stop the bugs biting. Tansy was also used in dyeing, producing a range of colours from golden yellow to olive green. Other garden plants that might be used by the house- wife for dyeing cloth included lady's bedstraw and madder for red, agrimony and goldenrod for yellow, and dyer's woad for blue. There was no need for expensive equipment, just a bowl for infusion and a fixative of alum.

The overall impression of these early gardens at the Downland Museum is of green, with occasional flashes of colour, like wildflower meadows. The massed colours that we are familiar with today would have been quite alien, although colour could be provided by utilitarian plants such as crimson-flowered Martock broad beans, or marigolds, used for food colouring and salads as well as for attracting predatory insects like ladybirds to keep down pests. In the mid-seventeenth-century gardens at Pendean and Walderton, some introductions show how plants were beginning to be grown for their decorative value, but even these had their uses; the gallica rose, for instance, would have provided not only colour but scent too, invaluable for a whole range of purposes, including fragrancing homemade soaps and ointments.

Alongside Walderton, a sunken track has been created. This important village feature allowed access between the back lane and the village street, so that animals could be moved around without intruding into the gardens. Gabriel Birch, the labourer at Upton-by-Southwell, would have used such a track to move his sheep and heifer from the common pasture to his strips when they were fallow. The landless labourer William Beacocke and his family must have lived in a dwelling of a similar size as the Weald and Downland Museum's Poplar Cottage. Without strips to cultivate, the household was totally dependent on the garden to produce food and grow herbs for strewing and medicinal purposes. Among the vegetables growing at Poplar Cottage are Carlin peas, a tall variety dating back to the fifteenth century, producing a yellow pea that was dried and ground up to make a kind of flour. But even in the garden of Poplar colour has not entirely been banished, with aquilegia, foxgloves, willow herb and of course the versatile marigold.

Poplar Cottage's garden looks delightful, but it is important to remember that the poorest families like the Beacockes led a precarious existence. The fate of William's wife, with her entire immediate family dead from the plague, is not recorded. Having lost the modest wage earned by her husband, she probably could not afford to pay the rent on her home, thus losing her means of survival from the food grown in the garden and the little holding of hens and pigs. This is a vivid example of how the garden represented the vital lifeline for thousands of late sixteenth- and early seventeenth-century rural households.

* * *

The first printed book in the English language that refers to gardening in the title was Thomas Hill's *Most Briefe and pleasaunt treatyse, teachynge howe to dress, sowe, and set a garden*. This little volume probably first appeared in London in 1560, but ran to nine editions. On the title page Hill described himself as a Londoner, and later claimed to have been 'always rudely taughte, amonge the Smythes of Vulcanus'.[15] Despite this show of diffidence, Hill had been taught Latin and Italian, translating popular works on science and the supernatural, and in his later gardening books he constantly quoted the writings of classical authors such as Columella and Varro. In *A Most Briefe and pleasuant treatyse* Hill explains that his intent 'is to please the common sort, for whose onelye sake, I have taken these paines and have published this Booke'. The modest format and the many editions suggest that his readership is indeed 'the common sort', particularly those who lived in cities and towns.

This was the period when London was undergoing a population explosion, moving from an estimated 50,000 in 1500, and 70,000 in 1550, to 200,000 by 1600, so that land for gardens came increasingly under pressure. The dissolution of religious houses in the 1530s had released open spaces within the central part of the city, but these were usually snapped up by the rich and powerful. Henry VIII's chief minister, Thomas Cromwell, went even further. Having acquired the property of the Augustinian priory in Old Broad Street, he decided to extend the garden by impounding sections of those of his neighbours. John Stow in his survey of London records with indignation how his father's garden was encroached upon: 'having some reasonable plot of land left for a garden, he [Cromwell] caused the pales adjoining the north part thereof on a sudden to be taken down; twenty-two feet to be measured forthright into the north of every man's ground; a line there to be drawn, a trench to be cast, a foundation laid and a high brick wall to be built'.[16] If Stow's father, a member of the Company of Tallow Chandlers, was unable to stop encroachment, one of the 'poorer sort' would have stood no chance of holding onto his garden as pressure was applied.

# YBP Library Services

WILLES, MARGARET.

GARDENS OF THE BRITISH WORKING CLASS.

Cloth     413 P.
LONDON: YALE UNIVERSITY PRESS, 2014


CULTURAL HIST. OF WORKING CLASS GARDENING SINCE
16TH CENT. W/ILLUS. & COLOR PLATES.
LCCN 2013-041145
  **ISBN** 030018784X      **Library PO#** SLIP ORDERS

|  |  | **List** | 40.00 | USD |
| --- | --- | --- | --- | --- |
| 6207 UNIV OF TEXAS/SAN ANTONIO | **Disc** | 17.0% | |
| **App. Date** 10/15/14  ARC.APR    6108-09 | **Net** | 33.20 | USD |

SUBJ: 1. GARDENS--GT. BRIT.--HIST. 2. GARDENING--
GT. BRIT.--HIST.
AWD/REV: 2014 NYRB
CLASS SB451.36        DEWEY# 635.        LEVEL GEN-AC

---

# YBP Library Services

WILLES, MARGARET.

GARDENS OF THE BRITISH WORKING CLASS.

Cloth     413 P.
LONDON: YALE UNIVERSITY PRESS, 2014


CULTURAL HIST. OF WORKING CLASS GARDENING SINCE
16TH CENT. W/ILLUS. & COLOR PLATES.
  LCCN 2013-041145
  **ISBN** 030018784X      **Library PO#** SLIP ORDERS

|  |  | **List** | 40.00 | USD |
| --- | --- | --- | --- | --- |
| 6207 UNIV OF TEXAS/SAN ANTONIO | **Disc** | 17.0% | |
| **App. Date** 10/15/14  ARC.APR    6108-09 | **Net** | 33.20 | USD |

SUBJ: 1. GARDENS--GT. BRIT.--HIST. 2. GARDENING--
GT. BRIT.--HIST.
AWD/REV: 2014 NYRB
CLASS SB451.36        DEWEY# 635.        LEVEL GEN-AC

Late sixteenth-century maps of London show gardens within the city walls, and a community of plant lovers has been identified as living in Lime Street, which curved between Leadenhall and Fenchurch Street, with substantial plots attached to their houses.[17] Astonishingly, some of the private gardens within the City survived until the twentieth century. A book published in 1907 described a collection off Fetter Lane: 'Even now in the heart of London, a small row of shabby old houses survives, each with a small garden attached to it ... A small wooden paling separates out the minute strips of blackened garden from a narrow paved pathway. There were many such gardens in this locality less than a century ago.'[18]

The pressure on space meant that many took 'garden grounds' outside the city, as John Stow makes clear in his survey, written at the turn of the seventeenth century. In the suburb outside Aldersgate, for instance, he describes how the area is 'replenished with small tenements, cottages and Allies, Gardens, banqueting houses and bowling places'. Recalling how in his childhood in the 1530s he was sent to collect milk from a farm by the Minories, to the east of the Tower of London, Stow records that by 1593 the area had been divided into garden plots, adding greatly to the profit of Goodman, the farmer.[19]

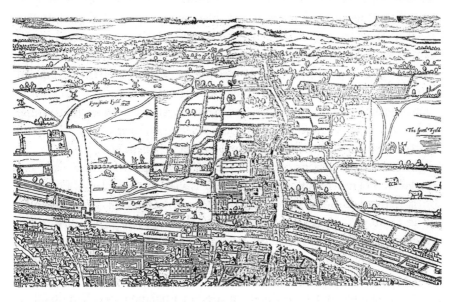

4 Detail of the 'Copperplate' map of London, from about 1559, showing the area just beyond the northern section of the City walls, with Bishopsgate Street flanked by houses and gardens, and fields and orchards beyond.

Some of the plots were attached to little cottages and thus would have been cultivated by labourers and their families but others were taken by the more prosperous, for he refers to elaborate buildings within them. Thus in Moorfields he talks of 'Gardens, wherein are builded many fayre summer houses, and as in other places in the suburbs, some of them like Midsomer Pageantes, with Towers, Turrets, and Chimney tops, not so much for use or profit, as for shewe and pleasure'.[20] According to the Puritan Philip Stubbes, these gardens provided a place for all kinds of sinful behaviour, but ordinary gardeners would not have had time for such indulgences.[21]

It was not only the pressure on land that caused gardeners to move out of the City: pollution from sea coal was beginning to affect the atmosphere. In the last years of the sixteenth century, the barber surgeon, John Gerard, moved westward to Covent Garden, followed by the apothecary John Parkinson, who went to Long Acre, close to the church of St Giles-in-the-Fields just south of what is now Tottenham Court Road. Parkinson has left us some details of his garden of about two acres. Originally he enclosed it with a hedge of white thorn, interlaced with dog roses, later building walls of brick and stone. The orchard was separated from the planting beds by household shrubs such as lavender, rosemary, southernwood and plashed cornelian cherry trees. The beds themselves were raised, with oaken inch boards or tiles to separate them. Parkinson noted that some people used the shank bones of sheep as separators, though didn't go as far as the Flemish, who used the jawbones. He tried to plant out the garden with knots, finding lavender cotton, recently introduced into the country, good for edging. Another recent introduction from the Continent was 'small, lowe or dwarf kind, called French or Dutch boxe'.[22] Parkinson, as an apothecary and enthusiastic horticulturalist, would have had a more elaborate plot than most, but he gives us a rare glimpse of what William Harrison might have described as an artificer's garden.

The spread of gardens can also be seen in seventeenth-century maps and perspectives of other towns and cities, such as a watercolour plan of Plymouth by Sir Bernard de Gomme, now in the National Maritime Museum (Plate V). As in London, such gardens were often detached grounds. A visitor to the 'western counties' in 1635 described how just outside Winchester 'some part of the ground within here is unbuilt, especially on the north and west sides, which is converted into orchards and gardens and little pastures'.[23]

Between 1500 and 1650 the population of England more than doubled, with the proportion of people living in urban areas rising from 2 per cent in the early sixteenth century to around 16 per cent by 1700. Compared to

London, however, towns and cities were relatively small. Norwich, England's second largest city, contained about 12,000 people in the 1570s, increasing to 20,000 in the 1620s, with a pause before rising to 30,000 in 1700. Plymouth's population doubled between 1550 and 1603, but then stagnated, so that there were only 8,400 people living in the city in 1740. The great rise in populations in the northern cities had yet to take place: Newcastle had only 4,000 people in the early sixteenth century, Liverpool 1,000 or less, Birmingham and Manchester around 1,500. The detached garden grounds were, therefore, well within walking distance of urban centres.[24]

In 1577 Hill's last gardening book, *The Gardeners Labyrinth*, was published. He had died three years before its appearance, and it was issued under the pseudonym Didymus Mountaine. This play on his name, mountain for hill, and a biblical reference to 'Thomas, which is called Didymus [twin]', may have been an attempt to raise Hill's status as an author, for it was his friend, the poet Henry Dethick, who saw it through the press. It is a much more elegant book than its predecessors, with some charming woodcut illustrations. Hill makes reference to garden grounds: 'It is right necessary (sayth Varro) to place gardens neare to the Citie, as well for the benefit of pothearbes and rootes, as all maner of sweete smeling floures that the Citie greatly needeth'.[25] One illustration depicts a prosperous couple, perhaps a merchant and his wife, in their detached garden, watching their gardener watering the knot garden with a kind of stirrup pump. Another picture shows men creating an arbour or herber around a table for outdoor meals. Hill explains how 'the herber in a garden may bee framed with Juniper poles, or the Willowe, either to stretch, or to bound together with Osyers . . . that the braunches of the Vine, Melone, or Cucumbre runing and spreading all over might so shadowe and keepe both the heate and sunne from the walkers and sitters there under'.[26] And yet another illustration in some editions shows the men sitting around a table having a welcome drink, suggesting that Hill was aiming the book at gardeners who worked their own plots as well as those who employed gardeners.

Both Tusser and Hill give us details of the tools used by gardeners at this time: Tusser calls them 'husbandlie furniture'. For watering small areas, a pot, usually of earthenware, with a sprinkling head like modern watering cans, was used. An example of an alternative design, which has no modern equivalent, can be seen in the Museum of London. This is shaped like a gourd, with a single hole at the top for filling, and ten or twelve holes at the bottom from which the water sprayed out, with the

THE SECOND PART OF THE
Gardeners Labyrinth , vttering ſuch skilfull experiences and worthie ſecretes, about the particular ſowing and re-
moouing of the moſt Kitchin Hearbes, with the wittie ordering
of other daintie Hearbes , deleᶜtable Floures , pleaſant Fruites,
and fine Roots, as the like hath not heretoſore been vttered
of anie. Beſides the Phiſicke benefits of each Hearbe
annexed , with the commoditie of waters
diſtilled out of them , right ne-
neſſarie to be knowen.

5 An illustration from *The Gardeners Labyrinth* by Thomas Hill, showing men training
climbers over an arbour. Below, a gardener is planting flowers in raised beds.

6 Gardeners at rest, from *The Gardeners Labyrinth*, treat themselves to a picnic in front of a trellis decorated with a flowering climber.

flow controlled by placing the thumb over the hole at the top. Hill describes this as a 'common water potte for the Garden beddes . . . [with] a narrow necke, bigge belly, somewhat large bottome, and full of little holes, with a proper hole formed on the head, to take in the water, whiche filled full, and the thombe layde on the hole to keepe in the aire'.[27] Tusser, addressing a rural audience, refers to the more down-to-earth method of watering in his verse on garden tools:

A pitchfork, a doongfork, seeve, skep and a bin,
A broome, and a paile to put water therein:
A handbarow, wheelebarow, sholve [shovel] and a spade.[28]

Fitzherbert in his *Boke of Husbandry* gave instructions for making garden rakes as a winter task: 'when the housebande sytteth by the fyre, and hath nothynge to do than may he make theym redye, and to the rakes with dry wethywode, and bore the holes with his wimble [gimlet] bothe above and under, and drive the tethe upwarde faste and harde, and than wedge them above with drye woode of oke ... they be most commonly made of hasell and withee'.[29]

Spades were of wood, cut from a straight-grained wood such as ash, with a handle shaped as a 'D' or a 'T', a straight shaft, and a footrest either single or double-sided. This structure would then be inserted into a metal tool edge, custom-made by the blacksmith. There was a wide range of regional designs, adapted to suit the particular nature of the soil. Thus in Devon, Cornwall and West Wales the spade or shovel would have a triangular blade and a 'long knob' shaft, while shorter handles were applied to spades made in the Midlands and South East England. Those working very wet and sticky ground might use narrower, open blades that were lighter to handle. Tined forks were also made by the blacksmith, to be inserted into a wooden handle. A formidable array of knives and cutting instruments were available, as shown in books of the period: bill hooks for pruning, hedge making and coppicing, knives for grafting fruit trees, scythes and sickles for cutting grass and tall plants, and mattocks for trenching, breaking up the soil and surface hoeing. A medieval French misericord carving even shows three-fingered weeding gloves that were worn for dealing with tough weeds such as thistles that would damage the hands, although these must have only been used in extreme conditions.

* * *

Not only were the poor being squeezed for space in London and to a much lesser extent in other cities, but they also had to cope with the twin threats of disease and dearth. Both descended with a vengeance in the 1590s. Outbreaks of plague in London in 1592 and 1593 were so severe that the authorities were obliged to close the playhouses. Two years later came the first of a series of disastrous harvests as a result of unceasing rain and tempestuous winds that rotted the corn. The situation was made particularly serious because the failure was European-wide: it was reported that Tartar women in Hungary were forced to eat their own children, while the poor in Italy and Germany resorted to whatever was edible, including cats, dogs and even snakes. In London the burial records of some of the poorer parishes show a doubling in the number of deaths in 1597 which is thought to have been the result of malnutrition.[30] William Shakespeare, who was living at this time in Shoreditch, just to the north of the City, probably makes reference to these terrible visitations when he has Titania describe the effects of her quarrel with Oberon in *A Midsummer's Night's Dream*:

> ... the winds, piping to us in vain,
> As in revenge, have suck'd up from the sea
> Contagious fogs; which, falling in the land,
> Have every pelting river made so proud
> That they have overborne their continents:
> The ox hath therefore stretch'd his yoke in vain,
> The ploughman lost his sweat, and the green corn
> Hath rotted ere his youth attain'd a beard;
> The fold stands empty in the drowned field,
> And crows are fatted with the murrion flock;
> The nine men's morris is fill'd up with mud,
> And the quaint mazes in the wanton green
> For lack of tread are undistinguishable. (Act II, Scene 1)

With the pressure on land within the city walls of London, many of the inhabitants, and especially the poorer, relied on food being brought in. The Privy Council was obliged to order authorities in the provinces to release grain and foreign ships were even hijacked in the English Channel, but given that the dearth pertained throughout Europe, other solutions had to be found. All major grains had been affected, along with peas and beans, so the answer lay in root vegetables. There was a considerable national prejudice held against these. Writing in 1548, William Forrest declared: 'Our English nature cannot live by roots/ By waters, herbs or such beggary baggage/ That may well serve for vile outlandish coats'.[31] The wealthy disdained vegetables such as carrots and turnips, considering them to be the food of the poor. The poor in turn disliked root vegetables, considering them to be food for animals. However, 'outlandish coats' – Dutch market gardeners – were now coming to the rescue of the starving poor with their skill with a range of vegetables, encouraged by the advocacy of writers such as Hugh Platt.

Platt was the son of a wealthy London brewer, enabling him to devote his time to writing an eclectic range of works. He was able to conduct horticultural experiments in his three gardens: near St Albans in Hertfordshire, in Bethnal Green to the east of the City of London, and in St Martin's Lane by Charing Cross to the west. In his treatise, *Sundrie new and Artificiall Remedies against Famine*, written in 1596 'upon thoccasion of this present Dearth', Platt explored various substitutes for conventional bread flours and suggested alternatives such as cakes made of parsnip meal.

The dearth also affected other parts of England, and another writer took to his pen in praise of vegetables. Richard Gardiner was a linen draper in Shrewsbury who in 1599 produced a treatise titled *Instructions for manuring, sowing and planting of Kitchin Gardens*. It is a modest little book, octavo in format, with just thirty pages providing practical advice on how to raise and save seeds of all kinds of vegetables, from cabbages and lettuce, to beans, artichokes, radishes and leeks. The carrot was his particular favourite, and he gives cooking tips such as cutting them up and boiling them to a broth with salt beef or pork. 'Carrets in necessitie and dearth, are eaten of the poore people, after they be well boyled, instead of bread and meate. Many people will eate Carrets raw, and doe digest well in hungry stomackes: they give good nourishment to all people, and not hurtful to any, whatsoever infirmities they be diseased of, as by experience doth prove by many to be true.'[32] At this period carrots came in a variety of colours – red, black, yellow and white. The modern orange carrot is said to have been bred from these colours by the Dutch as a tribute to the ruling House of Orange.

In the mid-seventeenth century the enthusiastic promoter of husbandry, Samuel Hartlib, looked back to the arrival of professional market gardening in England: 'About 50 years ago, about which time Ingenuities first began to flourish in England, the Art of Gardening began to creep into England'.[33] This sweeping statement ignores the fact that for centuries there had been a certain amount of market gardening in Britain. Wealthy owners of gardens, both secular and religious, sold off their surplus fruit and vegetables to urban markets, such as the one established near St Paul's Churchyard in London in the fourteenth century. Colchester in Essex had a vegetable market by 1529 when an order was issued that 'the pease and root market, with the onions, garlick, and cucumbers, and other garden stuff and wares should be held by St Nicholas' Church and nowhere else'.[34]

Cottagers in rural communities could offer some of their produce to their wealthier neighbours, as shown in the account records of aristocratic households. Thus the clerk of Lord William Howard of Naworth Castle in Cumberland noted payments such as 2s 6d to 'William Bird's wife bringing cherries' on 13 July 1612. Such a sum was substantial for a cottager, making Mistress Bird's journey well worthwhile, and presumably Howard appreciated his cherries in season.[35] Likewise, the diary of Sir Arthur Throckmorton records a similar payment to a woman bringing melons in September 1593 to his house at Paulerspury in Northamptonshire.[36]

An interesting example of a community of market gardeners from the mid-sixteenth century has been identified in the village of Stock in Essex.[37] Tudor Stock enjoyed several geographical advantages for trade: six miles from Chelmsford, it was located close to the main highway from Colchester to London. The land around the village had long been enclosed, and the community of about 300 people had a variety of commercial opportunities. Much of the village lies on the boulder clay area of Central Essex, from which the inhabitants made tiles, bricks and pottery. The higher grounds were light and sandy, so good for market gardening. Thus, although the villagers had no strips in open fields, they could make a living from one or other of these trades, and evidence suggests that some of them worked at both. Indeed, one aided the other, for the ashes produced by the pottery kilns could be added to manure from livestock to enrich the soil.[38] As early as the 1530s, a Stock potter, John Palmer, was supplying earthenware flower pots, often known as gallipots, to the new hothouses of Henry VIII's palace at Hampton Court, on the other side of London.[39] In January 1550 another potter, Robert Prentice, is recorded as producing '12 potts to set herbs in' along with 'a water pott for the Garden' in January 1550, and later in the year 'iiii pots for flowers'. Prentice had a good market among his fellow villagers, as well as trading connections with London.

At least eleven properties in Stock are described in contemporary records as non-domestic gardens, and these would have been planted with leeks, onions, garlic, cabbages and salads, as well as herbs and fruit trees. The gardeners not only sent their produce up to London every week, and probably to the market in Colchester, but also supplied tree stocks. The local landowner, Sir William Petre, for example, bought from Grey of Stock 'XIII crab tree stocks' for tenpence in January 1554.[40] Industrial crops were cultivated for dyeing, along with teasels for raising the nap on cloth, reeds, flax for linen and hops for beer.

When Dutch refugees began to arrive in England in the late 1560s and 1570s, escaping from religious persecution by the Spanish in the Netherlands, their vegetable-growing skills marked a significant development in market gardening. The diaspora of these Protestants represents one of the largest uprootings of population in late sixteenth- and early seventeenth-century Europe, involving approximately 180,000 people. Of these, 10,000 fled to England in the 1570s, 15,000 in the 1590s, and 10,000 in the early years of the next century.[41] Originally these refugees settled in East Anglian ports such as Norwich, Yarmouth and Colchester, and in Sandwich in Kent. At the beginning of Elizabeth I's reign, when Protestants from the Netherlands petitioned to practise their trades, 400 came to Sandwich. They were mostly weavers, but there were also gardeners. Two are specified in the records: Christian Lamot and Charles Hergebert, who grew teasels, flax and hops. Finding that the soil was sandy, and thus could heat up quickly, the Dutch gardeners of Sandwich turned to the cultivation of root vegetables. Regulations limiting numbers were applied to try to avoid outbreaks of xenophobia on the part of the native communities. Thus in 1565 Norwich permitted the introduction of 300 'Strangers', but within six years the number had increased to nearly 4,000, about one-third of the total population of the city.

In his study of the feeding of London's poor at this period, Malcolm Thick provides a picture of some of these gardeners.[42] He draws a distinction between the kitchen-gardener, who ran a small enterprise, and the more substantial farmer-gardener. Thus appearing among the Norwich inventories is Adrian Coesse on 2 December 1595, a kitchen-gardener with 'turneppes and roots', leeks, parsnips, herbs and 'sallets'. Among his possessions were unspecified seeds worth seventeen shillings, plus a measure containing 'roote seedes' worth five shillings, presumably for next season's sowing. Coesse kept five cows and a neat (an ox or a bullock, probably to pull the plough). His crops were grown in a garden of plots and beds, and he owned, among other implements, a plough, a rake, a hoe and spades. Francis van Dycke, whose inventory is dated 28 May 1597, was a farmer-gardener, with a mixture of field crops and vegetables: two acres of roots, four acres of barley, and two acres of wheat and rye.[43] Significantly, in both inventories roots represented more value as crops than grain. For Van Dycke, the roots were valued at £5 per acre, compared to wheat and rye at £2 5s, and barley at £1 5s. And roots, of course, travelled well so that market gardening even at a distance made good commercial sense.

From the coast the gardeners moved inland, drawn by the market opportunities, particularly those offered by the ever-expanding capital. In 1607 the topographer John Norden noted how the hot and sandy soils of Suffolk, Essex and Surrey were good for carrot roots: 'a beneficial fruit, as Orford, Ipswich, and many sea towns in Suffolk, as also inland towns, Bury, Framlingham, and others in some measure, in the same shire, Norwich, and many places in Norfolk, Colchester in Essex, Fulham and other places near London. And it begins to increase in all places of this realm, where discretion and industry sway the minds of the inhabitants.'[44]

While Fulham became particularly known for its carrots, on the opposite side of London, in Hackney, small turnips were the speciality. In his herbal of 1597 John Gerard noted how the village women took the vegetables to be sold at the market cross in Cheapside.

By the sixteenth century there were markets for fresh fruit, herbs and vegetables at Newgate and Gracechurch as well as Cheapside. In 1598 Hugh Alley produced his *Caveat for the City of London*, in which he provided charming illustrations of these markets, along with images of various officials of the City.[45] The illustration for Cheapside shows sellers of fruit and vegetables among other food vendors, in between pillars indicating their areas of provenance. Also shown is the Great Conduit and the Cheap or Great Cross, a decorated pillar surmounted by a cross erected by Edward I in memory of his queen, Eleanor. Alley was an informer, or as his editors describe him, a busybody, who wanted to enforce and augment the regulations governing the London markets, especially in the light of the scare caused by the harvest failures and dearth of the mid-1590s.[46] Regulations included the days on which various products might be sold: Sunday was added for 'timely fruits', such as cherries and strawberries which could easily rot. Other regulations covered the washing of root vegetables in the streets, and the routes allowed to basketmen and women hawking their wares. Sellers were restricted to three baskets per day. Attempts were also made to ensure that the vegetables offered for sale were fresh. A proposal made in 1593 advised 'restraint of those that let out cellars and sheds under stalls where herbs, roots, fruit, bread, and victuals are noisomely kept till they be stale and unwholesome for man's body, and then, mingled with fresh wares of the same kind, are brought forth into the market and there sold to the great deceit and hurt of the people'.[47]

The City managed to get through the scare of a complete collapse of food supplies in the 1590s but, with the population ever rising, it was clear that market gardening had to be encouraged. One of the factors that made the Dutch and Flemish so successful was their intense use of manure. According to Orazio Busino, the chaplain of the Venetian Ambassador at the court of King James I, these gardeners would dig through the gravel deposits which ringed London, selling the stone for ballast for ships and street repairs. The holes were then filled with 'the filth of the city', night soil and street sweepings 'as rich and black as thick ink'.[48] Once filled, the land was enclosed by palings, deep ditches of walls of soft mud with rotted straw and thatched on top. Similar in idea were the hotbeds for tender fruit and vegetables such as melons and cucumbers.

7 Cheapside Market, one of the drawings from Hugh Alley's *Caveat* issued in 1598. The elaborate pillar left of centre is Cheap Cross, erected in the late thirteenth century by Edward I in memory of his queen, Eleanor. The polygonal building on the right contained a water conduit. The six round pillars are shown with flags and captions indicating the source of the food being sold at their bases – an Elizabethan version of local sourcing. According to John Gerard, the village women from Hackney brought little turnips from their gardens to the market. They would have carried their vegetables in baskets on their backs, like the man in the foreground.

A whole new form of noxious husbandry developed as a result of this style of gardening: gong farming. Gong is derived from the Old English *gang* meaning 'to go', and in the medieval period was used to refer to a privy or its contents. In the Tudor period in London and other cities and towns, privies were usually located in backyards or gardens, with rear access by alleyways. The waste was loaded into barrels or pipes and taken on carts to laystalls, customarily on the edge of the town, for spreading on common land. In London much of the waste was taken to dumps on the banks of the Thames, such as Dung Wharf at Blackfriars. Londoners have always employed irony in the face of adversity, and so the massive dump by the Fleet River in Clerkenwell was named Mount Pleasant.

The increased value of manure is even reflected in the churchwarden records of the Cambridgeshire village of Foxton. The early sixteenth-century accounts stipulate: 'All persons who from the scouring of the roads accumulate earth and manure in heaps called "mire-heaps" and leave them in the streets shall cart them away before St John Baptist's Day on pain of a fine of 3s 4d, half to the Lady, half to the churchwardens'. By 1578, however, the mire heaps had become a worthwhile commodity: 'No one shall cart away the manure called "Compas" out of the street, on pain of a fine of 8s'.[49]

Sir Thomas Overbury, who was to acquire a terrible fame as the victim of poison in the Tower of London, was also celebrated in his day for his *Characters*, a series of satirical pen portraits of social types. One, called 'A Drunken Dutch-Man Resident in England' characterises him as a figure overfond of the brewhouses of St Catherine's, bloated like a herring and stinking of butter. But he is also marked out as a vegetable gardener: 'Of all places of pleasure [he] loves a common garden, and with the swine of the parish had need be ringed for rooting'.[50] Other Londoners thought that intensive cultivation would ruin the soil, so were reluctant to rent out their land to Huguenot gardeners.

Therefore the majority went to a ring around the capital including Fulham, Chelsea, Wandsworth, Battersea and Bermondsey, although Lord Southampton encouraged market gardeners on his estate in Bloomsbury: Shorts Gardens remains as a memory of one such. Opposition came from the Company of Gardeners, which had received its charter from James I in 1605. This charter had given them near-exclusive rights over the cultivation of 'plants, herbs, seeds, fruits, trees' within a six-mile compass around the City of London. But in 1616 the Company sought to exclude gardeners in Fulham, Chelsea and Kensington, whom they accused of pretending to be market gardeners, when they were really only husbandmen who had not served full apprenticeship. This, however, was a losing battle, for these descendants of Dutch immigrants were skilled men and were playing a vital role in feeding London's population, so the quarrel was resolved in 1633.

A revolution had taken place, not only in methods of market gardening, but also in the nation's eating habits. One hundred years earlier, vegetables were regarded as food for peasants and their animals, with the wealthy eating meat and fish dressed with rich sauces, followed by dishes of sweetmeats. By the early seventeenth century, new vegetables such as artichokes and asparagus were beginning to feature in the fashionable diet. Ben Jonson in a description of a trip up the Fleet in the summer, wrote of 'every clerke' eating 'artichokes and peason (Laxitive lettus and such windie meate)'.[51] Even the turnip was no longer dismissed. John Parkinson wrote in 1629 of how turnips were 'often seene as a dish at good mens tables', although he also pointed out that 'the greater quantitie of them are spent at poore mens feasts'.[52]

The demand for fresh vegetables to purchase was growing, not only because of changing tastes, but also because the urban population was rising, particularly in London. The next chapter will chart the development of market gardening to meet this increased demand and to prevent the recurrence of dearth. It will also look at the cultivation of medicinal plants to combat that other great threat, disease.

# CHAPTER 2

# Vital Remedies

WHEN THOMAS TUSSER drew up a list of useful seeds for the gardener in his *Five Hundred Pointes of Good Husbandrie* he included plants that might stock the housewife's medicine chest. Two dozen plants from 'annis' to 'woodbine' were recommended 'for Physick', though he did point out that herbs and flowers on the other lists could also be used.[1] The range of remedies that the housewife might be called upon to provide was dauntingly wide: for agues and fevers (including the plague), coughs, swellings and inflammations, problems with menstruation and childbirth, ulcers, vomiting and domestic injuries such as burns and cuts. She also had to deal with illnesses and injuries to the family's domestic animals.

A recorded example of an Elizabethan 'housewife' who practised physic is Grace, Lady Mildmay. At Apethorpe Hall in Northamptonshire she dispensed medicines to the local community, and at her death in 1620, along with her books and papers, she left her daughter a formidably long list of the flowers, roots and herbs to be grown in her garden.[2] Of course Lady Mildmay was no ordinary housewife, but given the paucity of available information, she must represent her humbler and silent sisters. Many of the medicines were based on herbal syrups that included garden flowers that we think of as decorative, such as cowslips, damask roses and violets.

In her autobiography, Grace Mildmay explained how she learnt about plants from a copy of a herbal given to her by her governess. This was William Turner's *Newe Herball*, the first truly Renaissance herbal written in English, with the first volume appearing in 1551. Grace, like most gentlewomen of the period, would not have had the benefit of a classical education, but at least she had access to books, a privilege denied most women, even if they could read. Instead they would have passed on their learning by word of mouth, and ballads, folk songs and proverbs give a hint, albeit brief and sometimes mysterious, of this oral tradition. This ballad, from East Anglia, 'Old Thyme', is probably referring to plants that can bring about abortion and provide contraception:

Come all young women and maids
That are all in your prime
Mind how you weed your gardens gay
Let no one steal your thyme.

Once I had thyme enough
To last me night and day,
There came to me a false young man
Stole all my thyme away.

And now my thyme is done,
I cannot plant no new,
There lays the bed where my old thyme grew,
'Tis all over-run with rue.

Rue is a running root,
Runs all across amain,
If I could pluck that running root
I'd plant my old thyme again.[3]

Similar in theme is an old Devon rhyme:

Boy's Love is Maiden's Ruin
But half of it is her own doing.

Boy's Love and Maiden's Ruin are local names for southernwood, *Artemisia abrotanum*, which, it was claimed, procured an abortion when made into an infusion.

The seventeenth-century diarist, John Aubrey, recorded the proverb, 'Eat Leekes in Lide [Lent] and ramsins in May/ And all the yeare after physitians may play'.[4] Ramsins were alliums, which even in the twentieth century were prescribed to be eaten for coughs and colds, as were roasted leeks. Proverbs and rhymes could be easily remembered even by those with only a modicum of education, as Tusser knew when he wrote his husbandry books in verse. Alongside these were aids to memory that gave an indication of the effects of certain plants. Thus a traditional name for dandelions was 'piss-a-bed', for juniper 'bastard killer' and for comfrey, 'knitbone'. The theory that God had left clues, known as signatures, in the leaves of plants, flowers and roots to suggest the disease of an organ may also have provided a memory aid.

An indication of some of the plants to be found in country housewives' gardens in the later seventeenth century is provided by John Worlidge, whose *Systema Horti-culturae or The Art of Gardening* was published in London in 1677. Worlidge was probably the woodward, or keeper of the timber, on the estates belonging to the Earl of Pembroke around Petersfield in Hampshire. Blanche Henrey, the twentieth-century authority on horticultural and botanical writers of the period, has described Worlidge's ideas as practical and enlightened. Worlidge sets out his stall in his preface: 'The affections of our Countrymen so naturally tending that way [towards gardening] have given great encouragement to such publications, some whereof are very large and voluminous, others there are that are more accurt'.[5] Worlidge chose the 'accurt', adopting an octavo format, hoping thereby to encourage 'the honest and plain Countryman'. Very unusually he provides a chapter 'Of some more Vulgar Flowers'. This is unusual because most horticultural writers of the period concentrated on flowers for expert breeders, florists, or on exotic plants. 'Vulgar' was used at this time for the common name of a plant as opposed to the Latin.

Worlidge's list of these 'Vulgar' flowers runs from aconites through to toadflax, including those that would have provided colour for the garden, such as 'blew-bottles', or cornflowers, nigella, sunflowers, and candytufts. Others would have proved useful for medicines and ointments, such as pilewort, or lesser celandine, whose name makes clear its use, and scabious which could be prescribed for coughs and shortness of breath, and for drawing of splinters. Amaranthus, also known as princes' feather and love-lies-bleeding, not surprisingly was recommended by herbalists for the staunching of wounds.[6]

Just as Grace, Lady Mildmay provides a rare glimpse of a medicinal gardener in Tudor times, so Goodwife Cantrey makes a tantalisingly fleeting appearance in the mid-seventeenth century. The wife of a Northamptonshire yeoman farmer, she planted a herb plot with fennel for an infusion to ease weak eyes, camomile for headaches, and goat's rue as an antidote to the plague. An idea of some of the flowers and fruit that she cultivated in her garden has also survived in the form of a receipt for plants

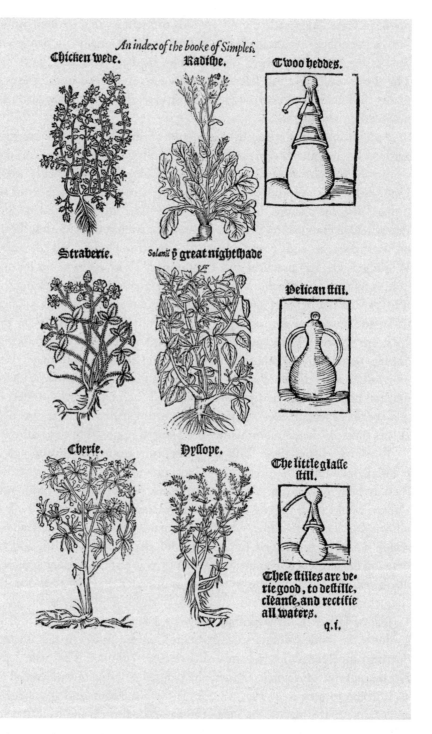

8 A page of medicinal herbs from William Bullein's *Bulwarke of Defence Against all Sicknesse, Soareness and Woundes* published in London in 1562. Alongside the herbs are alembics for distillation of medicines.

supplied on 28 July 1658 to the Hatton family of Kirby Hall. The list includes lupins, larkspurs, scabious, sweet williams, honeysuckle and 'double hollioake', along with four sorts of gooseberries – white, green, red and yellow – double currants and 'violette plumbe'.[7]

Grace Mildmay would have used an alembic for the distillations of herbs and other plants into waters and essences. Thirty-one large bottles of cordials and oils are recorded as being in her stillroom at Apethorpe, along with shelves of powders and pills. The country housewife had recourse to much less sophisticated equipment. An elderly lady from Essex, interviewed in the 1990s, recalled her grandmother using bottles of different tinctures on a sunny windowsill: one with marigold flowers in alcohol for sprains and sores, another of Madonna lily infused in oil to ease burns.[8] A traditional recipe was to pick the flowers of St John's wort (*Hypericum perforatum*) on 24 June, the saint's day, and put them on a windowsill in water until the sun turned the liquid red. The so-called blood of St John could then be used to treat skin complaints, as well as a balm against evil and the plague.

Lady Mildmay made her salves from sheep's suet, which was minced, clarified and strained before wax was added. Once cooled, the mixture could be rolled into balls and applied to the patient. This would have been similar to the way that the humble housewife made her salves, with herbs and flowers put in little pots of water with a grating of beeswax, or goose or bacon fat, and placed on the edge of the fire. Soap could be made from the essences of marigold, lavender, rose or elderflower, and then perco-lated several times using wood ash, before being boiled up with bacon fat.

Providing physic for the family and the community was a domestic matter in rural communities, but a rather different picture emerges for larger towns and cities, and above all London. As the population grew in these urban areas, so the possibility of having an extensive garden dimin-ished for all but the wealthy and powerful, and the provision of physic was in the hands of the medical profession. In the sixteenth and seventeenth centuries, there was considerable tension between what might now be regarded as the gentlemen and players of this profession. Gentlemen – and as ever, there were gradations of gentility – were the doctors, apothecaries and surgeons. Players were herb-gatherers, often known as simplers, who were invariably women.[9] Arguments about the merits of the latter ebbed and flowed in the sixteenth and seventeenth centuries. While the Tudor botanist William Turner felt that 'old wives' were more skilled in the use of herbs than many surgeons and apothecaries, a century later William

Coles in his *Art of Simpling*, published in 1656, dismissed them as 'silly hearb-women'.[10]

In 1518 Henry VIII granted a charter for the foundation of the College of Physicians at the instigation of his physician, Thomas Linacre.[11] The College sought to regulate the profession in London and the suburbs up to a distance of seven miles, issuing licences to administer medicine and oversee internal health to a limited number, estimated at between twenty and forty in the sixteenth century. Barber surgeons, who included the herbalist John Gerard, belonged to the London Company of Barber-Surgeons, which looked after wounds, amputations and external operations. They were estimated to number around 100. The apothecaries, who sold medicines to professionals, and increasingly to members of the public, were part of the Grocers' Company, which specialised in trading in 'gross' or exotic commodities such as spices and sugar. Again they numbered around 100 in Tudor London.[12] By the end of the century, London's population had reached 200,000, a huge constituency for this number of professionals to treat. An estimate of the number of medical professionals in Norwich in the Elizabethan period shows a similar ratio while in smaller towns it could be one medical professional for 400 people.[13] It is scarcely surprising therefore that many turned elsewhere for remedies that they could afford, and which they often preferred as being less drastic. As one lady trenchantly observed, 'Kitchen physic I believe is more proper than the Doctor's filthy physic'.[14]

Towards the end of Henry VIII's reign, in 1543, an act was passed allowing those experienced in the nature of herbs, roots and waters to practise and use them as a gesture of Christian charity. This caused much consternation in some quarters. The surgeon William Clowes fulminated about how a whole raft of tradespeople, from painters and glaziers to bawds, witches and soothsayers, 'without order, honesty, or skill, daily abuse both Physick and Surgery, having no more perseverance, reason, or knowledge in this art than has a goose'.[15] The College of Physicians summoned a series of women before their court for administering medicines and giving advice. But in one instance, when a poor woman, Margaret Kennix, was accused of supplying her friends and neighbours with herbal remedies, the Queen intervened in person. In a letter sent to the College via Secretary Walsingham, the Queen declared:

> It is her Majesty's pleasure that the poor woman should be permitted
> by you quietly to practise and minister to the curing of diseases and

wounds, by the means of certain simples, in the application whereof it seems God hath given her an especial knowledge. I shall therefore desire you to take order amongst yourselves for the readmitting of her into the quiet exercise of her small talent, lest by the renewing of her complaint to her Majesty through your hard dealing towards her, you procure further inconvenience thereby to yourselves.[16]

Given that many physicians and apothecaries could not grow their own medicinal herbs, they had to turn to women gardeners. Early seventeenth-century records show that the physicians of St Thomas's Hospital in London employed a herb woman to provide the raw materials for the medicines and ointments that the chief medical officer, the apothecary, prescribed for his patients. The difference in status between the medical men and the 'workers' is clearly demonstrated in the records. In 1629 it was noted that the apothecary was paid £60 per annum, the surgeon £35, and the doctors £30, while the man employed to cut bladder stones received £15 and the herb woman a mere £4. The apothecary was expected to pay for the ingredients of his drugs out of his salary, so the herb woman may have received additional money on top of her modest wages. The herbs were acquired in bulk, with wormwood (artemisia) coming by the horseload, others by the lapful, bundle, bag or flasket, so the woman must have cultivated her herbs in the style of market gardening to supply the demand. A recipe for 'snail water', dating from the early eighteenth century for the treatment of venereal disease, shows the large quantities of herbs used: a pound and a half each of wormwood, ground ivy and cardus (thistle); and half a pound each of pennyroyal, juniper berries, fennel and aniseed. These were mixed with three ounces of cloves and cubebs, eight gallons of spring water and spirit of wine, six gallons of snails, and three gallons of earthworms and distilled in an alembic to make a truly appalling concoction.[17]

In 1589 the College of Physicians had resolved to compile a 'Pharmacopoeia or Dispensary of Prescriptions to be followed by shops'. In order to keep this knowledge from the public, it was decided to produce the list in Latin, but apothecaries refused to cooperate, partly because they were not necessarily firmly grounded in Latin, but also because they felt that they, rather than the physicians, knew more about the ingredients of many medicines. When, nearly twenty years after this resolution, the College produced their *Pharmacopoeia*, it was found to be out of date and inconsistent in its information.[18] A new edition was finally issued in 1649, but at the same time a radical bookseller, Peter Cole, decided to produce

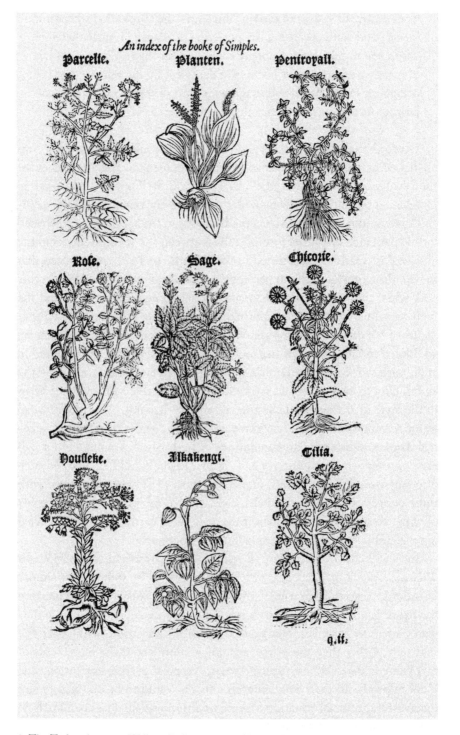

9  The Tudor physician, William Bullein, arranged his medicinal treatise as a dialogue, with a gardener explaining to a doctor how he cultivated herbs. The plants shown here were important ingredients in the sixteenth-century medicine chest, and included the useful pennyroyal, the houseleek (which could serve as a poultice for bad cuts) and the rose.

an alternative version in English. His choice of compiler for this was a momentous one, for he commissioned the apothecary, Nicholas Culpeper.

Like his publisher, Cole, Culpeper was a radical, from a staunchly Puritan background, although he was also convinced that lives were heavily influenced by celestial phenomena, observing that 'he had courted two mistresses that had cost him dear, but it was not the wealth of kingdoms should buy them from him'.[19] These ladies were physic and astrology. The third lady in his life was his wife, Alice Ford, daughter of a wealthy London merchant. In 1640 the couple set up home in the precincts of the old hospital of St Mary, now known as Spitalfields. Here, outside the City of London, and therefore able to practise without a licence, Culpeper would have been able to develop his knowledge by finding wild flowers and herbs and probably cultivating his own garden. His Nonconformist instincts influenced his dislike of the cant of the medical profession, and he threw down a challenge by offering help to all, however poor. After his death, a biographer noted 'To the poor he prescribed cheap, but wholesome Medicine; not removing as many in our times do, the Consumption out of their Bodies into their Purses; not sending them to the East Indies for Drugs, when they may fetch better out of their own Gardens'.[20]

Culpeper's English pharmacopoeia was published by Peter Cole in August 1649, with the title, *A Physical Directory*. The compiler noted on his title page that he had made hundreds of additions to the College's *Pharmacopoeia*, marking them with an 'A' to provide information about how ingredients and recipes should be used. Three years later Culpeper published his master work, *The English Physitian*, later known as his *Complete Herbal*. This was couched in simple, accessible language, and was aimed particularly at women as the main providers of non-professional healthcare. This can be seen from the wording of entries, such as the 'Herb True-Love' which Culpeper says should be found in every 'good Woman's Garden'. Also called One-Berry, 'Venus owns it. The leaves or berries hereof are good as antidotes against all kinds of poison, especially that of aconites, and pestilential disorders.'[21] It serves as a reminder that gardens could provide dangers as well as relief, for monkshood, an aconite, was highly toxic, and the housewife needed to be able to identify her plants. Culpeper's astrological beliefs convinced him that Herb True-Love was 'owned' by Venus, as was Featherfew (feverfew) because it expelled the afterbirth and strengthened women's wombs. Daisies were not only in the dominion of Venus, but also under the sign of Cancer, and good for wounds, internal and external. Pellitory, owned by Mercury, was proposed by Culpeper as one of the best purgers of the brain, as well as helping with gout and sciatica. The butter-flower, with its fiery and spirited nature, was under the dominion of Mars, and not to be given internally, but could draw a blister as an ointment.

Herbals were expensive at this time because they were usually highly illustrated. In the Huntington Library in California, a copy of Thomas Johnson's amended 1633 version of the famous herbal of John Gerard has a note inside the cover that the price was £1 17s 6d unbound, £2 8s bound. So precious were its illustrations to enable plant identification that women often specifically bequeathed it to their daughters in their wills, along with their Bible. Culpeper's herbal did not have the benefit of woodcuts, but was published at the very modest price of threepence, sometimes prominently featured on the title page to prevent booksellers from charging more. The power to heal and treat had been put into the hands of ordinary men and women, and this was to prove highly popular, with the book going into eighty editions, including pirated ones. His astrological beliefs drew criticism from contemporaries and from commentators ever since, but the book was one of the most successful ever to have been published in the English language, and is still available today.

Herbwomen would have found Culpeper's publications invaluable for their cultivation of the most effective medicinal plants. By the end of the seventeenth century an increasing number of herbwomen were acquiring a more respected social status, especially those able to rent stalls in London's markets where they sold not only medicinal plants, but also herbs for strewing and cooking. As a result these very humble women begin to be named in archival documents, and step out of the shadows. The records for the Fleet Market for the years 1737–38, for instance, identify Mary Leech and Judith Vardey as specialists in 'Phisick Herbs'. The records for the following years, 1739–40, go further, specifying the location of the gardens from which the herbs were gathered. Some herbwomen were located near the City, such as Hannah Smith from Grub Street in Finsbury, but most came from neighbouring suburbs such as Bethnal Green and Stepney Green, Bermondsey, Camberwell and Vauxhall.

Competition among the women selling herbs was fierce, and life could be precarious. A herbwoman, Elizabeth Gobbey, fell into arrears with her rent for her stall in Newgate Market, just above St Paul's Churchyard. Her petition to the market authorities tells how she had sold herbs there since infancy, had lost her husband 'leaving your Poor Petitioner in very low and meen Circumstances with two Smale children', and appealed to be allowed to return to her stall and pay off the arrears at two shillings per week.[22]

Some herbwomen fared better, appearing in the accounts of London Bridge House in Southwark, the administrative centre for the bridge's finances. As well as selling plants at the herb market in Covent Garden, the women were employed to strew herbs in the hall in Southwark. One woman who held a long tenure as a regular supplier of herbs to Bridge House was Mary Earle, who died in 1758, leaving bequests of £20 to each of her granddaughters, £30 to her grandson, and her remaining estate to her daughter-in-law, a substantial estate for a woman.[23]

But Mary Earle and her fellow Bridge House herbwomen were the lucky ones. When John Thomas Smith produced his *Cries of London* in the nineteenth century, his drawing of simplers shows women dressed in

10  Herbwomen trudging home from market, a drawing by John Thomas Smith, 1839.

ragged clothes, trudging home after a heavy day's work. They present a vivid contrast from the fresh-faced young women flourishing their watercress or strawberries, so often depicted in illustrations of city cries.

* * *

Gardening could provide vital remedies for the treatment of disease and injuries. Market gardening could also feed the poorest urban households in times of dearth, as shown in Chapter 1. The hard times of the 1590s were not the last, and market gardening was to become ever more vital as Britain's towns and cities grew in the seventeenth century. London in particular grew rapidly in the seventeenth and eighteenth centuries, creating a monster metropolis. By 1650 the population had doubled from an estimated 200,000 to 400,000. Despite the Great Plague and the Great Fire in the 1660s, the city continued to grow, to 575,000 in 1700, and 765,000 by 1750. Commentators noted that the years 1629–30 were particularly difficult as a result of the failure of the corn harvest, and more followed. In response, a ring of market gardens formed around the capital, spreading ever outwards like ripples when a stone is thrown into a pond.

Even so, to modern eyes London remained relatively compact, with market gardens in Battersea and Putney to the south, Whitechapel, east Smithfield and Stepney to the east, Hoxton and Hackney to the north, and Fulham, Chelsea and the Neat Houses of Westminster to the west. The last were located in the area now known as Pimlico, and took their name from the fact that they had been a rural retreat for the abbots of Westminster with a garden and farm. Nearby were pastures where cattle (neats) might graze and recover from their trek from the countryside before being driven to market. Ceded to the Crown in 1536 with the dissolution of monasteries, the Neat Houses became an area of commercial market gardens, and also a place of entertainment, providing food and drink. Samuel Pepys noted his visits to them in his diary. In September 1664 he took a boat upstream to the Neat Houses 'over against Fox-hall [Vauxhall] to have seen Greatorex dive'. Ralph Greatorex was apparently making experiments with diving bells on behalf of the Royal Society to demonstrate their usefulness in constructing the sea defences at Tangier. Two years later Pepys paid a more conventional visit, when he stopped off to buy a melon.[24]

By 1640 market gardens had been established around Oxford, Banbury, Henley, York, Nottingham and Ipswich, while the good soil of the vales of Evesham and Taunton Deane provided vegetables and fruit for Bristol. By the end of the century, gardens were established on the seaboard of Lancashire and Cheshire for the northern towns, and at Llandaff for Cardiff and Bristol. A key consideration was access to market. Some gardeners had their own boats on the Thames, sailing downstream at early light to Queenhithe and Billingsgate, the two major points of disembarkation for the City of London. Some used the coastal shipping routes from Kent and the East Anglian ports. Others had to use pack horses, for instance to travel from Evesham up to the Midlands. Roots, peas and beans travelled well, although it always helped to have good packing in wickerwork containers. Meanwhile manure was going in the opposite direction, for example, from Dung Wharf on the Thames, carried on barges to the ring of gardens around the capital.

It did not matter whether the fields for market gardening were open or enclosed. The communities in the Vale of Evesham, for instance, grew their produce side by side in their open fields. At Sandy in Bedfordshire market gardeners worked alongside farmers on small areas of freehold in the open fields. None of these enterprises was large in scale. Most would have employed an average of six labourers with one or two apprentices. Some gardens, however, were even smaller than this. High rents in Fulham, for instance, meant that gardens were often under three acres, yet it was possible with intensive use of labour and of manuring to return a profit. Thorough digging was undertaken to a depth of at least two spade blades, starting with a trench into which adjacent soil was turned, followed by careful weeding. The main digging season took place in winter, with more in spring to reopen the soil to the air. Manure was kept in heaps until quite rotted and odourless, when it would be added to the soil along with sand, soot, ashes and marls. Manure could also be used to heat the soil, by putting hot dung, still decomposing, into long beds three feet high and broad, on top of which a few inches of fine soil or mould was sprinkled to force crops such as radishes, mushrooms, cucumbers and asparagus.

Seventeenth-century commentators on agricultural and horticultural matters frequently urged the case for market gardening. During the Interregnum of 1649–60, a group of men of a radical Puritan persuasion formed themselves around Samuel Hartlib, a Polish immigrant who settled in London in 1628, and in the Civil War acted as an unofficial agent for the Parliamentarian cause. Describing himself as a conduit pipe, Hartlib employed scribes and translators to copy portions of letters and treatises for circulation to others on a diverse range of practical scientific matters, including horticulture, medicine and land improvement. His writings reflect his belief that God had given Man a talent that should be placed at the disposal of the commonwealth, as shown in the preface that he wrote for an anonymous pamphlet, *A Designe for Plentie, by an Universall Planting of Fruit Trees*, published in 1652. In it Hartlib argued that there should be a law establishing 'a generall and universall Plantation of such wholesome fruit (according to proportion) as might be for the relief of the poor, the benefit of the rich, and the delight of all'. Waste ground and commons should be planted with apples, pears, quinces and walnuts 'at the publique charge of every Town to which they belong', and the fruits could then given to 'the poor, and necessitous'.[25] Perhaps Hartlib's best-known publication was his *Legacy of Husbandry*, first published in 1651. In fact, this was probably not Hartlib's legacy, but that of a Royalist, Sir Richard Weston, who had fled to Europe during the Civil War, leaving his notes for his children. Hartlib on his title page, rather economical with the truth, describes the text as 'a Large Letter concerning the Defects and Remedies of English Husbandry' sent to him from France. The section on gardening bemoaned how the nation was dependent on imports that could easily be raised at home: 'it is known that Licorish, Saffron, Cherries, Apples, Pears, Hops, Cabages of England are the best in the world'.[26]

Saffron and liquorice were grown by market gardeners for their medicinal qualities. The English centre of cultivation of the *Crocus sativus*, from which saffron is produced, was based around Saffron Walden during the sixteenth and seventeenth centuries, although the flowers were also grown for production in other parts of Essex and in south Cambridgeshire by gardeners with small amounts of land in closes or garths. At Foxton in Cambridgeshire the crocuses were grown in open fields, in plots ranging in size from half a rood (one-eighth of an acre) to two acres. William Harrison explained how the bulbs were taken out of the ground in July, and then planted again in rows until September. At the end of that month the 'flowers are gathered in the morning before the rising of the sun, which would otherwise cause them to welk or flitter [dry up or wither]'. They were then dried in little kilns over a gentle fire and pressed into cakes. 'In good years we gather fourscore or an hundred pounds of wet saffron of an acre, which being dried doth yeild [*sic*] twenty pounds of dry and more'.[27] To set against this remarkably good return on investment, the gardener had to consider that it would take three years from first setting to final

11 Saffron crocuses from Crispin de Passe's *Hortus Floridus*, first published in Arnhem in 1614. According to Thomas Tusser in *Five Hundred Pointes of Good Husbandrie*, 'a little of grounde brings saffron a pound, the pleasure is fine, the profit is thine'.

gathering, with the first year producing only small bulbs, the second bigger, and the third the heaviest. Harvesting was also difficult, requiring skilled pickers, usually women or girls who could extract the tiny stamens. A Stock girl giving evidence at an Essex quarter session in 1579 declared that she was on her way to 'Waldon [Walden] for to picke saffron', so the skilled workers may have been peripatetic.[28]

Saffron was used extensively in medicine, as a poultice to relieve itchiness, and internally to strengthen the heart and relieve melancholy. It was also a flavouring for cakes and biscuits, and used to dye lace to make it look as if it were made from gold thread.[29] This style in clothing was very much in fashion in the reign of James I, but declined thereafter, which may partly explain why the cultivation of saffron was on the wane in England by the end of the seventeenth century. In 1720, when George I visited Audley End near Saffron Walden, no saffron could be obtained from the town, and his host had to send out to Bishop Stortford instead; by 1790 the cultivation in East Anglia had died out altogether.

Liquorice proved a much more durable cash crop. A native of southern Europe and parts of Asia, *Glycyrrhiza glabra* is a legume related to beans and peas, with the sweet flavour being extracted from the root. It grows best in deep valleys on well-drained soil, in full sun. Like saffron, it requires patience, for the roots can only be harvested in the autumn two or three years after planting. They are then boiled to obtain an extract. In the late sixteenth century, the market gardeners of Worksop in Nottinghamshire and Pontefract in Yorkshire found that the climate and soil was suitable for its cultivation, to be used in medicine both for flavouring and for the pharmaceutical properties of the plant. The tradition is that it was known as 'Spanish' in northern counties because monks from Spain had grown it at Rievaulx Abbey in Yorkshire during the Middle Ages. John Parkinson wrote in *Paradisi in Sole* that English liquorice was preferred to that imported from Spain because of its 'farre more weake sweete taste', while Culpeper wrote how it 'is planted in Fields and Gardens in divers places of this land, and thereof good profit is made'.[30] He prescribed it dissolved in rosewater for coughs, hoarseness, and consumption. This was an expensive concoction, and country women would replace the liquorice with fennel. By the mid-eighteenth century market gardeners in Norfolk and around London were also cultivating liquorice, attracted by its profitability.

A detailed description of the practices of eighteenth-century market gardeners is provided by Pehr Kalm in his account of his visit to England in 1748. Kalm was a Swedish botanist who had studied under Carl Linnaeus at the University of Uppsala, so he was naturally interested in horticulture. While staying at Woodford in Essex in February, he noted:

Market gardens appeared in several places, together with very large fields which the market-gardeners rented, and had sown with everything that is required in the kitchen. The length and breadth of beds was such as is usual in kitchen gardens, some with thin planks around them. They sloped although very little, towards the mid-day sun. Most of them were at this time covered with glass frames, which could be taken off at will. Under these were sown cauliflower seed, which was already come up four inches high. The cauliflowers stood in even rows across the beds, about eighteen inches between each row and each plant. As cold and snow had come, they had placed the frames over the beds, afterwards Russian matting over these, and straw over that, four inches thick. They had stood thus till today at noon, or a little before, when the straw and mats were cast off, and the frames raised quite up, so that the sun and the air could play freely over them . . . Of the rest

12 Coates Farm, a market garden in Bethnal Green, in a drawing dating from 1773. Bethnal Green, lying just to the east of the City, enjoyed good access to the capital's markets.

of the field, a great part was filled with large bell glasses, under which also cauliflower plants were set, three or four under each bell-glass.

Kalm meticulously recorded the dimensions of rows of vegetables – eighteen inches to two feet between rows of beans, peas and cabbages, and six to nine inches between each plant. The peas were grown on pea sticks, with the tops of the stalks cut off to increase shoots. Weeds were removed with small light hoes, about two inches broad, with a handle two feet long. These could get between the rows, and bank the mould around the vegetables, 'but it cost enough to the one who hoed, who was thus obliged to go very crook-backed, and stooping the whole day.' He also observed that the English were good at making use of the useless, so asparagus was grown in the necks of broken bottles which ensured straightness of the stalks, with the heat from the glass encouraging growth.[31]

A series of letters written in the early eighteenth century argued the case for market gardening in southern Scotland. John Cockburn was a landowner from Ormiston Hall in East Lothian. Elected an MP at Westminster in 1727, he spent much time in London. Many of his letters home to Ormiston were written to his gardener, Charles Bell, the son of a crofter. Charles's father held patches of arable land in common fields in the Scottish (Celtic) system known as rundale, where he cultivated strips in a three-year rotation of bere (barley), oats and pease, and one year fallow. In a letter written in December 1734, Cockburn urged Charles to get his father to be more enterprising and branch out into market gardening: 'It is commonly our Scots way to do little business but squeeze up high prices'. He suggests that on the strips he should grow vegetables for sale rather than 'get bad grain one year and worse the next'. In the garden attached to his croft he should grow raspberries, for brandy which would be snapped up by Edinburgh apothecaries. He also recommended gooseberries 'for Gentlemen may like a dish of fruit', along with artichokes, parsnips, carrots and beans, mulberries and quinces, apples and pears, 'early salading and fine collyflowers'. He even suggests neeps (turnips) served as fruit. Contacts for the Edinburgh market, which he calls Eden, are provided: 'All the people in Scotland are not so void of taste or their other senses as you incline to think them'.

Finally, Cockburn turns to the care and transport of fruit:

> I don't know if you have a carrier at Orm: but I am convinced one who understands his business would get Employment for a Cart such as the Higlers to the Gardeners who come to Covent Garden use. They would carry things cool and clean and one man with two horses in such a Cart would carry in as much as four carriers and four horses carry in one common way and if you put your things up in Baskets carefully as Gardiners do here, by which they'll not be wet, Bruised or Broiled in the Sun, the Cart being covered as the Garden stuff commonly is, in carrying to Eden.[32]

John Cockburn's advocacy of market gardening as a profitable enterprise is borne out by an analysis of the costs and returns for both kitchen and garden farmers. An annual outlay of £30 for a London market garden in 1773 brought in £70, a profit of more than 100 per cent. Against these high profits, however, the gardener also took high risks, with frost, drought, storms and pests presenting a range of threats.[33]

Higlers or higglers were seventeenth-century terms for itinerant dealers supplying city and town markets with all types of produce. The long-established London venues in the City, Stocks and Leadenhall were rebuilt after the Great Fire, and were joined in 1670 by Covent Garden where the 5th Earl of Bedford was granted by royal charter the right to hold a market for the sale of fruit, flowers, roots and herbs and to collect tolls from the dealers. This was a canny move on his part, for London was now expanding westwards, with smart new housing developments. In other parts of the country some produce was sold at the garden gate, especially by kitchen gardeners working in the suburbs of the larger towns, but also taken to the open markets.

The wide range of vegetables, salads and fruit being offered at markets, especially in London, reflects the change in taste that had begun in the late sixteenth century and grown through the seventeenth. The wealthy no longer regarded vegetables as suitable only for poor people and animals; indeed, in 1693 Gregory King in his 'Natural and Political Observations and Conclusions upon the State and Condition of England' reckoned that per capita consumption by the British was higher than the French. Of course, the dainty salads, cucumbers and asparagus, and soft fruit were the luxury of the rich, while root vegetables and cabbages, apples and pears were the diet of the poor. And as Emily Cockayne reminds us in *Hubbub*, her account of the less attractive aspects of English city life in the seventeenth and eighteenth centuries, fruit and vegetables were often not fresh, and at times were downright rotten. We must forget supermarket produce, beautifully presented with sell-by dates, and think of pears that were fresh in early autumn but ancient by January, fresh fruit that had rotted quickly in the summer heat, and vegetables that wilted on the higlers' barrows. But these vegetables and fruit kept alive many of the poorest in towns and cities. How close some of these people were to the edge is shown by popular sayings, such as 'All's good in a famine' and 'Hunger makes hard bones sweet beans', and tales of Londoners being reduced to eating cabbage stalks off rubbish tips. Market gardening had indeed become a vital remedy.[34]

\* \* \*

One of the concerns increasingly expressed by contemporary commentators was the effect of enclosures on the poorest. Enclosure was the process that ended traditional rights, such as grazing livestock on common land, or cultivating arable crops on strips in open fields. Once enclosed, the uses of the land became restricted to the owner. Enclosures began in the Tudor period, often to make sheep farming more profitable. Sir Thomas More famously described how sheep were devouring people and unpeopling villages and towns in his *Utopia* of 1516. In the years that followed, enclosures were more often made for the improvement of arable farming, and in the eighteenth and nineteenth centuries were undertaken by means of local acts of Parliament. Enclosure was a controversial subject at the time, and still constitutes a battleground for social and economic historians. Some argue that rich landowners used their control of state processes to appropriate public land for their own benefit, creating a landless working class. Others contend that enclosure enabled the more enterprising members of the peasant class to escape the perpetual poverty of subsistence farming. Both sides agree, however, that the poorest members of the agricultural community were the losers.

This is shown in some of the enclosure awards and charitable bequests in rural communities that have been identified during research into the origins of allotments. The earliest example is from Haddiscoe in Norfolk: 'an estate called Catfields, consisting of a messuage [a dwelling house] . . . and 12 acres of land in 20 pieces, given by will by Thomas Strange in 1556, for the purpose of paying the taxes, repairs of the church and highways and for the relief of the poor and needy'.[35] As Haddiscoe was not enclosed until 1814, these were probably separate strips in open fields, let to the highest bidder, with the income going towards the various charities. An example from the late seventeenth century is from West Haddon in Northamptonshire, where a charity estate was established in 1680 for garden plots for the poor. One of the traditional rights lost with enclosure was that of cutting furze for fuel on commons. When Clipston in Northamptonshire was enclosed in 1776, an allotment of fifteen acres was awarded to the rector, churchwardens and overseers for the use of the poor in lieu of this right. When Broadwell in Gloucestershire was enclosed in 1793, just over eight acres were allotted to the north of the village for letting, with the proceeds going towards buying coal for the poor. Fuel allotments became a feature of enclosure awards on this basis, with the money going to help the poor, but from 1832 a Fuel Allotments Act authorised parishes to let fuel allotments as garden allotments.[36]

From the later seventeenth century commentators proposed what the rural landless poor might grow in the gardens attached to their cottages. John Worlidge recommended various vegetables, which he called esculents: 'The meanest Cottager may well afford that little ground (if he hath any) that is contiguous to his Tenement, for the propagating of some or other of these Esculents'. Taking the traditional galenic humours, he goes on to describe the suitable soils: hot, dry and sandy for carrots, cold and dry for turnips, hot and moist for peas, beans and most sorts of tillage and cold and moist for cabbages and beans. He, like many of his contemporaries, advocated the practice of market gardening: 'The accidental or casual thriving of Plants or Seeds in the various sorts of Land hath, within the memory of man, very much encouraged our Rusticks to a farther improvement of this part of Husbandry'. But he goes on to point out that they have not only found 'a good Market for curious Pallets' but also how this gardening has kept them alive in times of dearth: 'frugal meats for their own Families and sometimes necessary also (which makes men ingenious) hath put them upon the propagation of these esculents which have served as Meat, Bread and Drink in such years that Corn has been Scarce'.[37]

Another promoter of such 'esculents' was Thomas Tryon, a remarkable figure. He was born in Bibury in Gloucestershire in 1634, the son of a tiler and plasterer. He received brief schooling but was soon set to work spinning and carding wool, earning two shillings a week. On Sundays and holidays he took to the hills to mind sheep, at the age of thirteen persuading his father to buy him a small flock which he managed so well that five years later he sold them at a profit of £3. Having taught himself to read, he set off for London in 1652 and apprenticed himself to a hatter at Bridewell Dock near Fleet Street. Flourishing at the hat trade, he settled in Hackney and began a prodigious output of publications on various subjects including vegetarianism. Perhaps his most famous work was first published as *Health's Grand Preservative* in 1682, and thereafter known as *The Way to Health*.

Tryon considered the way vegetables grew in the garden affected their influence on health. Thus colworts were 'of a more lively, opening and cleansing Nature and operation' than cabbages and cauliflowers 'because they grow open, so that the Air, with the Sun, has its free influence upon them; and this is also the Reason that they look of a greener and fresher colour than many other Vegetables'. Turning to root vegetables, he judged turnips to be 'of a very innocent and mild Nature' maturing in September and October 'at which time the central heat of the Earth being Weak, all its products are also weak and endowed with gross phlegm and cold Juice', and therefore not good for physic. However, the turnip and the potato, growing near the surface of soil, were 'better than other roots and more familiar to our natures than such as grow deeper in the ground [i.e. carrots and parsnips] because they participate more of the influences both of the air and sun than others'.[38]

Tryon's mention of the potato as a good root vegetable is an interesting one, for previous writers on horticulture, such as Culpeper and Hartlib, make no reference to what is today one of the principal, and popular, items in the British diet. The Virginian potato, *Solanum tuberosum*, was first described and illustrated in John Gerard's herbal of 1597. In fact, this type of potato probably came from Cartagena in Colombia, one of the plants brought back to England by Francis Drake in 1586. Gerard reported how it prospered in his garden, and recommended that it should be 'boiled and eaten with oile, vinegar and pepper, or dressed any other way by the hand of some cunning in cookerie'.[39]

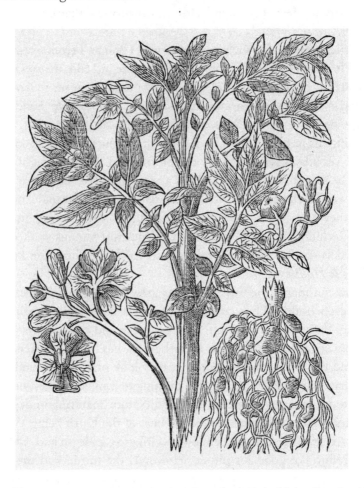

13 The Virginian potato, *Solanum tuberosum*, from the herbal of John Gerard published in 1597. This was the first illustration of the vegetable in an English book, and Gerard provided advice on how to cook and serve it. In fact, the potato was not to feature in the English diet for almost another hundred years.

Gerard also had his portrait engraved for the herbal, proudly holding the flower of the plant, but his keenness proved premature for it took many years for the potato to gain acceptance in England. Instead, it was Ireland that took up its cultivation with enthusiasm.

Traditionally Sir Walter Raleigh is attributed with the introduction of the potato to his Irish estates around the year 1585. Within fifty years it had become the principal staple of the island as the result of a whole set of circumstances. The Irish system of agriculture was based on the rundale, the Celtic equivalent of the open field system, but as society was organised in tribal groups, little attempt was made to cultivate and weed land between sowing and reaping because cottiers (peasants farming smallholdings) and their families were 'creaghting', that is, wandering through the mountains with their cattle looking for grazing land. The diet was dominated by meat, or for the poor, dairy produce. Early records make scant reference to gardening, and little mention of vegetables. Corn was burnt in the straw, with grain being winnowed from the ashes, and late varieties of potato could flourish on the potash following the burning of the corn. Cottiers rented a cabin and a small plot, usually around an acre, upon which to grow potatoes alongside the corn, oats and possibly flax. The subsistence character of agriculture meant that all surplus, especially the corn, went to pay rent. Food for the winter for both people and animals was an outstanding need, which the potato – easily cooked on cauldrons over an open fire – met perfectly. The climate, moreover, was ideal for cultivation.

The potato even suited the dreadful political climate: the sixteenth century had been fateful for Ireland, with civil war and ferocious treatment from the English. If the usual, above the surface, crops were sown, they might be destroyed, while potatoes could be cultivated and stored in a manner that might outwit destruction and malevolence by enemies. The pivotal role of the potato in the seventeenth century is shown by a proclamation issued by Lord Broghill at Youghal on 22 July 1644: 'Whereas the gardens in and near this town and liberties are in great hope to be a good help to the inhabitants, if care be taken that the roots [potatoes] and fruits growing in them be duly preserved from the violence of soldiers and other inhabitants who have of late most wrongfully entered and destroyed the same.'[40]

The scientist Robert Boyle, owner of lands in Cork and Waterford, made clear in a discussion at the Royal Society in 1662 how the potato had become the saviour of the Irish in times of famine: 'there were kept from starving, thousands of poor people by potatoes'. He went on to explain that the root, if mixed with wheaten meal, made good bread. It could also be made into a drink, feed poultry and other animals, and 'the very stalks . . . thrown into the ground, will produce good roots'.[41] The potatoes were grown in gardens or haggards attached to the cabins or cottages, or on small plots of land not available to plough. When the London bookseller John Dunton visited Ireland in the 1690s, he wrote: 'Behind one of their cabins lies the garden, a piece of ground, sometimes half an acre or an acre, and in this is the turf stack, their corn, perhaps two or three hundred sheaves of oats and as much peas. The rest of the ground is full of their dearly beloved potatoes and a few cabbages.'[42]

Later, potatoes were also grown on strips in rundale fields. The strips were usually four feet by twenty yards, although this was variable according to the lie of the land and whether it could be drained adequately. They came to be known as lazy beds because the ridge was built up by turning sods from either side of the ridge to lie inverted on a strip of untilled or 'lazy' ground. Manure was provided from cattle, sometimes from pigs, and from seaweed in coastal areas. Various kinds of spades were used, known as loys or facks, with one ear to the blade that measured about ten inches in length and four in width. The upper end of the blade expanded up into a socket bent at an angle of about 160 degrees. An ash pole about four feet in length was fixed into the socket, with no terminal handle. The spade would almost always be made entirely of wood, for most of the labourers worked barefoot. Once the lazy bed was made, sets of potatoes were placed on the manured turf and covered.

In 1739 came a forewarning of what could befall the Irish poor, so totally dependent on a single crop. A severe frost destroyed the potatoes, followed by fever and famine in the following two years. One-fifth of the population is estimated to have perished, yet in the next hundred years this loss was more than made up, by 1800 reaching 5 million and, by 1841, 8 million. The census in 1841 recorded 130,000 holdings of more than fifteen acres, and a massive 700,000 holdings of less than fifteen acres. In 1846 the population had reached 9 million. In August of the previous year a blight, the fungus *Phytophthora infestans*, was reported both in mainland Europe and in the islands of Britain. It hit with virulent speed. A man travelling to Cork to stay with relatives described how fields looked well on his way south. A week later, on his return, the whole parish was stricken as if by frost, with blackened foliage covering those same fields. In the famine that followed, over a million men, women and children died

14 Gardens in County Roscommon, from an article in the *Illustrated London News*, 15 May 1880, showing how potatoes were cultivated before the terrible Irish famine.

from starvation, typhus and cholera. Up to one and a half million more left the country as a direct result, setting a pattern of continuing emigration for the rest of the century, and fundamentally altering the history of both Britain and the United States.[43] This vital remedy had become a deadly poison.

The history of the potato in England, Scotland and Wales followed a very different course. From the time that the potato arrived in England, herbalists recognised that it was a member of the *Solanum* family with relatives that were both narcotic and poisonous, such as deadly nightshade, and that its berries should not be eaten. Another member of the family was the tomato, whose young or raw green fruit was also poisonous. Introduced to England from Mexico in 1596, the tomato was known as the love apple and credited with aphrodisiac qualities. The potato too was regarded as an aphrodisiac, with Shakespeare making Falstaff call upon the sky to rain potatoes as he prepares for a romantic assignation in Windsor Great Park in *The Merry Wives of Windsor* (Act V, Scene 5). Many not only feared that divine retribution would be dealt through eating forbidden fruit, but that potatoes carried leprosy, scrofula and fever.

However, the advocates of the potato were beginning to be heard. In 1662 the Royal Society discussed its possibilities as protection against famine, with Robert Boyle adding his views, as mentioned above. Two years later John Forster published the first treatise devoted exclusively to the potato, *England's Happiness Increased*, dedicated to Charles II with the alternative title 'A Sure and Easie Remedy against all succeeding Dear Years'. Forster maintained that by planting potatoes, 'ten thousand men in England and Wales, who knew not how to live, or what to do to get a maintenance for their families, may of any one acre of ground make thirty pounds a year'. In a wonderful combination of high politics and humble vegetable, Forster suggested that tubers should be imported from Ireland as seed and the King should have a monopoly to regulate planting, thus freeing corn for export abroad and encouraging trade. Foreign mercenaries could then be hired to maintain order within the kingdom, presumably fed on the potatoes. In 1664 when Forster wrote his treatise, potatoes were featuring in fashionable dishes on rich men's tables, and he provided directions on how to make potato bread, puddings, custards and cheese cakes.

Progress in the vegetable's popularity can be measured by the comments made by John Worlidge in different editions of his *Systema Agriculturae*. In the first edition in 1669 he considers the propagation of potatoes as food for animals. By the 1688 edition, he was advocating cultivating them as food for people:

> Potatoes are much used in Ireland, as in America, as Bread, and are themselves also an unusual food. They grow in mellow ground and are increased by cutting the roots in pieces and planting them as *scorsonera*. These and the Jerusalem Artichoke, which are by much the meaner food, although somewhat like them, may be propagated with advantage to poor people, a little ground yielding a very great quantity, as the many small Welsh territories adjoining the Highways of these parts, planted with them plainly demonstrate.[44]

Formby in Lancashire was the first English seat of cultivation, traditionally as a result of an Irish shipwreck off the coast. A special potato market was held in Wigan from the late seventeenth century, and the crop had become sufficiently established for local clergy to sue parishioners for tithes. The open field system had disappeared in the county, replaced by smallholdings and little enclosed plots. With the deep moss soil and mild climate, the potato flourished. The workers were relatively well paid, and thus could cultivate their own land to buy other foods, including the meat and onions that were combined with potatoes to make the local dish, lobscouse – a word that also meant 'sailor' and, later, a Liverpudlian.

Very slowly the rest of Britain began to adopt the potato as an important component of the diet, particularly in the 1760s when the price of meat and other foodstuffs began to rise while wages remained static. Even then there was resistance. In Lewes in Sussex in 1765, associating potatoes with despised Irish peasants, a popular slogan ran 'No potatoes, no Popery'. The conservatism of the rural poor was noted by Jane Austen's mother, when, around the year 1770, she advised a tenant's wife at Steventon in Hampshire to plant potatoes in her garden. 'No, no they are all very well for you gentry, but they must be terribly costly to rear', came the cautious reply.[45] The great naturalist Gilbert White was more successful with the village labourers of Selborne in Hampshire. He started growing potatoes in 1758, conducting experiments including the effect of various composts. After years of encouragement, including the award of premiums, he got the villagers to follow his example.[46]

In the 1760s the agricultural writer Arthur Young conducted his three great tours which he then converted into books: *A Six Weeks' Tour through the Southern Counties of England* (1768), *A Six Months' Tour through the North of England* (1770) and *A Farmer's Tour through the East of England* (1771). During his journeys, he noted where potatoes were being grown, both in fields for market and in gardens for private consumption. In the Midland counties he makes only one mention of potatoes, at Sandy in Bedfordshire, where they were being raised among other market garden produce. Sandy, with its light, sandy soil, had a long tradition of market gardening, stretching back to the Dutch immigrants in the late Tudor period. The only places where he found potatoes being grown in quantities were the Essex towns of Ilford and Brentwood, within easy distance of London. In the south-east he found one example of two acres in Kent and another acre in East Sussex. Both were noted as experiments by market gardeners. The picture continued like this throughout the south part of England, but was very different when he reached Yorkshire and the north, where he found potatoes being grown in quantity in fields, especially in the neighbourhood of industrial towns in the North and West Ridings, and in workers' gardens. Unsurprisingly, Lancashire abounded in potatoes (grown in gardens), as did Westmorland and Cumberland.

Young could find no correlation between potato cultivation and population density, nor (apart from in Yorkshire) industrial centres. But he found a significant difference between places with open common fields and those that had been enclosed: the availability doubled with enclosure. At this period of his life, Young was a strong supporter of enclosures, believing them to improve agriculture. Later, having seen the misery of landless agricultural workers, both in Britain and in Ireland, his views were to undergo considerable change.

Another influential writer on agricultural matters was Nathaniel Kent, who in 1775 published his *Hints to Gentlemen*, a work that was to prove highly influential among landowners concerned about the plight of their tenants, including the Earl of Winchilsea, one of the pioneers of nineteenth-century allotments. Kent provided detailed plans of model housing, but also advocated that around these cottages there should be half an acre for potatoes and carrots, plus three acres for a cow and pasture. A considerable body of opinion was thus building up to encourage the working classes to cultivate the potato.

Ultimately, however, it was want rather than desire that tipped the balance, and by the beginning of the nineteenth century, the vegetable had become one of the most important contents of a cottager's vegetable garden. This can be seen in the early nineteenth-century garden recreated at the Weald and Downland Museum, attached to a toll house built in 1810 to control the turnpike on the route through the South Downs to the fashionable resort of Brighton. The vegetable plot, which dominates the garden, is divided into three main areas: one for growing potatoes, followed by leeks, another for peas and beans and a third for root crops, with a three-year rotation.

\* \* \*

We are accorded only very rare accounts of what the gardens of agricultural labourers looked like in the eighteenth century. However, the description of a group in an Aberdeenshire hamlet has survived:

> About the place we find here and there an exceedingly rustic sort of garden. In these 'yards', which occur in no regular order – are so placed, in fact, that a stranger could hardly guess from the position of any one of them to which of the indwellers it belonged – may be found, besides certain useful vegetables, as 'kail', green or red, and 'syboes' [spring onions], a few old fashioned herbs and flowers. Some clusters of rich-

scented honeysuckle, a plant of hardy southernwood, peppermint, and wormwood; with, mayhap, also a slip or two of 'smeird docken', the sovereign virtues of whose smooth green leaves, in respect of sore fingers or broken shins, commend it to careful consideration.[47]

This garden combined the cultivation of vegetables for the pot and plants for the medical chest. 'Smeird docken' may have been Good King Henry, or more probably dock.

Another glimpse at an agricultural labourer's garden is provided by a pamphlet entitled *An Account of a Cottage near Tadcaster*, issued in 1797. It was written by Sir Thomas Bernard, a leading light in the Society for Bettering the Conditions and Increasing the Comforts of the Poor, founded in the previous year. He gives us the story of a Yorkshire agricultural worker, Britton Abbot, and a description of his garden, with a little woodcut engraving of the cottage and garden on the title page. Britton Abbot, born around the year 1730, was sent at the age of nine to work with a farmer. By the time he was twenty-two he had saved £40, married and taken a farm of his own at the rent of £30 per annum. But Abbot did not prosper and was obliged to take a cottage in the village of Poppleton with two acres of land, common rights and two cows. For nine years he worked as a labourer, but when Poppleton was enclosed, Abbot, with six children and a seventh on the way, was obliged to find a new home because of 'the arrangements made in consequence of it'.[48]

Abbot was very lucky to be given a piece of roadside land by Squire Fairfax, and, 'with a little assistance from the neighbours in the carriage of his materials, he built his present house; and planted the garden, and the hedge around it, which is a single row of quick [set], thirty-five years old, and without a flaw or defect'. The garden, a rood in extent (a quarter of an acre), contained 'fifteen apple-trees, one green gage, three winesour plum-trees, two apricot-trees, several gooseberry and currant bushes, abundance of common vegetables, and three hives of bees'.[49] The last can be seen in the engraving, behind the neat rows of vegetables. Mrs Abbot, in charge of the garden, seems to have organised some small-scale market gardening, obtaining an annual yield of around forty bushels of potatoes, along with other vegetables, and fruit worth between £3 and £4. She also occasionally went out to work, and spun at home. Despite his sixty-seven years, Abbot earned between twelve and eighteen shillings a week hoeing turnips, setting quick and other task-work.

AN

# ACCOUNT

OF A

# COTTAGE AND GARDEN,

NEAR TADCASTER,

WITH

## OBSERVATIONS

UPON LABOURERS HAVING FREEHOLD COTTAGES

AND GARDENS,

AND UPON A PLAN FOR SUPPLYING COTTAGERS
WITH COWS.

PRINTED AT THE DESIRE OF THE SOCIETY
FOR BETTERING THE CONDITION, AND
INCREASING THE COMFORTS OF THE POOR.

## LONDON:

PRINTED FOR T. BECKET, BOOKSELLER, PALL-MALL.

1797.

PRICE ONE SHILLING A DOZEN.

15 The title page of *An Account of a Cottage and Garden near Tadcaster*, published in 1797, showing the garden cultivated by Britton Abbot and his wife, with beehives, fruit trees and vegetables planted in rows.

Britton Abbot provided an ideal textbook example for Bernard, for he displayed industry throughout his life, never applying for parochial relief. Bernard wanted to show how the system was weighted against the small farmer and the landless labourer, and to appeal to both the philanthropic instincts of landowners and the economic arguments against the work-house system, increasingly an economic burden through the poor rates levied on every parish. He mentions how landowners in Rutland and Lincolnshire, such as the Earl of Winchilsea and Lord Brownlow of Belton, had annexed gardens to the cottages of their tenants, charged moderate rents, and sometimes supplied pasture for a cow. In capitals he emphasises how 'Five unsightly unprofitable acres of waste ground would afford habitations and comfort to twenty such families as Britton Abbot's'.[50] The remedy that he is proposing looks forward to the allotment movement that was to gain ground with the new century.

# CHAPTER 3

# Working Gardeners

'GARDENER' IS A term that covers a multitude of roles and diverse social status. Market gardeners were featured in the preceding chapters, but here those who earned their living working for private households will be the principal focus. As John Harvey points out in his pioneering study of nurserymen: 'At the professional end of the scale, as it were, was the landscape gardener or garden designer, who might well be the same person as the chief gardener to some noble estate. A few gardeners with exceptional botanical knowledge also took a high position. Beneath these in general estimation, but nonetheless commanding high pay, were a great many chief gardeners to the country gentry.'[1] These were the men – and they were always men – with relatively high status. Working under them were teams of assistants, reaching down to unskilled labourers, and here there were women.

Prior to the sixteenth century, these working gardeners were mostly anonymous figures, although as John Harvey memorably wrote, 'by no means nameless serfs provided with shovels'.[2] The reason for this is sparsity of evidence. Gardening skills in the Middle Ages in Britain lay very much in the hands of the Church, in the religious houses. Monks, nuns and their lay brothers grew flowers to adorn their churches and chapels, cultivated orchards and kitchen gardens to supply their refectories, and planted herbs to provide physic both for their infirmaries and for the care of the communities outside their walls. With the dissolution of the monasteries monks and priests were scattered throughout the kingdom, but some continued their horticultural craft. At the same time, Renaissance ideas were arriving in England, and the gardens of the wealthy and powerful were becoming status symbols. The most fashionable early sixteenth-century gardens were created by Henry VII (in contradiction to his miserly image) by Cardinal Wolsey, and above all by Henry VIII. It was important that their gardeners should be equipped with the requisite skills in design, plantsmanship and the management of their staff. Gardens, even more than buildings and furnishings, are dynamic, calling upon knowledge and experience to maintain them to the highest standards.

Some of the gardeners who worked for the Cardinal and the King would also have been nurserymen, running businesses dealing in living plants. Thus in the accounts of Cardinal Wolsey at Hampton Court there is reference to his gardener, John Chapman, supplying herbs in 1515. This would seem to have been a common practice throughout the profession, and there are many examples of gardeners retiring to run nurseries at the end of their careers. These nurseries often became important places for young gardeners to learn their skills.

When the King acquired Hampton Court from Wolsey in 1529, he inherited John Chapman, who had also looked after the Cardinal's garden at York Place on the south side of the Strand in London. This too passed to Henry VIII, and became known as Whitehall. Chapman would have been what we call a head gardener, with a team of men and women working under him. In the 1530s twenty-five garden workers are listed for Whitehall, assisted by nine under-gardeners and fifteen named labourers. Sometimes the team was supplemented by temporary help for short-term projects, so that Chapman prepared for a royal visit to the Cardinal's Hampton Court by introducing local labour, and at least six of his senior gardeners from York Place. When Chapman was succeeded at Hampton Court by Thomas Alvard, the royal clerk noted some of the tasks that were required. Roger Down organised the building of terrace walk embankments against the inner sides of the Privy Garden walls, assisted by nine labourers. John Hutton came up-river from London to work on the design of the Privy Garden's main beds, bringing with him rosemary plants and gillyflowers, mint and other sweet flowers for the knots. The plants were supplied by Agnes Hutton, who was probably his wife. Matthew Garret carried out much of the planting in the Privy Garden, with strawberries, violets, primroses and gillyflowers. He was helped in this task by a team of women, while others gathered strawberry and flower roots in the wild at threepence or fourpence per bushel.[3]

We do not know what training Chapman, Alvard and their teams had received, although a background in agriculture or husbandry would have provided a good grounding. A degree of specialisation is clear from the records, so that Roger Down was assigned construction works, while Hutton was skilled at design and Garret was a plantsman. One highly prized horticultural skill at this period was the cultivation of fruit. Richard Harris, an Irishman, was given land at Tenham (now Teynham) in Kent by Henry VIII, where he cultivated apple grafts, especially pippins, from France, and grafts of cherries and pears from the Low Countries. The King was concerned that England was too dependent on imported fruit, so the orchards in Kent formed a kind of Maginot line. This move was highly successful, for Kent became 'the garden of England', while orchards flourished throughout the country. Sir Thomas Tresham, owner of an ambitious garden at Lyveden New Bield in Northamptonshire at the end of the sixteenth century, dispatched his nurseryman, Andrewes, across the country to the fruit-growing counties of Gloucestershire, Worcestershire and Shropshire to acquire pear and cider kernels for his orchards. He also sent him lists of the fruits that he suggested should be planted. One was 'Normandy hawksbill peare ... one of petworth rootynge', which was probably obtained from the orchards at Petworth in Sussex, belonging to the Earl of Northumberland. Tresham was knowledgeable about the qualities of the different kinds of fruit, so that the Normandy hawksbill

16 Gardeners making and planting grafts in an orchard, from William Lawson's *New Orchard and Garden*, published in 1618.

ripened at 'hullontide' (All-Saints or Hallowtide, 1 November), while Dr Harvey's apple, he noted, kept until Candlemas (2 February).[4] Andrewes was clearly kept up to the mark.

The remuneration received by gardeners in royal and aristocratic service is duly noted in accounts. However, it is difficult to interpret as modern equivalents can be misleading. In his book, *Early Nurserymen*, John Harvey tried to provide some kind of modern comparison, reckoning that £12 in sixteenth-century England was the equivalent of £2,000 in 1973, his year of publication. Four decades on, the sum should be multiplied at least tenfold. Thus John Lovell, the principal gardener at Greenwich Palace in 1519, on an annual retainer of £3 0s 8d, was receiving today's equivalent of just under £5,000. His son, also John, was made keeper of the orchard and garden at Richmond in 1549, receiving a fee of £6 1s 8d, with an additional grant of £4 per annum for the weeding and sanding of the garden and the 'orteyard', or vegetable garden: today's equivalent of £16,600. These are not generous figures, but fare better when another form of comparison is applied. The average annual salary for a schoolmaster in the sixteenth century was £6 9s, and for a clergyman between £10 and £20.[5]

For those further down the gardening hierarchy, the picture is equally difficult to assess. The Statute of Artificers passed in 1563 gave the responsibility to county justices to make an annual wage assessment for every trade. They had to decide whether the rates should be fixed 'by the Yere or by the Daye Week Monthe or other-wise, with Meate and Drinck, or w[i]thoute Meate and Drinck'.[6] Not only did sustenance come into the equation, but also board and lodgings. Thus Philip Enys, the gardener at Greenwich in 1546, was paid board wages of 4d per day, while the two men he employed got 7d a day, presumably without board. If these men were paid six days a week for a year, then Enys received about £5 annually, while his assistants received £8 15s if they worked right through all the seasons.

The landscape historian W.G. Hoskins characterised the seventy years between 1570 and 1640 as the age of rebuilding in England.[7] Prosperity enabled yeomen, farmers, husbandmen and even cottagers in the countryside, and merchants and craftsmen in towns, to build new dwelling houses, while the nation's richest families built fine mansions in both. With these houses came new gardens and a growing number of working gardeners. A 'mystery' or fellowship of gardeners had existed in London from the mid-fourteenth century, ensuring that training took place through an organised apprenticeship system, and acting as a benevolent fraternity looking after members and their families. However, this fellowship did not enjoy the freedom of the City, nor the other privileges accorded to livery companies. In 1605 James I granted royal charters to gardeners and fruiterers to form two separate companies. When the fruiterers began their campaign to secure the charter, they asked the City's Court of Aldermen to draw up for them a set of ordinances. The gardeners took rather a different route, persuading the King to grant them near-exclusive rights over 'gardening, grafting, setting, sowing, cutting, arboring, rocking, mounting, covering, fencing and removing of plants, herbs, seeds, fruits, trees, stocks, sets, and contriving the conveyance to the same'.[8] This catch-all applied to gardeners within a six-mile radius around the City, greater than that which applied to most other companies.

From the very outset, the Company of Gardeners faced difficulties in the enforcement and control of their trade. Gardeners and labourers who had not come up through the Company's apprenticeship scheme were arriving in London from all over the country, drawn by the prospect of laying out and working on the gardens of the burgeoning population. Many did not enrol as members, and those that did often failed to pay their fees. In 1659 the Company put forward the proposal to incorporate 10 garden designers, 150 noblemen's gardeners, 400 gentlemen's gardeners, 100 nurserymen, 150 florists, 20 botanists, and 200 market gardeners. This plan was never implemented, but the numbers cited shows how the profession was expanding and attaining status.

The achievement of status is marked, for we begin to know much more about some of the head gardeners, and their relationship with their employers. One well-documented example is that of Robert Cecil and his gardener, John Tradescant. Cecil, Secretary of State to James I, created his last and most elaborate garden at Hatfield House in Hertfordshire in the first years of the seventeenth century. Tradescant was to become one of England's most famous horticulturalists, but it is sign of how quickly working gardeners were moving up the social hierarchy that his origins are obscure. Some accounts describe him as a Dutchman, but he was more likely to have been of Dutch descent, born in the 1570s, probably in Corton in Suffolk.

Tradescant began work at Hatfield on the first day of 1610, at an annual salary of £50, a substantial sum which suggests that he had built up a reputation in an earlier, unknown garden. Within the year Cecil had twice sent him to Europe to buy plants and to meet nurserymen in the Low Countries and France. In Paris, for example, he visited Jean Robin, one of the French King's gardeners, who had his own garden on the western end of one of the islands in the Seine. Robin gave him exotic plants including pomegranates, myrtles, oleanders and fig trees, helping him to pack them up and send them downriver to Rouen.[9]

Cecil died in May 1612, never living to enjoy his new garden at Hatfield. Tradescant went on to work for the Duke of Buckingham, the King's favourite, at his various gardens, and took part in three expeditions overseas. In 1618 he sailed to Archangel as part of a mission to persuade the Tsar to allow English merchants to travel through Russia en route to Persia. Two years later he took part in a naval attempt to crush the activities of the Barbary pirates of Algiers, and in 1627 accompanied Buckingham in his endeavour to aid the Huguenots of La Rochelle. All three adventures ended in failure, but Tradescant always got his plants. When Buckingham was assassinated by a disaffected soldier following the La Rochelle fiasco, Tradescant moved to Oatlands Palace to work for Queen Henrietta Maria before retiring with his treasures to his own garden and nursery in south Lambeth.

John Tradescant's son, also called John, was to make even more remarkable expeditions, to Virginia, in search of exotic plants. Most gardeners led less exciting lives, but the status established by the Tradescants was to continue. John Field was the head gardener to the Russell Earls of Bedford at their country house, Woburn Abbey, from the 1660s, making important changes, especially to the kitchen garden and orchard. In his book *A New Orchard*, first published in 1619, William Lawson had advised that the ideal gardener for an orchard should be 'religious, honest, skilful in that faculties and therewithal painfull'. By 'religious' he meant somebody who cherished learning, and above all the word of God. 'Painfull', or, as we would say, industrious, signified avoiding 'an idle or lazie Lubber', for the weeds always grow.[10] Field clearly filled the bill admirably for the Russells, for in correspondence he is described as 'dear', and sometimes 'very dear'. His staff consisted of men and women paid by the week at between 10d and 1s 6d, according to the nature of the work, but these workers were also supplied with food and clothes. For instance, in 1671 Field spent £1 3s on cloth to provide Francis Chandler a suit and coat, with an additional four shillings to have them made up. Lockram, a form of linen, was purchased for shirts for the men and boys, with laundry money set aside to wash these. Other men and boys were able to earn small sums two or three times a week for carrying loads and shifting gravel.[11]

Field himself earned a salary of £80 per annum. His wife was often called upon by the Russells as a sick nurse, so the couple probably lived in a house in the grounds of Woburn Abbey. Through his colleague Thomas Gillbank, the head gardener at Bedford House in London, he bought trees and plants from two nurseries located to the east of the City. Leonard Gurle, who ran a substantial enterprise between Spitalfields and Whitechapel, prided himself on his fruit trees of the finer and rarer kind, guaranteeing quality so that should any die, he would supply replacements. From James Rickets 'at the Hand in Hogsden [Hoxton] without Bishopsgate', Gillbank purchased lilies on Field's behalf. Seeds were acquired from George Field, who may have been John's brother. A trade in garden seeds had been established in London in the mid-sixteenth century, organised by the grocers, who had the monopoly on the selling of luxury goods such as spices. Thus, for example, when John Winthrop the Younger, the future Governor of Connecticut, wanted to acquire vegetable and flower seeds to take to the infant New England community in 1631, he sent a list to Robert Hill, grocer, who traded from the Three Angels in Lombard Street.

It would appear from the Bedford accounts that John Field did not have an apprentice. However, we do get a good idea of the training of young gardeners from a handwritten text, 'Directions for the Gardiner' among the papers of John Evelyn. The terms of apprenticeship varied, but were usually between five and seven years: Evelyn inscribes his text to 'Jonathan Mosse who came to me Apprentice for six yeares 24 June 1686'. John Evelyn was not only a diarist, but a courtier, scientist, passionate horticulturalist and creator of a fine garden at Sayes Court in Deptford, on the banks of the Thames downriver from the City of London. By 1686 Evelyn was in his late sixties, and wanted gradually to hand over the garden to his assistant.

In 'Directions' Evelyn covers all aspects of running a self-sufficient garden. He begins with 'Termes of Art used by Learned Gardeners', defining techniques such as lætation (dunging), repastination (shallow digging), semination (sowing) and plushing (cutting a branch nearly half through, to make it bendable for layering). The seasons are described: vernal (spring), estival (summer), autumnal, and hyemal or brumal (winter), along with the times attached to fruit and flowers: præcoce (early blossoming and ripening), median (middle term, applied particularly to tulips), and serotine (late flowering and ripening). We can only wonder at how bewildered and daunted Jonathan Mosse, probably from a humble background, must have been, faced with a knowledgeable scholar who was also a skilled gardener. Perhaps Evelyn recognised this, advising Mosse to set the plants for the physic garden in alphabetical order 'for the better retaining them in memorie'.

Mosse was given a full weekly regime, starting with a walk 'aboute the whole Gardens every Monday-morning duely, not omitting the least corner, and so [to] observe what Flowers or Trees & plants want staking, binding and redressing, watering, or are in danger; especially after greate stormes, & high winds and then immediately to reforme, establish, shade, water &c what he finds amisse, before he go about any other work'. Evelyn then provided a weekly calendar for mowing, reminding him that the weeders – women – must sweep and clean using the same methods recommended for the mower, 'and never to be taken from that work 'til she have finished'. Relationships with the other members of the household are also considered: providing 'Rootes, sallading, garnishing' for the cook; seasonal fruit for the housekeeper; giving notice to the mistress of the house for the fruits and flowers for the still house; and giving notice to the master when tools, which should be well cleaned and maintained, were broken or worn out. In his list of tools and instruments necessary to a gardener, he includes a calendar to maintain on the bees and their activities, and 'a paper-book to note when & where he sows & plants, & register the successe of Tryalls'.[12] This is an early reference to the idea of a gardener's diary, something that would become an important element of an apprentice's training in the nineteenth century.

The range of subjects covered by Evelyn in his instructions to Mosse shows the diversity of knowledge required by the head gardener of a substantial household: knowledge of plants, experience in cultivation of a range of areas such as orchard trees and kitchen garden vegetables and fruit, a grounding in surveying and a sense of design. Often it was necessary to look to London to find such a versatile expert. Thus Sir Thomas Smyth of Ashton Court in Somerset wrote from the capital to his steward: 'I have this night had a Gardyner in treaty with me, but wee can not yet agree'. Even before he had finished the letter, however, they had probably come to terms.[13] Although the London Gardeners' Company had its shortcomings, it was a professional body that provided information on gardeners. This was supplemented by the informal networks that can be seen in the records such as those for John Field, exchanging plants and trees with other gardeners in the area around Woburn.

17 A kitchen garden with raised beds for melons and cucumbers, from John Evelyn's *French Gardiner*, published in London in 1658.

A recent study of the salaries of the upper servants in seventeenth-century country houses shows that the estate steward stood at the top of the hierarchy, with the gardener, butler, coachman, cook and housekeeper usually reporting to him. Between 1660 and 1700, the annual salary of the gardener ranged from £4 to £20, the butler £3 to £10, the coachman £3 to £10, the cook £4 to £25 and the housekeeper £6 to £10.[14] From these figures it can be deduced that if the gardener and the cook were particularly skilled they could command a good salary, although some gardeners, such as John Tradescant and John Field, were even more highly paid. What marks the head gardener and the cook out from the other members of the household is that their skills were very much on display, and therefore they were a kind of status symbol, showing that their employer was a man of taste and distinction.

Moreover, because the gardener worked out on the estate rather than in the house, he could maintain a certain degree of independence, especially as he usually lived in a house or cottage on the estate with his wife and family. This independence sometimes tipped into truculence. The Reresby family of Thrybergh in Yorkshire seems to have had particular trouble with their gardeners. Some time after 1660, Sir John in London was informed by his wife that she 'cannot get the Gardener to worck as you ordered' so she had been obliged to resort to the gardener of a kinsman to prune the trees and vines. A later gardener, in 1686, complained that his spade was not good enough, so that the steward, Thomas Robotham, had to ask 'youar honor to get him one bought of London and to send it and rather than be without it he will pai himself for it'.[15] This independent spirit has enjoyed a long tradition, with P.G. Wodehouse depicting Lord Emsworth of Blandings Castle going in fear of offending his head gardener, the tyrannical Angus McAllister.[16] Not every gardener enjoyed such independence, and it must be remembered that the work was long and hard. A poignant record of this was made in the diary of Sir Henry Slingsby of the Red House in Yorkshire, on the death of his gardener Peter Clark, who had worked for him for more than a decade: 'he was for no curiosity [innovation] in Gardening, but exceeding laborious in grafting, setting and sowing, which extream labour labour shortn'd his days'.[17]

A fascinating glimpse into a gardening establishment at the end of the seventeenth century is provided by record books maintained by the Newdigate family at Arbury Hall in Warwickshire. Sir Richard Newdigate, the 2nd Baronet, was a controlling employer, carefully checking the estate accounts.[18] His wages book gives the salaries paid to the senior members of staff, including his gardener, alongside the clerk, the butler, the housekeeper, the cook and the coachman.[19] In 1692 the gardener was Joseph Bagley or Dagle (Newdigate's spelling of his servants' names is sometimes at variance with their own records). He was paid £4 10s each Michaelmas and Lady Day, compared to the clerk and cook, who received £5, the housekeeper and butler, £3 10s, and the coachman, £2. These salaries are generous when compared to those paid in other households, but of course Bagley's payment is very low when put against that of, say, John Field with his £80 per annum.

Newdigate's accounts show that he had a high turnover of staff. It was the custom for servants at this period to move after a few years, especially at the outset of their careers, in order to gain experience. But in Newdigate's case, a reason for the fluidity of his household may be detected from the

18  Arbury Hall, Warwickshire, with its walled gardens in a drawing by Henry Beighton in Aylesford's *Country Seats*, 1708.

forfeits that he imposed upon staff for breaching his rules – against, for example, bantering by maids or drinking by male servants. In August 1690 Joseph Bagley was forfeited two shillings for leaving beehives out in the rain to rot, having been twice instructed to put them away. Two shillings represented a substantial sum out of his wages. Newdigate, moreover, expected his head gardener to keep a record book in which he should detail the daily tasks undertaken by each member of his team, along with the wages paid at the end of the week. This must have proved an onerous task for a busy working gardener, who may not have found writing easy. Joseph Bagley clearly found it an imposition, for at the end of August 1691 Newdigate added a note: 'Jos If you keep this book no better you had as good not keep it at all. You should mention every particular thing you do about the Garden that is what you sowe set or remove, and write fairer. Enter for Saturday, Monday and send me the book again.'[20]

Bagley's hand was not very fair, but when he fell sick, Newdigate appears to have taken over the record himself, in much clearer writing. In one week, 11–16 October 1690 there were five members of the team working in the garden, two male gardeners and three female labourers. The two men, Jeofry Paul and William Warmingham, were paid 3s 6d per week. As it was autumn, they were gathering apples from the orchard and Warmingham was taking the crab apples to the 'Crabb Mill'. Currants and gooseberries were also being harvested, and the paved alleys in the kitchen garden were rolled. The three women, Goody Bass, Goody Wagster and Ann Suffolk, who earned about half the pay awarded to the men, spent their time clearing out the rooms above the stables, possibly in order to store the apples, helped Warmingham at the Crabb Mill, and raked and swept up leaves. (See Appendix, Table I.)

For Michaelmas 1698 John Risdall or Risden is recorded as the head gardener at Arbury, at an annual salary of £20. Unlike the unfortunate Joseph Bagley, his handwriting was good and clear, and he seems to have given Sir Richard much better satisfaction for there are no reprimands, and he remained head gardener until 1703. For the week beginning 20 April, Risdall and two of his male gardeners, William Sargent and J. Jacomb, attended to the lawns, mowing and turfing, and kept the tender plants, 'greens', well watered in the greenhouses. The second part of the week was spent by all five gardeners digging to find pipes in the kitchen garden, which suggests that they were creating a dipping pool.[21] (See Appendix, Table II.) The National Trust has recently recreated the kitchen garden at Packwood House in the West Midlands as it would have been in the 1720s, with just such a dipping pool in the centre to water the plants in the kitchen garden, and in the nursery, a protected area where the young seedlings were raised.

The Arbury records are particularly interesting in showing the range, albeit repetitive, of the tasks assigned to the women. Ann Suffolk and a woman named as Elizabeth were recorded working in the garden in April 1699, weeding and sweeping the grass. These two tasks took up a large proportion of their time throughout the summer, but they are also noted gathering herbs for the stillroom, carrying gravel, gathering strawberries and herbs for the kitchen, cutting rot out of apples, husking walnuts and cutting shreds. This last task refers to the lengths of cloth or leather that were cut into thin strips for fixing espaliers and climbers on walls. The women are recorded in February 1701 'straighting nails' for Risdall to use in the kitchen garden. During harvest time, they are often noted as absent, but appear in other account books for the estate, paid for bringing in the hay.

Not all working gardeners were part of teams attached to country estates. Some must have worked alone for an employer, as Peter Clark appears to have done at the Red House in Yorkshire (see above, p. 73), with perhaps a boy or casual labourer to help at busy times. Little is known of them, but the record of one 'jobbing' gardener from the seventeenth century has come down to us, and, remarkably, in his own words. Leonard

19 Women working alongside men in an engraving of 'Spring' by Pieter Brueghel the Elder, published by Hieronymus Cock in 1570. Women are often described as weeders, but here they can be seen moving earth, watering and planting out seedlings in the raised beds of a parterre.

Wheatcroft was a man of many parts: tailor, soldier, ale-house keeper, parish clerk and sexton, poet and gardener. He was born in 1627 at Ashover in Derbyshire, the eldest of nine children. His father was a tailor, also called Leonard, who died in 1648, leaving his son in charge of the large family.

In later life, Wheatcroft wrote his autobiography, a most unusual thing for a man of his status to do.[22] The first reference to gardening comes in 1651 when he planted an orchard for the rector of Ashover, Emmanuel Bourne. Thereafter there are notes of orchards created for members of the Derbyshire gentry, farmers, and merchants such as George Hodgkinson, a trader in lead. For Hodgkinson at Overton Hall in 1666 he noted making a garden set around by close hedges, planted with 'severall wall-trees and a codling hedge [apple trees of a hard type, so not to be eaten raw]'.[23]

While gardening and riding between jobs, Wheatcroft pondered a series of questions, such as: 'What is the reason that one man is not like another in phisogmony? Why have men beardes and women none? Why have sum women beards and sum none?' He also visited Chatsworth, where the 1st Duke of Devonshire was creating substantial new gardens in the Baroque style. Wheatcroft noted 'the famous hall where we was well received and withal had the happynes to view the hous within and without which was most amiable and famous to behold, and at last coming to behould those admirable gardens and platforms and those new invented water-workes'.[24] This, surely, is the earliest example of a working-class garden tourist.

\* \* \*

In 1681 John Field was asked to help found a nursery at Brompton Park in Kensington by his friend George London, head gardener to the horticultural enthusiast Bishop Henry Compton at Fulham Palace. Two other men were part of the enterprise: Roger Looker, gardener to Charles II's wife Queen Catherine at Somerset House, and Moses Cook, gardener to the Earl of Essex at Cassiobury in Hertfordshire. Field somehow managed to combine working on the layout of Brompton Park with his duties as head gardener at Woburn Abbey, and many of the fruit trees and bushes and flowering shrubs were, naturally, supplied by the nursery to the Bedfordshire gardens. But Looker died in 1685 and John Field in 1687 and Cook sold his share to Henry Wise, one of George London's protégés. Under the new partnership of London and Wise, created in 1690, the nursery flourished, to become not only the largest in the country but also to exert a major influence on the nation's gardens.

Brompton Park covered over a hundred acres of good soil, now occupied by the museums and institutes of South Kensington. By 1694 the firm employed twenty men and two women, with the foremen earning twelve shillings per week, other men eight shillings and women four shillings. The stock of plants was huge, valued at between £30,000 and £40,000 in 1705, with a substantial proportion accommodated in large greenhouses built of glass and wood against brick walls. In an advertisement in the front of the 1693 edition of his *Compleat Gard'ner*, John Evelyn declared that he had never seen such an enterprise at home or abroad. London and Wise were responsible for designing and stocking many of Britain's most prestigious gardens, including those belonging to the royal family, and Blenheim, in Oxfordshire, the gift of a grateful nation to the Duke of Marlborough for his victories over the French.

But the superlatives are not the only significant feature of Brompton Park. The origins of George London, the driving force behind the nursery,

are not known but presumed to be humble. His career took off after his
ability was noted by Charles II's gardener, John Rose, who sent him to
France to observe the great gardens being created for Louis XIV by André
Le Nôtre at Versailles, while his subsequent employer, Bishop Compton,
was known as the 'Great Encourager'. London wanted to give similar
opportunities to those studying under him, and is said to have taken his
apprentices to meetings of the Botany Club at the Temple Coffee House
where they could meet botanists and hear about the latest plant introductions. One of his 'students' was Stephen Switzer, who became an influential designer, pioneer of the irregular school of gardening, and a leading
author on practical horticulture during the first part of the eighteenth
century. In his first work, *The Nobleman, Gentleman, and Gardener's
Recreation*, published in 1715, he wrote: 'I have tasted both rough and
smooth (as we plainly call it) from the best business and books, to the
meanest labours of the scythe, spade, and wheelbarrow'.[25]

One of the striking features of English horticulture in the eighteenth
century was the proliferation of gardeners from Scotland. This may seem
strange considering that in the previous century Scotland was conspicuous
for the backwardness of its horticulture and botanical knowledge. In 1661
Robert Sibbald, having returned to Edinburgh from studying medicine at
Leiden and Paris, was horrified by the general ignorance of his countrymen and the poor standards maintained at the University compared to
those he had encountered in Europe. As a result he acquired land at
Holyrood for the use of a botanical garden. (A university botanical garden
had been founded in Oxford forty years earlier.) The first Scottish
gardening book, *The Scots Gard'ner*, was published in Edinburgh in 1683
by John Reid, gardener to Sir George Mackenzie of Rosebaugh. While the
big estates were cultivated in an up-to-date way, the smaller types of
gardens, so frequently found in England, were lacking. Paucity of opportunity may have been a factor in sending young, ambitious gardeners
southwards, in search of better pay and prospects, and a kinder climate.

One vociferous complaint about this influx came from Switzer who,
despite his name, hailed from Hampshire. In his *Ichnographia Rustica*,
published in 1718, he let rip:

> There are likewise several Northern Lads, which whether they have
> serv'd any time in the Art, or not, very few of us know anything of; yet
> by the help of a little Learning, and a great deal of Impudence, they
> invade these Southern Provinces; and the natural Benignity of this

20 The frontispiece to Thomas Fairchild's *City Gardener* published in 1721. The garden is possibly Fairchild's own in Hoxton, with a path between flower beds leading to a gate flanked by stoves for tender exotics. In the foreground are tubs containing an agave, banana, dwarf palm and cactus. This little book was intended to advise customers of the trees, shrubs and flowers suitable for all types of London gardens, and obtainable, of course, from the Hoxton nursery.

Warmer Climate has such a wonderful influence on them, that one of them knows (or at least pretends to know) more in one twelve-month, than a laborious South Countryman does in seven years.[26]

Switzer was exaggerating, for there were plenty of gardeners from other parts of Britain. However, one factor did play in the favour of Scots: their system of education that had been put in place by reformers in the sixteenth century to ensure that even the poorest of boys could read and study the scriptures. This was pointed out by Dr Alexander Carlyle, a minister from Inveresk near Edinburgh, who journeyed to England in 1758 and was shown the gardens of the aristocracy and gentry. Visiting the garden at Bulstrode, a seat of the Duke of Portland, he noted:

It was here that we discovered the truth of what I had often heard, that most of the head-gardeners of English noblemen were Scotch, for on observing to this man that his pease seemed late on the 4th of May, not being then fully in bloom, and that I was certain that there were sundry places which I knew in Scotland where they were further advanced, he answered that he was bred in a place that I perhaps did not know answered this description. This was Newhaills, in my own parish of Inveresk. This man, whose name I have forgot, if it was not Robertson, was not only gardener but land-steward, and had the charge of the whole park and of the estate around it; – such advantage was there in having been taught writing, arithmetic, and the mensuration of land, the rudiments of which were taught in many of the country schools in Scotland. This man gave us a note to the gardener at Blenheim, who, he told us, was our countryman, and would furnish us with notes to the head-gardeners, all the way down.[27]

So alarmed did the London Company of Gardeners become that a pamphlet *Adam Armed*, was published, probably in the 1760s, declaring that no apprentice from the north should be employed.[28]

One of the most influential gardeners of the period was Philip Miller, who, although brought up near London, was of Scottish origin. After working with his father in his nursery in Deptford, he opened his own business in St George's Fields in Southwark, where he specialised in florists' flowers and ornamental shrubs. In 1722, at the age of twenty-nine, he was appointed as gardener at the Chelsea Physic Garden. This four-acre garden had been founded upstream from the pollution of the City of

London by the Society of Apothecaries as a research facility for their apprentices and a source of rare ingredients for their medicines. The garden was in a neglected condition when Miller took over, but he quickly built it up into one of the most famous in Europe. He was supposed to be the man on the ground, under the direction of the *Praefectus Horti*, but Miller was very self-confident and strong-minded, and it was he in practice who made the decisions.

Miller was not only an experienced and skilful gardener, but also a great networker. Prolific correspondence was maintained with horticulturalists, plant collectors and fellow gardeners. Against the rules of the Society, he swapped plants and seeds, and during his reign of nearly fifty years at Chelsea, doubled the number of species cultivated in Britain. His Scottish father had provided him with a first-class education that included mathematics, drawing and natural history, as well as several foreign languages, so that when Stephen Switzer suggested that he should compile a dictionary for gardeners, he launched himself into an authorial career. The first edition of *The Gardeners Dictionary* was produced in 1731, providing a systematic, comprehensive and practical manual, and became an instant success.

Miller wrote in plain English, eschewing the florid style that so characterised the writings of his predecessors such as John Evelyn, insisting that the dictionary was intended 'to inform the Ignorant' rather than the learned.[29] The 1731 edition proved merely the beginning, with seven further editions appearing over the years. The dictionary was fairly modestly priced as there were no coloured plates to bump up the costs, although at £1 15s it was mostly purchased by aristocratic patrons to give to their head gardeners. In 1735 he issued his *Abridgement*, in a smaller format priced at 18s, but still containing much of the same information. More practical for the potting shed or greenhouse than the folio edition, it could be bought by nurserymen and working gardeners with constrained budgets.

In 1724 the Society of Gardeners was founded by twenty London nurserymen. Philip Miller was very much the leading light in this group, which also included Thomas Fairchild, whose nursery was in Hoxton, Robert Furber from Kensington, and George Singleton at the Neat Houses in what is now Pimlico. The group had coalesced in order to protect their interests, for nurserymen were being accused of misleading patrons through the confusion that existed over the naming of plants. Every month the men met at Newall's Coffee House in Chelsea,

21 'September' from the *Twelve Months of Flowers* produced in 1730 for Robert Furber, whose nursery was based in Kensington. Thirty-five varieties of flowers were offered for the month, including marigolds, primroses and geraniums. Individual plants were numbered with a corresponding key listing them by name at the bottom of the plate, so that customers could easily put in their order.

conveniently near to the Physic Garden, with a box packed with specimens. After wine and ale, new flowers, trees and shrubs were compared
and classified, and once agreement had been reached, entered into a plant
register. The original intention had been to provide an illustrated survey of
new plant introductions, but in the event only one volume of *Catalogus
plantarum* was published, in 1730, with Miller in charge of the work
and commissioning illustrations from the distinguished botanical artist,
Jacob van Huysum.

The problem of the accurate naming of plants had beset botanists for
centuries, with various efforts made to produce some kind of international
classification, becoming increasingly complex as more and more exotic
flowers, shrubs and trees arrived in Europe from all parts of the world.
Even as the Society of Gardeners strove to find some kind of system for
their publishing project, the Swedish botanist, Carl Linnaeus was tackling
the problem. The son of a keen gardener, Linnaeus first set out his ideas
in *Systema Naturae*, published in 1735. He divided flowering plants into
twenty-three classes, according to the number of male organs, the stamens,
which he called husbands. The classes were further distinguished through
the number of female organs, the pistils, which he called wives.

England had by this time become the most important European horticultural market, so Linnaeus realised that he had to get the nation's botanists and gardeners on his side. Unfortunately the Swede could outdo even
Philip Miller in his self-assurance, often rubbing people up the wrong way.
In addition, the horticultural establishment was shocked by the sexual
terms that he used. His meetings with Miller did not go well, with the
latter refusing to accept his theories, dismissing the system as of 'very short
duration'.[30] It was the Americans who liked his straightforward system,
especially as botanical books were often unavailable.

In 1753 Linnaeus published an even more important work, his *Species
Plantarum*, a survey of all known plants from information derived from his
European botanist acquaintances, along with specimens acquired by the
dispatch of his disciples, referred to as apostles, all over the world on
collecting missions. Wanting to avoid long names that would make international communication difficult, he devised a system that gave every plant
a two-word name. The 'surname' was the genus, to which he added a first
name to denote the individual species. The result of his strivings was a list
of 7,700 plants named and classified in a simple form of botanical Latin.

Again, the European establishment resisted his proposal, with the
Professor of Botany at St Petersburg predicting that the adoption of

Linnaeus's ideas would lead to 'worse than the confusion of Babel'.[31] But again the Americans accepted his ideas. Alexander Garden, a doctor of Scottish origin living in Charleston, South Carolina, wrote enthusiastically, 'Such neatness! such regularity! . . . more easy for beginners'.[32] However, although the Latin was simple, it mean that those without a classical education – which included almost every working gardener – might struggle to cope. Many writers of the period, and subsequently, would have preferred the classification to have been made in English. Miller refused to recognise the system for his new editions of *The Gardeners Dictionary*, but was finally obliged to bow to the inevitable, and in the eighth and final edition, published in 1768, the Linnaean system was adopted.

By the late 1760s, Miller's star was on the wane, and the minutes of the Society of Apothecaries record the differences of opinion that were opening up with their head gardener. His assumed authority had become an issue, although for years the laissez-faire attitude of the Society had provided a vacuum into which Miller had stepped. In November 1770 he agreed to resign, and died just one year later. His relationship with the Chelsea Physic Garden may have ended in sad circumstances, but the bequest that Philip Miller left is significant. Although the garden declined in quality following his departure, hundreds of exotic plants had been cultivated within its walls. The intellectual legacy was substantial, including a number of publications, and his dictionary, the most important horticultural book of the century, going into eight editions and with translations into French, German and Dutch. Among the assistants he trained up was William Aiton, who became gardener to the Dowager Princess of Wales at Kew Palace, while his son Charles Miller became the first superintendent of the botanical garden of Cambridge University.

The mantle of a centre for horticultural excellence passed to a commercial nursery, the Vineyard in Hammersmith, founded in 1745 by James Lee and Lewis Kennedy. Lee was yet another Scottish gardener, who acted as a central figure in the introduction and supply of new plants, including seeds from the second expedition made by Captain Cook to Botany Bay in Australia. Lee, who corresponded with both Joseph Banks and Carl Linnaeus, also established his name by publishing his *Introduction to Botany* in 1760, the first translation into English of Linnaeus's *Philosophia Botanica*. He was a canny businessman, and is famous for establishing the fashion for fuchsias in England. A client to the Vineyard Nursery told him how he had seen on the windowsill of a sailor in Wapping in east London a plant that resembled the *Fuchsia coccinea* that had recently been introduced from South America to Kew, though the Wapping plant looked far superior. Lee went immediately eastward and persuaded the sailor's wife to part with her plant for a fee and the promise of two more plants once he had propagated them. By the next flowering season, Lee had 300 plants, which he sold at a guinea a time.

Lee and Kennedy's nursery was on a much smaller scale than Brompton Park, occupying about three acres on the site of a former vineyard. Here the intensive cultivation of exotics was undertaken in heated houses, unlike at Brompton, where vast quantities of plants had been stored and labour provided to maintain the formal garden style. But the Vineyard Nursery provided a training ground for plenty of young apprentices, housed in a bothy (as the labourers' accommodation was called). They worked long hours, maintaining watch throughout the night over the fires and flues of the stoves that kept alive the tender and exotic plants. The daily routine included sorting out and packing seeds, and filling sacks with seeds of clover, flax and hemp to improve the soil of the nursery's clients. Lee would take apprentices to visit the gardens of these clients, and dispatch them to other nurseries to run errands and carry plants. Lewis Kennedy's role was financial, and he spent much time travelling, collecting debts and securing orders.

One of the apprentices who arrived at the Vineyard Nursery in 1768 was sixteen-year-old John Veitch from Roxburghshire, in the Scottish Borders. His father, Thomas, was a working gardener, and John Veitch not only benefited from the sound primary education provided in Scotland, but also received some teaching in Latin, which would be useful for his horticultural future. After working with his father, and for the first Scottish tree nursery, Robert Dickson & Sons, Veitch was ready to travel south to better himself, and after two years working for Lee and Kennedy at a weekly wage of eight shillings, he was appointed land steward and gardener to Sir Thomas Dyke Acland at Killerton in Devon. Acland had decided to create a landscape park as a fitting setting for his new mansion, and the teenage Veitch found himself in charge of a gang of gardeners and labourers, as he laid out a magnificent arboretum with trees from all parts of the world. In 1800, with the backing of Acland, John Veitch founded a nursery at nearby Budlake, which was one of the first to send plant hunters out in search of new discoveries. So the cycle of horticultural experience, training and discovery moved on.

* * *

Not all nurseries were large-scale enterprises. More modest London nurseries, for example, are mentioned in the records of the Hatton family, who were acquiring plants for their garden at Kirby Hall in Northamptonshire in the late 1650s. Charles Hatton, a keen botanist, acted as the London agent for his brother Christopher. From Mr Stepping's in Colman's Alley in Finsbury Fields and from Goodman Hilliard's in Brick Alley 'against White Crosse Street', both located just north-east of the City, he bought a wide range of plants that included prickly pears, musk roses, pomegranates and a Virginia climber.[33]

Even the largest of these early nurseries would have been comparatively small. Captain Leonard Gurle's nursery and garden plot, established between Spitalfields and Whitechapel to the east of the City in the 1660s was considered 'great' at twelve acres. London and Wise's Brompton Park Nursery, founded in the last decade of the seventeenth century, was exceptionally large, as noted earlier, and represents an unequalled precedent. The death of George London in 1714 marked not only the end of greatness for the nursery, but also the virtual monopoly of London nurseries. Improved road systems, the production of catalogues, and growing demand from owners of country-house gardens made it possible for provincial nurseries to sustain trade, especially around cities like York and Oxford which had a tradition of market gardening.

As the seventeenth century progressed, so the number of seed shops increased. John Worlidge provided a list of these in *Systema Horti-culturae*, in which he featured the 'big three': Thomas Fuller at Strand Bridge, Theophilus Stacy at the Rose and Crown at Bishopsgate and Charles Blackwell at the King's Head in Holborn.[34] The seed trade was closely linked to nurseries, with owners of the latter often running nearby shops. Seedsmen also bought trees and plants from nurserymen to sell in their shops, and in turn supplied the nurserymen with seeds for their customers. Vegetable seeds were being raised in quantity in the market gardens around London and certain areas became known for particular types – Barnes for peas, Battersea for cabbage and Deptford for onion. Further afield, three gardening areas in England raised vegetable seed in quantity – the Vale of Evesham, Sandwich and Colchester.[35]

Nurseries and market gardens frequently overlapped in their activities. In the seventeenth and eighteenth centuries non-specialist market gardeners sold small amounts of nursery wares to local customers, and Pehr Kalm makes no distinction between the two. In his diary for 27 March 1748, he noted:

The Market-gardeners around London have commonly the custom
that they do not employ their time in sowing and cultivating all sorts
of garden and kitchen-garden produce, but they mostly keep to something special. Thus some are only used to sow beans, peas and spinach,
and leave out other vegetables. Others again do not trouble themselves
about these but propagate other plants. Some do not devote themselves
to the planting and cultivation of any particular plants to sell for household use, but devote all their time and labour to sowing all kinds of
plants for kitchens and flower market gardens, so as to provide themselves with seed, which they afterwards sell, and make their living out
of that alone. Other gardeners only make it their business to keep nurseries, in which they have all kinds of plants to sell . . . Amongst these
who exclusively devoted themselves to sowing all kinds of purposes of
getting their seeds for sale was Mr Gordon, who had before been
gardener to the famous Sherard.[36]

The last was a reference to James Sherard, who had an important botanical
garden in Eltham in Kent full of plants recently introduced to England.
John Gordon went on to another highly prized position as head gardener
to Lord Petre at Thorndon Hall, another repository of new exotic plants
and trees, before setting up his nursery in the Mile End Road, with a seed
shop in Fenchurch Street.

Kalm's mention of Gordon is a reminder that Scotsmen were not only
prominent as private gardeners but also as heads of commercial nurseries.
Despite usually coming from humble backgrounds, they were able to draw
upon their primary education and their thrifty nature to build up their
businesses. The nursery owner had to combine a remarkable range of
skills: the ability to get seeds to germinate, flower and fruit; to select the
best seedlings or bud-sports; and to be expert on hybridisation. In addition
they needed business acumen, and the ability to network, compile catalogues and advertise their wares. Nurserymen were usually more prosperous than the owners of market gardens, but there were plenty of risks
involved, and many businesses failed, including a nursery established by
Philip Miller two miles from the Physic Garden at Chelsea.

The gardening trade in general was a very mobile one, with gardeners
who worked for private individuals moving into commercial nurseries and
taking up the sale of seeds. Apprentices, as shown earlier, went from
private gardens to nurseries, especially prestigious ones like Brompton
Park and the Vineyard Nursery in Hammersmith, in order to further their

training. The people of whom we know least, as ever, were the gardeners who were employed in a humble capacity in the nursery trade. The Neat House gardens in Westminster can, however, provide some kind of picture for the eighteenth century.[37] The enterprises here were small in scale, with a few labourers employed along with apprentices, the wives and grown-up children of the owners' families and their female servants. The number of people employed year round ranged between five and twelve, all living in. But in the summer months, casual labour was employed to weed and carry produce to market. Many of the casual labourers were women from Wales and the border counties such as Shropshire. This custom persisted through into the nineteenth century, with the *Illustrated London News* in 1846 noting how hundreds of women from Shropshire every summer were employed to carry baskets of strawberries from the beds in Hammersmith to Covent Garden.[38]

This was hard manual labour, but one commentator writing in 1798 observed how the casual workers were well fed with meat, vegetables and plenty of beer. Workers in the nursery trade were also noted to have been provided with good food by William Cobbett. A man of many talents, Cobbett is famous today as a political agitator, but his background was agricultural and horticultural. Born the son of a Surrey farmer in 1763, he began his working life as a ploughboy and gardener. From 1824 he kept a nursery at Kensington principally to raise considerable numbers of American trees. In a preface to his catalogue compiled in December 1827 he explained how he employed 'about thirty Englishmen, Irishmen and Scotchmen promiscuously, who, in these short days, give me their labour in exchange for 2lbs of bread'. Cobbett advocated bread as a staple in preference to potatoes, and provided the wheat to be ground by his men, along with 'good sound' Cheshire cheese and 2lbs of mutton or pork.[39]

He goes on to describe how the nursery work was organised:

> I myself, must be present with them, and also my foreman. Our time, and especially mine, is precious; and therefore I have done, in one day, by forty men, what another would have done in twenty days by two men. I bring the whole body together at their work, so as to have every man under my eye at one and the same time. I take notice of their different capacities and in short, about an hour after they begin, all having begun with the spade to take up trees, the distribution of the labour is made; some taking up trees; some sorting them, the large from the small; some counting them into hundreds and thousands; some

laying them by the heel in little rows, after they are counted . . . I began yesterday morning, and by this day week I shall be executed instantly, as there will be some men at Kensington constantly packing up trees, from this time to the middle of April.[40]

Cobbett's reference to 'these short days' echoes Hartlib's 'dear times' made two centuries earlier. These short days were to continue through the nineteenth century for some of the rural poor, as will be seen in Chapter 5.

# CHAPTER 4

# A Passion for Flowers

In 1623 Sir Henry Wotton, scholar, diplomat and observer of gardens, wrote to an acquaintance about 'some excellent Florists (as they are stiled)'.[1] This is apparently the first published reference to the term in English, but it was to resound over the next three centuries. Wotton was not using 'florist' in its modern sense, a retailer of cut flowers, a definition that dates from the nineteenth century. Instead he was describing enthusiasts who developed and exhibited pot-grown plants. These men, and very rarely women, were mostly amateurs, although some nurserymen mixed their profession with their passion. The original florists' flowers were recent introductions from the Middle East: the tulip, carnation, anemone and ranunculus. Later in the seventeenth century they were officially joined by the hyacinth and the auricula.

It is thought that the early florists were Flemish weavers, Protestants fleeing to England in the 1570s to escape persecution from the Catholic Spanish rulers of the Low Countries, bringing the precious bulbs and seeds with them in their pockets. Some of the craftsmen settled in Spitalfields, just outside the City of London, and William Shakespeare would have encountered them when he lived in Shoreditch in the 1590s. When he came to write *The Winter's Tale* in 1610 or 1611, he incorporated the passion that florists had for stripes and speckles in the petals of carnations and gillyflowers. In Act IV, Scene 3, Perdita explains to Polixenes:

> . . . the fairest flowers o'th'season
> Are our carnations and streak'd gillyvors
> Which some call nature's bastards: of that kind
> Our rustic garden's barren, and I care not

To get slips of them . . .
For I have heard it said
There is an art which in their piedness shares
With great creating nature.

By using the term 'nature's bastards' Shakespeare was hinting at the possibility that there was sexuality in plants just as in animals, although it had to be merely a hint: to press this too far would smack of heresy.

Garden writers, meanwhile, were exclaiming at the proliferating number of varieties of certain plants. Thus John Gerard in his herbal of 1597 grouped tulips into fourteen categories, protesting that to try to describe all the varieties was like trying 'to number the sands'. By the middle of the seventeenth century, John Evelyn was told by the French gardener Pierre Morin that there were no fewer than 10,000 kinds of tulip. [2] The tulip in particular was responsive to the selective process, as the Turks had discovered when they took wild species from various parts of the Ottoman Empire and applied targeted breeding. When the cultivated tulip was brought to western Europe by merchants and diplomats, the Dutch took up the breeding process with enthusiasm, entranced by the richness in variety of colour and pattern in the petals. To try to get stripes, some growers cut the bulbs of red-flowered tulips in half, binding them with halves of white-flowered bulbs. But this was to no avail, for the vivid breaks that made the tulips so fascinating and unpredictable was in fact caused by a virus carried by aphids, only identified in the 1920s.

In the 1630s the Dutch found themselves in the grip of a craze which they called 'the wind trade' and we now term tulipomania. This reached a climax in the winter of 1636–37 when a bulb of the rare *Semper Augustus*, of red on a white ground, fetched the staggering sum of 10,000 guilders (more than a skilled labourer at the time would earn in a lifetime). A spectacular crash followed, with the state of Holland trying to intervene to cancel debts and restore calm. There were further bouts of tulipomania in France and Turkey in the eighteenth century, and in England a bout of madness over hyacinths in the late seventeenth century, but these were mild in comparison.

Florists began to form themselves into societies. In Holland and the Low Countries these usually had religious affiliations, and were often dedicated to St Dorothy, the patron of flower lovers. In the 1970s and 1980s Ruth Duthie made painstaking investigations into the activities of English florists, and came upon three texts in the Bodleian Library. One was a play by Ralph Knevet, *Rhodon and Iris*, performed at a feast held by the Norwich Florist Society on 3 May 1631. The play's preface refers to the feast 'celebrated by such a conflux of Gentlemen of birth and quality in whose presence and commerce (I thinke) your cities welfare partly consists'.[3] This implies that the society was made up principally of gentlemen and merchants and was secular in character. Two poems have also survived, again pertaining to feasts in Norwich. The first is in a volume of poems of William Strode, chaplain to the Bishop of Norwich from 1632 to 1635, in which he was careful to counter accusations levelled by Puritans that such feasts were connected with the pagan deity, Flora:

. . . Our feast we call
Only with Flowres, from Flora not at all.[4]

The author of the second poem, Matthew Stevenson, had no such concerns, entitling his verse 'At the Florists Feast in Norwich, Flora wearing a Crown'.[5] Carousing and flagons of beer are mentioned, along with a series of named carnations. Sadly these are the only evidence of the Norwich florists, and apart from a reference to a London nurseryman, William Lucas, bequeathing in 1677 the cost of a gold ring to every member of his 'Society or Clubb of Florist', nothing more has come to light on other societies in seventeenth-century England.

Individual florists do, however, emerge from the credits given by gardening writers. Hugh Platt in his *Floraes Paradise*, first published in 1608, makes reference to Master Jacob of the Glass-house, who was able to use the stoves in his glass workshop to keep carnations through the winter. This was almost certainly Jacob Verzellini, a native of Murano who worked in Antwerp before coming to London in the 1570s. The apothecary John Parkinson mentions a whole list of people who supplied him with information, first for his *Paradisi in Sole*, published in 1629, and then his *Theatrum Botanicum* of 1640. Among these are gentlemen florists, merchants such as Nicholas Leate who had excellent contacts with their overseas counterparts, physicians and one woman, Mistress Thomasin Tunstall from Bull Bank near Hornby Castle in Lancashire. These are all people from the middle or upper classes. He did, however, include in his contact list some working gardeners, such as John Tradescant with his nursery in south Lambeth, and Ralph Tuggie with a nursery in Westminster where he was particularly known for his colchicums and auriculas, and above all, carnations. In *Paradisus* Parkinson included illustrations of two tawny carnations, 'Princess' and 'Rose gillyvor', raised by Master Tuggie.

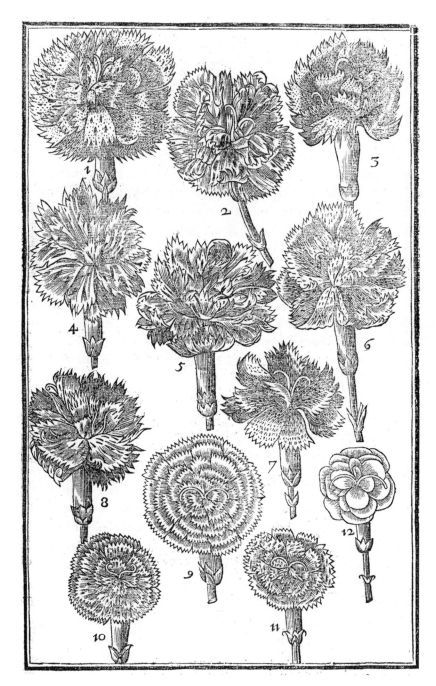

22  A page of carnations from John Parkinson's *Paradisi in Sole*, published in 1629. Among the flowers featured, Parkinson has included tawnies, 'Princess' and 'Rose gillyvor' raised by the florist Ralph Tuggie who opened a nursery in Westminster in 1620.

It is not surprising that humble florists go largely unrecorded. Practical manuals, such as *The English Husbandman*, first published by Gervase Markham in 1613, may claim to be for 'plain russet honest Husbandmen' to widen the possible market, but Platt and Parkinson needed either status, or claim of status and authority. Parkinson was particularly proud of his connection with the royal family, dedicating his first book to Queen Henrietta Maria and his second to the King, Charles I. As the century progressed, florist authors stood even more on their dignity. When Samuel Gilbert came to write his *Florists Vade-Mecum* in 1682, he dismissed rather haughtily 'the trifles adored amongst countrywomen but of no esteem to a Florist who is taken up with things of more value'.[6] The Royal Society had received its charter from Charles II in 1662, and clear water opened up between the members, who were very much gentlemen, and working gardeners who were the players. This is shown in the salutary tale of Thomas Fairchild. The Hoxton nurseryman had succeeded in creating Shakespeare's 'nature's bastard' with the Fairchild Mule, the result of crossing a carnation with a sweet william. When a paper was presented about the Mule to the fellows of the Royal Society, Fairchild was allowed to attend, but as a working man and thus not eligible to be a member, he had to have his paper read out by another.

Thomas Fairchild not only had to endure social discrimination with his Fairchild Mule, but he also needed to be wary of accusations from the Church of tampering with God's work. At his death in 1729 he bequeathed the annual sum of £25 to his parish church, St Leonard's in Shoreditch, for the preaching of a sermon on 'the wonderful works of God in the creation', thus signifying that humankind would never have been able to produce a new species. Disapproval of the activities of florists also came from another quarter, from botanists. Carl Linnaeus, the Swedish botanist who created the modern classification system, felt that the multicoloured and double varieties of flowers were monsters. The same term was used by the nineteenth-century Scottish weaver John Duncan, who condemned them as 'monstrosities, naething mair or less'.[7] Inveighing against florists, Linnaeus wrote: 'These men cultivate a science peculiar to themselves, the mysteries of which are only known to the adepts: nor can knowledge be worth the attention of the botanist: *whereof let no sound botanist ever enter their societies*'.[8]

Unabashed by such criticism, florists developed societies and put on entertainments right across England. Evidence of this comes from local newspapers which proliferated in the early eighteenth century. For example, an advertisement in the *Norwich Gazette* for 5 July 1717 announced: 'The Florists Feast, or Entertainment for lovers of Flowers and Gardens will be kept at Mr Thomas Riggs in St Swithin's Lane on Tuesday the 8th day of July next. Tickets will be had at 2s 6d each at the aforesaid Mr Thomas Riggs'. Local newspapers tended to carry advertisements rather than reports, but in the *Craftsman* of 16 April 1729 comes a description of a feast in Richmond in Surrey:

> On Tuesday last a great Feast of Gardiners call'd Florists was held in the Dog in Richmond Hill, at which were present about 130 in Number; after Dinner several shew'd their Flowers (most of them Auricula's) and five ancient and judicious Gardiners were Judges to determine whose flowers excelled . . . a Gardiner of Barnes in Surrey was so well furnished with good Flowers, that the Judge in the affair ordered him two Spoons and a Ladle.[9]

The report from a Hackney newspaper in 1749 makes clear that these feasts were quite a social event:

> Last Wednesday was held the annual Florists Feast at Mr Hugh Kennedy's, the White Horse at Hackney, where were present a great Number of curious Florists, and a Prize given to him that produced the best six whole-blowing [blooming] Carnations, which was decided in favour of Mr Monford of Lambeth. The Company made a grand Procession thro' the principal Streets of Hackney, the Stewards being adorned with Crowns of Flowers, decorated in a beautiful Manner, with a Band of Musick attending them; and the whole was conducted with the utmost Decency and Decorum.[10]

These newspaper records do not tell us the status of the participants of the feasts, apart from occasional clergymen and working gardeners.

From the early eighteenth century comes evidence of a floral society, the descendant of which is still with us today. A printed invitation has survived for 'the annual Feast of the Royal Society of Gardiners' in York. It is headed with the royal arms that predated the Hanoverian kings, thus dating it from before 1714, flanked on one side by the arms of the London Worshipful Company of Fruiterers. Why it should be a Royal Society, and how it is connected with the fruiterers, is a mystery. However, the florists enjoyed their feasts each year through the first part of the century. The

Ancient Society of York Florists was founded in its present form in 1766, launching its first show two years later. The society's avowed aim, which appears as a preamble in its first minute book, was 'Happiness', later explaining 'As the taste for Flowers and the disclosing of them to the View of others are almost inseparable, we consider these Cultivators as an agreeable Band or Society, who communicate with each other the observations their experience has enabled them to make'.[11] The preamble also talks of evils to be avoided, one of which was disputes over the awarding of prizes by the judges. John Roebuck, a founder member of the society, and a frequent winner of various classes, committed such an evil and was deprived of his membership for one year. In fact, he never returned.

Cross-checking trade directories with the early minute book has shown that in the eighteenth century members were tradesmen from the city, including apothecaries and druggists, a cutler, a butcher, combmakers, a wharfinger – a reminder that York was a port – and a bricklayer. Professional gardeners and scholars were also members, but very unusually it included no clergymen.[12] The year was mapped out by the various flowers, so that the season was launched with the auricula show in April or early May, where polyanthus and hyacinths were also exhibited, followed by the tulip in May, the ranunculus in June, and carnations in August. Pinks and anemones joined the select circle in the first years of the nineteenth century.

Even the tradesmen of York listed above were relatively well-heeled. However, a new breed of florists was making itself known. In 1770–71 William Hanbury, Rector of Church Langton in Leicestershire, described in his book, *The Whole Body of Planting and Gardening*, how weavers were winning prizes at feasts.

> The florists are now become more numerous in England than has been known in any preceding age . . . many clubs have been founded and feasts established, when premiums are allowed the best and fairest. These feasts are now become general, and are regularly held at towns, at proper distance, almost all over England. At these exhibitions, let not the Gardener be dejected if a weaver runs away with the prize, as is often done.

Hanbury attributes this social bouleversement to the fact that the time of handworkers was their own, and that they operated from home, while the businessman did not enjoy this advantage:

A very small shower, which may come unexpectedly, when he is engaged in other necessary work at a distance, will take off the elegance of a prize auricula or carnation; whereas your tradesman who makes pretensions to a show will ever be at hand; can put his pots into the sun, or again into the shade, can refresh them with air, or cover them at the least appearance of a black cloud.

Hanbury was not displeased by this situation, pointing out that looking after his flowers will 'be an ease and pleasure' to the weaver, enabling him 'to go to his work with more alacrity'.[13]

Hanbury was the first writer to describe the participation of the hand-loom weavers in the florist movement, but clearly they had been involved for some time before 1770. It is frustrating that we have no direct link between these craftsmen and the Protestant refugees arriving in England in the sixteenth century. There is, moreover, a persistent tradition that the silk weavers of Spitalfields in London, who were also Protestant refugees from France arriving in numbers after the Revocation of the Edict of Nantes in 1685, were florists, particularly cultivating tulips and auriculas in their backyards, on their windowsills, and even perched on their looms.

A floricultural map of Britain emerges, with areas of the country specialising in certain florist's flowers. Through her research into eighteenth-century provincial newspapers, Ruth Duthie concluded that almost all England had societies of florists, apart from the far south-west. Wales appears not to have been a florists' nation. In Ireland, the Florists' Club in Dublin was rather different from its English counterparts – confined to thirty members, all landed gentry or military officers. In Scotland there were lodges and friendly societies for the support of gardeners and their families in hard times, and it may be that these could function in a similar way to florists' societies south of the border. In England, florists' feasts were known as 'the ordinary' or 'a good ordinary', and were served at 1 p.m. Flowers were customarily submitted at midday, and after judging, were on view until 4 p.m. The most characteristic prize was a silver table spoon or a copper kettle, but sometimes the awards were in cash.

In a rough circle, taking in parts of Lancashire, Cheshire and Yorkshire and centring on the cities of Manchester and Sheffield, the florists special-ised in the cultivation of auriculas. The cool, moist climate here suited them, but care had to be taken, for the flowers could be easily spoilt by rain. The botanist Carolus Clusius had first come upon yellow auriculas in the 1570s while botanising in the woods near Vienna when he was prefect of the Hapsburg medical garden. He observed that the leaves were shaped like bears' ears, which he called *Auricula ursi*, and gardeners ever since have used the familiar name, bears' ears. Another common name for the flower is dusty miller, from the fine powder to be found on both the leaves and the flowers. John Gerard called them mountain cowslips in his herbal of 1597, explaining how people in the Alps used the roots as a cure for giddiness while climbing. He also noted how they flourished in gardens in London, assuring popularity among all levels of society. This garden auricula is thought to have arisen as a natural hybrid between *Primula auricula* and another alpine primula. The fashion in auriculas in the seventeenth and early eighteenth centuries was for double-flowered and striped forms. A red-flowered variety, polyanthus, appeared in the 1680s, and gold-laced forms were developed from this. But an 'auricula revolution' took place in the mid-eighteenth century, as a result of a break in the flower, producing a clear green edge to the petals with a centre ring of meal or paste. The first edged variety to gain publicity was the 'Rule Arbiter', but the hybrid flowers developed from the one break produced a new palette of colours, slate blue, cinnamon and green-grey.

It may be the highly distinct, clear-cut quality of the edged flowers that attracted the cutlers of Sheffield, known for their horticultural enthusiasm (see Chapter 6, pp. 145–7), but the auricula was also beloved by the silk weavers of Lancashire and Cheshire. The season for auriculas is a short one, from mid-April to early May, and these highly dramatic flowers kicked off the florists' year, with a feast to celebrate their showing. Some gardeners displayed the plants on 'theatres', consisting of tiered shelving and a roof, to protect them from the rain, but providing plenty of fresh air. Such a theatre has survived in a corner of one of the walled gardens at Calke Abbey in Derbyshire. Probably built in the 1770s, it has been restored by the National Trust with blue shelves to set off the brilliant colours of the petals and the grey-green leaves.

Pinks were also cultivated by florists in the Pitsmoor district of Sheffield. These were then taken up by the miners of Durham and Northumberland, and from there spread to the Paisley weavers in Scotland. Pinks can tolerate extreme cold, but do not like excessive wet. In 1770 a florist in Kent, James Major, raised a laced pink which he named the 'Duchess of Ancaster', with rounded edges to the flower rather than the traditional serrated petal. From the Duchess a number of seedlings were raised, including the famous 'Lady Stoverdale'. This was a double variety with a band of black around the outer edge, echoed by black in the centre, on a ground of pure white. Other laced pinks could have purple or crimson colouring, but always on white.

These pinks were cultivated with enthusiasm by the weavers of Paisley in the late eighteenth century, when the community was a collection of villages with a 'town centre' around the ancient abbey. Many of the houses were designed to accommodate a workroom alongside the living quarters. Industrialisation was rapid, so that the population of 4,400 in 1760s rose to 23,900 in 1800. A Florist Society was founded in 1782, with a motto from Cicero rendered as 'There is wondrous pleasure and delight in the cultivation of flowers'. The Society set about improving some of the plants from the seeds that the members had obtained from London. Strangely, no named Paisley pinks have come down to us, although there is a short list of Scottish pinks given by Thomas Hogg in his book on the carnation of 1822. Out of the eleven raisers of named varieties, four have names that echo those of society members, including 'Robertson's Gentle Shepherd' and 'Findlayson's Bonnie Lass', though these were common names in Lowland Scotland. 'Robertson's Gentle Shepherd' was also the name of a poem by Robert Tannahill, a Paisley weaver whose verse was almost as famous as that of Robert Burns. He does not appear in the records of the Society, but a Thomas Tannahill was a member.

The minute books of the Paisley Florist Society have survived from 1797, showing a complex series of rules and regulations.[14] These range from the conventional, such as maintaining attendance levels and the prohibition of swearing and abusive language, to some particular considerations. Rule xiii stipulated that 'whenever the club shall think it convenient to purchase flower roots or seeds in a general way they shall be laid out in lots and equally distributed among the members to plant or save their share of each roots or seedes', an indication that some of the members lived in straitened circumstances. This is also reflected in Rule viii: 'a book, called "The Florist's Directory" by James Maddock be provided for the club from funds, to be read by the members as they stand in point of seniority, each member to be allowed to keep it for one week'. In February 1804 the book was reported lost and subsequently found in the possession of James Bowie. 'It is therefore proposed that Mr Bowie should be spoke to, that the said book should be restored to the club as soon as possible'. It was agreed that in future the book should always be available at meetings for quick reference. When Maddock compiled his directory in 1792, he had accepted that pinks were a florist's flower, and showed illustrations of

PLATE 3.

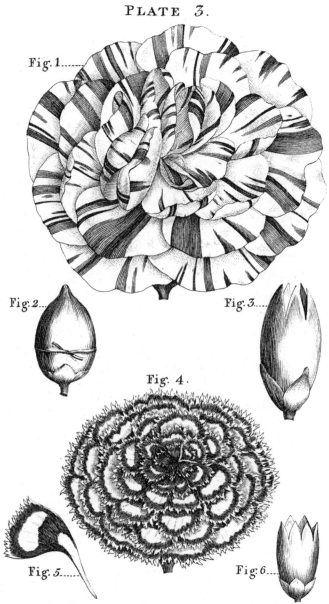

Fig. 1.......

Fig. 2...

Fig. 3.....

Fig. 4.

Fig. 5......

Fig. 6...

*Published as the Act directs by Jaʃ Maddock, Walworth 1ʃt June 1792.*

23 Carnations from James Maddock's *Florist's Directory*, published in 1792. Maddock was the first to acknowledge that the pink could be a florist's flower, and in Fig. 4 shows 'the corolla of a fine double laced pink of the middle size'. This provided invaluable information for the members of the Paisley Florist Society, whose speciality was the laced pink.

examples with lacing close to the edge of each petal, so his book was an important source for the Paisley members.

Competition played an important part in the life of the members, and although the society concentrated on pinks, other florist's flowers and 'border flowers' were also part of their year. John Findlay, a gunsmith rather than a weaver, recorded: 'Every Thursday evening from the flowering of the polyanthus, till the disappearance of the carnation, its members convene'. A complex tally was kept of the flowers shown, and 'at the end of the year the most successful florist receives perhaps a spade, the next a rake, and the third a trowel or knife'.[15]

Unusually, one of the traditions of the society was that a 'medal flower' should be agreed at the winter meetings, and the members were expected to make special efforts to grow that choice. Thus for 1814 the auricula was selected. The previous year it had been the pink, and the chairman, Archibald Duncan, presented a snuff mill in the form of a ram's horn mounted in silver for the twelve best blooms. After a series of adventures, the mill was returned to the society by a local jeweller in 1968, and is in the Paisley Museum. Unfortunately another element of the competitions has not survived. This was a half-size effigy of Flora that was dressed in finery and placed in a window to overlook the prize-giving ceremony, with silver medals on ribbons hanging over her hands. In 1804 it was reported that Flora had lost her head, and a group of deputies was appointed to obtain a new one. The minutes of 13 April record that the head-finding team has 'been directed to a celebrated head shop at the head of Queen Street [in Paisley] in which a variety of colossal and Lilliputian heads were exhibited'. Unfortunately none of these would fit, 'except the head of Mary Queen of Scots which by a little alteration might suit, but as the price demanded was two Guineas, they thought proper to decline the purchase, and being informed that it could not be got in Glasgow, poor Flora may perhaps remain sometime longer without a head'.[16]

Many of the Paisley florists worked in the mill of the cotton manufacturers, Coats, who specialised in shawls based on the traditional patterns brought back from Kashmir by soldiers serving in the East India Company. The dissenter minister for Paisley, the Revd W. Ferrier, drew an association between the interest of the weavers in horticulture and their work on the machines:

It is well known, that not only for the execution of the most delicate ornamental muslins, but for the invention of patterns, the operative

manufacturers of Paisley stand unrivalled. Their ingenuity is continually in exertion for the new and pleasing elegancies, to diversify their
fabrics. Now, where such habits obtain, the rearing of beautiful flowers,
which is an object very congenial to them, will easily be adopted and
pursued as a favourite amusement. On the other hand, it seems highly
probable that the rearing of flowers, by a re-action, must tend to
improve the genius for invention in elegant muslins.

Ferrier was quoted by John Claudius Loudon in his *Encylopaedia*, where
he waxes lyrical: 'The operatives of Paisley, taking them at large, exhibit a
condition of improvement very rarely, indeed, if at all to be paralleled
among persons of the same rank of life; and they are particularly remarkable in their taste for objects which please the eye by their beauty, for such
occupations for amusement as require nice attention, and for various intellectual gratifications'. Loudon goes on to praise the neatness of their
houses, the beauty and variety of their pigeons, the management of their
bees, and their verse-making. The only other working community that
could bear comparison as far as he was concerned were the literary miners
of Leadhills in nearby Lanarkshire (see Chapter 5, p. 130).[17]

The tulip, one of the most venerable of florists' flowers, had two principal geographical homes, one in the south-east of England, the second in
the north. From the mid-eighteenth century tulip shows were held in
towns in Suffolk, but at the beginning of the nineteenth century many of
the new kinds of 'fancy' tulips were raised by amateur growers in the area
around London. Tulips were shown in three main categories: Roses, with
scarlet, pink or crimson streaks on white; Bybloemen, with mauve, purple
or black on white; and Bizarres, with any colour of flame or feathers on a
yellow ground. Flaming took the form of a strong central bar up the
middle of each petal. Feathering was achieved when fine lines of colour
passed inwards from the edge of each petal, with no more than a fine line
of colour up the middle. One of the noted tulip growers was William
Clark of Croydon, who in the 1820s produced two famous tulips, the
Bybloemen 'Fanny Kemble' and the Bizarre 'Polyphemus', both long used
as parents in crosses. 'Fanny Kemble' had very deep purple, almost black,
markings at the edge of the white petals, while 'Polyphemus' had purplish-
brown markings on a lemon ground. When the latter was acquired by the
Lancashire growers, they referred to it affectionately as 'Polly'.

*An Account of the Different Flower Shows*, produced in 1826 by Thomas
Cunningham of Ashton-under-Lyne provided a list of the prize winners

at florists' meetings in that year.[18] Although the title page specified the categories of auriculas, tulips, ranunculuses, star pinks and carnations, prizes were also recorded for the best cucumber, mushroom, new potato, and so on, and for stove plants, baskets of flowers and even ericas. Given that Cunningham was based in Ashton, most of the shows he recorded were held in the industrial cities of Yorkshire, Lancashire and Cheshire, but places further south, such as Chelmsford and Oxford, were also included. Twenty-seven shows were held by tulip societies in that year, and the number of these societies increased through the century, but of the hundreds that existed, only one survives, in Wakefield in Yorkshire. This was founded in 1836, with its membership dominated by shoemakers. The account of the shows explains that there were classes for single blooms in Roses, Bybloemens and Bizarre, with feathered and flamed within each.

The run-up to shows posed a series of challenges to the growers, for it was difficult to get all their blooms at their best at the same time, and so they had to grow them in large numbers to provide a good selection. The usual time of planting near London was the Lord Mayor's Day, 9 November. Each variety was planted in rows according to its class and height, with the tall in the centre, and dwarf near the edge. Most gardeners planted their tulips in 'boxes', beds that were four to five feet in width, and any length available. These would be surrounded by planks of wood raised nine inches above the ground, and palings were often erected to protect the tulips from cold winds. In April it was the custom of handloom weavers to erect canvas sheeting or garden lights over the tulip beds to provide further protection from hail and rain. The temperature in May was difficult to predict: if warm, florists had to continue with their canvas shelter, this time against the sun; if cold, then the blooms would be cut, taken indoors and put by the kitchen range. Florists often stayed up all night before the show to watch the weather, and to guard their prize blooms from thieves.

The Ottoman Turkish concept of the perfect shape of the tulip flower was thin of waist, with pointed petals fanning out like needles. In complete contrast, the ideal for nineteenth-century English florists, both in the north and the south, was round and shallow. However, differences of opinion developed between growers. The features of the tulip that attracted the northern florists were symmetry and the beauty of marking. For southern florists the important qualities were the shape of the flower and the purity of the bottom colour. To help reconcile this divide, the National (later Royal) Tulip Society was formed in 1849, and continued

24 Groom's Victoria Regina tulip with Harrison's Madonna and Goldfinch seedling fuchsias, from Joseph Harrison's *Floricultural Cabinet*, from about 1843. Harrison had worked for several years as head gardener to Lord Wharncliffe at Wortley Hall near Sheffield in Yorkshire before taking up journalism. Florists used the illustrations in his journal as the source for the development of their particular speciality. For Victorian tulip growers, the flower shape to aim for was round and shallow.

until 1936, when it handed over its assets to the Wakefield and North of England Society, which still holds tulip shows each May. Originally the Society showed individual tulips in stone jars; now they are exhibited in brown beer bottles.

Steered by the tulip growers, florists imposed upon themselves an exacting regime bound by rules and regulations. Mr Kendall, a gardener of Stoke Newington, then a village to the north-east of London, noted '[the florist] loves nature . . . but not in deshabillé; for him she must be clad in all her charms. He takes the wild beauty from its rustic homes, sees hidden charms beneath the rustic guise, makes it his fondling.'[19] The Scottish florist Thomas Hogg, who had settled in Paddington Green in London, quoted some of the regulations from the shows in Islington and Chelsea in his *Concise and Practical Treatise on the Growth and Culture of the Carnation*, published in 1822. The annual subscription was £1 11s 6d, divided equally among the three shows, auricula, pink and carnation. In addition each member had to pay for a dinner ticket for the three shows. On show days all flowers had to arrive by one o'clock; the judges had to declare they had not seen or helped to dress the blooms, and the exhibitors that the flowers had been in their possession for the last four months. Exhibitors who questioned the awarding of prizes would forfeit a guinea or be expelled from the society. If any member created a quarrel or disturbed 'the harmony of the company on show days', his conduct would be reviewed and if felt to be inappropriate by the majority, he too would be expelled. As most florist societies were open to all England, these rules pertained across the country.

The Ancient Florists of York had declared their founding aim was happiness. Passion does not, of course, always bring happiness, and Hogg accompanies his rundown of the rules and regulations with a cautionary tale, 'A Flower Christening'. This is his fictional account of the experiences of Samuel Greenhorn, a novice florist. 'One of the most important and wished-for events in the life of a florist, in a florist's estimation at least, is the raising of a fine flower from seed; his joy in first beholding it is equal to that of a lord in first viewing the infant heir of his title, wealth and honours.' First, the florist had to fix on a name for his infant bloom:

The unlettered florist, on such an occasion, is frequently obliged to consult the parson, the schoolmaster, or the doctor, as high authorities, for some learned and astounding name; but the summary of the proper names of the heathen gods and goddesses, illustrious heroes and heroines, and celebrated worthies and beauties of antiquity, discovered at the end of Entick's Spelling Dictionary, has obviated much of the difficulty heretofore complained of.

Sam had raised a number of seedling carnations, as yet unnamed, from the categories laid down by florists: Flakes with broad stripes of one colour; Bizarres with stripes of two or three colours; and Picotees, with tooth-edged petals tinged with colour. Selecting twelve of the best, he travelled fifty miles to present them at a flower show where a silver cup was in contention. Hogg locates this somewhere between Battersea and Chelsea, 'places noted for the cutting of simples and cabbages, as well as the curing of simpletons'. Sam's seedlings were duly examined by the wily florists, who suggested names for each, such as Greenhorn's Emperor, Greenhorn's Queen and Lovely Margaret after Sam's wife. Each new name was toasted in wine, until the sixth bottle when the innkeeper arrived at 10 p.m. to ask who would pay for all the drink and tobacco. Sam went down to settle up, which he could just about manage, and made his escape, leaving his Emperor, Queen, and the Lovely Margaret behind. The florists, realising what had happened, rushed into the street, to bawl after the retreating and humiliated Sam with the greatest insults they could muster. His Emperor is a mere button, his Queen a buttercup, and his lovely Meg a dirty red garter. Hogg ends the piece, 'Further, I dare not report'.[20]

This cautionary tale not only tells us of unkindness to the naive, but also that much alcohol was consumed at these feasts. Just as the outrageous sons of George III were succeeded in 1837 by the respectable Queen Victoria and her family values, so the floral feasts gave way to a much more disciplined calendar of shows of various kinds in the 1830s and 1840s. These shows will be considered in Chapter 9. Florists, however, continued to flourish, and Ruth Duthie concluded that the period between the 1820s and the 1860s was the golden age for the industrial workers as gardeners.

William Howitt, social commentator and poet, wrote in his 1844 edition of *Rural Life in England* about the florists whom he encountered on his travels, finding them not only in towns but country villages too:

Many cottagers ... are most zealous and successful florists. So successful that they were amongst the first to raise fine flowers before floral societies and flower-shows were in existence, and the names of some of these village florists are attached to some of the finest specimens. Hufton, Barker and Redgate, appellations which some of our finest carnations, polyanthuses and ranunculuses bear, are those of old Derbyshire villagers, well known to me, who scarcely ever were out of their own rustic districts, but whose names are thus made familiar all the country over.[21]

John Hufton was a stocking-maker who lived in a cottage on the estate of Squire Munday at Shipley in Derbyshire. The *Midland Florist* in 1851 described his garden as 'facing south and sheltered from the north-east by extensive woods'. From the woods, he was able to collect decaying leaves, and 'willowdust', a material collected in old pollarded willows and much treasured by florists. Hufton's speciality was carnations, one of which he named after his landlord, another, 'Hufton's Magnificent', a flake in red and white, was one of the most prized varieties of the nineteenth century. To show his carnations, Hufton would walk to Nottingham, carrying a dozen pots in wooden boxes hanging from a yoke, like a milkmaid with her pails. After a celebratory meal at the inn, hopefully buoyed up by his success, he would make the journey home in the cool of the evening.

The excitement of the successful florist was captured by George Crabbe in his long narrative poem of 1810, *The Borough*, describing life in a country town, based on Aldeburgh in Suffolk. The florist is a weaver, keen on butterflies and flowers:

He both his *Flora* and his *Fauna* shows.
For him his blooming in its rich array,
The glorious flower which bore the palm away.
In vain a rival tried his utmost art.
His is the prize and joy o'erflowed his heart.
'This, this my glory! Cast, O pray, your eyes
On this my glory! See the grace – the size!
Was ever stem so tall, so stout, so strong.
Exact in breadth, in just proportion long;
Three brilliant hues are all distinct and clean,
No kindred tint, no blending streaks between;
This is no shaded, run-off, pin-eyed thing.
A king of flowers, a flower for England's king!'

The reference to pin-eye reveals that the winning flower was an auricula. If the stigma protruded beyond the tube, or was visible, then it was not of show standard. Crabbe brilliantly conveys the reason why this flower lent itself so well to competitions.

But the circle of florists' flowers was expanding. Pansies now were considered worthy. In the early nineteenth century, gardeners had taken the wild pansy or heartease, with its small, heart-shaped flower known to florists as 'horse-faced', and developed it into a large round form, which might be called 'moon-faced' (see Plate X). It was the miners of Yorkshire, Derbyshire and North Staffordshire who concentrated on the pansy, for the flower was happiest in the north, blooming more freely and over a longer period. These were known as 'fancy pansies', raised for show rather than bedding, because of their straggling habit.

Another flower which was a potential candidate for the florists was the hollyhock, but the possibility was firmly scotched by *The Gardener and Practical Florist*:

[It] is not and never can be a florist's flower, any more than a horse can be a lap-dog. It is essentially an outdoor plant . . . A lady would as soon think of having a pig in a parlour as a ramping spike of Hollyhock in a bouquet; and even a coachman, who on state days is expected to wear a nosegay as large as a cauliflower, would look awkward, with six feet of Hollyhock stuck in his buttonhole.[22]

Fruit joined flowers in many shows. Miss Mitford in *Our Village* introduces a retired innkeeper, who lent 'his willing aid . . . at pink-feasts and melon-feasts', and they were also shown at the same time as carnations. [23] Melons required a hotbed for ripening, and therefore were beyond the means of many working-class gardeners unless they could heat them in their compost heap. Gooseberries, however, were not difficult to grow, and became a favourite at shows in industrial areas, where the aim was to produce the heaviest fruit rather than being concerned about flavour.

Two exotic introductions became wildly fashionable florist's flowers: the dahlia and the chrysanthemum. Although the dahlia was first observed and described in Mexico in the 1570s by the Spanish physician Francisco Hernández, who defined it by its Indian names, 'acocotli' and 'chicipathi', the flower did not arrive in Europe until the end of the eighteenth century, where it was named after the Swedish botanist Andreas Dahl. The Abbé Cavanilles, director of the Royal Gardens in Madrid, began to cultivate the flowers, carefully crossing and selecting them to create a palette of different colours and forms. The exciting, vibrant results, which reached

Britain after the Napoleonic Wars, created among all levels of society a frenzy that in its fervour approached the Dutch tulipomania of two centuries earlier.

In 1833 Joseph Harrison launched a monthly magazine, *Floricultural Cabinet*, which gives a good indicator of the really popular flowers of the time. Tulips, pansies and dahlias throng the pages. An early issue of the magazine contains an article by a Nottinghamshire florist, 'On the Culture of the Dahlia' which begins, 'Having very extensive journeys to take during the summer season through most districts of the kingdom ... none has arrested my attention so forcibly as the Dahlia in all its splendid varieties of colour and form, and no other plant of recent introduction has spread so rapidly through the country, which is full proof of the superiority of the flower'.[24] The ideal pursued by florists was the ball shape, a sphere of geometrically arranged petals, known as 'fancy' or 'show' dahlias (see Plate XI).

The first chrysanthemum to be recorded in England was the Old Purple at a nursery in the King's Road, Chelsea in 1796. It had been brought from China several years earlier by a Marseilles sea captain, Blanchard. This purple double flowerer, *C. morifolium*, along with the yellow single, *C. indicum*, became the ancestor of all early and late flowering varieties. In 1846 the plant hunter Robert Fortune introduced the Chusan daisy, which became known as the pompone because it resembled the bobbles on the caps of French sailors. The first form to appeal to florists was the Gold-bordered Red, with incurving petals. A Chelsea florist, writing in another early issue of *The Floricultural Cabinet* in June 1833, makes the point that florists had always held stripes and streaks as important qualities in their flowers: 'Chinese chrysanthemums have not hitherto ranked with true flowers of the florist because, however well formed, in many of the varieties, they are all, save the Gold-bordered Red, of self or uniform colours; and the florist requires yet another colour or colours to be distinctly depicted upon the first or ground colour of every petal to constitute his favourite flakes, bizarres and picotees'.[25]

The first show of chrysanthemums was held in Norwich in 1843, and three years later the first society to concentrate on the flower was established in Stoke Newington (see Chapter 9, p. 225). The florist tradition would seem to be flourishing all over the country and at all levels. The gardening press provided regular columns advising on the cultivation of florist's flowers and advertising the dates for shows. However, just as a flame burns brightest shortly before extinction, so the golden age of florists, especially from the working classes, was nearing its end. It is ironic

25 A Spitalfields handloom weaver working alongside his family, from the *Queen*, 21 September 1861. In the window can be seen the two hobbies that brought colour and sound to their lives: flowers growing in pots, and a singing bird in a cage.

that at the very time that the Revd Hanbury introduced the concept of florist handworkers in 1770, machines powered by steam were being developed by Richard Arkwright, Samuel Hargreaves and Samuel Crompton that would revolutionise the textile industry. Not only did these machines create a factory system that removed workers from their gardens, but their furnaces were powered by coal that polluted the atmosphere and ruined many a horticultural activity. This can be seen in the example of the Paisley weavers. The introduction of the jacquard machine into the mills put paid to their handlooms, while the smoke from the mill chimneys created increasingly adverse growing conditions for their pinks.

A century after Hanbury, another clergyman florist, Francis Horner, observed with sadness how urban development had led to the loss of gardens: 'There stands many an old house, now deeply embedded in a town, that used to have its garden, oft-times a florist's. Here, for instance, is the very window – curiously long and lightsome – at which a hand-loom weaver worked behind his loom, able to watch his flowers as carefully as his work, his labour and his pleasure intermingled, interwoven as intimately as his silken threads.'[26] He was talking about his particular passion, auriculas, and the silk weavers of Lancashire and Cheshire, but the trend was national. The *Horticultural Magazine* in 1846 had noted of the East End of London:

> Those who look upon the thousands of houses which already cover the space that used to boast of the gaudy tulip beds of the working man would scarcely think it possible to have seen so great a change. Yet there are many small gardens, even now, in the Mile End Road with their canvas houses looking, in season, like an encampment, which are doomed at no short distance of time to give way to brick and mortar buildings (and to factories).[27]

Roy Genders in his book on florists and their flowers notes a sudden decline around the year 1855.[28] In the previous year, a florist, John Groom of Clapham Rise in London, had offered in his catalogue tulips at huge prices: the 'Duchess of Cambridge' was being priced at 100 guineas, while many of the other varieties were 10 guineas and upwards. The following year, the entire stock of more than a quarter of a million bulbs was sold at rock-bottom prices as they stood planted in their rows. The decline was probably not as sudden or spectacular as this, but was inexorable. Worst affected were the societies dedicated to auriculas and polyanthus, with only the carnation societies faring better. According to William Paul, who ran the Royal Nurseries at Waltham Cross in Hertfordshire, the artificial devices adopted by competitors at shows to improve the appearance of their exhibits were no longer acceptable:

> the show goer stands in ecstasy over a group of Dahlias, unconscious of the fact that this or that flower before him is made up of two or more individual flowers, and 'dressed' with all the artistic skill of an accomplished milliner. I have seen Hyacinths shown for competition with small pins sticking the flowers close to the stems, and the drooping flowers of a loose truss brought to look you in the face by the flower-stalk being tied to the stem by an almost invisible ligature of fine green silk.[29]

For the working classes, especially in urban areas, new interests were beginning to absorb their leisure time, and the term florist took on a new meaning, a retailer of cut flowers, or somebody who creates arrangements with them. In 1871 the Football Association was inaugurated, and seven years later the Football League was established, with the game quickly developing into a national obsession. Evenings could now be spent at the music hall, and later the cinema, rather than under the watchful gaze of Flora.

CHAPTER 5

❧❧❧

# Two Nations

ONE OF THE most familiar images of a nineteenth-century village or
hamlet garden is represented by paintings of artists such as Helen
Allingham or Myles Birket Foster. A charming, flower-filled space is set
before a picturesque cottage with thatched roof and roses climbing up the
walls. A woman and child in impeccable dress are often shown amid this
lovely scene. This image is echoed by much of the poetry and literature of
the time. But how true is it?

The question is simple enough, but the answer is quite the reverse. The
challenge facing any examination of the gardening practices of nineteenth-
century rural families is that the picture is hugely complex. First, there
were regional differences in the farming landscape which had a knock-on
effect on horticulture. If a line is drawn across England from the East
Riding of Yorkshire down to Devon, to the north and west farming was
primarily pastoral, to the east, arable. The counties around London
concentrated on dairy and garden produce. Farms in Devon and Wales
were family affairs, resulting in much smaller economic divisions than the
large-scale enterprises prevailing in East Anglia.

The system of landholdings was also an important factor, with close and
open villages. In close villages the social stratification was more obvious,
with the principal landowner at the top, followed by other gentry, clergymen, substantial farmers, rural craftsmen, shopkeepers and smallholders.
At the bottom of this triangle were agricultural labourers. The community
was firmly regulated, and conformity was important: cottagers could be
ejected for cutting down a tree in their garden without permission, for
instance. Most villages in England were of the open kind, with ownership
widely dispersed, the parson as the only 'gentleman', and less rigid social

divisions. These communities sometimes suffered from overcrowding, as they were used as 'dumping grounds' for undesirable inhabitants from estate villages. New-built cottages were often poorly constructed by speculative builders and let at comparatively high rents. Insecurity of tenure in both types of village had the effect of the tenant regarding certain gardening activities, such as the planting of fruit trees, to not be worth the expense.

In the Scottish border counties, and Northumberland and Durham, a bondage system often operated. The Duke of Northumberland, for instance, had his cottages numbered and assigned to the labourers, who were known as hinds, allowed to keep a cow, plant a certain quantity of land with potatoes, and granted a quantity of oats, barley and peas for the household's consumption. In return the hinds gave their labour all year round, and furnished a woman labourer at a shilling a day during harvest, eightpence a day for the rest of the year. The agrarian commentators William Cobbett and William Howitt, seeing this system in action during their studies of rural life, thought it smacked of serfdom. As he looked upon a landscape populated by houses without gardens, Howitt reflected on the contrast with Surrey, the county where he lived. Here, just fourteen miles from London, the rural cottages had 'their walls covered with vines, and gardens and orchards'.[1]

Although the substantial majority of cottagers living in nineteenth-century villages were agricultural labourers, there were industrial workers too. The move from cottage industry to big mills varied across industries, and wool combers could be found around Bradford, lacemakers in Nottinghamshire, nail makers in the Black Country, file cutters and scythe makers around Sheffield, bootmakers around Northampton, framework knitters in Leicestershire, and miners in South Wales, the East Midlands, the North East and Cornwall.

In the early nineteenth century there were still manors that had not been enclosed. Walter Rose, the village carpenter of Haddenham in Buckinghamshire, looked back in his autobiography to the time of his great-grandfather who was a peasant farmer, with ninety-seven acres of grazing.[2] When the parish was enclosed in 1830, the holding was reduced to forty acres, and the various manorial rights were lost. The Rose family was able to survive because of their carpentry trade. Flora Thompson, almost an exact contemporary of Walter Rose, was born in 1876 at Juniper Hill, a hamlet on the border of Oxfordshire and Northamptonshire. Juniper Hill was transformed into Lark Rise in her famous trilogy, *Lark Rise to Candleford*. Among the inhabitants was 'Old Sally', based on Sarah

Moss, born in 1812, who was able to recall the hamlet in pre-enclosure days when her family's house stood in a wide expanse of open heath and they were able to exercise commoners' right, with animals turned out to graze, furze cut for firing and even turf collected to make a lawn for somebody's garden.[3]

Even the definition of a garden can vary: land attached to a cottage, a detached ground which could be an allotment, a potato field, the open spaces provided by the creators of model communities, and the ground cultivated by self-help settlements. All of these will be considered in this chapter.

As noted in Chapter 1, in 1589 Elizabeth I issued an act requiring new cottages to have at least four acres of land attached. This legislation was never enforced, but it is interesting to note that at the time four acres was considered a suitable amount of land to sustain a cottager. By the end of the eighteenth century, despite significant emigration to towns and cities through industrialisation, so great was the pressure on land with a rising rural population that such a generous provision was not available to most cottagers. The enclosure movement, by depriving the rural poor of common rights such as pasturing a cow and collecting wood for fuel, had seriously affected living standards at a time when wages for agricultural labourers were low and declining. Therefore for many the land around the cottage, whatever its size, represented a vital source of food, and inevitably vegetables had to take precedence over the cultivation of flowers. Some cottagers, however, were better off. Artisans in open villages, such as the blacksmith or the carpenter, might have sufficient income not to be dependent on growing their own food, as might miners and domestic outworkers in industrial villages. A key factor in the equation could be the allotment. If a family had an allotment, then there was less pressure to use the cottage garden for production of vegetables and herbs, and thereby an opportunity to cultivate flowers and fruit.

The term 'allotment' begins to appear in enclosure acts, making some land provisions for the poor. Thus at Armley near Leeds in 1793 the act made allotment to cottagers of eight and a half acres in 'six or more distinct and separate places'.[4] In the first report of the Society for Bettering the Conditions and Increasing the Comforts of the Poor (SBCP), founded in 1796, George Finch, 9th Earl of Winchilsea, wrote:

As land cultivated as a garden will produce a greater quantity of food for man than in any other way, and as four-fifths of the labour bestowed upon their gardens will be done by the labourers at extra hours, and when they and their children would otherwise be unemployed, it may not be too much to say, that 100,000 acres, allotted to cottagers as garden ground, will give a produce equal to what 150,000 acres cultivated in the ordinary way would give; and that, without occupying more of the time they would otherwise give to the farmers who employ them than the cultivation of 20,000 acres would require.[5]

Lord Winchilsea is now noted in reference books as a pioneer of English cricket, but was an influential landowner, with estates in Rutland and Northamptonshire, and showed concern about the lot of agricultural workers.

In that same year, 1796, Arthur Young in the first volume of his *Annals* describes how 'in the parishes of Ashley and Newton, in the county of Wilts, and Shipton Moyne, in Gloucestershire, the landlord gave every cottager fifteen perches [approximately one-tenth of an acre] of ground, enclosed in one large piece, containing acres sufficient in that proportion for every cottage; thus thrown together in one piece to save the expense of separate enclosures'.[6] This idea of dividing a piece of land into small plots surrounded by an external fence, but without partitions, may well have been adopted on sites earlier in the eighteenth century, and it is sometimes suggested that allotment strips, organised side by side, were a miniature offspring of the acre strips of the pre-enclosure, open-field system.[7]

The land at Shipton Moyne was given by Sir Thomas Estcourt, who is described as the 'inventor of allotments', and this part of the country would appear to be the cradle of the movement. One of Estcourt's neighbours, the Revd Stephen Demainbray, set aside eight acres when the parish of Great Somerford was enclosed in 1806, while George Law, the Bishop of Bath and Wells, was a generous benefactor of land. In 1836, a local apothecary wrote a letter extolling 'the beautiful splendid sight, now blooming, of a kitchen garden full of the bounties of Providence, of one hundred acres subdivided, from four to five hundred industrious, I will not say poor, but happy allotment tenants just now gathering in the profits of their own and their children's labour'.[8]

Although philanthropy was an important factor in the launching of the allotment movement, motivation was not entirely altruistic, as Winchilsea made clear in his report when he suggested that the land thus cultivated would be more productive. The turn of the nineteenth century, moreover, not only witnessed extremely difficult years for the rural labouring classes with a series of poor harvests, but landowners also retained alarming memories of revolution, and the threat of invasion from the French, with whom Britain was now at war. In the years that followed, the allotment movement developed gradually, gaining momentum after the idea was proposed in the late 1820s for a new organisation, the Labourer's Friend Society (LFS). Its founder was not a member of rural society, but a London surgeon, Benjamin Wills, who proposed the concept of a general enclosure bill permitting a proportion of land to be taken 'for the nation', to be divided into small farms, let rent-free for the first thirty years. Enclosure commissioners would add some land to every existing cottage so that all agricultural cottages would have two acres. This was regarded as a dangerously radical idea, but Wills was able to form the LFS in 1830, the very year that social unrest was breaking out in Europe, echoed by the Captain Swing riots. Captain Swing was the name appended to threatening letters sent when labourers, particularly in Kent, protested violently against the introduction of threshing machines. The Captain was characterised as a hardworking tenant farmer faced with destitution.

The LFS set out its aims in its magazine, *Facts and Illustrations*. This was stirring stuff:

> [Let us place] the labourer in a situation in which he can employ himself during his spare days and hours; he will then feel that he has an interest in the soil and that he is indeed a member of, and not an outcast from, society; he will then become attached to the land of his forefathers, and be once more reinstated in that just standing in the social system, to which as a British-born subject he is fully entitled.[9]

The magazine was circulated to landowners and clergymen giving substantial information, while a pamphlet, *Useful Hints*, was provided for the labourers themselves, although the latter tended to be full of improving stories and crude information, limiting severely its effectiveness. Travelling agents were sent out to lecture on benefits, form auxiliary societies and to raise subscriptions.

The LFS took an interest in Ireland from the outset, supported by one of the leading agricultural improvers, Martin Doyle from County Wexford. He was concerned about the family custom of dividing farms into small parts, writing that labourers should not fancy themselves small farmers, being tempted to marry too soon 'on the prospect of two or three barrels of potatoes'.[10] The spectre of total dependency on potatoes in Ireland was

*The Committee, having been furnished with the above lithographed Sketch, free of expence, by a zealous friend to the Society, have great pleasure in presenting it to the Subscribers.*

26 Frontispiece to the 1835 volume of the *Labourer's Friend Magazine*. The head of the household, wearing a remarkably elegant shirt and waistcoat, is shown digging his allotment, watched by his wife and child. The house in the background is symbolic of the domesticity that it was hoped allotments could promote.

to dominate gardening experts there long after the Great Famine had wrought its terrible damage. Doyle commended the example of Grogan Morgan of Johnstown Castle in Wexford, who 'has built twenty-four slated cottages two stories high of which thirteen are exclusively for his labourers; to each of these houses is attached 1A[cre].3R[od].13P[erch] of land . . . When the necessary offices are added, and the gardens under a strict course of *rotation crop* (an essential point), a complete specimen of the allotment system will be here exhibited.'[11]

In England, a dynamic was forming among the three main social groups involved: landowners, farmers and labourers. Owners of great estates, such as the Dukes of Bedford, Newcastle and Richmond, began to let out thousands of plots. The generosity of these powerful aristocrats has to be tempered by the fact that their ancestors were the principal winners in the enclosure lottery, with their wealth and parliamentary influence. Nevertheless, their support, at a time when government intervention was notably lacking, helped the movement to develop and become regarded as socially beneficial. Support came from all the main political factions, including Sir Robert Peel, Sir James Graham and Benjamin Disraeli, whose 'Young England' friend, W.B. Ferrand, established allotments at Bingley in West Yorkshire and Methwold in Norfolk, while another, Lord John Manners, was the son of the Duke of Rutland, an allotment duke.[12]

In 1841 at the annual general meeting of the Banbury Agricultural Society, Sir Henry Dryden, who had inherited the Canons Ashby estate four years earlier, at the age of nineteen, caused a furore by attacking the allotment system and suggesting that labourers were thieves because this gave them the opportunity to claim corn had been grown on their land, when in fact it had been stolen from their employers. Not only was Dryden rebuked by the chairman, with three other speakers recording their dissent, but the *Northampton Herald*, in its report of the meeting, wrote a defence of allotments and put down Dryden's views as the naïvety of youth.[13]

While landowners might be sympathetic to the allotment movement, and some actively supportive, the farmers as a group were opposed, often adamantly so. An example of this bitter antagonism can be seen in the experience of John Stevens Henslow, rector of Hitcham in Suffolk. Henslow had become Professor of Botany at Cambridge at the age of 29 in 1825, ushering in a golden age for botanical science at the university. Charles Darwin, for instance, described Henslow's remarkable power of making the young feel completely at ease, though 'we were all awe-struck with the amount of his knowledge'.[14] Henslow's arrival in Hitcham in 1837 must have come as a shock both to him and to his parishioners, for the community was impoverished, with a high level of unemployment and much criminality. The new rector began to organise self-help clubs, founding a village school where he taught botany and was criticised for being irreligious. A herbarium was built up with the help of the school-children, and botanical excursions organised, including an outing to Kew Gardens.

A local historian of Hitcham recorded how, even with industry and frugality, the villagers' diet 'consisted principally of bread and potatoes. There are, however, some who when their families are grown up, by putting their earnings together, occasionally get a piece of meat at their supper time and their Sunday dinner.'[15] Henslow sought to vary this diet by providing quarter-acre allotments to grow vegetables, incurring wrath, which sometimes spilled into violence, from local farmers who hated the idea of their workers enjoying any kind of independence, and threatened not to employ any allotment holders. They also accused them of stealing seed, the charge that got Sir Henry Dryden into such trouble. Henslow continued unfazed by this opposition, calling upon his distinguished bota-nist friend, John Lindley, who provided guano to manure the plots, while the owner of an ironworks in Ipswich sent him vegetable and flower seeds.

One of the most active of the agents for the Labourer's Friend Society was James Orange, who campaigned for allotments for the frameworkers in the villages of the East Midlands. Born around the year 1800 in Chesterfield, Derbyshire, the son of a joiner, by the early 1830s Orange was a leading figure at Salem Independent Chapel in Nottingham and was emerging as a significant force in the civic life of the city. In 1840 he wrote 'A Plea on Behalf of the Poor', motivated by the unemployment and low wages of the handloom weavers and lacemakers, in which he advocated the provision of allotments both to supplement incomes and to improve health. Establishing the Northern and Midland Counties Artisan's and Labourer's Friend Society, he secured the creation of allotments in the urban area of Nottingham, but was also forming local allotment societies in villages. In evidence to a select committee in 1843, he described the effects of the introduction of allotments in the Nottinghamshire village of Lambley, where the inhabitants had been wont to talk politics and neglect their Sabbath duties. 'After the rector granted 17½ acres in allotments, the church became well filled spontaneously. The parishioners stopped talking about politics.'[16]

The politics that these labourers were discussing was Chartism, with their six points for parliamentary reform.[17] Orange encountered opposition from the Chartists, who disliked his message because they felt that the provision of allotments represented a distraction, a 'sticking plaster' solution to fundamental social problems that should be solved by political action. At Ilkeston, for example, Orange addressed a meeting with apparent success in January 1842, but found on his return the following month that the enthusiasm for allotments had entirely vanished, and the committee had failed to carry out a single action. On looking into the mystery, he discovered that the committee had been packed by Chartists intent on frustrating his plans.[18] However, as Jeremy Burchardt points out in his history of the allotment movement, the relationship was a complex one, and as the Chartists' political activism declined following the failure of their petition in 1842, many became enthusiastic advocates of allotments, organising themselves into societies and lobbying local landowners.[19]

James Orange was a man of immense energy, as can be seen from the journal he kept from 1842 to 1844, which was published in the *Labourer's Friend Magazine*. Hundreds of meetings are recorded including some in the open air, as he contended not only with the weather but opposition from clergy who would not allow him use of the local schoolroom, farmers banning him from their barns, and even the framework knitters themselves, taken aback at the novelty of his plans. The evidence given to the Royal Commission on the Framework Knitters in 1844–45 shows how important allotments had become. Thus James Clarke, a framework knitter from Ruddington, declared 'It would be a great benefit if we had them [allotments]; there is not a vegetable in the place, only what is brought from Nottingham and other places'. Thomas Hillard, a framework knitter from Horsley Woodhouse, similarly reported that the allotment system 'is a thing that is very much desired, I believe, generally throughout the parish, and I believe it would benefit the condition of the framework knitters throughout the three counties [Nottinghamshire, Leicestershire and Warwickshire] if they had small allotments of ground at a low price, as it would enable them to grow a few potatoes for themselves'.[20]

James Orange, with his indefatigable enthusiasm and determination, prevailed, and by 1873 there were nearly 35,000 plots in the East Midlands, an astonishing personal achievement. During the middle years of the nineteenth century wages increased and the repeal of the Corn Laws in 1846 took much of the sting out of the political tension. The number of allotments doubled across England, with the number of parishes that had them rising from one-quarter to one-third – so still a minority.

While clergymen like Henslow were often supporters of the idea of providing allotments, others played a less admirable role, as recorded by Joseph Ashby. Ashby was born in 1859, the son of an unmarried servant, and brought up in the Warwickshire village of Tysoe, in his stepfather's cottage. When his stepfather died, the family was supported by the parish on a weekly total of six or seven shillings, just below the income of many earners in the village. Like the villagers of Hitcham, Tysoe's labouring families lived on bread soaked in hot water and salted and peppered, vegetables and lard. When Joseph Ashby was aged just fourteen, Joseph Arch, leader of the farmworkers' union, came to Tysoe to address a meeting. Recalling the event many years later Ashby described how the vicar and the resident steward of the largest local landowner, 'almost furious with rage' came on the scene, 'trusting their combined powers to prevent any effects from the meeting'. Arch clashed with the vicar, who accused him of stirring up trouble, while villagers in their turn accused the vicar of obtaining land for allotments at £2 per acre, and letting them out at double the sum. More clashes took place with the vicar over the size of allotments, which he felt should be no more than ten poles, one-sixteenth of an acre.[21] As a result of this meeting, Ashby became a staunch supporter of Arch and the union, and an outspoken advocate of the provision of adequate allotments.

An alternative to the allotment was the potato field or ground. These were patches of land which were resting as fallow, which farmers offered to labourers, usually on a temporary basis either free or at a rent if the labourer was not in the farmer's employ. The size of these grounds varied, but were usually small, around ten poles. Farmers much preferred this system to allotments, as they retained control of the land, which the labourer manured for them, and cleansed with their potatoes.

The potato, after the slow start described in Chapter 2, had become a staple part of the diet in England, Scotland and Wales, and often vital to keep the agricultural labourer's family alive. This dependence is shown in a passage from Thomas Hardy's *Tess of the d'Urbervilles*, when Tess realises that she is late with her sowing: 'It was now the season for planting and sowing: many gardens and allotments of the villagers had already received their spring tillage, but the garden and the allotments of the Durbeyfields were behindhand. She found, to her dismay, that this was owing to their having eaten all the seed potatoes, – that last lapse of the improvident'. Having obtained some seeds, she began to work on the allotment-plot rented in a field just outside the village. 'She and her sister worked on here with their neighbours till the last rays of the sun smote flat upon the white pegs that divided the plots . . . Nobody looked at his or her companions. The eyes of all were on the soil'.[22]

The importance of potatoes is also reflected in an analysis of crops grown on allotments between 1830 and 1849. Potatoes come right at the top of the list, grown in 87 per cent of the allotment records examined, followed by 55 per cent for wheat. In descending order thereafter come beans, peas, barley, cabbages, root vegetables such as turnips, onions and carrots, with a few mentions of lettuce, fruit and just two references to flowers.[23]

This mix is also attested by Flora Thompson, although she also makes clear that her village had allotments so that flowers might be cultivated in gardens. Some social historians have expressed concern that Thompson painted a romantic picture of the village life of her youth, but it would be fairer to say that she has been romanticised by others. A recent television series has provided a sentimental version that is very different in tone from her original text, which was plainly but beautifully written, displaying a shrewd rather than a romantic view.

She describes how the allotment plots were divided into two, 'one half planted with potatoes, the other half with wheat or barley'. She also emphasises that the practical must be the priority in the garden adjoining the cottage: 'Proud as they were of their celery, peas and beans, cauli-flowers and marrows, and fine as were the specimens they could show of these, their potatoes were their special care, for they had to grow enough to last the year round'. However, she does also talk of 'green vegetables, currant and gooseberry bushes, and a few old-fashioned flowers'.[24]

That cottagers did grow flowers in their gardens is borne out by the descriptions recorded by Joseph Ashby in a series of articles written for the *Leamington Chronicle* in the 1890s. Of one of the prettiest villages in Warwickshire, he wrote: 'I have more than once wandered through Combroke during the summer months and have never failed to be struck with the floral tastes and care of the cottagers. All the varieties of garden flowers which cottagers might reasonably be expected to cultivate are spreading their foliage and their glowing petals to enhance the beauty of the corner, bed, or border in which they are planted'. The expectation referred to here was that perennials and hardy annuals were the staple of these gardens, for the villagers would have had limited access to seeds, although there was plenty of swapping of cuttings, and local head gardeners could be generous with plants. Colour was an important factor, with villagers seeking to cultivate beauty, even in a modest space.

Of the gardens of Ashby's own village of Tysoe, he was more specific:

> Here and there tall hollyhocks spread their honours over grey walls beneath the sombre thatch. On the eaves of which cheeky sparrows chirrup ominously to the labourers in their gardens as the corn grows golden in their allotments. Annuals have more than usual favour . . . Here and there roses are in evidence, but not quite so much as in some old Warwickshire villages. Chrysanthemums spread their luxuriant foliage in every garden to make base or back ground for these perennials which honour the summer with their beauties.[25]

Images of people working either on their gardens or their allotments are rare, but the frontispiece of the 1835 volume of the *Labourer's Friend*

27 Gertrude Jekyll's photograph of an old labourer, from *Old West Surrey*, published in 1904. He is wearing a smock-frock with a large collar that he could pull up to protect his neck from wet weather and burning sunshine.

28 A cottager admiring the roses in her garden, in a 1904 photograph taken by Gertrude Jekyll. She is well protected from the sun by a bonnet with a deep 'curtain' hanging over the back of her neck.

*Magazine* depicts a father forking his plot, watched by his wife and child (Figure 26). He is wearing remarkably smart clothes, more appropriate to one of Jane Austen's young clergymen. Flora Thompson tells us that when working in the fields, the older labourers still wore traditional smocks, but that by the 1880s most men wore stiff corduroy trousers and unbleached drill jackets known as 'sloppies'. Just such an outfit is worn by a cottager in a photograph taken by Gertrude Jekyll for her book about the villages of West Surrey. The man's wife wears a bonnet, but for working in the garden she would have had the additional protection against the sun of a second bonnet with a deep 'curtain' to cover the neck. Jekyll also took a photograph of an old labourer in his smock-frock, with a hefty collar to keep out the wet in inclement weather.[26]

Nineteenth-century rural gardens contained not only plants, practical or decorative, but also livestock of several kinds. William Howitt in his *Rural Life of England*, described how cottagers kept rows of thatched hives in their gardens, cultivating the kinds of flowers that the bees appreciated.[27] Straw beehives were the traditional form, but back in the seventeenth century experiments had been conducted with glass set into hives. The budding architect Christopher Wren created glass beehives in the gardens of Wadham College in Oxford when he was an undergraduate. This enabled the study of the bees – a matter not only of intellectual concern, for it also made it possible for the beekeeper to observe when the bees had moved on and thus procure the honey without injuring them. George Borrow, in his novel *The Romany Rye*, first published in 1857, described the beehives of an old man:

> In the garden was the habitation of the bees, a long box, supported upon three oaken stumps. It was full of small round glass windows, and appeared to be divided into a great many compartments, much resembling drawers placed sideways. He told me that, as one compartment was filled, the bees left it for another; so that, whenever he wanted honey, he could procure some without injury to the insects.[28]

The honey could be used to make mead, as described by Flora Thompson. Known as methaglin, 'it was a drink almost superstitiously esteemed, and the offer of a glass was regarded as a great compliment . . . Old Sally said that some folks messed up their methaglin with lemons, bay leaves, and suchlike; but all she could say was the folks who'd add anything to honey didn't deserve to have bees to work for them.'[29]

Cottage gardeners would often try to make some profit from their gardens: not on the scale of market gardening, but something that would add to their meagre income. John Clare tells the poignant story of how his family had a single russet tree in their tiny Northamptonshire garden, and would sell some of their apples. When the harvest failed one year, his family was obliged to enter the workhouse. The housewives of the Vale of Aylesbury, and in some Oxfordshire villages, reared and fattened ducklings for the London market. This trade dated back at least to the eighteenth century, but reached its peak in the 1890s when birds were dispatched in hampers and transported in carts or by railway. The cottage gardens were divided by planks into pens, with shedding to protect the birds. When the garden was used for 'ducking', an allotment was essential to grow the vegetables for the family. Walter Rose, who lived in one of the ducking villages, Haddenham, warned that a cottage garden given over to breeding was not an inviting sight, 'and the stench after a warm June shower was even worse to put up with'.[30]

Chickens were not often a feature of nineteenth-century rural gardens, for they were rarely part of the poor man's diet. Corn seed was much too valuable for agricultural labourers to use as feed. Cows needed too much pasture land for grazing, so it was the pig that was the poor man's best friend, the meat equivalent of the potato. An old saying was that every part of the pig could be used except the squeak: black pudding was made from the blood; soft entrails could become chitterling pie; the head and tongue were made into brawn; even the gristly ears, tail and snout could go into a soup or stew; the lard was an indispensable ingredient in any cooking; and the meat could be salted or smoked inside the chimney to last through the winter. Walter Rose described how the pig could be fed on 'waste from the garden, trimmings of cabbages, peelings from potatoes and turnips, all and sundry were put by for its meals', and in turn it provided excellent manure. So important a place did it play in the villagers' lives that 'To call on a neighbour without asking "How's the pig a-doing?" was a plain breach of courtesy not to be lightly excused. The walk round the garden on Sunday, or of an evening, the detailed examination of the growing cabbages, the savoys, the sprouts, the beans and the peas, would have seemed incomplete without a long and interested pause at the sty.'[31]

The pig was not the only provider of the fertiliser vital to crop yields. Children would be sent out onto the roads to collect horse manure, and this would be supplemented by vegetable compost, ashes, nightsoil, fish and seaweed in coastal areas, hooves and bone, and even, in Kent, by woollen rags torn up and buried in the ground until they decomposed.

If the husbandry, fruit and vegetables crowded out the flowers, the cottager could always plant climbers to run up the walls of the house, and practise what was known as window gardening. Gertrude Jekyll wrote: 'There is scarcely a cottage [in West Surrey] without some plants in the window; indeed, the windows are so often so much filled with them that the light is too much obscured. The wise cottagers place them outside in the summer, to make fresh growth and gain strength.' She also described one cottage where staging had been put up on the roadside:

There were hydrangeas, fuchsias, show and zonal geraniums, lilies and begonias, for the main show; a pot or two of the graceful francoa, and

29 An elderly couple photographed in their cottage garden, from an early twentieth-century postcard. The couple clearly loved their flowers, for dahlias peep out from behind the man, while his wife holds a couple of blooms, and flowers can be seen in the window. Itinerant photographers toured with their equipment to take the images that could then be printed on one side of the card, allowing the message and address to be put on the other.

half hardy annuals cleverly grown in pots; a clematis smothered in bloom, over the door, and for the protection of all, a framework, to which a light shelter could be fixed in case of very bad weather. It must have given pleasure to thousands of passers-by; to say nothing of the pride and delight that it must have been to its owner.[32]

* * *

Some poor rural gardeners found themselves part of a rich man's vision. While certain landlords enclosed land to increase their agricultural wealth, others were inspired to do so by the birth of landscape gardening, often demolishing entire villages to achieve an exquisite piece of pastoral scenery. The landowner could include a model village as a charming feature.

At Houghton in Norfolk the politician Sir Robert Walpole landscaped his estate in around 1730, building new cottages with large gardens just outside the park gates. When the house was built at Nuneham Courtenay in Oxfordshire in the 1760s, the villagers were rehoused in cottages in rows flanking the road. This transplantation was not only the basis for Oliver Goldsmith's lament 'The Deserted Village'; proponents of the picturesque movement, William Gilpin and Uvedale Price, also criticised the new accommodation for its street-house-like straight lines and regularity.

Irregularity, roughness and variety were the watchwords of the picturesque movement. These can be seen in what has been described as the first fully picturesque village, Blaise Hamlet in Somerset. This was designed by John Nash in 1810 for John Scandrett Harford, a Quaker banker and owner of Blaise Castle. Nine cottages, with names like Jessamine and Sweet Briar, were arranged around a village green of one and three-quarter acres, each with a garden well hidden behind hedges. In about 1820 a set of lithographs was published with this lyrical introduction:

> The Air of Comfort diffused over those little Dwellings; the play of Light and Shadow produced by their Projections and Recesses, which afford shelter to a variety of Creepers; the highly Ornamental and varied Character of the Chimnies; and the Beauty of the surrounding little Gardens, glittering throughout the Summer with Flowers of the brightest hues, and guarded from the intruding hand by Hedges of Sweet-Briar, suggest the most pleasing Images to the Fancy, and shed a romantic and poetical Character over this favoured Asylum.[33]

A favoured asylum it may have been, but it was a very carefully stage-managed one, with the villagers playing bit parts. At Harlaxton in Lincolnshire, where George de Ligne Gregory had the village remodelled in the 1830s to match his extravagantly picturesque house, the cottage gardens were planted by the head gardener with no two gardens allowed to have the same climbers. What the cottagers thought of this is almost never recorded. However, 'Old Cottages', a poem written in 1863 by the playwright and comic writer, Tom Taylor, gives some idea, for Taylor himself was the son of a Cumberland farm labourer.

The cottage-homes of England! Yes, I know
How picturesque their moss and weather-stain,
Their golden thatch, whose squared eaves shadows throw
On white-washed wall and deep-sunk lattice pane . . .
All these I know – know, too, the plagues that prey
On those who dwell in these bepainted bowers:
The foul miasma of their crowded rooms,
Unaired, unlit, with green damps moulded o'er,
The fever that each autumn deals its dooms
From the rank ditch that stagnates by the door;
And then I wish the picturesqueness less,
And welcome the utilitarian hand
That from such foulness plucks its masquing dress,
And bids the well-aired, well-drained cottage stand,
All bare of weather-stain, right-angled true,
By sketches shunned, but shunned by fevers too.

At the end of the century Lord De L'Isle laid out a model estate village at Penshurst Place in Kent with the help of his agent and architect, George Devey. When a picturesque 'old' well was installed on the village green, the conversation of two inhabitants was reported in *Country Life*: 'Might so well have gied us a pump, mighn't he?' The reply: 'Lord love ye, that wouldn't have been quaint fashioned enough.'[34]

Another kind of model village with gardens was provided by industrial entrepreneurs. A very early example of this kind of project is provided by Leadhills. In 1734 James Stirling of Garden, Stirlingshire, was engaged by the Scots Mining Company as the manager in the Lanarkshire village of Leadhills. Stirling was a mathematical genius who had fled from Venice with a price on his head after trying to discover the secrets of the glass-making techniques. He brought the company back from the verge of bankruptcy by proper management and attending to the welfare of the miners. Their lives were extremely harsh, working in the lead mines high up in the Lowther Hills during the summer months and spending their winters down in the valleys with their families. Stirling cut the miners' working hours from twelve to six per day, started a health insurance scheme, inaugurated schooling for their families, and established a reading society which still exists. The men were encouraged to build strong stone cottages and to keep gardens, so that their leisure hours could be divided between horticulture and reading.[35]

A similar community was established in 1753 in the north of England by the London Lead Company, which was owned by a group of Quakers. At Nenthead in the remote North Pennines a new village was developed, and by the 1820s some 4,000 people relied on the company for their livelihood, with cottages, a market hall, school, and chapel set in a large acreage of fields, gardens and plantations. All the original eighteenth-century cottages were rebuilt with adjoining gardens which were considerable in their size, the smallest of 350 yards, the largest of 700 square yards. In addition, sixteen acres of allotments were provided for the miners, at an annual rent between 2s 6d and 10s.[36] Such generous provision of land for horticulture was vital for growing food in an isolated community, but the company also needed to recruit a skilled workforce, and allotments and gardens were attractions, along with good wages, housing and schools.[37]

A furnace and forge had been established in Staveley in Derbyshire in the mid-eighteenth century, but the village was developed by Richard Barrow a century later with housing and other benefits. At first his houses were built 'blind back' on a grid pattern with no backyard or stairs to the upper floors, with access by ladder, but when he provided more housing at his mining works at Barrow Hill in the early 1850s, these were planned in blocks of three with generous gardens. In addition Barrow provided a mechanics institute, a sick club, school, allotments, and in 1869 a horticultural society. He also opened the gardens of his house, Ringwood Hall, each Sunday, for families to enjoy. He was determined to improve the life of his coal hewers, who were offered a rise in pay if they arrived for work on Monday and Tuesday after a heavy weekend of hard drinking, dog fighting and rabbit coursing. Horticulture was one solution, and the life of his workers was described as centred on the two chapels, the football pitch, the gardens and allotments, the pigsties and chicken runs.[38]

Some idea of what the gardens of these industrial workers might have looked like can be gained by visiting the St Fagans Natural History Museum outside Cardiff. Six cottages from a terrace, Rhyd-y-car in Merthyr Tydfil, have been relocated here and their gardens recreated in the style of various periods. Iron-working had taken place over the centuries at Merthyr Tydfil, at the top of a valley on the border of the Brecon Beacons, but in the mid-eighteenth century it was still a remote settlement mainly devoted to the rearing of sheep. This changed rapidly over the next fifty years, and when Richard Crawshay opened his ironworks it was one of five at Merthyr. Like the ironmasters of Derbyshire, he was anxious to attract skilled workers, so offered them accommodation in two terraces of sixteen and thirteen houses, forming an L-shape in a site constrained by the narrow valley and the Glamorgan Canal.

The Rhyd-y-car gardens, separated from the cottages by a narrow, cobbled alley, were long and narrow, 100 feet by 30 feet. When the museum recreated the 1800 garden, a cinder path was installed, running down to the pigsty, and the plot was divided from the next with wattle fencing. The planting is entirely utilitarian, with edible plants for the kitchen: broad beans, curly kale (traditionally known as cow cabbage), and 'lumper' potatoes. The last are large, knobbly, susceptible to blight and good for cooking – the variety that was much favoured in Ireland. The herbs, such as rue and comfrey, could be used for medicine. Colour is provided by the flowers of the herbs, like the brilliant yellow of the rue. By the mid-century, life had changed for the community. The ironworking industry had slumped, and coalmining taken over, with the standard of living for the workers in decline. Cholera had struck Merthyr Tydfil in 1849 and 1854, killing nearly 2,000 of the population, including six from the terrace. In the 1855 garden, horseradish has been planted nearest to the house, the plant's rampant habit constrained by a cobbled pavement leading down to the cinder path. The inhabitants of Rhyd-y-car would have enjoyed little roast beef, but the young leaves could be used for salad and the older for stews. Further down the path are more vegetables and currant bushes, with wild strawberries as border planting. Privet hedging divides this garden from that of 1895, which sports a donkey stable and a coop for hens as well as the pigsty, along with an outside toilet. The cholera scare had at last persuaded householders to abandon the bucket, the contents of which were usually thrown into the nearby canal. The utilitarian nature of the garden did not change, however, and the planting now includes goose-berries, rhubarb and runner beans along with the potatoes and broad beans.

At Beamish, 'the Living Museum of the North' in County Durham, a terrace of coalminers' cottages is on display. These date from the 1860s, and have been transferred from Francis Street in Hetton-le-Hole. This was a period of considerable expansion in the output of the coalfields of the North East of England, with a proliferation of small colliery villages. The Hetton Coal Company wanted to attract not only local agricultural labourers, but also workers from Ireland and Wales. Thus they offered houses free to those working in the colliery (so they were like tied agricultural cottages), with a garden in front, separated by wooden fences.

The miners were prodigious gardeners, often cultivating an allotment as well as the garden. Their horticultural activity must have stood in stark contrast to the terrible conditions in which they worked underground. Mrs Storey, interviewed in 1976 when she was eighty-nine years old, told how she had worked as an agricultural labourer at the age of seven, working eleven hours for ninepence a day. Her father had begun work even earlier, at the age of four or five, carried to the pit on the back of her grandfather. Mrs Storey had married a miner, and recalled their garden in Lyons Street in Hetton-le-Hole, which the interviewer noted:

> was an important source of cheap home-grown vegetables . . . leeks, carrots, potatoes, cabbages, etc. Flowers were grown in small numbers in flower beds against the front of the house. A path from the front doors straight down to the end of the garden . . . Most of the garden was given over to vegetables. Some pansies were grown and some strawberries. Did not keep any animals or birds – pigs were banned (at some stage). But towards the bottom of the garden the pig cree [the local name for a sty, and for pigeon lofts] still stood. Next to them was the garden shed – which was used to keep tools, etc. No trees or shrubs.[39]

Mrs Storey's recollections have enabled the museum to recreate the Victorian gardens.

In 1845 Benjamin Disraeli published his novel, *Sybil, or the Two Nations*. This was written to promulgate the ideas of 'Young England', with the two nations in the title being 'the Rich and the Poor'. Among the crowded cast of characters is the brutal estate owner, Lord Marney, who boasts how he is 'tremendously fierce against allotments', and declares 'I will take care that the population of my parishes is not increased. I build no cottages, and I destroy all I can.' In contrast, Disraeli introduces a humanitarian mill-owner, Mr Trafford, who builds a model village near his mill, with gardens to every cottage, encouraging his men to buy their leases. Trafford is described as of 'gentle blood' and 'Old English feelings'. His employees are 'proud of their house and little garden, and of the horti-cultural society, where its produce permitted them to be annual competi-tors'. His own house stands in the middle of the village, with beautiful gardens to give an impetus to the horticulture of the community.

Urban mills represent a later development of the Industrial Revolution. Earlier mills were established where there was a source of power from water, often in remote river valleys. One of the first was a textile mill established by Richard Arkwright in the early 1770s at Cromford in the

Derwent Valley in Derbyshire, developing a former lead-mining village. Arkwright had built a water frame that produced cotton yarn strong enough to be a warp thread, thus making possible an all-cotton cloth, and he needed to lure workers to this remote, sparsely populated site. This he did by building cottages with small back gardens and detached plots of land scattered around the village where his workers could cultivate allotments and keep pigs in 'pig-cotes'. Arkwright was one of a group of Derbyshire mill-owners with a strong sense of responsibility towards their workers. It is ironical therefore that when Arkwright's patents for his water frame were set aside in 1783 the textile equivalent to a gold rush took place, with 200 Arkwright-type mills opening in different parts of Britain. As a result, mills were built in cities and towns, and the opportunities for workers to have gardens and allotments evaporated, as will be seen in Chapter 6.

The degree of enlightenment of the mill-owners was of course comparative: they were also determined entrepreneurs, and the balance could be a fine one. At Quarry Bank Mill in Cheshire Samuel Greg, the son of a prosperous Belfast merchant, believed that he should provide for his workers the ordered and familiar life of a village rather than the chaos of the rapidly developing towns. Taking advantage of the setting aside of Arkwright's patents, Greg established his cotton mill in the isolated Bollin Valley, about ten miles south of Manchester, in 1784. Some of his first workers were child apprentices, brought from as far afield as Hackney and Chelsea, although by 1830 most were provided by the workhouses of Liverpool. An Apprentice House was built for nearly a hundred children, and the National Trust has recreated their garden, where they grew their vegetables to supplement their diet of bread, milk, porridge and potatoes. Older workers lived in the village of Styal, many in houses owned by the Gregs, with rent deducted from wages. Each house had a long garden, probably planted with fruit and vegetables, although today they are filled with flowers. The young Samuel Greg, more altruistic than his father, created another community at Lowerhouse Mills in Bollington, where he took further the ideas of social responsibility, refurbishing existing cottages and dividing meadows and pastures into allotments for fruit and vegetables. His venture, however, proved financially disastrous.

One man who managed to combine altruism with spectacular profits was Titus Salt. Salt made his fortune from using alpaca wool in the manufacture of worsted. Probably influenced by Disraeli's *Sybil*, he carried his ethical views into practice with a model village at Saltaire outside Bradford.

Schools, chapels, a mechanics institute, a hospital, laundry and park were all provided, though Salt, with his Congregationalist views, banned public houses. For his workers he provided allotments, and for his pensioners gardens around their almshouses fronted by gardens and walks, and creeping plants by the windows. We have to remember, however, that although the almshouses may have looked like Italian villas, they were in practice back-to-backs, with strict qualifications for admission – good moral character and incapacity for labour by reason of age, disease or infirmity.

In complete contrast to the paternalism of these enlightened but controlling industrialists, some working-class gardeners were part of self-help movements. Perhaps their spiritual godfather was Gerrard Winstanley, the seventeenth-century political activist who during the Protectorate of Oliver Cromwell founded the Diggers. Under the rallying cry, 'With spades and hoes and ploughs, stand up now, stand up now. Your freedom to uphold', Winstanley led his followers onto the waste and common lands in Surrey, which had been enclosed, depriving labourers of free fuel and the opportunity to forage for fruits and nuts. The Diggers' plan was to cultivate crops free of restrictions and rents, in the belief that no man should own land or property, but in common according to needs. The first settlement, at St George's Hill at Weybridge, was abandoned after harassment from the lord of the manor and the loss of a court case in 1649. Further attempts to establish more Digger communities also failed, to be followed by legislation which sought to ensure that the poor stayed in the parishes of their birth to prevent a recurrence of such activities.

The Diggers' idea of a community based on self-help may have ended in failure, but their legend lived on. In the early nineteenth century William Allen, a chemist with strong Quaker principles, bought a tract in Sussex to set up a smallholding community. By 1831 the colony at Lindfield consisted of twenty-five cottages, with a school and workshop. Each cottage had a garden of one and a quarter acres, with larger holdings of six acres added later. Although the soil was poor, the experiment proved a success, and was an important influence on Feargus O'Connor when in 1845 he decided to direct the Chartist movement away from direct political activism towards land colonies. The Chartist Co-operative Land Society was set up to settle working-class families on plots of between two and four acres on which it was hoped they could earn a reasonable income. About 70,000 members from all over England paid subscriptions of around £2.50 in the hope of being successful in a lottery to allocate the plots.

The first Chartist colony was begun following the purchase of 103 acres at Heronsgate in Hertfordshire, with well-proportioned cottages and a schoolroom with accommodation for a teacher. Although the ideas were good, the practicalities were not so well considered – only one well for the entire community and no nearby market where the colonists might sell their produce. More communities were established at Lowbands in Gloucestershire, bought in October 1846, followed by Snigs End and Minster Lovell (renamed Charterville), and Great Dodford at Bromsgrove near Birmingham. However, finances were shaky, the soil often poor, and the people recruited into the new villages were drawn from the cities, and were therefore not experienced in agrarian and horticultural practices. A select committee of the House of Commons reported that the Land Company whereby the properties were purchased was illegal, and in 1851 an act was passed to dissolve it. On top of all this, O'Connor was growing increasingly erratic in his behaviour – he would later become insane.

The most successful of the colonies was at Great Dodford. Chartist colleagues from the West Midlands lent practical help, bringing tools on regular visits. A special 'Dodford digging fork' was made in Stourbridge to deal with the heavy red soil. With access to the Birmingham and Black Country markets, the villagers were able to earn revenue from market gardening with their flowers, fruit, peas, beans and shallots. Garlic was supplied to Lea & Perrins for Worcestershire Sauce. One of the colonists, John Wallace, realised that with careful treatment of the soil, strawberries could be cultivated, and early in the 1860s, the village made this their staple crop, with 'Joseph Paxton' the favourite variety. Up to 1922 an annual Strawberry Wake was held on the second Sunday of July, when visitors could eat as much fruit as they wanted for sixpence. Such was the success of Great Dodford that Jesse Collings used the colony as an example in his land reform campaigns in the 1880s: 'These small cultivators are only acquainted with poor rates from the fact that they have to pay them. What I want to see, and what the working classes, if they are wise, will insist on securing, is that there should be three or four thousand Great Dodfords in England.'[40] Great Dodford lost its radical character when plots were bought as rural retreats and better wages could be found in the factories of nearby towns and cities. Rosedene, one of the Great Dodford cottages, with its garden and orchard, has recently been acquired by the National Trust. Built in 1849, the cottage has undergone little alteration and provides a good example of what these Chartist colonies were like in the nineteenth century.

A similar experiment in self-sufficiency was conducted at Whiteway in the parish of Miserden near Stroud in Gloucestershire. This community was founded in 1898 by a Quaker journalist, Samuel Veale Bracher, inspired by the philosophy of Tolstoy. Bracher purchased forty-one acres, along with seeds, tools and provisions, and the colonists then burnt the property deeds on the end of a pitchfork as a symbol of their rejection of the notion of property. The colonists built their own homes, wooden shacks, and cultivated the land: one member in 1935 described how 'if our feet were down in the potato trenches our heads were up with the stars'.[41] The community still exists, with over sixty homes, although these are now privately owned and sold at market value.

Another experiment was established in 1895 by a small international group as the Clousden Hill Free Communist and Cooperative Colony, just outside Newcastle upon Tyne. The Clousden Hill colonists were influenced by the Utopian ideas of William Morris and of the Russian anarchist, Peter Kropotkin. Both Morris and Kropotkin held high-minded views that were often not very practical. The latter, for instance, maintained that vineyards could be constructed in Durham heated by local coal. He also wanted to grow oranges, lemons, bananas, and tomatoes 'just to prove how wonderfully full of colour we could make the coal-mining areas if only we gave the miners full opportunity to use the coal they bring up from the depths'.[42] At Clousden Hill work was voluntary and, as Kropotkin had predicted, hard, often an average of nineteen hours a day including Sundays. Four acres were cultivated intensely with peas, cauliflowers, cabbages, celery and carrot. Fruit trees were planted – 120 apple and 25 cherry – along with 2,000 berry and currant bushes. A quarter of an acre was set aside for strawberries. Flowers were also grown, such as chrysanthemums and roses, and a colonist from Brussels even raised orchids in the greenhouses that the colonists built. Within three years, however, conflicting political views began to lead to the break-up of the colony, although the site is still used for allotments.

The Diggers had attempted to be part of the venerable tradition of squatters. Other makeshift communities formed on wasteland by roadsides, others at the edge of heathland, some on the fringes of forests, others on the outskirts of towns and cities. The inhabitants were often in migratory occupations, such as hop-picking, harvesting and picking fruit in market gardens. An example of a squatter's cottage can be seen in Blists Hill Victorian Town at Telford in Shropshire. The early nineteenth-century cottage of sandstone and brick, which would have been constructed in a matter of days, originally stood on roadside wasteland at Burroughs Bank, Little Dawley. In 1861 it was the home of Michael Corbett, a cobbler, his wife Sarah, and their six children. The triangular shape of the garden that surrounds the cottage at Blists Hill reflects the original site, and is planted mainly with herbs, vegetables and fruit bushes that would have provided the sustenance for a family living both physically and economically on the edge of society. The garden also contains the outside privy and a sty for the squatters' pig.

The squatters' settlement at Headington Quarry, just outside Oxford, was the subject of study by the social historian Raphael Samuel in the late 1960s. For centuries the stone to build the university colleges had been extracted from Headington, leaving a landscape of various levels, and in the nineteenth century brickmaking had also been conducted on the site, so that the layout was higgledy piggledy, quite unlike the nucleated settlements lined on either side of the main highway, or the neat arrangement of estate communities.[43] As one villager told Samuel, it was 'all 'oles and alleys and 'ills, that's what Quarry is, all up and down'.[44] This must have made gardening a difficult task, but because this was a 'free' village, the inhabitants could extend their gardens as much as they wanted: 'up went the fence, that was theirs'.[45] The gardens were, moreover, large enough to accommodate all kinds of activities. William Green, a builder's labourer and navvy, was remembered by his son as having 'something of everything' in the garden. 'We had . . . fruit trees all down the centre . . . vegetables – potatoes and so on . . . pig sties half way down . . . hen houses . . . something of everything . . . we never bought vegetables'.[46]

Charles Snow, a stonemason, kept a diary of his gardening, showing how it was his constant leisure occupation. According to family tradition he would get up at four on a summer morning, work in his garden for an hour, and then set off from Headington Quarry to Oxford. The year 1882 is in its original pocket book form, while 1884 survives as a photocopy.[47] Every day he noted the weather, usually followed by short notes, written in pencil, of his gardening activities. Sometimes other subjects are also included, such as killing a pig, cleaning a clock, buying a new hat or shoes for the children, and births and deaths in the village. He worked at various colleges, with wages of £1 16s per week, although he mentions being laid off or getting the sack, so the income was erratic. Expenses are listed on the opposite page to the 'week to view' of the diary.

When in work, almost all his wages were given over to Mrs Snow, and the rest spent on things for the garden and occasionally on beer. Thus on

30 Henry Taunt's photograph of the squatter settlement at Headington Quarry, just outside Oxford, taken in 1906. Space was not at a premium because of the nature of the settlement, so that keen gardeners, such as the stonemason Charles Snow, were able to cultivate large gardens, running right down to the mouth of the quarry workings.

23 January 1882 he spent two shillings on hyacinth and tulip bulbs, paid a penny for a button hole and one shilling for flower pots. On 31 January, a fine day, he planted currant trees at the top of the garden. On 15 February, a very wet day, he cut and fresh-potted fuchsias and attended a Band of Hope tea. Two days later, when the weather was fine, he planted single gladiolus and sweet pea, and sowed a pot of celosia seed. And so the diary proceeds through the year, showing that Snow grew a wide range of vegetables, herbs, fruit and flowers in his garden, as well as keeping ducks. He noted the various kinds of potato he planted, including Elephants and Beauty of Hebron. He made parsnip wine and pickled his broccoli, buying vinegar and curry powder to do so. Given his erratic employment, he must have welcomed the extra money he could earn from selling his produce, such as strawberries and gooseberries in July. He provides, in this rare survival of a working-class gardener's diary, a picture of a keen and knowledgeable gardener. There must have been many like him whose devotion to their gardens and allotments is lost to us.

* * *

To return to the question posed at the top of the chapter, it is clear from the descriptions provided by writers such as William Howitt and Flora Thompson, and the diary entries made by Charles Snow, that working-class rural gardens were not just for vegetables. Flowers and fruit were also present whenever possible. It is impossible, moreover, to talk of *the* cottage garden when looking at the horticultural activities of nineteenth-century rural workers. The cottage garden means something quite different in garden history, as will be seen in Chapter 10.

The appearance of the gardens of rural workers depended upon a concatenation of factors: tenure, economics, climate and sheer good fortune. On a journey from Swindon through Wiltshire, William Cobbett in his *Rural Rides* described 'all through the county, poor as well as rich, are very neat in their gardens, and very careful to raise a great variety of flowers'. But earlier, on the road to Marlborough, he had come upon a group of women labourers presenting 'such an assemblage of rags as I never before saw'.[48] Seventy years later, Joseph Ashby, in his articles on the villages of Warwickshire, provided examples of prosperous villages with flourishing gardens just down the road from communities sunk in abject rural poverty.

It also has to be remembered that Helen Allingham was a commercial artist, who needed to sell her pictures to people who were unlikely to want hanging on their drawing-room wall a picture of a destitute garden with a woman in torn clothes accompanied by a grubby child. Nevertheless, the 'father' of the school of picturesque cottage painters, Myles Birket Foster, showed the other side of the coin in a watercolour of a cottage vegetable garden (Plate XIII). It is a gritty scene, but colourful roses still climb defiantly up the wall of the tumbledown dwelling.

CHAPTER 6

❦

# Hard Times

JOHN WARD, A cotton weaver from Clitheroe in Lancashire, noted in his diary a journey he took, beginning on Good Friday of the year 1860. His purpose was to revisit the industrial villages to the east of Manchester where he had been brought up twenty-eight years earlier: 'Villages have grown into large towns, and country places where there was nothing but fields are now covered with streets and villages and large factories and workshops everywhere. I made enquiries many a place after people who had lived there, but they were either dead or gone to America or gone somewhere else.'[1] Statistics bear out his observations. In 1700 two-thirds of the population of Britain were engaged in working on the land. By 1800, this had been reduced to one-third, and was dwindling rapidly. Developing industrialisation in the latter part of the eighteenth century moved nearly 400,000 men, women and children from the countryside into cities and towns, and in the next fifty years this figure doubled.

Social historians sometimes question whether the rural labouring classes suffered worse living conditions than their urban cousins, a fairly fruitless debate as both often had to endure the most appalling deprivation. However, urban gardeners had to cope with one problem that did not afflict their rural counterparts: pollution. This started to be a problem in the late sixteenth century, when thousands of London establishments, both domestic and industrial, burned what was known as sea coal, brought down by ship from Newcastle and other north-eastern ports. In his gardening book published in 1629 John Parkinson wrote of 'unwholesome ayre . . . where there is so much smoake, especially of sea-coales, which of all other is the worst, as our Citie of London can give proofe sufficient, wherein neither herbe nor tree will long prosper, nor hath done ever since the use of sea-coles beganne to bee frequent therein'. [2] Abraham Cowley expressed this in more poetic terms in his poem 'The Garden', in which he asked:

> Who, that has Reason, and his Smell,
> Would not among Roses and Jasmin dwell,
> Rather than all his Spirits choak,
> With exhalations of Dirt and Smoke?
> And all th'uncleanness which does drown
> In pestilential Clouds a pop'ulous town?

Cowley's poem was reproduced at the beginning of the 1679 edition of John Evelyn's famous horticultural work, *Sylva*. In 1661 Evelyn had sought to turn back the clock with his book *Fumifugium*, in which he proposed that plantations should be set around London 'supplied with such *Shrubs* as yield the most fragrant and odiferous *Flowers*, and are aptest to tinge the *Aer* upon gentle emission at a great distance'.[3] But all in vain – the problem just got greater and more widespread with the onset of the Industrial Revolution.

Realising that nothing could be done to alleviate the polluted atmosphere of towns and cities, gardening writers turned to proffering advice on which plants could best cope with smoke. In his *City Gardener*, published in 1722, Thomas Fairchild begins by noting: 'I find that every thing will not prosper in London: either because the Smoke of the Sea-Coal does hurt to some Plants, or else because those People, who have little Gardens in London, do not know how to manage their Plants when they have got them'.[4] More than a century later Shirley Hibberd, in his book *The Town Garden*, a manual for city and suburban gardens, began: 'It is generally thought that a city garden is an impossibility! that vegetation cannot be reconciled to the close air, the darkness, and the smoke of towns; and that all attempts to mingle the rural with the urban must, like Brummel's forty neck-cloths, turn out failures'.[5] In Preston in Lancashire, it was reported that the smoke pollution from the cotton mills was so intense that additional labour was required in the market gardens to remove the soot from the surface of the soil.

Although, with the exception of London, most British cities in the early nineteenth century were within walking distance of the countryside, the deprivation of trees and flowers, and of fresh air must have been intensely felt. In his poem 'The Task', written in 1783, William Cowper evokes this sense of loss:

. . . man, immur'd in cities still retains
His inborn inextinguishable thirst
Of rural scenes, compensating his loss
By supplemental shifts . . .

These 'supplemental shifts' were what were known as window gardening, one way that urban gardeners overcame their difficult conditions:

The most unfurnish'd with the means of life,
And they that never pass their brick-wall bounds
To range the fields and treat their lungs with air,
Yet feel the burning instinct: over head
Suspend their crazy boxes, planted thick,
And water'd duly. Their pitcher stands
A fragment, and how the spoutless tea-pot there;
Sad witnesses how close-pent man regrets
The country . . .[6]

In *Little Dorrit* Dickens has Mrs Plornish, the wife of a poor plasterer living in 'virtually an urban pigsty' in Bleeding Heart Yard, employing a man to paint a mural on the wall leading from the shop to the parlour, depicting the exterior of a thatched cottage, about which old-fashioned flowers, the modest sunflower and hollyhock, were 'flourishing with great luxuriance'.[7]

William Cowper was a romantic poet, and Charles Dickens is often labelled as a sentimentalist, but the following verse was written by a working man, a Leicestershire house-painter, William Whitmore, and he too expresses the nostalgia of the urban man for the countryside of his youth:

To one who hath long pined, shut from the sky,
Immured amid bare walls, how full and strong
The feel of life, how wild the bounding joy,
At length, released, to roam at large among
The woods and hills, imbathed with sunshine, flowers and song![8]

In 1854 Charles Dickens published his novel *Hard Times*, based on his impressions of the Lancashire weaving town of Preston, which he called Coketown. The book not only features Thomas Gradgrind, the misguided exponent of Utilitarianism, but also records how the lives of men, women and children were being transformed by the Industrial Revolution. Eighteenth-century views of Preston show long narrow gardens, burgage plots, belonging to privileged townsmen. But half a century later a very different vista was displayed. The gardens had been infilled as the town underwent rapid economic growth and an enormous increase in population. At first the cotton weavers worked in their own cottages, on looms in their cellars where the damp conditions were necessary for the thread, but the Preston-born Richard Arkwright's water frame (see Chapter 5, pp. 133–4) required a power source and could only be used in a factory: the first cotton mill in Preston was opened in 1777 to be followed by a whole series of others, and the fate of the handloom weavers was sealed.

Ten years before Dickens visited Preston, the Revd John Clay wrote a report on the sanitary conditions of the town, in which he described in graphic terms the housing conditions of the millworkers: 'overcrowding of rooms and of beds; filthiness of apartments, persons, clothing and bedding; prevalence of damp, yet want of water; absence of proper and decent accommodation as to privies; keeping of pigs in or too near dwellings; and pervading all a sickening smell'.[9] Alongside this text he reproduced an illustration of a typical street, showing little terraced houses with not a chance of a garden, just tiny yards leading into a rear passage.

For its poorer residents Preston was a horticultural desert – an experience shared by many towns and cities overtaken by the Industrial Revolution. The early presence of large mills and factories in the development of these urban areas meant that workers' lives were not their own. Handloom weavers and outworkers had always worked long hours, but

31 Detail of a prospect of Preston in Lancashire, from Buck's *Antiquities*, 1774. The long narrow gardens running down from the houses take the distinctive shape of burgage plots.

were in charge of their own time. This change was reflected in a song by
John Grimshaw, a Lancashire cotton weaver, comparing the hand loom
with the power loom:

So come all you cotton weavers, you must rise up very soon,
For you must work in factories from morning until noon:
You mustn't walk in your gardens for two or three hours a-day.
For you must stand at their command, and keep your shuttles in
    play.[10]

It is significant that Grimshaw singles out the loss of time to enjoy a
garden.

But not every city experienced this pattern of industrialisation. The
long burgage plots shown on the eighteenth-century views of Preston were
common to almost every town in England; these were tracts of land allo-
cated to the freemen entitled to practise a trade and to elect members of
the ruling council. Their long, narrow form is thought to be based on
ploughland strips of earlier agrarian settlements and are still to be seen in
some modern towns, such as Chipping Campden in Gloucestershire and
Cricklade in Wiltshire, where the properties have a narrow frontage on a
main street with a long garden behind. Sometimes these plots were not
attached to the property, but were stand-alone garden grounds on the
outskirts of the urban area. In many industrial towns the burgage plots
disappeared under bricks and mortar, but not in every instance. Sheffield,
for example, shows a very different pattern.

The Yorkshire city had for centuries been the principal centre for the
manufacture of cutlery outside London. Chaucer, for instance, makes
reference to a Sheffield dagger in the Reeve's Tale. In the 1740s a crucible
process made it possible to produce steel implements and the town developed rapidly, so that by 1801 the population had reached just over 60,000.
However, the working pattern of the cutlers, making a whole range of
scissors, knives and blades, was centred on small workshops, with the
master as a working craftsman rarely employing more than two or three
journeymen and a couple of apprentices. One of the principal leisure
activities of these men was gardening, cultivating allotment gardens on
many acres of land around Sheffield.[11] The first references to land being
leased to craftsmen date from 1712 to 1730 when thirty-five parcels were
let at will on various sites. The agreements for some of these include
records of the occupations of the tenants: by far the majority are cutlers,

but also button makers, shoemakers, bakers, innkeepers and a school-master. These tenants were leasing between 150 and 200 square yards, and being charged threepence per square yard, the equivalent of £6 per acre.[12]

A physician, William Buchan, wrote about these gardens with great enthusiasm in his *Domestic Medicine*, published in 1769: 'the very smell of the earth and fresh herbs revive and cheer the spirits, whilst the perpetual prospect of something coming to maturity delights and entertains the mind'. He continues in this vein:

> It may seem romantic to recommend gardening to manufacturers in great towns; but observation proves that the plan is very practicable. In the town of Sheffield in Yorkshire where the great iron manufacture is carried on, there is hardly a journeyman cutler who does not possess a piece of ground which he cultivates as a garden. This practice has many salutary effects. It not only induces these people to take exercise without door, but also to eat many greens, roots, &c of their own growth, which they could never think of purchasing.[13]

In all, over ninety acres of gardens were scattered around Sheffield by the late 1780s, probably offering at least 1,200 plots for families.

The enthusiasm of the Sheffield cutlers for the cultivation of auriculas was noted in Chapter 4. It would seem from Dr Buchan's comments that the working men of Sheffield also relished the growing of vegetables. The accounts of Joseph Rowbotham, keeper of the Horse and Garter Inn and tenant of a small garden survive from the 1760s. In the spring of 1763 he bought from William Perfect of Pontefract one pound each of best onion seed (2s 6d), radish (1s) and parsley (1s), with 'Best Lettuce of Sorts' (4d). In the autumn of 1766 he took delivery of 800 cabbage plants in two baskets for 8s, and the following April a peck of long Hotspur peas at 2s; in May two quarts of Ledman's dwarf peas at 8d, plus another parcel of seeds, and in June four quarts of kidney beans at 2s 6d.[14] Dr Buchan made the point that these gardeners could have bought their vegetables from local market gardeners who had stalls in the town, but preferred to grow their own. This was not for subsistence, as the craftsmen earned good wages (up to twenty shillings per week for journeymen in the eighteenth century), and even ordinary labourers earned more than their counterparts in Barnsley and Wakefield. An account of the Sheffield gardeners also describes the observance of 'Saint Monday', prolonging the weekend by an extra day. This practice was not confined to Sheffield, but was to be found in cities and towns where the workers were in charge of their own destiny and management of their time. The cutlers were famous for working hard and putting in extra hours, but the additional time spent in their garden plots and resulting produce justified the cost of the rent, as well as ensuring good fresh food, a healthy lifestyle, camaraderie and friendly competition.

Birmingham, like Sheffield, had a long history as an industrial community. According to the Tudor topographer, William Camden, the town was 'resounding with hammers and anvils, for most of them are Smiths'.[15] The metal trades, often described as toy manufactures, were predominantly small in scale, with masters running workshops. Locally known as 'shopping', these were often built on what had originally been burgage plots and subsequently back gardens of town houses. The loss of these private gardens stimulated the demand for similar land elsewhere, known as 'guinea gardens' which first developed in the late seventeeth or early eighteenth centuries.[16] On William Westley's 1731 map of Birmingham, he shows twenty-three separate garden sites, which rose to thirty-five by 1778. The owners of such land found that they could get a better return from letting the sites for gardens than for agricultural purposes. By the early nineteenth century, the return was £16 per acre, compared to £4 per acre for farming. The high point for this arrangement was reached in the 1830s when there were 2,000 gardens ringing the urban centre. A decade later, the numbers began to fall as landowners

32 Durham, from Buck's *Antiquities*, 1774, showing detached garden grounds. Many cities had such grounds on their outskirts, but the particular site of the city of Durham made these vital for the citizens.

found that they could make even more money by leasing for building development.

The price of £16 per acre is considerably higher than the £6 pertaining in Sheffield, and the status of the gardeners who leased these plots has been a matter of debate. Some were middle class, but others were from the working class. A study of five streets in Birmingham's town centre in the 1820s and 1830s gives an indication of the occupations of tenants of gardens in the Snow Hill area. These included members of the middle classes, such as a grocer, surgeon, victuallers and a fancy gilt and black toy manufacturer. However, there are also working-class tenants, such as a tin-plate worker, a currier, a burnisher and a plane maker.[17] In 1833 the Select Committee on Public Walks reported that in Birmingham 'it was the custom for the working man to have gardens at about a guinea a year rent, of which there are a great number round the town, and all the better parts of the workmen spend their leisure hours there'.[18] The individual plots were surrounded by hedges or close-boarded fences, with access via lanes or walks lined with hedges. Some were ornamental, others more practical according to a late eighteenth-century historian of the town: 'Health and amusement are found in the prodigious number of private gardens . . . from which we often behold the father returning with a cabbage and the daughter with a nosegay.'[19]

Advertisements give us more details. For instance, one on the Oozells Estate near Broad Street, posted in 1802: 'To be disposed of, a garden, lately belonging to Mr John Smith, diesinker deceased, with an excellent summer house, a choice collection of fruit trees, flowers, shrubs, well fenced, etc, situated near the Cottage of Content.' The cottage was occupied by a gardener who oversaw the site and showed plots to potential tenants. Another advertisement describes a garden 'in the highest state of very great forwardness; the fruits (of which there is great Plenty) are all of the best and in their prime. There is also a Collection of choice flower roots, variously dispersed and a number of auricular plants in pots, likewise a handsome brick Summer house and other conveniences and several painted garden screens, etc.' These accoutrements suggest that the gardener had been a florist.[20]

The working men who cultivated such plots were skilled with their hands, and thus able to build their summerhouses. These were sometimes well furnished, with sash windows, cupboards, and even a cooking kitchen, making it possible for families to use them as weekend retreats. One observer was critical of the appearance of some of these little buildings, though he approved of their social benefit:

Many of the little fabrics, dignified with the name of summer-houses, though in general built in sovereign contempt of all the orders of architecture, contain accommodious repository for their favourite beverage; and in all of them it is accounted a luxury to smoke a pipe . . . Is it probable that a race of Savages should erect altars to Flora, or that people fond of riot, confusion or plunder should take delight in the tranquil recreations of a garden?[21]

His question refers to the riots that shook Birmingham in 1791.

By the 1840s, the centre for guinea gardens had moved out from the centre to Edgbaston on the south-eastern side of the city, where Lord Calthorpe was leasing 250 gardens on several sites, in plots between one-eighth and one-sixteenth of an acre. An example of such a leasing agreement was made on 26 March 1846 with William Taylor, a glass cutter of No. 6 Court, Islington Street. Taylor undertook not to use his plot as a trading garden, and to maintain fences and hedges, scour and cleanse gutters, drains and watercourses. He was not to injure timber trees, nor erect any buildings, and not to dig or cultivate land or take in manure on a Sunday.[22] The number of gardens was increased when the Botanical Gardens got into financial trouble and more land was released. However, by 1878, a book written about the recent history of Birmingham noted how 'little plots of ground let for a guinea per annum, laid out with flowers, or planted with vegetables, currants and gooseberry bushes, strawberries and other useful "garden stuff"' were disappearing, as 'the continually increasing town has spread its limbs on all sides like a huge octopus, and shabby suburbs have long since covered the pleasant artisans' gardens of seventy years ago'.[23]

Remarkably, eighty-two of these plots have survived. These were rescued by the Westbourne Road Leisure Gardens Association against all the odds after, in 1972, bulldozers were sent in to demolish hedges, sheds and summerhouses ready for building development. A good idea of how these gardens looked before dereliction and demolition can be gained from a visit to the Hill Close Gardens in nearby Warwick. Unlike Birmingham, Warwick did not become an industrial centre, but endured rather as a historic market town. The Hill Close Gardens lie to the south-west of the town centre by the race course, and thus retain a semi-rural character. They too were threatened by the arrival of bulldozers in the summer of 1993 but local resistance to the proposed development forced the importance of the gardens to be recognised. Of the hundreds of such sites that had once existed across England, Hill Close was one of only four now remaining. Four of the summerhouses were listed as Grade II*, and the gardens themselves were later designated as of historic importance.[24]

As at Birmingham, many of the Victorian gardeners were shopkeepers and men with businesses who often 'lived over the shop' and therefore walked out to their gardens for recreation. But research has revealed that others were working-class, such as Reuben Lively, a servant from Northgate Street who acquired Plot 12. The only one on the site that has been continuously cultivated is Plot 25. A description made in 1870 mentions hawthorn hedges, paths with edging tiles and a cucumber frame. There were four plum trees, three standard and one espalier apple, a cherry, twenty-nine gooseberries and thirty-two currant bushes, along with two standard rose bushes. Not only was there a summerhouse, now gone, but also a pigsty, that has survived. The pretty summerhouses that remain might even have gained approval for their architecture, and are furnished with fireplaces so that they could be occupied overnight and during week-ends by the family. The level area at the bottom of the gardens was culti-vated in a similar style to allotments in the Victorian period.

The distinction between garden grounds and allotments is a fine one, usually defined by whether there were dividing hedges. One provision of gardens for workers in which the distinction is blurred was the land provided by Matthew Boulton at his Soho Works, the manufactory where he made cut-steel luxury goods and developed his Sheffield plate process. Boulton had taken a lease on an extensive area of ground around Handsworth Heath, to the north-west of Birmingham town centre, in 1761, and over the next five years built his manufactory. In 1801 he secured enclosure of the remainder of the heath and determined to lay out gardens for his employees.

William Cheshire, his agent, was in frequent correspondence with him to confirm his wishes, mentioning in a letter of 18 April 1801: 'I under-stand each guinea garden is to contain one eighth of an acre'. This is an interesting use of the term guinea, as the workers were in no position to pay such a rent, suggesting that it was used as a general term. A lottery was organised and workers invited to put down their names to apply to be tenants, including Cheshire himself, who expressed the hope that his enquiries might not appear selfish. He goes on: 'I have heard that you express'd an Intention of assisting the Garden Speculators by ploughing, cross-ploughing, harrowing, & cross-harrowing . . . & some of them have hinted, that if you are dispos'd to grant them a Boon equivalent to the

Expence of Ploughing it would be more acceptable to them in Manure; but in reply to this I have signified that Manure is of greater value to you than Money.' A letter written two weeks later refers to digging wells and continuing trenching, with a piece of land near the Mill Pool being levelled for the planting of potatoes. Cheshire was worried about the amount of land that should be assigned to each plot, sending Boulton a plan so that he might make a judgement, with a walkway twelve feet wide indicated for wheelbarrows. These plots, then would not be divided by hedges, but laid out in the allotment style.[25]

Boulton's workers, and the guinea gardeners mentioned above, were the lucky ones. In the early nineteenth century Birmingham had a population of around 80,000, out of which only around 1.5 per cent was able to afford to lease the gardens. The city was growing fast, doubling in population by the middle of the century, with many workers crammed into the notorious back-to-back housing. This type of housing was even denser than the terraces with their backyards described earlier. The wall of one house, sometimes just half a brick in width, was shared by another, with dwellings grouped around a court with shared facilities for washing and lavatories. The chance for these residents to enjoy gardening went no further than a flower-pot or window box on a sill, or a tiny bed.[26]

With the exception of London, Nottingham is the urban area which has the most descriptions of working-class gardening in the nineteenth century. Earlier views show many garden grounds surrounding the city centre, and as the city expanded, more ground was made available, mostly to the north-east of the city, including Hunger Hills, Mapperly Hills and Thorneywood. Some of these plots, as in Birmingham, were described as 'guinea gardens', cultivated by a mixture of middle-class residents and craftsmen, such as lace-makers and framework knitters. Knitting hosiery on a frame is thought to have been introduced in 1589 by William Lee, and by the eighteenth century Nottingham had become the leading manufactory in Britain. The framework knitters worked either in small workshops or in their own homes, with the women and children of the family winding yarn onto bobbins and seaming the flat pieces to make the finished hose. Some lived in outlying villages to the north-east: Arnold, Burton Joyce, Calverton, Woodborough and Lambley. But the early nineteenth century was not a kind time for these workers, who resisted the incoming factory regime. Hit by falling wages and a series of bad harvests between 1809 and 1811, the knitters launched attacks on unscrupulous employers. Along with workers in other industrial areas, they invoked Ned

Ludd, or the fictional General Ludd who was said to live in Sherwood Forest. By 1817 these disorders were over, but the workers were suffering bitter poverty, crowded into courts and alleys, and more than 6,000 back-to-back houses. Further rioting followed in 1831, with many supporting the Chartists, and the Duke of Newcastle's castle in the centre of the city was attacked when the Reform Bill was rejected by the House of Lords. To alleviate the misery of the framework knitters James Orange established in 1842 the Nottingham Independent Garden Society, providing land for 400 gardens at a rent of £1 per annum.

The magazine *Horticultural Register*, founded in 1831 by Joseph Paxton and Joseph Harrison, included in its second issue a letter from 'A.J.' of Nottingham. This suggested that the new publication should be:

> the monthly companion of our artizans, and to hear its pages read over carefully, and its contents examined in most of the little summerhouses on Mapperly-hills, or the sides of our ancient forests. For we are here Horticulturalists and Floriculturalists to a great extent: and our Frame-work-knitters and Twist-hands, when they have completed the labours of the day, adjourn to their hundred yards of land on the outside of the town to superintend the blowing of an auricula or a tulip, to mark the first folding of the leaves of a cabbage, or the gradual growth of a favourite cucumber, each vying with its neighbour in producing the best or largest specimen.[27]

This description is echoed by William Howitt, who had lived in the city for many years. In his 1844 edition of *Rural Life in England*, he described his visits to some of the gardens:

> There are, in the outskirts of Nottingham, upwards of 5000 gardens, the bulk of which are occupied by the working class. A good many there are belonging to the substantial tradesmen and wealthier inhabitants; but the great mass are those of the mechanics. These lie on various sides of the town, in expanses of many acres in a place, and many of them as much as a mile and a half distant from the centre of the town. In the winter they have rather a desolate aspect, with their naked trees and hedges, and all their little summer-houses exposed, damp-looking, and forlorn; but, in spring and summer, they look exceedingly well, – in spring, all starred with blossoms, all thick with leaves, and their summer-houses peeping pleasantly from among them.

Howitt emphasises how important gardening is to the Nottingham workers in comparison with other cities transformed by the Industrial Revolution:

> When steam-engines abound, and are at the foundation of all the labours of a place, as in Manchester, for instance, there you will find few gardens in the possession of mechanics. The steam-engine is a never-resting, unweariable, unpersuadable giant and despot; and will go on thumping and setting thousands of wheels and spindles in motion; and men must stand, as it were, the slaves of its unsleeping energies ... the slave of the steam-engine must be at the beck of his tyrant night or day, with only such intervals as barely suffice to restore his wearied strength and faculties: therefore you shall not see gardens flourish and summer-houses rise in the vicinity of this hurrying and tremendous power. But where it is not, or but partially predominates, there may the mechanic enjoy the real pleasures of the garden. And how many are these pleasures!

He continues with a detailed description of the calendar of these gardeners:

> Early in spring – as soon, in fact, as the days begin to lengthen, and the shrewd air to dry up the wintry moisture – you see them getting into their gardens, clearing away the dead stalks of last year's growth, and digging up the soil; but especially on fine days in February and March are they busy. Trees are pruned, beds are dug, walks cleaned, and all the refuse and decayed vegetation piled up in heaps; and the smoke of the fires in which it is burnt, rolling up from many a garden, and sending its pungent odour to meet you afar off. It is pleasant to see, as the season advances, how busy their occupants become; bustling there with their basses [baskets] in their hands and their tools on their shoulders, wheeling in manure; and cleaning out their summer-house; and what an air of daily-increasing neatness they assume, till they are one wide expanse of blossomed fruit-trees and flowering fragrance.

The little houses on these plots would seem to resemble the summerhouses to be seen today at Hill Close Gardens:

> Every garden has its summer-house; and these are of all scales and grades, from the erection of a few tub-staves, with an attempt to train

a pumpkin or a wild-hop over it, to substantial brick-houses with glass windows, good cellars for a deposit of choice wines, a kitchen and all necessary apparatus, and a good pump to supply them with water. Many are very picturesque rustic huts, built with great taste, and hidden by tall hedges in a perfect little paradise of lawn and shrubbery – most delightful spots to go and read in of a summer day, or to take a dinner or tea in with a pleasant party of friends.[28]

A decade later these gardens were visited by Samuel Reynolds Hole, who became Dean of Rochester, and is familiarly known as Dean Hole. From Caunton, a village near Newark in Nottinghamshire, he was a dedicated rosarian, author of *A Book of Roses*, founder of the Rose Society, and hailed as 'the Rose King' by the Poet Laureate, Alfred, Lord Tennyson. Having established the first National Rose Show in July 1858 at St James's Hall in London's Piccadilly, Hole was invited the following year to judge a very different rose show, organised by mechanics in Nottingham. After judging the exhibits (see Chapter 9, pp. 229–30), he went to see the gardens where the roses had been cultivated: 'tiny allotments on sunny slopes, just out of the town of Nottingham, separated by hedges or boards in size about three to the rood'. Ironically, the city's pollution helped, eradicating black spot. Along with the roses, the Nottingham gardeners cultivated a whole range of flowers and shrubs, from the Christmas Rose and winter jasmine, through to laburnum and wisteria. He also noted splendid cabbages, lettuce, rhubarb and celery.[29]

Roses were not only grown on these little plots for exhibition; they were also a very useful source of income to offset the cost of rents. Twice a week in season, roses were sent for sale to the markets in Manchester and Liverpool. Harry Wheatcroft, the famously flamboyant rose-grower, was also a Nottingham man. Born in 1898, he was able to walk with his father from the centre of the city into open country, to the 1,200-yard allotment on the Thorneywood Estate. The Wheatcroft family had a summer-house, that 'Father had knocked together . . . out of bits and pieces of wood, and during the summer we would go up at weekends, taking a picnic meal, and have a thoroughly good time'.[30]

The artisans of Leeds were not so fortunate. The *Labourer's Friend Magazine* for 1843 reported that a meeting was held on 8 February 'for the promoting of the small Allotment System'. The chairman, James Garth Marshall, reported that to date only he and two other landowners had provided plots, at Headingley and Holbeck. Most of the tenants that had taken up the offer were destitute but not paupers, and had duly paid their rents. At the rent suppers they received free literature related to cottage gardening. However, he was obliged to declare that other landed proprietors were not prepared to go to the trouble of dividing up some of their land for 'numerous small occupants'. The meeting agreed to acquire a small quantity of land and let allotments to working-class tenants, and if this proved a success, then they might overcome the objections. It was agreed too that an advertisement should be placed in the *Leeds Intelligencer*.[31]

In the city centre another scheme to encourage horticulture was introduced some decades later. Catherine Buckton was a Unitarian and the wife of Joseph Buckton, wool merchant and manufacturer. Among her philanthropic activities, Mrs Buckton sat on the Leeds School board, and gave lectures on 'Laws of Health'. Some of these lectures were turned into books, including *Town and Window Gardening* published in 1879. In it she details the window gardens produced by the schoolchildren, with the hope that 'the rising generation will be brought up with a love and respect for plants, so that no gentleman having beautiful gardens and grounds may object to allow their being visited by those who have no gardens, and who spend their lives in the midst of the smoke and dirt of a large town'.[32]

One of the pupils could not afford a window box, which would cost 1s 6d from a shop, acquiring instead a soap box for threepence from the grocer. He managed to rear a fuchsia from a tiny cutting in his bedroom by keeping the window glass so clean that the plant benefited from every ray of the sun. Another box contained Virginian stock, French marigold, fuchsia, musk, nasturtium, pansy and marigold, all of which thrived even though the window looked north. The boy's mother told Catherine Buckton that she had always lived in the countryside before coming to Leeds, and had long sighed for the sight of a little green. The father, who could neither read nor write, bought a window box for his lad, and delighted in the results. Yet another pupil explained how he made up the soil to go in his box. First he filled the base with ashes and cinders to aid drainage, then added decaying leaves from the street, sand from a street grate, and some common soil. This was chopped with a spade, mixed, and sifted, providing a good combination to receive small plants of mignonette, saponaria, musk, sweet pea, convolvulus, golden feather and lobelia. The boy had spent twelve to fourteen hours ornamenting his box, with grass and moss collected from waste ground, willows grown in his own garden, and rough wood picked up in the street. His total outlay was eightpence.

Catherine Buckton provided practical advice on which plants to try to grow for those with low incomes. Cowslips, primroses, snowdrops and violets would not grow in a smoky atmosphere. For sitting rooms she suggested dracaenas, explaining: 'The leaves are often beautifully coloured. These plants come from the colonies, where rain seldom falls. When rain does fall, these plants store up a good quantity in their leaves and stems, which they live on until the rain comes again.'[33] However, she did warn against having plants in rooms which were lit by gas. For those with very little money, she suggested planting the foliage from carrot tops, wrapped in moss, in saucers of wet sand. She also proposed hanging baskets, telling her readers to visit St Andrew's Chambers in Leeds to view the simple wire structures displayed under a skylight at the top of stairs, where moss and ferns had been brought in from neighbouring woods.

* * *

Although Britain's industrial cities grew enormously in the nineteenth century, they were far outstripped by London's development. In 1650 the capital's population stood at 400,000, rising to 575,000 by 1700 and 765,000 by 1750, larger than Paris and Constantinople. By 1800 it had reached a huge 959,000, on a par with the oriental cities of Peking and Edo (Tokyo) and continued to grow by one-fifth each decade throughout the nineteenth century so that by 1900 the population stood at a massive 6,600,000. Comparisons with other British towns are startling – the next largest conurbation in 1750 was Bristol, with a population of 50,000. Even in 1801, when the populations of the industrial cities of Birmingham, Manchester and Liverpool were each approaching 100,000, they represented less than a tenth of London – around the same number of inhabitants as in Southwark, south of the Thames.

The effect of this huge growth in London's population can be seen in written accounts, and in images. The little gardens depicted within the city walls in Tudor maps were largely gone, although Pehr Kalm in the mid-eighteenth century was still able to record that:

At nearly every house in the town there was either in front to the street, or inside the houses and buildings, or also in both places, a little garden. They had commonly planted in these yards and round about them, partly in the earth and ground itself, partly in pots and boxes, several of the trees and flowers which could stand the coal smoke in London.

They thus sought to have some of the pleasant enjoyments of a country life in the midst of the hubbub of the town.[34]

But the hubbub grew ever louder as the inner-city population inexorably grew, with gardens being gobbled up as every available space was filled up by new, often badly constructed, buildings.

In *The Old Curiosity Shop*, published in 1841, Charles Dickens describes the journey out of London made by Little Nell and her grandfather, bringing the urban map to life. They start in the long and deserted streets of the City itself, moving into 'the labyrinth of men's abodes' where:

> servant girls looking lazily in all directions but their brooms . . . listened disconsolately to milkmen who spoke of country fairs and told of wagons in the mews. This quarter passed, they came upon the haunts of commerce and great traffic . . . and again this quarter passed, they came upon a straggling neighbourhood, where the mean houses parcelled off in rooms, and windows patched with rags and paper, told of the populous poverty that sheltered there . . .

Here they came upon brickfields:

> skirting gardens paled with staves of old casks, or timber pillaged from houses burnt down . . . mounds of dock-weed, nettles, coarse grass and oyster shells, heaped up in rank confusion . . . At length these streets, becoming more straggling yet, dwindled and dwindled away, until there were only small garden patches bordering the road, with many a summer-house innocent of paint and built of old timber or some frag-ments of a boat, green as the tough cabbage-stalks that grew about them . . . To these succeeded pert cottages, two and two with plots of ground in front, laid out in angular beds with stiff box borders and narrow paths between.

Beyond, at last the two voyagers reached the open countryside.[35]

In 1864 Samuel Hadden Parkes, the senior curate of St George's Bloomsbury, published a book about the gardening experiences of parish-ioners. In this work he reproduced two drawings of Coram Place, the first showing the courtyard in 1800 with little gardens in front of all the houses, the second in 1860, with the former gardens inhabited only by clothes-lines. The accompanying text explained:

33 & 34 The disappearance of gardens from the poorer parts of London during the nine-teenth century is graphically shown by two illustrations in Samuel Hadden Parkes's *Window Gardens for the People*, published in 1864. In the first picture he shows Coram Place in Bloomsbury in 1800, with little gardens in front of the houses. Sixty-four years later the scene was very different, 'since the houses have passed into other hands, and been let out in single apartments, the gardens have been altogether neglected, and are used as yards merely to dry clothes'.

formerly . . . it was no uncommon sight to see the little gardens in front of the house of the poor carefully cultivated. But now, since the houses have passed into other hands, and been let out in single apartments, the gardens have been altogether neglected, and are used as yards merely to dry clothes. The only green thing which remains in some of these gardens is horse-radish, a root which it is difficult to extirpate. 'And it's just the sort of thing' said one man, 'that poor people hasn't no call for . . . you see, they ain't not overdone with joints of beef, nor rump steaks'.[36]

The disappearance of working-class gardens is echoed by the experiences of Hector Gavin as recorded in his book, *Sanitary Ramblings*, published in 1848. Despite the rather unprepossessing title it was an important work. Gavin was a physician with a medical practice in the Hackney Road in east London. As he lived close to his surgery, he became only too aware of the terrible sanitary conditions prevalent in this part of city due to the industrial pollution, overcrowding and squalor of the housing, and was determined to secure the eradication of typhus fever. Gavin's ramblings were accounts, street by street, of the alleys, courts and slums of Bethnal Green. Garden Place and Pleasant Place sound places of delight, but this was a terrible illusion. Of the former he wrote:

It is entered by a narrow alley, three or four houses are stuck on the damp clay, with small yards in front, on which every kind of refuse is thrown ... Fever has been very prevalent in this place, in one house nearly every inmate has been attacked. In the alley leading to these horrid and neglected spots is a large pig-stye; it is close to the houses, and emits the most disgusting and sickening odours. I could not remain to make notes of this place, so overpowering was the abominable stench.[37]

Yet, to Gavin's great surprise, he did find amid all this horror a horticultural island, Whiskers' Gardens.

This is a very extensive piece of ground, which is laid out, in neat plots as gardens. The choicest flowers are frequently raised here, and great taste, and considerable refinement are evidently possessed by those who cultivate them ... The weary artisan and the toil-worn weaver here dedicate their spare hours, in the proper seasons, to what has always been considered a refined, as well as an innocent recreation, the cultivation of beautiful flowers.

The irony of the situation was not lost on the doctor:

The love of the beautiful, and the sense of order which are readily accorded to the artisan, or weaver, in his neat garden, surrounded by the choicest dahlias or tulips carefully cultivated, are denied to him when visited in his filthy, dirty street. When seen in his damp and dirty home, he is generally accused of personal uncleanliness, and a disregard for the commonest appearances of decency and regularity; yet, in his garden he displays evidences of a refined and a natural order.[38]

Dahlias and tulips were florists' flowers, and an account of life in the East End of London pointed out that weavers liked form in their flowers, keeping fuchsias on the frame of their looms, and dahlias in the back garden.[39]

A very similar site, described as Saunderson's Gardens, was noted a few years earlier by an assistant commissioner reporting on the conditions of the handloom weavers of Spitalfields. The gardens

may cover about six acres of ground. There is one general enclosure round the whole, and each separate garden is divided from the rest by small palings. The number of gardens was stated to be about one hundred and seventy: some are much larger than the rest. In almost every garden is a neat summer-house, where the weaver and his family may enjoy themselves on Sundays and holidays ... There are walks through the ground by which access is easy to the gardens.

The commissioner found that vegetables such as cabbages, lettuces and peas were cultivated, but pride of place was given to the flowers. 'There had been a contest for a silver medal amongst the tulip proprietors. There were many other flowers of a high order, and it was expected that in due time the show of dahlias for that season would not fail to bring glory to Spitalfields. In this neighbourhood are several dealers in dahlias.'[40]

In *Great Expectations*, Charles Dickens describes the little gardens to be found in the district of Walworth, in south London. 'It appeared to be a collection of black lanes, ditches and little gardens, and to present the aspect of rather dull retirement'. One of these gardens belonged to Wemmick, a clerk, and thus a member of the middle class, but his fellow gardeners well may have been working class, and to have shared his desire to turn the dull retirement into miniature fantasies. Wemmick created a little castle fitted with Gothic windows and door, mounted by a gun which was fired every night at nine o'clock.

'Then, at the back' said Wemmick, 'out of sight so as not to impede the idea of fortifications – for it's a principle with me ... At the back, there's a pig, and there are fowls and rabbits; then I knock together my own little frame, you see, and grow cucumbers; and you'll judge at supper what sort of a salad I can raise.'[41]

Having a garden plot or allotment beyond the built-up limits of the city was clearly a custom for many Londoners. In the Old Bailey records for 1810, John Pittard, who lived in Church Street (now Fournier Street) in Spitalfields, described how a table was stolen from the summerhouse in his garden on the Hackney Road after it was broken into.[42] The use of distant plots continued right through the century, for when the Royal Commission on the Housing of the Working Classes gathered its report in 1884, the curate of St Philip's in Clerkenwell described how some of his parishioners had small gardens in the country, where they went on Saturday and stayed until the Monday – probably in little summerhouses.[43] Lord Salisbury, to whom the commission made its report, also took what were known as 'Saturday to Mondays', his political weekends in country houses, but the parallel was no doubt lost on him.

35 The Bavarian artist George Johann Scharf is celebrated for his series of drawings, watercolours and sketches of everyday London from the 1820s, so it is thanks to him that we get a rare glimpse of working-class gardens of the period. A pencil sketch of 1825 shows part of Woolwich looking towards the Thames. In the foreground, roughly delineated, are the back gardens of some of the houses, while men can be seen working on their vegetable plots in the middle distance.

It is not easy to reconstruct a working-class suburban London garden, as artists did not bother with such trifles, and pioneering photographers had more important images to capture, but some idea of a typical modest garden can be gained from Appleby Road in Hackney. In the mid-nineteenth century, Hackney was growing fast. Much of the development was middle class, but interspersed with the terraces of houses and rows of villas were cottages for workers. Appleby Road, which lies just on the fringe of London Fields, was developed in the 1850s, and census records show that the first residents were a mixture of lower middle class and working class: clerks and a retired schoolmistress alongside warehousemen, shoe-makers and carpenters. The flat-fronted houses had little front gardens with wooden picket fences. The back gardens were bigger, long and thin, 90 by 14.5 feet. A wash-house was attached to the rear of each house, and some of these survived into the 1980s – green painted, with a copper and an outside privy. Beyond these were the gardens themselves, with paths that probably were originally cinder. A tiny patch of lawn, and flower beds led down to an area that might be devoted to vegetables and fruit bushes.

The census returns for Appleby Road show that, despite the small size of the houses, they were often multi-occupied, and some still retain miniature kitchen ranges in the upper floor. However, these dwellings, with their gardens and the open land of London Fields beyond, were positively luxurious compared to the terraces just a mile to the south, near the Regent's Canal on the border of south Hackney and Bethnal Green. The houses here – two-up, two-down – led straight onto the pavement, with a backyard rather than a garden. This form of housing was recorded by Walter Southgate in his autobiography. Southgate was born in 1890 in North Street (now Northiam Street), in a 'cottage' built in the 1830s for brickmakers employed in the area of Bonner's Fields, just around the corner from Victoria Park.

> The backyards were all alike (you could hardly call them gardens, although many were the efforts some cottagers made to bring anaemic-looking plants to flower in a sunless zone). The yard measured 12 feet by 16 feet, and contained a back-to-back water closet . . . Every year Father planted a few geraniums and blue lobelia plants, but with the soot, lack of sun and cinder ash in the soil they lingered to a premature death. Nevertheless he persisted and encouraged mother to plant her favourite pot of musk (which had scent in those days) and creeping jenny. If a tuft of grass appeared in the crevices of stone and clinker she would tend it as if it was a lily so divorced was she from the country scene. It reminded her, she said, 'of the country'.[44]

If cultivation at ground level was not possible, then some people created roof gardens. Thomas Fairchild in his *City Gardener*, published in 1722 and specifically focusing on plants that 'thrive best in the London gardens', advised that currant trees could cope with the city smoke: 'There are many Instances of their growing well in close Places, such as Tavern-Yards, and even upon Leads on the Tops of Houses amidst the Chimneys'.[45] He assured his readers that with gentle and regular watering, they would survive.

One well-documented rooftop garden from the early nineteenth century belonged to Elizabeth Kent. It was set high up above St Paul's Churchyard, where her stepfather ran his bookseller's business. In *Flora Domestica, or, the Portable Flower-Garden*, published in 1823, she wrote of how she managed to grow flowers, shrubs and small trees in pots and tubs, and recommended which ones would do well. She may well have inspired Charles Dickens to include the roof garden of Mr Riah, the Jewish moneylender 'of noble and generous nature' in *Our Mutual Friend*. Dickens describes how Jenny Wren and Lizzie Hexam sat on his rooftop, leaning against a 'blackened chimney-stack over which some humble creeper had been trained . . . A few boxes of humble flowers and ever-greens completed the garden; and the encompassing wilderness of dowager old chimneys twirled their cowls and fluttered their smoke.'[46] Leigh Hunt, Elizabeth Kent's brother in law, was the model for Harold Skimpole in *Bleak House*, and Dickens must have been familiar with the house in St Paul's Churchyard. He repeats the idea of a rooftop garden in a short story, 'The Country Cousin' published in 1874. Here Hetty grew tulips 'which flourished wonderfully between sloping roofs in a nook where the chimneys luckily stood aside, as if to let the sun across many obstacles upon the garden'.[47] Hetty's father was a second-hand bookseller, rein-forcing the connection with Elizabeth Kent.

An article in *Floral World* in 1871, aimed at indoor servants who had no chance of using the household's main garden, suggested that they could garden on a flat roof, a balcony, or even the area below street level. 'The gratification of this addition to urban pleasures, will be duly appreciated by all those who are capable of estimating the difference between a look-out upon bright foliage and flowers, or upon stucco fronts and brick walls; and of comparing the fragrance wafted through windows so adorned with the natural whiff of the streets'. The author advised container planting, but warned against choosing pots that were too ornate: 'They require consid-erable taste and judgement to fill them to advantage, their brilliant colours and ornate patterns having a tendency to make them principals instead of simple accessories, and to *kill* the flowers, unless ingeniously harmonized or contrasted therewith; indeed they may be termed too ornamental in themselves, and are only suitable for positions of pretension'. In other words, these gardeners should not get above themselves.[48]

Catherine Buckton talked about flashes of colour on windowsills and balconies as her coach toured the streets of Leeds in search of potential window gardeners. The splash of horticultural joy – though no colour – can be seen in old black-and-white photographs of London. Samuel Parkes was keen to encourage the parishioners of St George's Bloomsbury to maintain window gardens and displays of flowers in their homes. Coram Street represented one of the poorest localities of the metropolis:

'Little Coram Street ... is a narrow street, with a number of courts stretching right and left, containing about 1,700 persons. The inhabitants of these courts are persons who generally obtain their living by selling watercresses, fruit, and small toys in the streets, with a larger number who obtain their living no one knows how.' In his book, Parkes reproduced a cutaway image of a typical eight-roomed house, with one family to each room. When Parkes asked a resident how the man managed, the man replied, 'Well, the fact is, I don't live – I muddles'.[49]

The Revd Parkes was determined to make these desperately poor people into urban gardeners. His determination was, of course, inspired by Victorian evangelism. He believed horticulture would hold off the debasing influences of the music hall, the gin shop and the beer house, uniting the family by giving the man a recreation: 'and I consider it is an unquestioned truth that a love of indoor plants and flowers is indicative of good character and healthy taste, as well as of the domestic and industrial habits of the London poor'.[50] Some of his stories take on the character of proverbs. For example, he tells of a poor, aged woman living in a room at the top of a house, dependent on 2s 6d per week. A city missionary spotted a strawberry plant flourishing in a broken teapot, and pointed out that the woman could soon get fruit. The woman replied: 'I'm very poor, too poor to keep any living creature, but it's a great comfort to me to have that living plant; for I know it can only live by the power of God, and as I see it live and grow from day to day, it tells me that God is near'.[51]

Parkes found that the favourite plant for window gardening was balm, with its aromatic leaves, and spikes of small lilac flowers that bloomed in August. Cuttings grew quickly and could be trained up window frames. Other good candidates were thyme, bergamot, peppermint, lavender and musk, all plants with scent. Dahlias grew well, as did sweet william, common yellow stonecrop, creeping jenny, ferns and Virginia creeper. 'Major convolvulus [morning glory] has been seen to give great pleasure to the poor infirm women of a ward in the workhouse. It was trained on either side of the window, and the poor women watched day after day for a bud to appear.'[52] Scarlet runner beans provided a splash of colour, but did not bear fruit. Of the different types of geranium, Parkes recommended the horse-shoe rather than fancy kinds, which tended to last for only a few days and attracted large numbers of insects.

An evangelical magazine, the *Day of Rest*, reinforces Parkes's observations:

even in the low courts and mews where the roughest costermongers and
street Irish congregate, scarcely a window is without its pot or its bower
of flowers. We say 'bower', because many of these windows are
actually darkened by Virginia creepers, nasturtiums, the pretty yellow
'canariensis', and even common scarlet-runners (these much affected by
stablemen and weavers). A favourite fashion is to surround the ledge of
the windows – more especially in stable mews – with tiny green palisades, joined by little miniature imitations of five-barred gates painted
white. Within these palisades, and along the ledge are set pots of any
cheap and favourite flowers. Oftentimes a large box is filled with
mould, and deep set with common red tulips in spring, mignonette in
summer, and marigolds and chrysanthemums in autumn.[53]

In the second half of the nineteenth century, model dwellings were
built for 'the industrious poor' in various parts of London. Many of these
projects were blocks of flats, such as the Peabody Estates, with little or no
garden, especially on inner-city sites. Some of the companies that built
flats as model dwellings did, however, add gardens. One surviving example
of this is Allens Gardens in Stoke Newington, named after Matthew Allen
who was in partnership with the Improved Industrial Dwellings Company.
The development of ten blocks of three-storey flats was built in 1874 on
Bethune Road. The communal garden, running behind the flats, was for
the use of residents, with greenhouses and wash-houses, along with
recreational facilities.[54]

A very interesting Victorian housing experiment survives in Battersea.
On 3 August 1872 the philanthropist Lord Shaftesbury delivered an inau-
gural speech, opening the estate named in his honour, Shaftesbury Park. The
event was held on a Saturday afternoon, to suit the working men, and the
project was hailed as the 'Workman's City'. The housing development was
the brainchild of the Artizans', Labourers' and General Dwellings Company,
founded in 1866, which promoted itself as a working-class initiative with
co-operative principles, unlike the conventional philanthropic investment
companies with a return usually of 5 per cent. When the Company was
incorporated in January 1867 the stated aim was 'to assist the working classes
to obtain improved dwellings, erected from the best designs at the lowest
possible cost; to become owners of the houses they occupied; to raise position
in the social scale; to spread moral influence over their class, tending to foster
habits of industry, sobriety and frugality'. The sobriety was taken seriously,
and no public houses were built. The Company was able to attract the great

and the good as supporters, including Shaftesbury and Cardinal Manning of Westminster. Shareholders included politicians such as the Duke of Devonshire and Lord Salisbury, bankers such as N.M. Rothschild, and writers such as Charles Kingsley, John Ruskin and Charles Darwin.

Despite the grand claims, matters went wrong early on, with the secretary and directors accused of fraud, and by 1877 social radicalism had to give way to the more conventional philanthropy plus 5 per cent method of finance. But the cottage-style estate was being built on an area of forty-two and a half acres of Battersea, each house provided with a small front garden and a yard at the back. The Company planted lime trees along the roads, and there was a strong emphasis upon gardening for health and self-improvement. Displays of flowers and shrubs in the front gardens and window gardening were encouraged. According to Samuel Carter Hall in the *Social Review* for February 1875: 'I saw houses well constructed with a modest approach to architectural grace, each with a little well-kept garden in front, some of them with decorative vases, and most with blooming and carefully tended flower-pots in the windows'.[55] In many ways Shaftesbury Park looked forward to the cottage estates developed by the LCC in the early twentieth century, as described in Chapter 12.

Individual philanthropy also provided homes with gardens. Two examples that can still be seen are Eden Grove in Walthamstow and Redcross Gardens in Southwark. In 1862 Ebenezer Clarke, in association with Benjamin Rowbotham, bought ten building plots in Eden Road to build eighteen houses for the labouring poor, with each semi-detached cottage given gardens back and front. Walthamstow is now a part of north-east London, but in the nineteenth century it was a kind of satellite village in Essex, five miles from the City, accessible by omnibus and railway from Lea Bridge station. Clarke, a builder, was a keen advocate of freehold land schemes, whereby workers might borrow money from building societies and repay in instalments. He gave an example of a mechanic who, instead of paying 5s per week for rent, could borrow £125 from the building society, repaying 5s 6d each week, and thus complete the purchase of his own home within fourteen years. Not only did he build his houses in Eden Grove in the teeth of opposition from the local gentry and farmers who felt that they would lower the tone of the village, but he also wrote a history of Walthamstow which gives fascinating details about life there in the nineteenth century.[56]

Three decades later, Octavia Hill built the Redcross Cottages just behind Union Street in Southwark. Hill, a founder of the National Trust, was a tireless campaigner for open spaces to be provided as 'green lungs' in urban environments, especially in London. Her cottages, built in 1887, embody her belief that the working classes deserved a civilised environment rather than the tenements common at the time. The cottages sport a picturesque variety of gables and upper bay windows in the Tudor style, while the gardens were originally laid out by Emmeline Sieveking for the Kyrle Society.[57]

* * *

One of the most famous music hall songs of the late nineteenth century was 'If it Wasn't for the 'Ouses in Between', written by Edgar Bateman and made famous by Gus Elen around the year 1894. Subtitled 'The Cockney Gardener' it featured an east London costermonger who worked in Leather Lane, but had a garden in Bethnal Green or south Hackney. With the facetious humour that was a Cockney characteristic, he described his little garden:

If you saw my little backyard, 'Wot a pretty spot' you'd cry,
It's a picture on a summer day;
Wiv the turnip tops and cabbages wot people doesn't buy
I makes it on a Sunday look all gay.
The neighbours finks I grow 'em and you'd fancy you're in Kent,
Or at Epsom if you gaze into the mews.
It's a wonder as the landlord doesn't want to raise the rent,
Because we've got such nobby distant views.


*Chorus*
Oh it really is a wery pretty garden,
And Chingford to the eastward could be seen,
Wiv a ladder and some glasses
You could see to 'Ackney Marshes
If it wasn't for the 'ouses in between.


We're as countrified as can be wiv a clothes prop for a tree,
The tub-stool makes a rustic little stile;

Ev'ry time the blooming clock strikes there's a cuckoo sings to me
And I've painted up 'to Leather Lane a mile'.
The backyard looks a puffick mass o'bloom
And I've made a little beehive wiv' some beetles in a pail,
And a pitchfork wiv a handle of a broom.

The sentiments contained in these verses would have chimed with the working-class audiences who sang along to the chorus. Despite all the privations, and the terrifying speed with which towns and cities were being built up, the urban gardener was determined to cultivate his or her garden or detached plot, a backyard, or even a windowsill. They might be working long hours to earn a living wage, lectured on their way of life by the great and the good, but this was their domain. The 'beehives' and the other rustic touches, gently mocked though they might be, were reminders for many of their rural life, just a generation or two in the past.

CHAPTER 7

❧

# Climbing the Wall

I left London by the Comet Coach for Chesterfield; arrived at Chatsworth at 4.30am in the morning of the ninth of May 1826. As no person was to be seen at that early hour, I got over the greenhouse gate by the old covered way, explored the pleasure grounds, and looked round the outside of the house. I then went down to the kitchen gardens, scaled the outside wall and saw the whole place, set the men to work there at six o'clock; then returned to Chatsworth and got Thomas Weldon to play me the water works, and afterwards went to breakfast with poor dear Mrs Gregory and her niece. The latter fell in love with me, and I with her, and thus completed my first morning's work at Chatsworth before nine o'clock.[1]

THIS EPITOME OF a red-letter day was recalled by Joseph Paxton. Aged twenty-two, he had been appointed by the 6th Duke of Devonshire as Superintendent of his Gardens at Chatsworth in Derbyshire. Paxton became one of the great head gardeners of the nineteenth century, famous not only for transforming the grounds at Chatsworth, but also designing and building the huge glass house for the Great Exhibition of 1851 in Hyde Park. He designed and laid out one of the first 'people's parks' at Birkenhead in 1847 and published two influential horticultural journals, the *Horticultural Register* and the *Gardeners' Chronicle*. His relationship with the Duke developed into a close friendship, he became an MP, received a knighthood and died a rich man. In 1827 he wed Sarah Brown, Mrs Gregory's niece, a marriage that proved happy and fruitful. Given all this, Joseph Paxton would seem a questionable example of the working class, yet these were precisely his origins.

Paxton was born in 1803, the seventh son of William, a farm labourer, in the village of Milton Bryant on the edge of the Russell family's Woburn Abbey estate in Bedfordshire. The impoverishment of the Paxton family was increased with William's death in 1810. As Joseph was later to observe, 'you never know how much nourishment there is in a turnip until you have had to live on it'.[2] Despite this poverty, Paxton was able to attend a school that had been refounded in 1808 by the 6th Duke of Bedford. Eighty boys were taught in eight classes run on the pupil teacher system, learning their three Rs. This was the most basic of education, but it provided the foundation on which Paxton was able to build his remarkable career as a gardener. Like many young gardeners, he worked in a series of gardens before making the momentous move in 1823 to the Horticultural Society's experimental gardens at Chiswick as one of the first entrants in their training scheme.

The Horticultural Society of London had been conceived in the year of Paxton's birth, 1803, following a meeting of seven men at the bookshop of John Hatchard in Piccadilly. This was the brainchild of John Wedgwood, son of the famous potter, Josiah, with the blessing of Sir Joseph Banks, the highly influential President of the Royal Society, and founder members that included William Forsyth, from the royal gardens at Kensington and St James's Palace, and William Townsend Aiton, who had succeeded his father as superintendent of the gardens at Kew. Wedgwood's aim in forming the Society was to work towards the improvement and co-ordination of horticultural activities. A prospectus was compiled, classifying horticulture as a practical science, and dividing plants into the useful, the priority, and the ornamental. An emphasis was put upon good plant selection, and quality in design and construction of glasshouses, along with the standardisation of plant names.

An important element of the early Society was to encourage the training of gardeners from every social level. Periodicals and publications, beyond the means of gardeners and labourers, were made available in the Society's room, leased from the Linnaean Society in Regent Street. In 1822 the Society took a significant step forward when thirty-three acres of land were leased from the Duke of Devonshire at Chiswick House, with the purpose of providing a national school of horticulture. A report drawn up the following year explained:

the head gardeners will be permanent servants of the Society, but the under gardeners and labourers employed will be young men, who

36  George Cruikshank's cartoon of 1826, showing a meeting of the London Horticultural
Society, often characterised by fierce debates among the members. On the left at the top
table sits Joseph Sabine, the Society's Secretary, who admitted the young Joseph Paxton as
a labourer in the Society's gardens at Chiswick. The picture on the wall on the left depicts
'An Irish Potatoe Plant with young ones dress'd in their Jackets after the fashion of the
Country'. This may have been an imaginary image, but it presages the disaster that was to
overcome the impoverished Irish in the 1840s.

having acquired some previous knowledge of the rudiments of the art
will be received into the establishment, and having been duly instructed
in the various practices of each department, will become entitled to
recommendation from the Officers of the Society to fill the situations
of Gardeners in private or other establishments.[3]

The first young men accepted as under-gardeners and labourers are
recorded in a *Handwriting Book*, kept from 1822 to 1829, and now in the
RHS Lindley Library. Every entry is introduced by the Society's Secretary,
Joseph Sabine, followed by a statement from the candidate, giving a brief
account of his life, his father's occupation, where he had worked before
being admitted and a declaration that he was unmarried. The handwriting
of these men is very fine, raising the possibility that this was one of the
criteria on which their application had been accepted. Most had begun
work at the age of fourteen, and had moved around, often gaining experi-

ence in a nursery. The majority were the sons of gardeners, and a large proportion came from Scotland, or North Britain as they put it. One came from New York, another from Vienna where his father was gardener to the Emperor, and another – the son of the King of Bavaria's gardener – from Nymphenburg, so this was truly an elite group. However, the sons of a brickmaker, a stonecutter and a shoemaker also appear among the successful candidates. One of the first applications was received from Joseph Paxton, with his entry dated 13 November 1823. He falsified his date of birth, adding two years, presumably in the hope that the extra schooling thus implied would redound in his favour: an uncharacteristic deceit, but a demonstration of his determination.

By the beginning of the nineteenth century, just as the number of rooms in great houses had proliferated, so grand gardens had become divided into a whole series of departments: for example, the pleasure grounds, the walled kitchen gardens, the ornamental flower gardens, glass-houses for vines, fruits and exotic plants, and so on. It is not known in what part of the Society's garden Paxton began his training, but after six months he became a labourer under the ornamental gardener, Donald Munro, looking after the new plants that were being introduced from all over the world, such as the brilliantly coloured verbenas, petunias and dahlias from South and Central America. In 1825 he moved on to the arboretum as an under-gardener, with his wages rising from fourteen to eighteen shillings per week. Here again, he would have encountered trees new to Britain, such as the Sitka spruce, the Monterey pine and the Douglas fir, all introduced by the plant hunter, David Douglas.

One of the conditions of the lease between the Horticultural Society and the Duke of Devonshire was that the latter should have a key to a private door for access into the garden. It is probable that Paxton first came to the Duke's notice while the Duke was letting himself through this door. George William Spencer Cavendish, 6th Duke of Devonshire, son of the famous beauty, Georgiana, inherited his title in 1811 at the age of twenty-one. Although he was immensely rich, the most eligible man in England, he never married and is known to posterity as the Bachelor Duke. Why exactly he took the leap in the dark and offered the job of superintendent of his gardens in Derbyshire to the twenty-two-year-old Paxton – whom he of course thought was twenty-four – is not known. His judgement, however, was shrewd, for the young man more than fulfilled his potential, and over thirty years transformed the grounds at Chatsworth: the relationship ended only with the Duke's death in 1858.

Paxton would have provided a model example for John Claudius Loudon, who believed so passionately in the education and encouragement of young gardeners, although ironically the two men were quite often in contention. Loudon, the son of a well-to-do Lanarkshire farmer, was born in 1783. Although the precocious Loudon liked making walks and beds in the garden his father provided for him, he refused to study Latin or French, even though a master was brought from Edinburgh to teach him. Later he overcame his aversion to Latin, and even later to French, keeping a daily journal from the age of thirteen, in which he often wrote in French to familiarise himself with the language.[4] This combination of obstinacy and indomitability was to mark his character throughout his hectic, workaholic life. Loudon began his career working in nurseries in Scotland, at the same time entering the University of Edinburgh, where he attended lectures on agriculture as well as classes in botany and chemistry. According to his wife, he developed the habit of staying up two nights each week to study while at university.

Moving to London, Loudon launched himself into his prolific authorial career. His most ambitious project, *An Encyclopaedia of Gardening*, was first published in 1822. A voluminous work, it covered plant culture, botany, garden design, an international survey and a history of gardening, along with practical information for the owner of a garden in his employment of staff, and for the head gardener in managing his team. Education for gardeners was one of his watchwords: 'The knowledge of languages, history, geography, arts, sciences, and literature, which a gardener daily occupied with his profession may acquire, provided he begins at the commencement of his apprenticeship, and continues to employ his leisure hours in reading till he is twenty or twenty-five years of age, is by no means inconsiderable.'

Loudon was no elitist, and a firm believer in self-help:

The terms knowledge and ignorance are entirely relative; the knowledge of a modern chemist's porter would have subjected him to be hanged and burned in the days of the first popes; and any bricklayer's labourer who reads the London newspapers, has more correct ideas on the principles of political economy than nine-tenths of the nobility in Russia or Spain ... The intelligence of the miners in Scotland and Sweden may be referred to as proofs. The miners at Leadhills have a regular library and reading society; and the works they make choice of are not only histories, voyages, travels, &c but even works of taste such as the British classics, and best novels and romances.[5]

He was to follow up these observations by his editorial contributions to the *Gardener's Magazine* which he launched in 1826. In the introduction to the first issue he wrote:

> Finally, there is one subject which, more than every thing else, will tend to improve gardening and agriculture, – the better education of gardeners. . . . As gardening has advanced, and its productions and its province extended, the situation of head gardener has become more and more important; he has become a more confidential servant, entrusted with more power, and more frequently consulted and communicated with by the master and mistress of the family.[6]

In his directions to his apprentice gardener, drawn up in 1686, John Evelyn recommended him to keep 'a paper-book' in which to maintain a record of his work. This had become a common practice by the beginning of the nineteenth century, as Loudon noted in his encyclopaedia. This was partly so that the apprentice could refer back to it when he had to organise the tasks for the year in his later career. It also enabled some employers and head gardeners to keep an eye on what their young apprentices were doing. In his encyclopaedia Loudon reproduces a page from the pocket memorandum-book of J. Gott, apprentice at 'Aubrey Hall', that is, Arbury Hall in Warwickshire, home of the Newdigate family. The entries for 27 and 28 January 1821 provide a wonderful combination of earnest endeavour and comic relief. For the first day, he noted that 'Last night's frost and this day's sun have killed the peas in the south border: but those sown in the north side of the wattled hurdles escaped being shaded from the sun'. A note added later explains that these were covered with drill hand-glasses, and the crop by 2 June was fit to gather. In a second entry for 27 January Gott claimed to have caught a new species of lizard with no tail. When he presented this to the foreman at Arbury, Henry Twigg, it transpired that this was simply a common lizard which had accidentally lost its appendage.

For 28 January, after recording the idea of a conic iron tree which could be covered with climbing roses, Gott notes that 'Gurkin O'Doolittle caught distilling parsnip whiskey in the tan-shed: discharged without a character. His still two watering-pots placed top to top, and closed with a wet cloth: the top kept cool by pouring water on it.' This careful note (for future reference?) is followed by a visit from the parson, Torriel Joss, who said:

there are two ways of getting new ideas; by shuffling what ideas we have together, like a pack of cards, (which is to be done by a free glass of wine, opium or tobacco) when new combinations may occur to the mind accidentally: or by a studied selection of ideas suitable to the subject on which it is desired to invent, which can only be done by scientific persons, as Sir H. Davy in his invention of the safety-lamp.[7]

The Newdigate family had established the idea of keeping a daily record book of the gardening activities at Arbury at the end of the seventeenth century, as noted in Chapter 3, but no later books have survived. However, the Newdigates would seem to have continued the tradition, for Loudon used one of the pages kept by the head gardener in 1821 as a textbook example in his encyclopaedia. As with the earlier books, this provides an excellent picture of the activities in a sizeable garden of the period. The week recorded ran from 8 to 15 June 1821.

Henry Twigg, the foreman, spent some of the week reorganising the pinery, introducing peach trees from the ice-room, and washing the leaves of orange trees, as well as preparing cuttings of hard-wood plants and making up a hot bed for salading. One of the gardeners, J. Green, spent a day digging in the parterre, transplanted China asters, and shifted plants to Lady Almeria's glass closet. This presumably was a conservatory, a form of Wardian case. The other gardener, C. Fisher, spent two days working on a 'sinarium', a word that has disappeared from dictionaries, but would appear to have been a miniature conservatory in which desert plants might be cultivated. He also nailed creepers in the Dry Stove Dome, and repaired box edgings in one of the shrubberies. Green is recorded as earning 3s per day, and Fisher 2s 6d. The labourer, R. Fraser, was paid £1 6s for the entire job, which was digging and trenching. The apprentice, J. Gott, worked alongside the rest of the team, but on Friday swept the sheds and gathered mushrooms. A. Teisel spent her week in the lowly jobs always assigned to female workers: searching for insects, worms, snails and slugs, weeding turnips, and gathering gooseberries for wine. For these she was paid 1s per day. (See Appendix, Table III.)

The head gardener, who is not named, added remarks, yet again introducing some unlikely characters: 'There have been only two days of sunshine this week, when the thermometer was at 50 deg and 52 deg, the rest of the week cloudy and cold, the thermometer not above 48 deg. The Russian ambassador Count Bubkynowski, called on Tues, and Baron Schmutzighoff on Friday. Teisel wishes her weeding gloves repointed.

Much pleased with the Amazon working dress given her by my Lady Almeria.'[8] Weeding gloves often had metal tips to the fingers so that the gardener could scrape out weeds from between paving stones, but the Amazon working dress remains a mystery. The extraordinary names of the visitors must have been made up by the head gardener, for Loudon was not a man blessed with a great sense of humour.

Loudon explained the significance of the various levels of gardeners at this period:

> The lowest grade in the scale of this class is garden labourers. These are occasionally employed to perform the common labours of gardening, as trenching, digging, hoeing, weeding, &c. Men for the more heavy, and women for the lighter employments. They are not supposed to have received any professional instruction, farther than what they may have obtained by voluntary or casual observation. In all gardens where three or four professional hands are constantly employed, some labourers are required at extraordinary seasons.

He then moves on to apprentices:

> Youths intended for serving, or tradesmen gardeners, are generally articled or placed under master or tradesmen gardeners, for a given period on terms of mutual benefit; the master contracting to supply instruction, and generally food and lodging, or a weekly sum as an equivalent; and the parents of the apprentice granting the services of the latter during his apprenticeship as their part of the contract. The term agreed on is generally three years; or more if the youth is under sixteen years of age ... The period of apprenticeship being finished, that of journeyman commences, and continues, or ought to continue till the man is at least twenty-five years of age.

Journeymen, as the name suggests, were peripatetic, moving from one job to another to develop their skills. Finally Loudon noted, 'In extensive gardens where a number of hands are employed, they are commonly grouped or arranged in divisions, and one of the journeymen of longest standing employed as foreman, or sub-master, to the rest'.[9]

With his passionate belief in education, Loudon advocated that a library should be introduced into households, and in 1827 compiled a preliminary reading list, pointing out that the provision of books would prove both

37 A journeyman gardener in his summer costume, with straw hat and cotton trousers and jacket, from the *Gardener's Magazine*, 1826.

helpful to young gardeners and inculcate in them a feeling of loyalty to their employer. His reading list was made up of seventeen sections, with 167 titles covering a whole range of practical and inspirational subjects. He pointed out that trainee gardeners would no longer have to purchase the books for themselves, and so would be able to put their saved money towards food – thus not only improving their living standards but also enabling them to work harder. Unfortunately, few employers could be persuaded to lay down their money in establishing such libraries.[10]

Loudon was also very concerned that employers should pay a proper wage. The huge disparity between the wages earned by gardeners at every level had long existed, although the figures have to be treated with caution, as some gardeners acquired status as designers and thus were able to command generous salaries. When Capability Brown became the gardener at Stowe in Buckinghamshire in 1739, he received a salary of £35 per annum plus £9 for lodgings. When he became the King's 'Chief Gardiner' at Hampton Court, he received a colossal £1,107 with additional payments for raising pineapples and forced fruits. Meanwhile John Morris, the head gardener at Dunster Castle in Somerset in the mid-eighteenth century, was paid one shilling per day, making his annual salary a mere £18 5s. But Morris may have received perquisites in kind, such as board and lodgings, and profits from the sale of surplus fruit and vegetables after the household had drawn their supplies.

Not only was there a disparity between gardeners, but also a disparity between their pay compared with other professions and crafts. In the second issue of the *Gardener's Magazine*, Loudon printed the observations of an architect, I.P. Burnard, of Formosa Cottage, Eden Grove in the suburb of Holloway in north London:

> If we take a carpenter, bricklayer, mason, or smith, and compare the wages usually paid them through their apprenticeship, and while they are journeymen, with the wages of a gardener during these states of progression; and compare also their intellectual state, the difference between the two classes is almost incredible. A bricklayer who cannot write, and who has not the least knowledge of figures, or geometry, receives from five to seven shillings a-day, as the common price given by master builders. A journeyman gardener in one of the first nurseries, who has gone through a course of practical geometry and land surveying; has a scientific knowledge of Botany, and has spent his days and his nights in reading books connected with his profession, gets no more than two shillings or two and sixpence a day.[11]

Loudon continued to battle on behalf of gardeners and their remuneration, his task made even more difficult in the 1840s when wages were depressed right across the country. His own life by this period had become precarious. His health was never robust, and his right arm became permanently contracted following an attack of rheumatic fever when he was a young man. An attempted operation fractured the arm, and it was amputated in 1825. He managed, nevertheless, to continue with his prolific writing. Three years later he reviewed an anonymous novel, *The Mummy*, expressing his enjoyment of the account of scientific and technological advances made in its imagined future. When he met the author, he was surprised to find it was a young woman, Jane Webb, whom he married in

September 1830. She proved an ideal companion, writing botanical books in her own right, and acting as Loudon's amanuensis as his health began to fail. John Claudius Loudon died in December 1843, and his last book, on the subject of self-instruction for young gardeners, was published two years later. In the preface, Jane noted that 'our kind friend' Joseph Paxton had persuaded her to publish it as 'my poor husband's last legacy to gardeners'.[12]

Paxton, who had enjoyed good fortune with his salary of £65 and a cottage provided by the Duke of Devonshire at the outset of his career, was instrumental in setting up the Benevolent Institution for the Relief of Aged and Indigent Gardeners and their Widows in 1839, which became Royal in 1860. It was unusual for a pension to be paid on retirement, and head gardeners had often to leave their tied accommodation. For many working gardeners in old age, and those who fell ill or incurred injury, the dreaded workhouse represented the future. The need for such a charity is made clear by a sad note first inserted among the advertisements on the front page of the *Gardeners' Chronicle* on 4 September 1852: 'A few friends to the family of Mr. James Carton, once gardener at Syon House [belonging to the Duke of Northumberland], and now wholly destitute, having formed a small purse, in order that he may emigrate with his family to Australia, solicit some further aid in order to complete their arrangements.' Donations were to be sent to John Edwards Esq, founder-secretary of the National Floricultural Society. As funds were gradually accrued by the Benevolent Institution, pensions began to be paid out: by late 1840 there were just three, sharing £75 as an initial instalment; by 1852 over £500 was being paid out yearly on caring for pensioners with the average age of seventy-seven; by 1861 the income had reached £1,000. The society was dependent on voluntary contributions and an annual dinner as a fundraising event.

The move to improve education for working gardeners continued. A correspondent calling himself 'Linager' proposed in the *Gardeners' Chronicle* in 1860 that a three-tier set of national examinations should be established. The Preliminary Examination, to be taken between the ages of eighteen and twenty-one, would require 'little more than what every decently educated lad must learn if he is to rise to the level of labourer' along with tests in book-keeping, land-surveying and timber measuring. The Pass Examination, which had to be taken by those over the age of twenty-three, would be based on candidate's practical skill as a cultivator, including botany. The third tier, the Examination for Honours, would be accessible only to men over twenty-five, and would include papers on vegetable physiology, plant geography, climate, and two optional subjects, pomology (the study of the cultivation of fruit) and mathematics, 'not to go beyond the first book of Euclid'. The editor of the *Chronicle*, John Lindley, knew that some of his readership would not like these proposals, which were aimed not at students but at employees who were working long hours, often more than sixty per week. Not only did he condense the 'rather long communication', but also pointed out that the system was not intended for 'mature gardeners of England'. However, the anticipated reaction followed. A gardener from Birmingham, William Prestidge, for example, wrote to ask what class of men such schemes were aimed at, 'for only the sons of middle-class men could ever afford the time and money to be educated as he proposes, and they will hardly go through all the high degrees mentioned in order to enter even a nobleman's garden at wages varying from £50 to £100 per annum, when they can clear above £1,000 per annum in trade with less education than he insists on their possessing'.[13]

Despite this, moves were made towards a more realistic national system of examinations. The Royal Horticultural Society (it had acquired royal status in 1861) combined with the Royal Society of Arts to arrange the first examination of gardeners in April 1866. The first level was a three-hour written exam organised by the RSA, followed by a practical test supervised by the RHS in London. Those who passed with a first- or second-class certificate in 'the operations of the Fruit and Vegetable Garden' or 'in the operations of the Flower-garden' had their travelling expenses reimbursed and were admitted as Associates of the RHS. Although additional incentives to sit the examinations were offered by the *Gardeners' Chronicle* to 'bona fide' professional gardeners taking first-class certificates, RSA records show that they were not well subscribed – just a few dozen of the thousands of apprentices eligible applied. Trainees gained no benefit from sitting the examinations, employers were not exercised by the lack of a paper qualification, and above all, apprentices and journeymen continued to learn their craft through experience with a good head gardener.

A group of gardeners who had reached positions of eminence were asked by the *Gardeners' Chronicle* in 1874 and 1875 to contribute notes about their early experiences for a series, 'British Gardeners'. Again and again they mentioned the training they had received from head gardeners and foremen at the outset of their careers, remembering them with respect and often with affection.[14] However, not all were as exemplary. John Clare, the poet, recalled his time as a working gardener with no pleasure.

Around the year 1807 he was apprenticed to the master of the kitchen garden at Burghley House, home of the Marquess of Exeter. When he arrived with his father, the master was so well dressed in white stockings and neckcloth that they thought him a gentleman of great consequence. Clare was given an informal apprenticeship for three years, beginning with wages of eight shillings per week. The apprentices were shut in the garden house at night to prevent them stealing fruit, but being able-bodied youths they could easily escape out of the window. The master, despite his fine clothes, was foul-tempered, so Clare absconded, along with the foreman. He later wrote, 'to give him his due, he used me better than he had done others and even after I left him gave me a good word as a willing boy'.[15]

Even in well-run gardens, conditions for young lads were hard, and hours long with little time for leisure. This style of life is described in a rare survival, the diary of an apprentice gardener, kept by John Donaldson of Banff in Scotland, who went to work at Duff House in the autumn of 1873.[16] Donaldson was born on 12 July 1855, near Banff, the son of a farmer. He attended school until the age of ten, then worked on a farm, but at the age of eighteen became an apprentice to the head gardener at Duff House, Joseph Mackie. The great house, which stands just outside the harbour town of Banff on the north-east coast of Scotland, was built in the late 1730s by William Adam for William Duff, Lord Braco, who became 1st Earl Fife. Before the ambitious design could be completed, Adam fell out with Braco over money, so that the wings were never built, but the flamboyant classical centrepiece rises dramatically above the surrounding flat landscape of the estuary of the River Deveron.

Donaldson begins his diary on 31 October 1873: 'It appears to be a very difficult task for me to get a commencement on this book but as I don't intend to write this for public inspection it does not matter what I commence it with'. The young man's sense of independence is already established, and he then begins with the task of putting forty-one different varieties of potatoes in a pit. Every entry ends with remarks on the weather, with rough meaning windy, fine for still: this part of the north-east coast was frequently lashed by formidable storms that made the lives of the fisherman so precarious. John Donaldson's existence was more protected, but still hard to modern eyes. Sometimes he rose at 4 a.m., with breakfast followed by forenoon (morning). Lunch was eaten at midday (he called this dinner), with the last meal being taken at 5 p.m., unless he was invited out to a later meal, which he refers to as supper. Sundays were usually free, although he was sometimes required to undertake tasks.

Church attendance was noted, including the text of the readings. The number of staff working under Joseph Mackie is difficult to calculate, though references are made to foremen and other apprentices. His wages were noted in his diary as £5 8s a quarter.

Mackie had a substantial house next to one of the gatehouses, where Donaldson and his colleagues were expected to work in his garden, although the Mackie family helped out at harvest time in the orchards of the great house. The unmarried members of the garden staff slept in bothies, of which there seemed to have been two. The lower bothy can still be seen, next to the vinery glasshouse, in the part of the garden hard by the town. The glasshouse has been recreated, but the area where the stoves were kept is located right next to the bothy, so that the gardeners could keep them stoked all night through if necessary. The accommodation must have been fairly basic, for one diary entry refers to the bothy leaking, so that Donaldson was soaked to the skin on one side. A reference to 'making our meat ourselves now we gave Mungo the kick yesterday' suggests that one of the other lads did the cooking for them.[17]

In the walled garden, next to the lower bothy and glasshouse, was a long border and formal beds set into the lawn, one of which must have been shaped like a horse-shoe. In early November Donaldson talks about the bedding plants:

> Put in some more Penstemons, Blue Salvias up at the wall side and cleared out the Horse shoe. Took down what was in it and here they are Cerastium at the outside, Verbenas next, but they did not do well at all. Blue Salvia next did very well. Trentham Rose Geranium did well, Antirrhinum they did not do well. A lot of them did not come and we had no others to fill up the spaces. African Marigolds do very well for the centres scarlet Penstemons, next Jerolla Calceolarias, Dwarf Nasturtium, Alyssum. The inside of the Shoe looked very well.[18]

The brilliant colours evoked – blues, oranges, scarlet, yellow and white – were very fashionable at this period. Donaldson was clearly interested in flowers, making careful observations for future reference. In later entries in the diary he talks of making bouquets for the ladies of the house to take to balls and for the local horticultural show, and, when he had moved to his next placement, at Vogrie House, a large table bouquet for a dinner party. The task of supervising the arrangement of flowers for the house was usually assigned to the head gardener, but Donaldson must have had an eye for the art. In later life, he became president of the New York Cut Flower Exchange.

In strong contrast to the delicate job of flower arranging, in February Donaldson had to clear out and fill the ice houses down by the River Deveron. Ice houses had become an important component of estates not only for making ice creams and cooling wines, but also for the preservation of meat, fish, fruit and vegetables. The ice was cut into blocks from the river, and shovelled into the brick-lined pits of the little igloo-like houses, firmly packed in, with straw added to stop the ice forming into one solid mass. Enough ice would be stored to last right through the summer months, but this was a hard job in icy conditions. It took Donaldson and his colleague, Bagra, two days to do this, with respite only to boil willow withies in order to skin them and make them into baskets.

August would seem to come as welcome relief, when work in the garden was slack and the flower shows were held, and he talks of Joseph Mackie going off to the nearby show at Turriff to act as a judge. The Banff show took place at the beginning of September, with Donaldson digging up carrots and picking currants and gooseberries and carrying them up to the town in the morning. Nonchalantly, he records, 'A good [day], we had about 39 prizes, 19 first, 18 seconds and the rest thirds'.[19] The big house, with its glass houses and walled gardens, was bound to dominate such events, which must have caused frustration among gardeners with modest plots.

In November 1874 Donaldson left Duff House, after just one year. As Loudon makes clear in his encyclopaedia, it was common practice for young gardeners to move about, working for comparatively short periods in one job, so that they might experience different kinds of gardening. On 9 November Donaldson collected his character reference and pay from Mackie, and left Banff the following morning, taking the train to Edinburgh. It would seem that he went to David Laird, a placing agency, to find his next job, at Vogrie House near Dalkeith, the home of the Dewar family. Despite the grandness of their title and of their house, the Duff Earls of Fife had encountered financial problems, and by the beginning of the twentieth century, despite, or perhaps because of their marriage into the royal family (one of the daughters of Edward VII, Princess Louise, married Lord Duff, who became a duke), the problems only increased. The household for whom Donaldson now worked was rather different, for during the eighteenth and nineteenth centuries the Dewar family had made a great success of a series of commercial activities, including a coal mine, a gunpowder mill, and a famous whisky distillery.

The Vogrie estate consisted of about 2,000 acres, where Colonel Dewar was to rebuild the house in a baronial style in 1876, after Donaldson's departure. The wealth of the family comes through in the diary, for Donaldson mentions houses for peaches and muscats, three vineries, a Plum Wall, a Blackcurrant Border, melon frames, potato borders, a Long Flower Border, and a fernery. Under the head gardener, Mr Gibson, a team of gardeners is mentioned, though Donaldson seems to have particular affection for the female labourer, Isa, who washed crocks and netted currants among other tasks. His pay had risen to £3 per month, so Donaldson would now have been regarded as a journeyman.

Donaldson's time at Vogrie lasted just under a year, with the final entry in his diary coming on 28 September: 'I believe I am through with this month. Don't think I will complete another. However, if I had another month with this book it would have been more complete. I think it has done quite well with one year and eleven months. I am safe to conclude with saying: Amen!' The young man travelled down to London to work as the gardener in the Zoological Gardens, before emigrating to the United States of America, where he died in 1949.

Another gardener's diary of this period has also survived, that of William Cresswell, who was born in 1852 at Grantchester, just outside Cambridge, the second son of a professional gardener who doubled as the church clerk. William was thus brought up in Clerk's Cottage, and attended the local school 'for the education of the poorer classes', where he was lucky to have a well-qualified teacher. He probably began his career apprenticed to his father, but after his twenty-first birthday he went as journeyman to the Yeo family who lived at Elm Lodge in Streatham, to the south of London. Here he was the single-handed gardener, in charge of three acres of garden, and a vegetable field. One of the early entries in his diary records this double role: 'Began taking up Potatoes, took up those on bank under Fruit trees and got many bad ones. Second crop of Turnips sown. Dung prepared for mushrooms by wetting, turning and shaking up into a heap to ferment.'[20]

Cresswell moved on in late 1873 first to Carters' nursery at Forest Hill, and then to Audley End in Essex as second man in the kitchen garden. The Victorian love of organisation is shown in this position. As the number of departments in gardens proliferated, so the gardeners were graded by seniority like the footmen in the house. Cresswell worked to Mr Bryan, in charge of the kitchen department, and as second man would be in charge of several gardeners. His wages were 16s per week, with only

38 Older, and often old, women were employed to look after the teenage boys who lived in garden bothies lest bad behaviour should ensue. In this cartoon, 'The Gardener's Offering' by Thomas Rowlandson, a young gardener declares his love to the daughter of the house.

Sundays off, though he was expected to take his turn in watering, heating and ventilation of the glasshouses on the Sabbath. He lived in the bothy at the back of the Vinery range, along with the third man, James Bedgegood. The men cooked for themselves, and the diary records how Bryan gave him knives, forks, tablespoons, and a quart saucepan. Clean linen was provided by a garden woman, Mrs Brown, for which she was paid 11d per day. In his book on head gardeners, Toby Musgrave tells how the job description for the woman who looked after the bothy boys at Wimpole Hall, a near neighbour of Audley End, was that she should be employed for her advanced age and lack of attraction, lest temptation should befall her charges.[21] Whether Mrs Brown fitted this description is not known.

Audley End at this period was the home of the Braybrooke family. The 3rd Lord Braybrooke had undertaken considerable changes to the garden in the 1820s and 1830s, returning a certain degree of formality with flower beds in a parterre, and extensive walled kitchen gardens with a range of glasshouses. Orchard House was built in 1856 to the most up-to-date design for the cultivation of fruit trees. Although his department was the

39 Potting up bedding plants was the work of many days for workers in large gardens at the end of the nineteenth century, as described by William Cresswell in his diary. These young men were photographed in 1904 on an unnamed estate.

kitchen garden, Cresswell worked with flowers as well, and bedding schemes play a big part in his activities, so that in March 1874, when the wind was from the north, and snow fell from 11 a.m. to 3 p.m., he worked in one of the glass houses, potting off pelargonium geraniums in huge quantities: 1,196 Lord Palmerston, 1,719 Cristine, 1,154 Vesuvius. He also repotted Achines and Calaliums. The two vine houses had to be protected from the bad weather, and he reported that the temperature of the first was 75°F by day, 65°F by night, while the second was ten degrees lower. With the grounds covered in snow, and a strong frost, fires were made up just before midnight to heat all the houses and pits.[22]

April through to June was the time of the horticultural shows. At the show in Cambridge on 23 April, Cresswell received first prize for azaleas, hyacinths, primroses, and three plants in bloom, and second prize for best plant. A month later, at another show in Cambridge he won first prize for his amaryllis, second and third for foliage plants, which were now very fashionable for decorating houses, a second for azaleas, and an extra for a collection of dracaenas and grapes. For the local show at Saffron Walden in June, he records taking a van-load of plants and foliage to decorate the tent.[23]

On 30 September 1874, Cresswell noted tersely in his diary 'Left the service of Lord Braybrooke, left Audley End for Cambridge by 7.35pm train'. He went on to work at the Cambridge Botanical Garden, and ceased his diary two months later. The book was fortuitously found at a second-hand book market and proved invaluable in the restoration of the gardens at Audley End by English Heritage. In particular it helped in the restoration of Orchard House, and the area where Cresswell worked, including the bothy, with its three rooms and kitchen-and-living area, which has been recreated to look as it would have in the 1870s.

Although Audley End and Vogrie employed quite substantial numbers to work in the gardens, even they are dwarfed by Waddesdon Manor, the home in Buckinghamshire of Baron Ferdinand de Rothschild, where the head gardener, John Jaques, supervised a team of over a hundred gardeners. The overwhelming majority of households, however, employed either a single-handed gardener, or a couple of gardeners. One such garden owner was the novelist H. Rider Haggard, who was deeply interested in both agriculture and horticulture. In 1903 he decided to keep a gardening diary for Kessingland, his garden in Norfolk. His 'head gardener', Mason, was assisted by Charles, aged twenty-one. The odd-job man of the house, Freaks, over seventy years of age, could be called upon to help, along with a labourer from the village. Haggard obviously enjoyed a good relationship with Mason, writing of the sympathy and co-operation that had been established, 'which are often lacking when the bond is one of money alone, and in their separate stations both strive together for a common end. In this matter they become friends, the link between them being the welfare of the plants and flowers in which they take an equal pride.' He also described the network that operated among gardeners: 'On the morning of Wednesday nineteenth [of August], Mason took the pony and cart, and made a solemn round of calls upon the gardeners of the neighbouring houses. This is more or less an annual ceremony . . . good that gardener should meet gardener; also he returns, bringing his sheaves with him, in the shape of various flower roots and cuttings.'[24]

For those who could not employ somebody full-time there were jobbing gardeners, who enjoyed rather a mixed press. In his book, *The City Gardener*, published in 1722, Thomas Fairchild warned against ignorant jobbing gardeners along with sellers of plants at London markets: 'I and others have seen Plants that were to be sold in the markets that were as uncertain of growth as a Piece of Noah's Ark would be'.[25] A jobbing gardener who doubled up as a supplier might be tempted to neglect plants in a customer's garden to create a market for replacements. Shirley Hibberd warned that the jobbing gardener 'fiddles away his employer's time and his own earnings in the low enjoyment of beer', and went on to observe:

40 Middle-class garden owners often employed just one gardener, sometimes assisted by his boy. This photograph was taken in Walsall in about 1880.

Periodical digging, 'as a matter of course', such as the jobbing gardeners designated 'turning in', has for its sole object the destruction of plants; but that object is disguised by describing the operation as 'making things tidy'. When you are tired of herbaceous plants, let the jobbing gardener keep the border tidy, and you will soon be rid of the obnoxious lilies, phloxes, ranunculuses, anemones, hollyhocks, paeonies, and pansies, without the painful labour of pulling them up and burning them.[26]

The poor jobbing gardener rarely got the chance to put his case, but one, Archibald M'Naughton from Hackney, is an exception. In a letter, 'On the Life of a Jobbing Gardener', to the *Gardener's Magazine* in 1826, he described his career, which took a rather different turn from those of the eminent head gardeners who usually populated such publications. Leaving Edinburgh in 1777, he travelled down to London, working for a time in a nursery in Fulham before getting 'a very good place with a Mr Rolls, a great stock-broker, whose affairs went wrong after I had been six

[TOM MAKING THE ACQUAINTANCE OF A "FANCY GARDENER."]

41 Nineteenth-century commentators often criticised jobbing gardeners for deliberately neglecting plants or grubbing them up needlessly so that they could supply new ones, as they often doubled up as plant sellers. Some were also accused of drunkenness, as shown in this sketch.

years with him, and I was obliged to quit'. After a stint with a seedsman in St James's, he worked for Mrs Wilson at Putney, 'where I remained till her daughter married, when her husband having an aversion to Scotch servants, I was obliged to leave'. After more adventures, 'not liking to go into servitude again, I began jobbing on my own account, and a poor business I have found it ever since. When I first began, the highest wages I could get were 3s a day, and obliged to find my own tools. I had a good deal of employment at first, partly from the circumstance of being a Scotchman, being called by the people who employ jobbers, a professed gardener.' Clearly being a Scot was a mixed blessing for gardeners. M'Naughton's difficult life continued:

> My wife also took up a greengrocers shop about this time, and we did very well till we lost our only daughter, which obliged us to take in a maid-servant, who let in some fellows into the house one Sunday afternoon when we were at chapel, and took away all my savings, most of my wifes clothes, and concealed the bedding in an outhouse, to be taken away no doubt at night ... After doing nothing for some time, I began the jobbing again at Paddington, and my wife took in washing; but she falling ill, we removed to Hackney, on account of the air, where I have been ever since, being just able to gain a livelihood, by laying out the gardens for the new buildings going on in the neighbourhood.

M'Naughton ends his tale of woe by explaining that he is now a widower approaching seventy years of age, with only the prospect of the workhouse if he falls ill. His final advice was 'never give up any place whatever for the condition of a jobbing gardener, for that is greater slavery than being a common labourer'.[27]

Many working gardeners at the outset of the careers, as journeymen, spent stints employed in nurseries to gain experience before going back to the gardening departments of large houses. Others were involved in the supply of plants, shrubs and trees as nurserymen, and seeds as seed merchants for their entire working lives. The Victorian period saw a huge increase in the number of nurseries and seed businesses, catering for a rapidly growing market, especially amongst the middle classes. Businesses moved out of urban centres to escape worsening pollution, and to cater for the new suburbs, taking advantage of the development of the railway system to send their plants and seeds across the country, and securing their orders from mail catalogues and advertisements in gardening journals.

The great London nurseries established in the eighteenth century continued, more or less. Brompton Park Nursery, made famous by George London and Henry Wise, was taken over by Gray, Adams and Hogg, but closed in 1852. The following year, the Exotic Nursery of Knight and Perry in Chelsea was bought by James Veitch, to give a London dimension to his Exeter business. The Vineyard Nursery in Hammersmith, begun in the mid-eighteenth century by James Lee and Lewis Kennedy, continued under James's grandson, Charles, into the 1860s and 1870s. Perhaps the most important London nursery of the early nineteenth century was Loddiges of Hackney, bought by a German, Conrad Loddiges, in 1771, when Hackney was made up of a series of rural villages. By 1852, however, growing industrialisation around the River Lea brought such severe pollution that the great nursery with its show houses and arboretum was forced to close, with much of the stock going to Paxton's Crystal Palace site at Sydenham.

But nurseries came in all sizes. William Bull of King's Road in Chelsea advertised exotic tree ferns along with hundreds of varieties of fuchsias, chrysanthemums and pelargoniums. William Paul ran a nursery specialising in roses at Waltham Cross with easy access into London. Youell & Co., with their Royal Nursery at Great Yarmouth in Norfolk, used advertisements in gardening newspapers and mail-order catalogues to offer 'Communications by steamer and railway to all parts of England, Ireland and Scotland, as well as to the continent. All orders of £2 upwards delivered carriage free to London, Newcastle and Hull, as well as any railway station within 150 miles of the nurseries.' Shirley Hibberd was critical of some of the smaller nurseries: 'In the suburbs of London, there are numbers of small nurseries, where "a little of everything" is to be had at a moment's notice – fruit trees, evergreens, roses, &c, &c. The way in which most of these are grown is such that they are utterly unfit to be removed when sold.'[28]

By the nineteenth century some businesses trading in seeds had become considerable enterprises. Suttons started life as corn merchants based in Covent Garden but moved to Reading in 1837, branching out into the sale of flower and vegetable seeds and establishing seed-testing laboratories and nursery trial grounds. Carters Seeds, founded around 1816 by James Carter, chose to retain their High Holborn address, although their seeds were mainly grown on farms near Colchester in Essex. Here ninety-six acres were set aside for cabbages, 70 for beans and an immense 814 for peas. In the 1870s the *Gardener's Magazine* provided a series of detailed descriptions of Carter's business, including how the seeds were prepared by woman workers in Holborn ready for dispatch:

> The sorters are placed beside great benches, on which the seed is poured out in quantities. At the end of the bench is a small slit, and beneath the slit hangs a great bag. The sorter draws forward the seed and rolls through the slit into the bag every grain that is the proper size and shape and colour, but quickly detects and throws out every seed that is small or misshapen or badly coloured or in any way wrong ... [Those detected are] cast out for feeding pigeons and other such purposes.[29]

An enterprise that combined supplying seeds with nursery and market gardening was Robinson's Seeds and Plants. Founded in 1860 by William Robinson on a twenty-two-acre site near Preston in Lancashire, it was originally a nursery and market garden with bushes and fruit trees alongside vegetables. Manure was provided by cows and horses, with the latter doubling up for transport. William Robinson's son started to improve the size of onions and leeks through selection, giving his varieties of vegetables the prefix 'mammoth', and the business, which still flourishes, is known as the 'Home of the Giant Onion'. Some of the Victorian glasshouses have survived, along with old varieties of fruit in the orchard.

Market gardens, great and small, were also established throughout the country in the nineteenth century, especially around the new suburban districts of large industrial areas. A watercolour painted in 1852 of the Kingsland Road in Hackney shows market gardening side by side with a brickmaking enterprise (Plate VII). New houses created from the latter would within a couple of years swallow up the former, driving the market gardens further north to Tottenham, Edmonton and out into Hertfordshire. Fruit was brought into the London markets from Kent and the Vale of Evesham rather than from the environs of the capital, thanks to the railway network.

The discovery of a diary kept by a young market gardener in Oxfordshire provides a fascinating glimpse into running such a business in the mid-Victorian period. Joseph Turrill began his diary in 1863 at the age of twenty-two, and kept it for four years. His market gardening was based in the village of Garsington, where he rented an allotment from the North Manor Estate, owned by the Morrell brewing family. Joseph's mother was the licensee of the Red Lion public house, and he used the garden there, along with other small plots, for his cultivation of fruit and vegetables for sale at the market in Oxford.

As well as providing his livelihood, gardening in general interested him. Thus the entry for 25 February 1867 runs: 'The gooseberry trees are out in leaf but no bloom yet. The red early potatoes are shot well. Trained young plum trees up. Rhubarb not shot up much. Crocuses out in bloom.'[30] For 22 April 1866 he noted:

> My first planting of peas up in full drill and look well and the onions are up in drill and Parsnips . . . Got one more row of peas to plant in Common and a few potatoes and that's all . . . Peas and Shallotts and onions up well but rhubarb backward. Potatoes coming up and plum and damson trees out in bloom but not much this year. . . . The briar stocks shooting well and tulips out in blossom. The flower garden looks gay now. The garden wants hoeing. Bees work well now and shudded [probably lopped] the trees in the garden and sowed celery seed.[31]

He kept pigs, and recorded their purchase and killing, and helped his mother out in the Red Lion. Little wonder he recorded working by moonlight – known as the parish lantern – during some of the early winter months.

Nevertheless Turrill had plenty of leisure interests. He took the *Oxford Chronicle* and followed carefully the passage of the 1867 Parliamentary Reform Bill. He was a keen cricketer, writing reports of Garsington's team matches and feasts for the *Chronicle*. One match is recorded against Headington Quarry, so he may well have known the stone mason gardener, Charles Snow (see Chapter 5, pp. 138–9). He makes several references to flower shows, including the Royal Oxford Horticultural Show held in the gardens of New College. Here he singled out one flower, a geranium named 'The Cloth of Silver', which he found 'extraordinary good'. On the way home, he and his sister called in at the University's Botanical Garden.[32]

Turrill was lucky that he was able to rent an allotment and use it for commercial enterprise, as the regulations often stipulated that the land was to be used only for domestic purposes. A report of another allotment holder who was able to operate a small gardening business is provided by the *Flower, Fruit and Vegetables Magazine*, a monthly journal 'of Popular

Gardening'. In the January edition for 1898, it offers a profile of Henry Dearlove, a Surrey labourer from the village of South Park near Reigate, who was making a comfortable living from half an acre of allotment land.

> His holding is situated in the centre of the village. He has 120 feet of glass, and in the houses he grows strawberries in the spring and tomatoes in the summer. One year he gathered 90lbs of strawberries in eight days from his biggest house, and three years running he has raised more than a ton of tomatoes each season. Out of doors he grows strawberries, rhubarb and peas and beans for market. The forced strawberries he sends to Covent Garden, and the other produce is disposed of locally.

It was noted that his net profits averaged £80 per annum.

Another portrait, in words and picture, of a modest market gardener was depicted by the photographer, P.H. Emerson. Emerson was very concerned about the lot of the poor, and set out to photograph and describe their lives in East Anglia in the 1880s. His photographs are like paintings, and he had an eye for the romantic and the picturesque, so that his description of the premises of a Jewish market gardener from near Beccles in Suffolk, begins: 'The garden was beautifully kept, perhaps a little too neatly for our purpose.' His photograph shows the gardener potting out plants. Behind can be seen his garden:

> carefully pruned and trained apple-trees, loaded with white apple-blossom tinctured with the faintest rosy flush, met us at every turn, while beneath these grew the yellow buds, rosy stalks and broad green leaves of the rhubarb plant. Lettuce and young onions were springing up from the brown earth, and strong plants of horse-radish grew in rank luxuriance, their biting roots buried deep and cool in the earth. The old gardener – of Hebrew origin – joined us, and pointed exultingly to his spring potatoes, the 'Pride of Hebron' as he had named them with naive anachronism. He was a venerable old man, with flowing white beard and clear, dark eyes. His face was honest and kindly, and the gentle work of all his life – tending and caring for his plants – seemed to have left its impress on his character.[33]

42  P.H. Emerson's photograph of an old market gardener in Suffolk, taken in the 1880s. He is shown potting up plants, assisted by his granddaughter.

Emerson found him very tired, and noted that the old gardener died that summer. His epitaph was to point out that it was heart, character, sympathy and affection, not intelligence or knowledge, that makes the real happiness of life.

*  *  *

In 1913 the education of gardeners was at last put on a formal basis with the establishment by the Royal Horticultural Society of a National Diploma, and the first examinations were held the following year. These best-laid plans were, however, thrown into disarray by the outbreak of the First World War in the late summer of 1914. This terrible conflict also spelt the end of many large-scale country-house gardening establishments. Hundreds of gardeners were killed in the war, and those who did return to Britain found a very different kind of society, as we will see in Chapter 13.

# CHAPTER 8

# Sources of Inspiration

WORKING-CLASS GARDENERS have for centuries encountered three principal obstacles when seeking to develop their horticultural activities: want of literacy, poverty and lack of opportunity. By the mid-nineteenth century it was estimated that 40 per cent of men in Britain were illiterate, with slightly higher figures for women – scarcely improved since Elizabethan times. For those who could read, books were often beyond their straitened means. The lack of opportunity to view a range of plants being grown and find the latest varieties was noted in 1860 by a head gardener in London: 'I am sure that many of the working classes have a wish to cultivate flowers and would do so, were they taught in what manner they should raise those kinds suitable to the climate of the town'. As so often was the case, he went on to add a moral dimension: 'The backyard, where a few flowers bloom, would soon prove an antidote to the gaudy gin-palace'.[1] Leaving aside the social prejudice, those who were determined – and it has amply been shown how working-class gardeners could be determined – all three obstacles might be overcome with increasing efficacy as the nineteenth century developed.

Just such a gardener was John Duncan, a linen weaver, whose biography by the educationalist William Jolly was published in 1883. This in itself was very unusual, because Duncan was born into a life of extreme deprivation: the kind of person who is nearly always a silent witness of the times rather than a protagonist. The biography also tells us of the sources of inspiration on which he was able to draw to overcome his lowly circumstances and acquire the information to become an eminent botanist and skilled horticulturalist. Duncan was born in 1794 at Stonehaven in Kincardineshire, the illegitimate son of a weaver, John Duncan, and Ann

Caird. His mother decided to support herself and her child by weaving stockings and harvesting. John Duncan never attended school but wandered in the countryside collecting rushes to make wicks to sell. From the age of ten he worked as a herd boy on local farms, and at eighteen, resolving to be a weaver, he was indentured to Charles Pirie, pugilist, gin smuggler, and a man of violence who treated him cruelly. However, Pirie's wife possessed a collection of books, and secretly began to teach the young man to read. After her death, Duncan continued his education with the help of other villagers and by following the biblical texts in church, although he did not learn to write until he was thirty-four.

Finding Pirie's behaviour intolerable, Duncan ran away to live with his mother, earning his keep by weaving. Through frugal living he saved up to buy a copy of Culpeper's herbal, the first book in what was to be his modest library. In 1836 he met Charles Black, gardener to local gentry at Whitehouse overlooking the Vale of Alford in Aberdeenshire. Black was to be an important influence, teaching Duncan the system of plant classification established by Linnaeus, and together they scoured the countryside for plants to build up a scientific herbarium. To identify their rarities, they needed W.J. Hooker's *British Flora*, but could not afford the purchase. Instead, they were able to consult the book while drinking in the local inn, where a copy had been left by the landlord's deceased son, a gardener.

Duncan was a figure worthy to have featured in the novels of Dickens. His wardrobe, which lasted him half a century, consisted of two tall hats, two best suits of his own design and weaving, and work clothes which were worn with tam-o'-shanter bonnets topped by large tassels. His trousers were worn rolled up to keep them from wear. He was so short-sighted that he was obliged to crawl along the ground while botanising. Charles Black's brother James, a gardener at Chatsworth, described him as 'human proto-plasm, man in his least complex form . . . a survival of those "rural swains" who lived in idyllic simplicity'. However, his last years were far from idyllic, for Duncan was destitute and obliged to apply for poor relief in 1874 to supplement the tiny wages he earned from weaving. In 1880 this desperate state was discovered by William Jolly, who had written a brief account of Duncan's life two years earlier, and a nationwide appeal was launched, raising £326, including a contribution from Queen Victoria. Duncan died the following year and was buried, shrouded by plants symbolising his life, at Alford. William Jolly then wrote a full biography of his friend: previously he had written a life of Robert Burns, somebody of whom Duncan did not approve. With his outspoken Calvinist views, he dismissed the poet as a 'filthy loon'.

The main sources of information and inspiration open to gardeners before the advent of radio and television was the printed word and observation of practice. John Duncan's illiteracy was common in the early nineteenth century, although Scotland provided a better system of primary education for all levels of society than was to be found in the rest of the British Isles. Gardening in particular provided pitfalls even for those who could read and write. As Duncan found, the Linnaean system of plant classification required some knowledge of Latin. Despite his very late start in literacy, John Duncan taught himself the classical languages in his adult years. Jolly recorded Duncan's method of learning Greek and Latin words: 'Ow ye see, I had aye a gweed memory. But when I got a noo plant and fund oot its name, I used to write it doon on a bit o' paiper, and lay it on the wab afore me as I wis wirkin', to glance at it noo and nan and say it ower to mysel', without disturbin' my wark.'[2]

A classical education was the acquisition of a few, almost invariably men. Jane Loudon in exasperation pointed out in *Botany for Ladies*, published in 1842: 'It is so difficult for men whose knowledge has grown with their growth, and strengthened with their strength, to imagine the state of profound ignorance in which a beginner is, that even their elementary books are like the old Eton grammar, when it was written in Latin, they require a master to explain them'.[3] This exasperation is echoed by the Curate, one of Dean Hole's gardening characters in his *Six of Spades*. He tells of 'a bilious old gentleman' who suggested that the children at the local show should record Latin names and classifications for the wild flowers to be exhibited. The Curate's response was:

> Botany is a grand science for those who have the head and time for it, but it's about as useful to a ploughman's child as a ball-room fan to an Arctic voyager: and therefore, so far from rewarding any of my young rustics for Latinizing our dear old country flowers, I should be inclined to award for the precious pedant transportation to Botany Bay. Carry out your idea, and we shall have the labourer's child no more exclaiming, 'Oh, faythur, there's a dandelion!' but 'Aspice, O paterfamilias dilecte, ubi Leontodon taraxacum flavescit!'[4]

The gardening writer William Robinson wrote in a similar vein: 'It is best to speak of things growing about our door in our own tongue, and the practice of using in conversation long Latin names, a growth of our own century, has done infinite harm to gardening in shutting out people who have a heart for a garden, but none for the Latin of the gardener'.[5]

Latin was not the only pitfall facing those interested in plants. Jolly described how unlearned gardeners called rhododendrons 'Roderick Randoms' or 'Rosy Dandrums' and the Gloire de Dijon Rose 'Glory to John'. This habit was noted by the Yorke family of Erddig near Wrexham in North Wales who commissioned portraits of their servants, and composed poems to accompany them. The one for James Phillips, their head gardener in the early nineteenth century, ran:

> Old fashioned, in his notions, he
> With foreign names, did not agree
> 'Quatre-Saisons' 'Quarter-Sessions' meant
> The 'Bijou' as the 'By-Joe' went.[6]

In response to the call for a formal qualification for professional gardeners the Royal Horticultural Society instituted examinations in 1866, as noted in Chapter 7. Amateur working-class gardeners would learn their craft from observing their fathers and other members of the family, an excellent but limited form of education. However, there were the beginnings of practical instruction in horticulture from institutions such as mutual improvement societies that sprang up in the nineteenth century. John Duncan, who cultivated his own garden and particularly grew drug plants in a wild flower plot, gave lectures at the mutual instruction class in the village of Auchleven. Unfortunately William Jolly does not give us the gist of the practical gardening advice provided by Duncan, concentrating rather on his introduction of the subject based on the garden of Eden, 'a most beautiful and charming spot, enclosed and planted by God Himself'.[7]

Floricultural societies also held lectures from invited experts. In east London, the Tower Hamlets Society met in 1864 to hear a lecture on ferns given by the head gardener of Victoria Park, W.S. Prestoe. Sometimes one of the members might speak. In 1866 the *East London Observer* reported on the lecture programme of the East Tower Hamlets Society. At meetings held monthly at the Coach and Horses Tavern on the Mile End Road, a paper was read on the cultivation of a particular flower or plant, followed by questions and comments: 'February's subject was "The Cultivation of the Grape" and in March Mr. C. Parker spoke on

"The Lilium auratum" – the last new importation from Japan, and for the possession of bulbs of which there has been a decided rage in floral circles.'[8]

At the end of the century, Dean Hole was advocating that the newly created county councils should advise and assist cottage garden societies. He describes how John Wright in Kent had acted as a horticultural instructor, giving lectures that were intelligible to all on the culture of flowers, fruit and vegetables, illustrated by diagrams and lantern slides. He also personally inspected gardens and allotments, superintended the award of prizes and established school gardens to provide boys with tools and seeds so that they could grow up to be allotment holders. Surrey County Council also employed John Wright, and set up a technical education committee with lectures not only on the growing of vegetables, but also on how to cook them. The committee recognised 'that Horticulture is the oldest of the Arts, and the foundation of all others', and therefore 'is especially anxious, and has made arrangements accordingly, not only for gardens in which boys may be taught while they are at school, but for "Continuation Gardens", in which they may receive further instruction, when they have left it'.[9]

In 1906 county councils in Ireland also set up committees of agricultural and technical instruction. The Monaghan County Committee, concerned by the traditional lack of variety of vegetables grown in Ireland, declared in the report for that year: 'We must sincerely congratulate the Technical Education Committee and their earnest and hardworking horticulturalists upon the successful carrying out of a most useful and far-reaching scheme of instruction in practical gardening.'[10] The Kildare County Committee claimed that they were the first to appoint a Horticultural Instructor, William Tyndall, who organised a team, including one woman, to go out and advise cottage gardeners, give practical demonstrations and evening lectures. This was regarded as a key part of developing Ireland as a nation.

Our knowledge of working-class private libraries in the nineteenth century is minimal, but we do know that John Duncan began his book collection with the long-standing staple, Culpeper's herbal, and it is mentioned by other sources as a feature of the cottage bookshelf to provide information both on horticulture and home medical treatments. The poet John Clare, who was a keen botanist and gardener, had as his chief work of reference John Abercrombie's *Practical Gardener's Companion* in its 1823 edition. Abercrombie's father owned a market garden near Edinburgh,

*Isaac Taylor del et sculp!*

43 The title page of the second edition of John Abercrombie's *Every Man his Own Gardener*, published in 1767, showing gardeners digging and hoeing. This book proved a great success, running to many editions, and its low price meant that it could be afforded by gardeners of modest means.

and the young John worked his way up the horticultural ladder before setting himself up as a nurseryman in Hackney. He was also the author of at least fifteen books of horticultural interest, and new editions of his most popular books, *Every Man his Own Gardener*, *The Practical Gardener's Companion* and *The Gardener's Pocket Journal* continued to be published for more than fifty years after his death in 1806.

While books were expensive and usually beyond the purse of most working-class gardeners, *The Gardener's Pocket Journal* cost a comparatively modest one shilling. Moreover, Abercrombie wrote in a clear, practical style. A story runs that in 1770 a bookseller, Lockyer Davis, and the poet Oliver Goldsmith invited Abercrombie to dine with them in the hope that he might produce 'an original work on "Practical Gardening"'. The gardener agreed on condition that his manuscript should be revised and the style improved by Goldsmith. However, when the poet received the text, he returned it unchanged, pointing out that 'Abercombie's style was best suited to the subjects of which it treated'. Abercrombie took the lesson on board, and in *The Universal Gardener and Botanist*, published in 1778, advised his readers: 'Some apology may be necessary for the style; but when it is considered, that perspicuity ought to be preferred to elegance, the good-natured reader will pardon little mistakes in language if the meaning is clear and obvious.'[11] His readers clearly agreed, for his books sold in great quantities. One working gardener who owned a copy of the 1813 edition of *Every Man his own Gardener* duly noted his name and place of work on the fore-edge. Joseph Mott was probably a gardener at Hackwood House in Hampshire, in the employ of the Duke of Bolton. As the current owner of the book points out 'its shoddy condition [is] a testament to frequent use in the garden or potting shed'.[12]

John Duncan, being a keen botanist, acquired a herbal by the Frenchman Joseph Pitton de Tournefort, *Elemens de Botanique*, first published in 1694, in which the author attempted a system of plant classification focusing on the shape of petals. He also owned a more modern herbal, that of John Hill. The first English writer to adopt the Linnaean system, John Hill incorporated it in his *Useful Family Herbal*, issued as a serial publication in fifty-two parts. Partworks of this kind were more accessible to those of limited means, and John Duncan and Charles Black shared the price of the sixpenny issues between them. The first botanical partworks published in Britain had been produced by William Curtis, the *Praefectus Horti* and Demonstrator of Plants at the Chelsea Physic Garden in the 1770s. In 1787 he launched *Curtis's Botanical Magazine*, sold in parts, with coloured plates, which he was able to affordably price at one shilling. This proved a great success, and indeed is still going today.

Where Curtis's magazine led, a whole raft of periodicals followed, aimed at three principal markets: botanists, florists and gardeners.[13] Their production was dominated by four men of strong, and sometimes differing, opinions: John Claudius Loudon, Joseph Paxton, John Lindley and George Glenny. Loudon launched his *Gardener's Magazine* in 1826 as a quarterly, priced at four shillings, but it developed into a monthly, at 1s 6d. Paxton, in association with Joseph Harrison, a professional gardener from Sheffield, started his monthly periodical, the *Horticultural Register*, five years later. Many of the topics in the *Register* were considered by Loudon as *his* territory, and he thought Paxton was throwing down the gauntlet by offering a cheaper alternative. According to Jane Loudon, sales of the *Gardener's Magazine* instantly decreased and never recovered.[14]

The animosity between Loudon and Paxton was, however, nothing to the ill feeling engendered by George Glenny. While Paxton and Loudon had begun their careers as professional gardeners, Glenny came from a very different background: he was a watchmaker from Clerkenwell, who had prospered through a good marriage and the sale of insurance. As an amateur florist, he was irritated by the Horticultural Society's reluctance to feature florists' flowers at their shows, so in 1832 he founded the Metropolitan Society of Florists and Amateurs to promote floriculture through competition. The following year he turned his first periodical, the *Royal Lady's Magazine*, into the *Horticultural Journal and Florists' Register*. Defiantly, he declared:

> Our object, therefore, is merely to supply that information which no other work supplies, and which there are still many persons who think degrading. Be it so until we show the contrary. We shall go on in our humble way till we can prove that florists' flowers belong to the highest instead of the lowest grade of floriculture; and that tailors, tinkers and weavers, who knew them and grew them a century ago, though not one in a hundred could read or write, were better judges than botanists of what constituted a good thing.[15]

Botanists' and florists' differences of opinion had a long history – as shown by the comments of Linnaeus (see Chapter 4, p. 94) – and was still very much alive. Dean Hole, a man of moderate views and good humour, remarked in his book on roses: 'I honour Dr Lindley, but I do not envy, because, strange as it may seem, he is very rarely an enthusiastic gardener; I never remember to have seen a scientific botanist and a successful practical florist under the same hat.'[16] George Glenny was neither a man of moderation, nor, it would seem, possessed of a strong sense of humour. He has been described by his biographer as a horticultural hornet, and his stings were sent in all directions. Loudon's *Gardener's Magazine* was described as having 'every appearance of decay'. Of Joseph Harrison's new magazine, *The Floricultural Cabinet*, he went even further, muttering of 'mere overflowing of imbecility and folly'.[17]

In 1837 Glenny founded another periodical, this time a weekly, the *Gardener's Gazette*, in which he continued his criticisms, aimed in particular towards John Lindley, the associate secretary of the Horticultural Society. So immoderate were these that he was banned from the Society's shows. To silence Glenny, Joseph Paxton and Lindley in 1841 launched a second weekly, the *Gardeners' Chronicle*. Priced at sixpence, it consisted of sixteen pages that included other news, and was published on a Saturday, ready for the day of rest.

Loudon's pioneering *Gardener's Magazine*, even with its reduced price of 1s 6d, was well beyond the means of ordinary gardeners, and in practice was a way of providing news and information for garden owners to pass down to their head gardeners. When Paxton and Harrison brought out their *Horticultural Register*, they made the point that although professional gardeners had been able to publish their experiences in existing publications, these were so expensive that the information 'was thus out of reach of many persons in the humbler classes of society', an allusion to Loudon's magazine. George Glenny certainly aimed his *Horticultural Journal* at working-class as well as middle-class florists, and Paxton and Lindley claimed a very varied market, writing in their prospectus for the *Gardeners' Chronicle*: 'a weekly record of everything that bears upon horticulture or garden botany . . . thus the gardener, the forester, the rural architect, the drainer, the road-maker, and the cottager, will all have the improvements in their respective pursuits recorded'.[18] Nevertheless, their periodical was more likely to appeal to professional gardeners, nurserymen and gentry, and even sixpence represented a considerable sum to pay out each week for a cottager who was working within the most constrained of circumstances.

By the mid-nineteenth century, however, the prices of publications right across the board were coming down. The *Cottage Gardener*, established in 1848 by George Johnson, adopted a newspaper format and sold for threepence. The *Gardeners' Hive*, begun in 1850, sold for twopence, as did Shirley Hibberd's *Gardener's Magazine*, launched in 1865 and taking up the title that had ceased with Loudon's death eighteen years before.

The *Edinburgh Weekly Journal* in 1848 was probably the first general newspaper to include a regular gardening column, by George Glenny. Four years later, the popular *Lloyd's Weekly London Newspaper* followed suit. This periodical, owned by Edward Lloyd, had been founded ten years earlier as *Lloyd's Illustrated* in direct competition to the *Illustrated London News* at the price of twopence, but fell foul of the stamp law and had to be revamped with the price raised to threepence. Edward Lloyd was a fascinating figure. The son of a Welsh labourer who died in Lloyd's infancy, he overcame his impoverished background by studying shorthand at the London Mechanics' Institution and opened shops in London selling comic valentines and penny story-books. His market was the working classes, and among the sensational literature that he produced for them were plagiarisms of the works of Charles Dickens, such as *Nikelas Nickelbery* and *Oliver Twiss*. These, like Dickens's real novels, proved a great success, and he went on to introduce the world to Sweeney Todd, instructing his illustrators 'there must be more blood, much more blood'.[19]

Carrying the banner 'Measures not Men', *Lloyd's Weekly* was published in Salisbury Square off Fleet Street every Sunday, reaching a circulation of 350,000 in the 1860s with the newly invented Hoe's rotary press making it possible to meet demand. The abolition of the stamp and paper duties in 1861 allowed the price to be reduced to one penny. This was the first of the cheap Sunday newspapers, and although the great majority of customers lived in London, it was distributed throughout the country. With its wide readership and reformist tone, it provided a perfect platform for its gardening correspondent, George Glenny.[20]

Glenny had experienced a chequered journalistic career; having been forced to sell the *Gardener's Gazette*, he revived it, and then lost it again. But he had lost none of his fire and competitiveness. In February 1852 he set out his stall by declaring:

> We have undertaken the horticultural part of a newspaper which circulates *ten times* as many copies as the *Gardeners' Chronicle* and *sixty times* the number of the *Gardener's Journal*. In short, we have harnessed ourselves to the leading Journal of Horticulture, and we have once more to write on gardening for the million. Aware of the responsibility we have incurred, we shall endeavour to make the Horticultural Department of this vast paper as far excel its contemporaries in real usefulness as it

does in circulation. We have no room for nonsense, and as for controversy, we may safely leave that for those who are fond of it. We hold
ourselves quite capable of settling such matters in a paragraph.[21]

Those who had had dealings with Glenny knew that avoidance of controversy was highly unlikely to be maintained. Only six weeks later, he
declared: 'We own that we only have one column of garden news where
others have twelve, but nobody will deny that we give as much USEFUL
information as any of them; nor about tom tits and snakes, and eels, which
are not necessary in a garden; but we let no facts escape us. We write for
67,000 people, the majority of whom are buyers, not sellers of flowers.'[22]
This last dig is at the gardening press being used as a medium of publicity
for nurserymen.

Despite his aggressive tone, Glenny provided good practical advice in
simple language for the whole range of gardeners, from those with
hotbeds, glasshouses and pine stoves to those with modest plots, for whom
he provided a regular feature. Thus, 'anyone with ten feet square of ground
can make a garden', with annuals such as 'sweet peas, mignonettes, French
marigolds, Virginia stocks, nasturtiums, dwarf larkspurs, candy tuft,
convolvulus minor. Scarlet beans are recommended to climb up a fence or
wall, and look gay all the summer.'[23] Of course, given his background, he
provided information about florists' flowers and notices of the shows, but
also about allotments and the cultivation of fruit and vegetables.

The main rival to *Lloyd's Weekly* was *Reynold's News*, launched in May
1850, appearing each Sunday at the price of 1½d. The founder, George
Reynolds, was a dedicated supporter of the Chartists, and aimed his paper
firmly at the working class. One man recalled how his grandfather would
club together with a group of eleven men to buy the paper, and he would
then read it to them in his nailshop. By 1855, *Reynold's Weekly*, as it was
now titled, started an occasional gardening column consisting of a couple
of paragraphs which became a regular item by 1861. Ten years later, it had
expanded again, into a weekly calendar, written by George Glenny's son,
also called George, who ran a nursery at Paxton House in Fulham.

The year 1871 marked the arrival of an important new periodical, *The
Garden*, edited by William Robinson. Robinson, born of humble Protestant
parents in Ireland in 1838, had by the age of twenty-one become foreman
in the gardens of the resplendently named Revd Sir Hunt Henry Johnson-
Walsh, 3rd Baronet, of Ballykilcavan, Vicar of Stradbally. Following a
mysterious quarrel during the severe winter of 1861, Robinson drew the

fire from the entire glasshouse range, opened the windows and by the following morning arrived in Dublin. His career, however, did not collapse: within two years he was in charge of the herbaceous section of the Royal Botanic Society's gardens in London's Regent's Park, and by 1871 had become an influential author.

Samuel Reynolds Hole described how he sat 'with my friend, William Robinson, under a tree in the Regent's Park, and suggested *The Garden* as a title for the newspaper which he proposed to publish, and which has been so powerful in its advocacy of pure horticulture of the natural, or English, school, free from rigid formalities, meretricious ornaments, gypsum, powdered bricks, cockle-shells, and bottle-ends'.[24] Robinson was an important advocate of the natural style of gardening, promoting the virtues of the traditional cottage garden, as described in Chapter 10. The other influential advocate of this style, Gertrude Jekyll, was to contribute pieces to *The Garden*. Not only did this weekly, priced at fourpence, have a new message to promulgate, but it was also revolutionary in its appearance, with decorative headings to the articles, and illustrations, including colour plates. The other papers were obliged to change their appearance and make themselves more attractive to their readers. By 1875 there was a whole range of mass-produced cheap papers, full of information and news. Importantly they could be bought at bookstalls in railway stations and stationers without a subscription. This must have made them more accessible and affordable to those on limited means who could not necessarily invest in a subscription.

William Robinson was to go further and in 1879 founded another paper, *Gardening Illustrated*, costing just one penny and aimed at what he called 'the smaller class of gardens', including window gardeners. Like Glenny a generation earlier, Robinson could be highly provocative, maintaining a long-running feud with Shirley Hibberd, beginning with an asparagus competition, continuing with circulation figures and ending with mutual racist remarks, presumably because Robinson was Irish and Hibberd was English. However, the garden periodical establishment had to go where Robinson led, and two new weekly papers appeared in 1884, both costing a penny. In its first issue the *Gardening World Illustrated* asked the pertinent question of why they were launching yet another paper for gardeners. Its answer was that there were 'fully a million persons deeply imbued with a love for gardening'. The second paper was *Amateur Gardening* 'For Town and Country, For the Home Garden, Villa Farm, Poultry Yard, Bee Shed and Housekeeper's Room', under the editorship of Shirley Hibberd. The subtitle would suggest that the working-class gardener was not the likely target, but a new paper from Robinson, *Cottage Gardening*, might well have been aimed at this market. A review in the *Country Gentleman* for 13 January 1894 described it as a 'publication emphatically one for households of poorer classes', with its price of one halfpenny.

It is very difficult to know how many working-class gardeners did take one or more of these papers, with the picture muddied by the fact that cottage gardening had become the fashionable style. However, the formation of village garden societies and local gardeners' groups in towns and cities made it possible for members to club together to take out subscriptions on even the more expensive periodicals. Strangely, although *Lloyd's Weekly* had introduced George Glenny's gardening column back in 1852, other national newspapers did not follow suit until the beginning of the twentieth century.

Gardening periodicals not only proliferated during the nineteenth century, but also influenced the production of books. In the *Gardener's Magazine* for May 1834 John Claudius Loudon provided a list of useful books to promote horticultural skills among cottagers. For those who could hardly read, he recommended Charles Lawrence's *Practical Directions and General Management of Cottage Gardens*. For those who could read *and* think, he commended John Denson's *Peasant Voices* and his own *Cottage Manual*.

Charles Lawrence, a member of the Council of the Royal Agricultural Society of England, published his book in 1831. 'In setting out allotments of land to supply all of you with gardens, I have been guided as to quantity, chiefly, by the number of persons in each family; my intention has been to allot to each of you just as much land as I thought each family might be able to cultivate properly, without interfering with their regular labour for *wages*.' Lawrence advises that there should be a rotation of crops, providing a plan for one-quarter of an acre, with each bed laid out. Eleven beds are recommended, with alleys a foot wide between each, and lists of vegetables are given in what he considers the descending order of nourishment, beginning with lentils, going through beans and peas, to potatoes, carrots, turnips and greens. He strongly advises keeping a pig, with advice on how to house and feed it. Even the duties of the gardener's wife are laid down: she should 'have a regular time, every day, allotted for the performance of her various duties; and should so arrange them, as to devote as much time as possible, of the most favourable part of the day, to the garden'.[25]

Lawrence writes clearly, in the tone of a teacher talking to a pupil, and does not seem to be someone who could 'hardly read'.

John Denson, a smallholder and self-styled peasant, came from Waterbeach, a fen-edge village a few miles north of Cambridge. His book is similar in its message, advocating spade husbandry and self-sufficiency, but is contingent on having enough land on which to cultivate the garden. Loudon's *Cottage Manual* contains a series of essays submitted as a result of a competition held in the *Gardener's Magazine* in 1827.[26] The winner, 'the Cottarman's Friend' from Perthshire, demonstrated how a family could produce not only food, but also fuel, malt, sugar, cider, wines and spirits, tobacco, substitutes for tea and coffee, opium and other medicines. It is highly unlikely that any of these publications would have been purchased by the gardeners themselves. Much more probable is that they were provided by their landlords or the local clergyman to supplement the knowledge passed down from family forebears. The provision of such advice was a continuing practice. For example, George Johnson, the editor of *Cottage Gardener*, offered in the issue of 1857 his 'Manuals for the Many', which were sold at discount to 'clergymen and gentlemen who wished to distribute them to their parishioners'.[27]

In the gardening column of *Lloyd's Weekly*, George Glenny offered illustrated treatises on individual flowers, such as calceolarias and fuchsias, published, naturally, by Edward Lloyd and sold at the amazingly cheap price of one penny. He also offered monthly gardening guides for a penny, or bound up for a whole year for 1s 6d. Technical advances, such as linen bindings, cheaper sources of paper and rotary presses made it possible for books to be produced at moderate prices, within the means of working-class readers. At the end of the century, Samuel Reynolds Hole was able to recommend gardening books produced in a series by Macmillans, priced at one shilling. One, *Garden Flowers and Plants: A Primer for Amateurs*, was written by John Wright, the Chief Instructor for the county councils of Surrey and Kent (see above, p. 202). Hole was now Dean of Rochester, so was able to attend Wright's lectures in Kent.[28] In the preface to *Garden Flowers and Plants*, published in 1895, Wright made the familiar claim that his book would inform and inspire a wide range of readers, from 'ladies and gentlemen who manage their own gardens', to 'tradesmen and cottagers'. However, he went on to note how 'The importance of domestic gardening is now recognised by the Board of Education as a legitimate subject for teaching in elementary and continuation schools, and a great impetus will thus be given to the work in its various aspects, including

Floriculture'. At last this claim to reach working class gardeners, in towns and the countryside, would seem to be justified.

Being taught and reading about gardening were important sources of inspiration, but so too was direct observation. John Duncan, so deprived in many ways, was fortunate that among his friends were professional gardeners, in particular Charles Black. He was thus able to visit the gardens looked after by his friends and acquaintances, and see the growing habits of the plants, the ideal sites and conditions for planting. Charles Black's brother worked in the gardens of the Duke of Devonshire at Chatsworth in Derbyshire, and these gardens were in fact opened to the public. Robert Aughtie, an under-gardener at Chatsworth, recorded in his diary how the opening of the railway line to Rowsley in June 1849 made possible day trips from Derby. On 20 June he wrote: 'A large company of Derby folks came today by a special train to see Chatsworth – they were taken round in parties of from twenty to thirty. The Duke seemed much pleased with them, walking about and among them.'[29] Although entrance to the grounds was free, the trips were organised on Wednesdays, so the visitors were likely to be artisans and shopkeepers. A report some years later in the *Gardener* described a Whit Monday open day at Chatsworth: 'Here were pale-faced men and women from the cotton factories of Manchester, dark denizens of the Staffordshire potteries, and the sharp, active-looking mechanics of Leeds, Bradford, and Halifax, all brought hither on special trains, and, in the full heyday of an English holiday, rushing through the gorgeously-fitted-up rooms of the ducal mansion – admiring the conservatories, rockeries and fountains.'[30]

Other stately homes also opened up their grounds on occasion, but these were regarded as days out rather than horticultural experiences. There were, however, more opportunities on offer to urban working-class gardeners through botanical gardens and public parks. The first parks in London to open to the public in the seventeenth century were former royal hunting grounds, St James's, Hyde Park and Green Park, to be followed later by Kensington Gardens and Regent's Park. In the early nineteenth century it was recognised that urban communities needed open spaces for recreation, especially as towns and cities were becoming densely populated, and walking out into the surrounding countryside was increasingly difficult. The working class was regarded by many in authority as a potential political threat, especially following the unrest surrounding the passing of the Great Reform Bill of 1832, the rise of Chartism, and subsequently of trade unions. The Parliamentary Select Committee on the Health of

Towns reported in 1840 that improvement in the provision of parks was essential not only for the welfare of the poor, but also for the safety of property and security of the rich.

For those who lived in east London, it was possible to visit the famous London nursery belonging to the Loddiges family, established off Mare Street in Hackney in the mid-eighteenth century by John Busch from Hanover, and taken over by fellow German émigré, Conrad Loddiges. Successive generations of the Loddiges family added to the nursery, and by 1820 the greenhouses and walks had become a popular public attraction. Loudon, who designed a magnificent camellia house for Loddiges, described the arboretum, the first of its kind in England: 'The arboretum looks better this season than it has ever done since it was planted . . . We walked round the two outer spirals of this coil of trees and shrubs; viz from Acer to Quercus. There is no garden scene about London so interesting.'[31] The nursery was free to the public for their educational benefit every Sunday, the one day when the working classes were able to visit. This custom was continued in other nurseries: in Devon, for instance, Charles Sclater, Luccombe & Pince, and Veitch in Exeter all opened their establishments to the public.[32]

The opening of the first new public park in England was an honour claimed by the city of Derby, where an arboretum designed by John Claudius Loudon was opened in 1840. The land was given by a local textile manufacturer, Joseph Strutt, who stipulated that 'the artisans' should have free access on two days a week. He wanted them to 'enjoy a rare opportunity of expanding their minds by the contemplation of nature', but as the days were Wednesday and Saturday, working days, this rather limited their visits. Loudon, as ever, was much keener on expanding minds by education, and laid the arboretum out with serpentine paths winding their way round mounds where the trees were planted, so that visitors could study individual specimens. The trees were carefully labelled, with more written information available on request. In 1847 the first municipal park available for the free recreation of local residents was opened in Birkenhead. Known as the 'People's Park', it was designed by Joseph Paxton. Each half of the park contained an irregularly shaped lake with an island. Rockwork and shrubberies concealed and channelled views, a style adopted in other parks that were established in cities all over Britain, fuelled by civic pride.

Botanical gardens were also opened, such as Sefton Park in Liverpool and West Park in Wolverhampton, with extensive glasshouses containing collections of exotics and tropical plants informatively displayed, reflecting the increasing interest in science. In 1841 William Hooker opened the Royal Botanic Gardens at Kew on weekday afternoons, despite the opposition of the Queen, who claimed that they provided her only place to exercise. In the first year 9,000 visited, but the numbers then rose rapidly, and when the gardens were opened on a Sunday over 64,000 people visited. By the end of the century, the figures had reached over a million. For those who could not travel easily westwards to Kew, there were the gardens at Crystal Palace on Sydenham Hill, opened by Joseph Paxton. He offered cheaper tickets on a Sunday for working men, provoking a fierce debate in the press, with the *Morning Herald* seeking to terrify readers by suggesting that this was 'an introduction to that Continental view of the Sabbath' which began with Popery and led to the riots in Paris, Munich and Berlin in 1848.[33] *The Times*, on the other hand, pointed out that it was stupid and inhumane to suggest that 'the working Londoner ought to spend his Sunday in his own dark and dismal hole, breathing the reeking atmosphere of close courts and yards'.[34]

Working-class families certainly enjoyed these open spaces as an escape from a life of overcrowding, squalor and ill-health, but would have found the identification of trees and exotic plants in glasshouses of little relevance to the cultivation of their small gardens and backyards. However, flower beds also began to be introduced into public parks and botanic gardens. At the Botanic Garden in Birmingham, for instance, Loudon arranged borders apparently borrowed from the patterns of old-fashioned muslin and printed calicoes.

Extravagant bedding displays, especially of pelargoniums and calceolarias, became the fashion. The *Cottage Gardener* in 1858 noted with a certain amount of disdain that brilliant masses of the strongest colours were the most likely to attract the attention of the crowd. A more charitable response came from the *Gardener's Chronicle* when flower beds were introduced to London's Hyde Park in 1859: 'Flowers are wanted in the people's parks just because the people's houses have no gardens, and ninetenths of those who frequent the parks have no opportunities of seeing growing flowers anywhere else'.[35]

Undoubtedly the best example of the combination of recreation and horticultural inspiration for the working classes was Victoria Park, in the East End of London. The royal parks were all located in the western part of the capital, but the most densely populated areas lay to the east. The development of the docks along the Thames east of the Pool of London drew a huge workforce and, by the 1830s, 400,000 people were living in east London. These included the Irish around the docks, poor Jewish immigrants in Whitechapel, and the silk workers, many facing destitution, in Bethnal Green and Spitalfields. Not only were they crammed into over-crowded accommodation, but were also prey to outbreaks of disease such as cholera and typhoid, as described by Dr Gavin in his *Sanitary Ramblings* (see Chapter 6, pp. 159–60). In 1839 the sanitary reformer William Farr wrote:

> A park in the East End of London would probably diminish the annual deaths by several thousands . . . and add several years to the lives of the entire population. The poorer classes would be benefited by these measures, and the poor taxes reduced. But all classes of the community are directly interested . . . for the epidemics . . . which arise in the east end of the town do not stay there, they travel to the west end and prove fatal in wide streets and squares: the registers show this.[36]

When even this call to the self-interest of the Establishment did not get immediate results, the locals began to act. On 10 June 1840 George Frederick Young, MP, convened a meeting of some 'gentlemen of Tower Hamlets' at his home in Limehouse, where it was resolved: 'That consid-ering the density of the population of the Eastern districts, it was of the highest importance that a large open space should be secured for the purpose of forming a park.'[37] A subsequent public meeting at the London Tavern in Bishopsgate drew up a petition that attracted 30,000 signatures after circulation in Tower Hamlets.

This petition, addressed to the Queen, pointed out that:

> while the Artisans, Manufacturers, Labourers and others, composing this vast population are, by their ceaseless toil contributing to these important advantages [the docks, the silk trade, and noxious industries such as sugar refining] adding wealth to the community and stability to the Crown, we feel assured, that it cannot fail to excite your Majesty's generous sympathy, to be informed, that a large proportion of them are exposed to privations and calamities, of which we would gladly spare your Majesty the recital.[38]

The text was not entirely sparing, for it goes on at length, mentioning epidemic diseases and pointing out that Victoria's predecessors had allowed inhabitants of western London to use the royal parks there.

44 & 45 Gardeners working on the scroll beds in Victoria Park, east London, around 1900. The plants favoured for this type of decorative bedding were sempervivums, cerastiums and pyrethrums.

However, it did gain the Queen's generous sympathy and the proceeds of the sale of a house in St James's Palace that had belonged to her bankrupt uncle, the Duke of York, were set aside to buy land for the park.

The site chosen lay between the densely populated area of Tower Hamlets to the south and the semi-rural villages of Hackney to the north. In earlier times it had been the hunting park of the bishops of London, a point of contention with local residents who also wanted to hunt deer and course hares and rabbits there. A reminder of this past was Bonner's Fields, named after Mary Tudor's bishop, notorious for burning Protestant martyrs. By the early nineteenth century Bonner's Fields had become the location for prize fights, gambling and political meetings, including Chartist rallies. The land, nearly 300 acres, had been mostly used for market gardens, grazing and gravel extraction. The principal landowners, St Thomas's Hospital and the estate of Sir John Cass, agreed to sell without demur, but some of the individual market gardeners proved more awkward and the locals grew so impatient at the negotiations that they started to use the park in 1843 before the borders had been defined. The original intention had been to sell off some of the land around the periphery for building houses for upper-class clientele, but this never

materialised, and Victoria Park is surrounded by more modest terraced developments.

Despite financial support from the Crown, Victoria Park was run by the Metropolitan Board of Works, and the man appointed to create the landscape was James Pennethorne, architect to the Commissioners of Woods and Forests. Pennethorne, who had worked with John Nash on the layout of Regent's Park, was dismayed at the flatness of the terrain, so wanted to make good use of trees. His first permanent superintendent, Samuel Curtis, editor and proprietor of the *Botanical Magazine* and son of William, ran a nursery and orchard out in Essex, at Coggeshall, and was particularly knowledgeable about trees. He suggested a whole series of trees and 'coarse shrubs' such as lilac, spirea, guelder rose and tamarisk, so that from the very beginning Victoria Park had both colour and scent.[39]

The park was an instant success, and not only among the local working classes. The *Illustrated London News* reported in 1846: 'On Sunday and for many weeks past the visitors have exceeded 10,000, and amongst them were many from the west-end, upward of thirty carriages being outside the principal lodge entrance on Sunday between four and six o'clock. Three coroneted carriages were there at one time – an event, perhaps, unknown in the previous history of the parish.'[40]

Snobbish prejudices abounded, with assumptions that working-class visitors would invade the flower beds and steal the plants, but they were proved wrong. The vicar of St Philip's, Bethnal Green, in a letter to *The Times* observed:

> There is, I believe, a very general opinion entertained, though I think it a very erroneous one, that the poorer classes in this country cannot be trusted, unless under the *surveillance* of the police, in any place of public amusement, from a wanton disposition to injure or destroy whatever is beautiful in nature or curious in art . . . Now when it knows that there have been planted in various parts of the park roses and other flowers of various kinds entirely unprotected, and that in only one solitary instance throughout the summer has a rose or flower of any kind been plucked or injured, this fact alone is sufficient to refute the unjust aspersion that the poorer classes are not to be trusted in public places without the dread of the police before their eyes.

George Glenny concurred in *Lloyd's Weekly*, declaring that unlike some of the parks to the west and south of London, where the behaviour of the public was not always all it should be, at Victoria Park '20,000 men, women and children enjoy themselves on a summer's evening, and appear to hold the floral beauties sacred'.[41]

Just in case there should be outbreaks of bad behaviour, rowdy sports were not encouraged in Victorian public parks. Instead, genteel activities such as bowls, archery and cricket were permitted, along with the provision of facilities such as lakes for boating and bathing, refreshment areas and bandstands. Victoria Park had all of these: the old gravel pits were transformed into lakes, tea rooms were introduced and regular concerts were held. But the old spirit of Bonner's Fields had not entirely disappeared, and rallies were frequently held in the park, some religious, others political. After William Morris spoke at a Socialist League rally under the banner 'No Coercion' on 21 May 1887, he wrote to his daughter Jenny how he had had to compete against the noise of a brass band, and that in his grey cloak he was regarded as a picturesque oddity, with passers-by shouting after him, 'Yah Shakespeare!'[42]

George Bernard Shaw addressed a similar meeting and has left a vivid description of the park and its facilities:

> Near the outer end of the Hackney Road is a Park of 217 acres, fenced in, not by railings, but by a wooden paling, and containing plenty of greensward, trees, a lake for bathers, flower beds which are triumphs of

I Poplar Cottage at the Weald and Downland Museum. The cottage, brought from Washington in Sussex, dates from the early to mid-seventeenth century and probably belonged to a landless husbandman. The garden has been recreated to show how it was given over to practical plants, cultivated in beds separated by narrow paths, which would be used in the kitchen, the medicine chest, and for dyeing and brewing.

II  Bayleaf Farmstead at the Weald and Downland Museum. This timber-framed hall house, dating from the 1540s, was brought from Chiddingstone in Kent. It would originally have been the home of a yeoman farmer. Its extensive garden of vegetables, herbs and fruit is protected by a fence of intertwined hazel branches.

III  Bee skeps of plaited straw in the garden of Bayleaf Farmstead. Hives are depicted in early gardening books, such as Thomas Hill's *Gardeners Labyrinth*, standing in shelters like this to protect them from the wind and rain.

IV The back garden of a seventeenth-century house from the Sussex village of Walderton, which is now at the Weald and Downland Museum. In the centre is one of the beds for the cultivation of vegetables and salad herbs, while the wooden planks on the right protect a bed for the cultivation of pompions, or pumpkins.

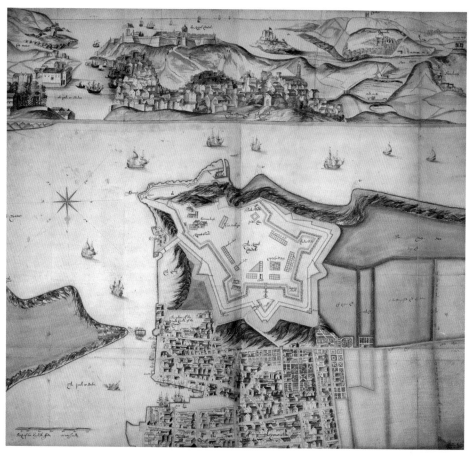

V  Sir Bernard de Gomme's plan, in ink and watercolour, of the citadel and town of Plymouth in Devon in 1672. On the outskirts of the town, gardens are shown; some of them were clearly detached grounds.

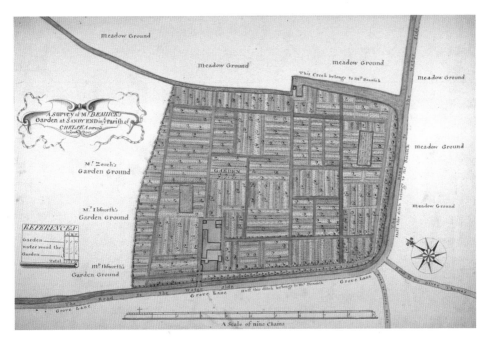

VI Mr Beawick's market garden near Grove Lane in Chelsea, from a survey made in 1744. The garden was just over seven acres in area, laid out in strips with walkways and two 'dipping pools'. The locality was particularly favourable for market gardening, with sandy soil and a surrounding creek to supply water.

VII Watercolour by C.H. Mathews of Kingsland Road in Hackney. The artist painted the picture in 1852, but it shows how the area would have looked at the beginning of the nineteenth century when the market gardens, on the right, were giving way to terraces of houses constructed with the bricks being manufactured on the left.

IX 'King's Cross, London: The Great Dust-Heap, next to Battle Bridge and the Smallpox Hospital', a watercolour by E.H. Dixon, 1837. The heap, which evokes the enterprise of the Golden Dustman in Charles Dickens's *Our Mutual Friend*, was finally removed in 1848 to make way for the railway terminus of King's Cross. Allotments can be seen cheek by jowl with the rubbish.

VIII A watercolour by George Johann Scharf of Unity Place in Woolwich, 1825. The tiny front gardens are enclosed behind picket fences, and pots of flowers are shown at some of the windows. Estate agents would now describe these as 'bijou urban cottages'; in the Regency period they would have been the homes of the artisans and lower middle classes.

X Three different varieties of pansies, from Joseph Harrison's *Floricultural Cabinet*, from about 1835. Pansies had become the object of interest to florists, who developed the heart-shaped flower of the wild pansy, or heartsease, into an increasingly stylised circular form.

XI The dahlia made its first appearance in British gardens in the early nineteenth century and proved a sensational success. The ideal for florists was the ball shape, with a sphere of geometrically arranged petals. These were known as 'show dahlias' or 'fancy dahlias'. This chromolithograph made around 1870 shows the Dr Frampton dahlia.

XII  A gardener scything in a grand formal garden in the 1860s.

XIII  A cottage garden depicted in a watercolour by Myles Birket Foster. Unlike similar images from the Victorian period, this has no romantic connotations, showing an elderly lady tending her vegetable patch, with washing drying over a dilapidated fence.

XIV  Helen Allingham's painting of Peacock Cottage in West Horsley, Surrey, from *The Cottage Gardens of England*, written with Stewart Dick and published in 1909. As the name of the cottage suggests, one of the features is a topiary peacock, and there is also a monkey puzzle tree on the right.

XV & XVI Late nineteenth-century stone gnomes from the garden of a country house in Scotland.

XVII 'Pests in the Garden', a cartoon from the 1930s showing the perils that might befall an inexperienced urban gardener.

XVIII  An allotment in Bethnal Green, painted in 1943 by Charles Ginner.

XIX  The luxuriant balcony garden of a high-rise block in Tower Hamlets, photographed in the late 1970s.

XX 'Barrington Colliery, Bedlington' by the pitman painter, James MacKenzie. In front of the Durham colliery is the row of miners' cottages with their narrow back gardens, some filled with flowers.

XXI James MacKenzie's 'Howicking Preparing Leeks on Show Day, Alexandra Road, Barrington'. The leeks for show are traditionally displayed in pairs. One of the miners is carefully measuring his prize specimens.

the admired cockney art of carpet bedding, and a sandpit, originally imported from the sea-side for the delight of children, but speedily deserted on its becoming a natural vermin preserve for all the petty fauna of Kingsland, Hackney, and Hoxton. A bandstand, an unfurnished forum for religious, anti-religious and political orators, cricket pitches, a gymnasium, and an old fashioned stone kiosk among its attractions.[43]

The style of planting described by Bernard Shaw as the 'cockney art of carpet bedding' can be seen in old postcards where they are described as scrolled flower beds, with flat rosettes of cacti forming the border and agaves used as punctuation marks. The ornate nature of these plantings was also shown in Robert Thompson's *The Gardener's Assistant*, where he reproduced in colour designs used at Victoria Park in 1875.[44] This style was inaugurated under the supervision of John Gibson, who had worked at Chatsworth with Joseph Paxton. He recognised that with increasing air pollution short-lived, seasonal planting was more practical than attempting anything more permanent. Gibson's head gardener, William Prestoe, had 'learnt the art of embroidering nature's carpet in gorgeous masses of colour' while working at Kew Gardens, according to one newspaper article in 1863. It went on to describe how Prestoe was 'offering to the working man such flowers as he could most easily cultivate in his own little garden . . . fuchsias, dahlias, geraniums, asters, verbenas . . . It is to these flower-beds that the working man is attracted as if by some magic spell, and from their contemplation he learns how best to cultivate those little home gardens which, where possible, form the delight of his leisure hours.'[45]

Thirty-five years later Lt-Col Sexby made a similar observation:

at Victoria Park the hard-working artisan is a bit of a horticultural critic in his way. Somehow in the small back gardens and crowded yards he manages to rear many a choice specimen, so that the flowers in the adjoining park have to be kept up to the mark. The ornamental gardening alone is well worth going to see; at almost every season of the year there are bright flowers to be seen. In the spring the beds are gay with tulips, hyacinths, and other showy bulbs imported from Holland to brighten our flower-gardens. These in summer give way to every possible variety of bedding-out plants. The area is so large, and the beds so numerous, that the skill of the officials is taxed to the utmost

46 The distribution of surplus plants to residents of east London in Victoria Park, depicted in the *Illustrated London News*, 8 November 1879. The accompanying text extols this 'laudable custom at the close of the floral season, of distributing gratuitously to respectable people, households or lodgers in the inferior quarters of London . . . for small gardens or window-boxes'. Tickets or letters of introduction were issued by clergymen and managers of hospitals and orphanages. The favourite flowers 'cherished with fervent enthusiasm in parts of east London' were geraniums, calceolarias and lobelias.

to infuse sufficient variety into the whole of the large surface. Something like 200,000 plants are bedded out annually.[46]

In 1860 government instructions were issued to distribute plants to the poor after they had been removed from the beds of public parks at the end of the summer, and an engraving in the *Illustrated London News* for 8 November 1879 shows the distribution of plants from Victoria Park to locals, including boys taking a cartload to the workhouse. These plants were exhausted and needed a greenhouse to keep them going through the winter months, but as one writer wryly pointed out, 'the backstreet horticulturalist does not believe in looking a gift-horse in the mouth. He takes what he can get and makes the best of it.'[47] Victoria Park continued the tradition of giving out plants right through to the 1930s.

Shirley Hibberd, living in Stoke Newington, knew Victoria Park well, and in the *Gardener's Magazine* in 1862 provided substantial descriptions of the annual bedding schemes, including plans of the main beds with names.[48] He explained that the designs were possible to reproduce on a small scale in a modest garden, and that identifying labels were provided in the park to enable visitors to buy the same varieties for themselves. He also detailed the resources available to William Prestoe: a span-roofed house, about 40 by 12 feet, and a frame ground of 1,000 square feet, with enough lights to cover about half.

> Of course in such a place as this propagating goes on all the year round. The little house is now filled with cuttings [of geraniums], mostly three or four cuttings in fifty 4-sized pots, in which they are to be wintered, and be shifted into separate pots in spring. In the pits are reserves of asters, perillas, etc. In the rear of one of the shrubberies, and quite out of sight of the public, is a small piece of nursery ground. Here we saw a fine stock of . . . calceolaria, turned out expressly to furnish cuttings for beds next year.[49]

In 1892 a small version of Paxton's Palm House at Kew was bought from Battersea Park. Local gardeners were so keen to view the exotic plants and palms that it was opened to the public, and in the winter months it proved with its heating system a popular place for courting couples and those who simply wanted to get out of the cold. A famous collection of chrysanthemums was accommodated in another glasshouse, and surplus cuttings were given free to local residents. In 1898 a scheme

47 Although the garden squares in west London were rarely open to members of the public, with access only to key-holding residents, a more relaxed policy was applied in other parts of the capital. This Edwardian postcard shows Carlton Square in east London.

was introduced whereby local schoolchildren could learn botany from twenty beds laid out with different specimens. In 1910 a miniature garden, made for the influential Japanese-British Exhibition at Shepherds Bush by Yokohama Nursery Company, was given to Victoria Park by the Mayor of Tokyo. Measuring nine by four feet, the tiny tea garden had trees that were over a hundred years old, mounted on a wheeled trolley so that it could be moved outside in fine weather.

* * *

By the end of the nineteenth century literacy figures had risen dramatically, as a result of Forster's Education Act of 1870 which aimed to provide all children with a rudimentary education. For men, the rate was now 97.2 per cent, and for women, 96.8 per cent. Technological improvements to printing and the manufacture of paper brought down the cost of books, journals and newspapers, so that sources of horticultural information were within the pockets of most gardeners.

Opportunities to see plants growing had also burgeoned, with many municipal parks providing not only displays of flowers in summer, but also examples of exotic plants in conservatories. Lectures were available, with experts able to provide information at first hand. Even social attitudes were shifting, so that in urban parks it was no longer assumed that working-class visitors would steal the flowers. And important sources of inspiration, as well as offering keen competition, were the flower shows that blossomed with the century, as will be shown in the next chapter.

# CHAPTER 9

# The Spirit of Competition

'HORTICULTURAL AND FLORICULTURAL Exhibitions . . . have within these few years been working a change in tastes and recreational pursuits of the inhabitants of this densely populated island, such as by any other cause would have defeated all the legislators of Europe', by contrast with the former public taste for 'a bear-baiting, a bull-baiting, a cock-fight, a dog-fight, or mayhap two animals in human form similarly engaged – such being the *amusements*, as they were termed, which Floricultural Exhibitions have superseded'.[1] This dramatic and sweeping claim was made in 1838 by Robert Marnock, then the curator of the Sheffield Botanicical Gardens.

Although far-fetched, it carried a ring of truth, for in the nineteenth century the whole nation became addicted to flower shows in all forms and sizes. Earlier, competitions for prized blooms had been held by florists at their feasts. It was they who set the horticultural calendar, kicking off with shows for auriculas in late April, where polyanthus and hyacinths were also exhibited, followed by the tulip show in May, sometimes also featuring anemones. In June came the turn of ranunculus, with carnations in August. In the Victorian period, the vogue for the dahlia and the chrysan-themum extended the showing season through into autumn.

At a national level, three societies were founded in the opening years of the nineteenth century: the Horticultural Society of London in 1804, the Caledonian Society in 1809 and the Hibernian Society in 1830. Declaring that the Horticultural Society of London was not catering for florists, in 1832 George Glenny set up the Metropolitan Society of Florists and Amateurs. Within a few years, Londoners were spoilt for choice. The Horticultural Society began their annual show first at Chiswick, and then in the 1860s in Kensington. The royal gardens at Kew, reorganised as the

Royal Botanic Society, held their show in the inner circle of Regents' Park. Joseph Paxton, having moved the Crystal Palace from its original site in Hyde Park to Sydenham Hill in south London, founded the Crystal Palace Company.

According to the *Gardener's Magazine* in 1836, at the Horticultural Society's Chiswick shows 'the principal part of the English aristocracy are present, and mix indiscriminately with the tradesman, the mechanic and the gardener'.[2] Like Marnock's claim this, too, was surely far-fetched, for working-class gardeners would have felt out of place and would be unlikely to be able to afford the price of admission to such events. It was working gardeners, as opposed to working-class gardeners, who took part in these grand competitions, where there were often quarrels about the fairness of judging, the status of nurserymen as opposed to amateurs, and accusations of 'purse gardening'.[3]

The burgeoning gardening press in the 1830s and 1840s was also full of reports about the activities of florists. Most of the old florists' feasts were in decline but their place was taken by organisations that concentrated on individual flowers. For example, the first society devoted to chrysanthemums was established in Stoke Newington, then a semi-rural village to the north-east of the City of London. Many of the chrysanthemums introduced into Britain by the plant hunter Robert Fortune in 1846 were acquired by Samuel Brookes, whose nursery lay to the south of Stoke Newington, and he specialised in their cultivation and sold them to local gardeners. Meeting at the Rochester Castle tavern in the village's high street in that same year, a group of professional gardeners formed the Stoke Newington Florists' Society for the Cultivation and Exhibition of the Chrysanthemum. A competition for a stand of twelve blooms was held in an upstairs room, with a dinner to follow. The society's formation was watched with interest by Shirley Hibberd, also a native of Stoke Newington, who later reported its history in the *Gardener's Magazine*.[4] Other societies followed in Bermondsey, Kennington and Camden Town. Shirley Hibberd felt that the London interest was due to the fact that in the month of November, with practically no daylight thanks to soot and fog, the golden flowers shone out, and even looked good by gaslight. More money was taken during one hour after 6 p.m. at a chrysanthemum show than at any other time of the day.

These societies were dominated by working gardeners. But a few miles south of Stoke Newington, floricultural societies with a very different class composition were being formed. Although the 'hamlets' of Tower Hamlets, which included Whitechapel, Stepney, Bethnal Green and Poplar, had enjoyed a strong tradition of horticulture, housing developments to accommodate the huge rise in population had subsumed many of the gardens. One newspaper in 1863 reported:

> Hollybush-place, Green-street, Pleasant-place, and other neighbourhoods, which now consist of ruinous tenements reeking with abominations, were outlying decent cottages, standing on or near plots of garden ground, where the inmates reared prize tulips and rare dahlias in their scanty leisure, and where some of the last of the old French refugees dozed away the evenings of their lives in pretty summerhouses, amidst flower-beds gay with virginia stocks and creeping plants.[5]

However, the horticultural appetites of the inhabitants had not been sated. The first annual dinner of the Tower Hamlets Chrysanthemum Society was held on 5 December 1859 at the Eagle Tavern in the Mile End. Chairman of the society was the gardening journalist George Glenny, who noted with satisfaction how floriculture had 'never made such progress among the people as within the last 18 months'. He also quoted another guest at the dinner, Samuel Broome, head gardener of the Inner Temple, that the chrysanthemum 'was the only flower the working man could successfully cultivate without an expense beyond his means'.[6] Broome's magnificent displays of the flower each autumn at the Temple's gardens on the Thames were a potent attraction for working-class gardeners, and he was a great supporter of floral societies, later being described as 'the floral oracle for the working classes'.[7] In 1861 he wrote to the editor of the *Penny Illustrated Paper*: 'The working classes are getting passionately fond of flowers, and those among them who enjoy the advantage of a sunny spot of ground out of town cultivate them in their leisure hours on summer evenings as an amusement. They form themselves into little societies. They exhibit their productions in friendly rivalry with one another, and those who are successful go away highly delighted with their prizes.'[8]

The prizes were worth the delight. The East London Amateur Horticultural Society, based in Bow, not only gave money at their shows but also 'various articles of household use and ornament' such as 'a handsome timepiece and tea and coffee services, and a pair of lustres, a chased cup; and a cruet stand', according to the *Gardener's Magazine*. The paper

went on to observe: 'Such a mode of connecting home comfort with horticulture is to be commended and we hope many other societies will follow
the good example set by the friends at Bow.'[9] The East London Society's
two particular innovations were establishing a show for spring flowers, and
setting the tradition of giving fuchsia cuttings to the children of local
schools, who could then exhibit them for prizes in the summer show.

George Glenny, as has already been observed, was 'the horticultural
hornet', and just as his journalism stirred up all kinds of arguments, so his
presence in the Tower Hamlets Society brought about controversy. The
Chrysanthemum Show in November 1863 was expanded to run for three
days, and thus coincided with the first Great Chrysanthemum Show held
at the Agricultural Halls in Islington. One member therefore removed his
winning plants early from the former to take to the latter, where he once
again was awarded first prize. At the annual dinner Glenny declared that
he had broken the rules of the Tower Hamlets Society, while the current
chairman, William Eickhoff, felt that the awarding of the prize in
Islington had brought them honour. Glenny used his column in *Lloyd's
Weekly* and in other magazines to continue the debate to such effect that
in August 1864 two rival societies held their shows at almost the same
time: the Tower Hamlets Society at the Eagle Tavern, and the East Tower
Hamlets Society in the Edinboro' Castle in Stepney. The debate raged on,
with the local press carrying accusations of all kinds of malpractice.
Eickhoff, now chairman of the East Tower Hamlets Society, kept a file of
the insulting names used by Glenny, such as 'bounceable young gentlemen',
'scavengers who have scraped together the refuse of chrysanthemum societies' and 'men of incapacity and of miserably low grade of intellect who can
neither write a sentence in plain English nor spell the most common
word'. Glenny's last lash at Eickhoff was to describe him as the 'hired
chairman of a pot house in Whitechapel'.[10] This unfortunate episode
shows how seriously members of floral societies took their flower growing
and showing, and how important it was for them to observe the rules that
governed floral societies right across the nation. It also underlines the
crucial point that these were societies for working men, run by working
men, without being imposed upon by those who considered themselves
their moral and social superiors.[11]

Another east London group was the Lea Bridge Horticultural Society,
formed in 1864. These gardeners were not so much florists as holders of
allotment gardens. The following year an article about them appeared in
the evangelical magazine, the *Day of Rest*:

We know of one long plot of land at Lea Bridge station, on the Great Eastern Railway, which is entirely let out in small strips to 'Londoners', who build a little summer-house at one end, and come down of an evening, or on a Saturday half-holiday, to 'do their gardening', and on Sunday bring their friends to admire the result; which, by the way, is very creditable, for we have often seen some fine beds of tulips and other flowers, which would have done credit to many a nobler ground. Every summer, too, a 'show' is held, and a brass band is engaged to finish the day with a dance in an adjoining field.[12]

The Lea Bridge Society made a feature of floral decorations and miniature gardens at their shows. While the category for floral decorations was one in which women could compete, miniature gardens were very much the territory of men. Some idea of the ingenuity of these gardens can be found in one of Gertrude Jekyll's books, in which she told of a lad who 'minded his mule' in a mill in one of the great northern manufacturing towns, who wrote to her asking for somebody to help him with a window box through advertising in a mechanical paper. Jekyll decided to be his patron, sending

48 'An East End Flower Show' as recorded in the *Day of Rest* for 1873, held in a local church hall.

him a box three by ten inches in size, containing little plants of mossy and silvery saxifrage, a few small bulbs, and some stones (it was to be a rock garden with hills and a valley). Correspondence ensued, with Jekyll advising him to stop killing his plants by kindness with liberal doses of artificial manure.[13]

The trend in the late nineteenth century was for national societies to be established for individual flowers. The Stoke Newington Society became the National Chrysanthemum Society in 1883, while the Hammersmith Heartsease Society, founded in 1841, was transformed into the National Pansy and Viola Society in 1911. The move to have a national society for roses went down a rather different route. The first national rose show was held in St James's Hall in Regent's Street in London on 3 July 1858, but it was to be another twenty years before a National Rose Society was established. However, it was the same man who inaugurated both, Dean Hole, who was a native of Nottinghamshire. The county was famous for its roses, and Hole inherited this attachment to the flower, growing around 400 varieties at Caunton Manor, his home near Newark.

Dean Hole comes over in his writings as a genial man, possessed with good sense, and he was certainly no snob. In 1859, a year after establishing the national rose show, he was invited by the framework knitters of Nottingham to judge their local show. His description of this is contained in his *Book about Roses*, which he published in 1904, where he provides a vivid account of a working-class competition. The show was to be held on Easter Monday, an unseasonable time of the year for roses, so Hole at first took the invitation as an April Fool's joke. However, he was assured that 'the Roses in question were grown under glass – *where* and *how*, the growers would be delighted to show me, if I would oblige them by my company'. He was met from the station by the landlord of the General Cathcart Inn, who sported a 'Senateur Vaisse' in his buttonhole, 'which glowed amid the gloom like the red light on a midnight train'.

The competition took place in a long narrow room, where the roses were set out on tables, with single blooms displayed in the necks of beer bottles. Hole was astonished by the quality of the blooms: 'I have never seen better specimens of cut Roses, grown under glass, than those which were exhibited by these working men'. He appreciated that among the exhibits were specimens of moderate quality, or even failure, such as 'a small and sickly exposition of Paul Ricaut, who, by some happy coincidence which warmed my whole body with laughter, was appropriately placed in a large medicine-bottle, with a label requesting that the wretched invalid might be well rubbed every night and morning. Poor Paul! A gentle touch would have sent him to *pot-pourri!*' After delivering his judgement, Hole was taken to see the workers' little allotments and glass-houses: '*Houses!* Why, a full-sized giant would have taken them up like a hand-glass . . . [I] was unable in most of them to stand upright, and into some to enter at all. That "bit o' glass" had been, nevertheless, as much a dream, and hope, and happiness to its owner as the Crystal Palace to Paxton.' He noted that a timber merchant on the road from Nottingham offered five-guinea greenhouses, glazed, painted and complete, a substantial outlay for a stockinger's pocket. Most of the rose-growers, being practical men, had resorted to their own constructions.

In conversation with the gardeners, Hole found that although they habitually had to walk a mile from their home to the allotments, nevertheless during the winter months they were tending their flowers before and after work. This reminded him of how a lady living near Nottingham who went about much among the poorer classes, found that the coverlet was missing from the bed in one home. Her immediate reaction was that it had been pawned, but the wife revealed it had gone to keep the frost out of the green-house. 'And please ma'am, we don't want it, and we're quite hot in bed.'[14]

For those who lived in the centre of cities, with no chance of even the smallest plot of land and with the tiniest of incomes, there were still flower shows. One great proponent of Window Garden Shows for the Poor was the Revd Samuel Hadden Parkes, the senior curate at St George's Bloomsbury, whose observations on window gardening were noted in Chapter 6. In June 1862 he read a paper before the social economy section of the National Association for the Promotion of Social Science at London's Guildhall in which he talked of the recent innovation of flower shows for the poor in towns, where 'garden ground there is none, where the air is impure, where the sun's rays can scarcely pierce through the dust and smoke'. Under such conditions, it might seem that such a project would be impossible, but flower shows had been tried twice in his own parish, and each time 'have been crowned with marked, and almost unexpected success'.[15] Parkes reminded his audience that his parishioners were some of the poorest in the capital. In a later book he described the living conditions: 'The houses in which these people generally dwell contain six or eight rooms, each of which is occupied by one family. Some of these houses are in a fair state of repair, but the majority are in a very unhealthy and dilapidated condition. The cellars are almost invariably inhabited, and in some instances there are families residing in both the front and back cellar or kitchen.'

To prepare for the first show, held in 1860, he had handbills printed to remind exhibitors that they must have their plants in their possession for at least four weeks in advance, and an inspector was sent round to check, just in case they had visited Covent Garden to make a covert purchase. Cash prizes, much more attractive than useful domestic articles, were offered, ranging from one to five shillings. The competition was confined to fuchsias, geraniums and annuals in three classes: for fathers and mothers not flower dealers, for flower dealers and for children. The entrance fee to the show, which was held in the Bible Mission Room, was one penny for adults and a halfpenny for children. Forms were arranged in tiers around the room, decorated with green tissue paper to look like 'real' flower shows. The flowers arrived in a collection of broken tea-pots, jugs 'with dilapidated noses', and washing basins, but the exhibitors had taken pains to present them attractively: 'nearly all the flower-pots were either freshly raddled, or tastefully adorned with old scraps of gaily coloured paper'.[16] A total of 140 plants were registered four weeks before the show, though only 94 reached the Mission Room, as some had flowered too early, and others had not flowered at all. The aim of the show was not to reach the heights of horticultural quality, but to bring colour and scent and recreational interest into lives that were bedevilled by hardship. And, as Parkes was a clergyman, he believed that 'flowers speak of God and for God where God is too often entirely forgotten', a reference to beer shops and other temptations.[17]

A second show was held the following year, on a larger scale and with great success, this time in the National Schoolroom. Various categories were added so that the inhabitants of the smaller courtyards and darker dens of Coram Street did not lose out. Only the mews produced a disappointing contribution. The best class proved to be domestic servants, with the judges pronouncing that 'some of the plants would have done credit to any green-house'.[18]

The success of these shows inspired others. Parkes was able to report at his Guildhall lecture that the Revd Coxhead in the parish of St Clement Danes and Miss Oxley, the Honorary Secretary of the Fitzroy Market Ragged School, had organised similar events. The philanthropist Lord Shaftesbury presented the prizes at the latter, something he was going to do with increasing frequency. The *Penny Illustrated Paper* covered the event, which it described as 'a novel and interesting addition to the ordinary operations of a ragged school' and set the scene in the room 'crowded throughout the day by visitors, who seemed astonished that such choice

49 A working man tending his window box in anticipation of the local flower show, an illustration from Samuel Hadden Parkes's *Window Gardens for the People*, published in 1864.

floral productions could be reared by the poor inhabitants of such a district'.[19] The event was completed by the presence of the band of the Grotto Passage Ragged School.

The third Bloomsbury Show in 1863 was yet more ambitious, held in Russell Square in a spacious tent. Although Samuel Broome had been opening the gardens of the Temple so that the public might enjoy the displays of chrysanthemums and there was general access to the London parks, the capital's private squares were off-limits to all but the residents of the surrounding houses. A report written on 5 May, previewing the Bloomsbury show, asked with some exasperation:

> And where does the reader suppose this flower show is to be held? On the top of a house? In a stable? In the Museum Reading-room? Or in the sanded parlour of a public house? In none of these places, but in one less likely than all, but the most suitable for the purpose imaginable. The inhabitants of Russell-square have consented to allow the exhibition to be held in their garden, which sounds as if the end of the world was near at hand.[20]

This was an early shot in a long battle, which included high-profile supporters for greater access, such as Octavia Hill, who talked about green lungs for ordinary people, and William Robinson, who had been inspired by Napoleon III's reforms to the open spaces in Paris.

The event was illustrated in the *Penny Illustrated Paper* for 18 July 1863, as was the fourth show in the *Illustrated London News* the following July. Both pictures showed remarkably well-dressed people thronging the tent and the surrounding gardens. These were presumably the middle-class residents of the area, who were able to attend in the afternoon by purchasing shilling tickets. Exhibitors were offered a free ticket both for the afternoon and the evening, while other, poorer parishioners could only attend the show from late afternoon until 8 p.m. According to Samuel Parkes, 'Upwards of 3,000 persons, rich and poor together' were entertained by two bands.[21] The 1864 show was attended by Charles Dickens, who described in *All the Year Round* how the marquee was filled with roses, fuchsias, geraniums, balsam, convolvulus, mignonette and dahlias.[22] The event was also covered by the *Holborn and Bloomsbury Journal*, which detailed some of the exhibitors and their exhibits. Local schools took part, entering not only flowers but also walnut, oak, date, locust, orange and lemon trees taken from pips and stones. A special category was limited to domestic servants, and one of the prize-winners was a cook from a household in Woburn Square. Another winner was a very poor army tailor, whose entry transformed an old fish-basket into a small garden of annuals edged with stonecrop. A miniature garden was also created by Annie Roberts from Southampton Mews. This featured a little front garden of a villa, 'Bloom Grove': 'A beautifully pointed brick wall, with a neatly constructed gate, enclosed the front of the garden, and a gravelled path, leading to the mansion, was bordered with flowers of every description, including verbenas, stocks, and fuchsias, mostly in bloom, and here and there was placed a little piece of statuary; indeed, the whole exhibited great taste and attracted much attention.'[23]

In Westminster, flower shows for the poor were organised by Lady Augusta Stanley, wife of Arthur Stanley, Dean of Westminster. When the social investigator Charles Booth created his 'Social Map of London, 1899–1900', it was coloured street by street to indicate in detail the social and economic standing. For Westminster, his map shows areas of gold and red, for the wealthy and the well-to-do, cheek by jowl with blue for the very poor and black for the semi-criminal. Just a few streets separated the gracious houses of Queen Anne's Gate overlooking St James's Park from the notorious rookeries off Great Peter Street in the shadow of Westminster Abbey. The *Graphic* for November 1884 depicted competitors from these mean streets and courts looking remarkably dapper, taking their exhibits into Dean's Yard for Lady Augusta's show.

Dean Stanley was one of the supporters of the Shaftesbury Park project in Battersea (see Chapter 6, pp. 166–7), and flower shows were also an important feature of life in the cottage estate. These were organised by the Secretary of the Artizans, Labourers & General Dwellings Company, William Swindlehurst, who had the whole estate decked with flags and banners, ending the day with a concert. The flowers were judged where they grew in the gardens and yards, or on windowsills, by professional gardeners from Kew and Battersea Park – a tradition that continued into the twentieth century in council cottage estates.

Another advocate of window gardening, Catherine Buckton, organised shows for children of the board schools in Leeds. The *Yorkshire Post* sets the scene for the show in July 1878:

> The flower boxes, which, by the bye, in many instances were soap and powder blue boxes, in some cases neatly got up with paper and paint, and ornamented, were ranged in tiers round the spacious room; the contributions from each school being kept separate and duly labelled. Not the least interesting feature of the exhibition was the delighted faces of the parents, who with pardonable pride pointed out 'their Jem's' or 'our Sally's' pet plant, whose bright blooms and summer-green leaves had gained a prize . . . Dwellers in the country know not fully the joy the sojourner in the town derives even from a common wild flower.[24]

50 Competitors taking their exhibits into Dean's Yard, Westminster, for a window gardening show organised by Lady Augusta Stanley, 8 November 1884. The artist who drew this illustration for the *Graphic* has made the exhibitors look positively dapper, considering the tenements from which they must have come (Figure 51).

Buckton set the rules: 'Additional prizes will be given for the best box or pot of mignonette, the best box or pot of musk, best arrangement of climbing plants, best hanging pot or basket of plants; and also for the best bouquet of fresh cut wild flowers and grasses.' The judge of these categories was a professional gardener, and a collection of the prize-winning entries was etched for Buckton's book, *Town and Window Gardening*, which was published in 1879 (Figure 52).

51 Parker Street, Westminster, in 1907. This was one of the notorious London rookeries, with the eighteenth-century houses turned into lodging houses. Despite the chronic poverty, several of the windowsills boast pots of flowers and singing birds in cages.

The Ancient Society of York Florists, entering its second century of existence in 1866, continued the tradition of showing only flowers, unlike many other floricultural and horticultural societies which had moved into fruit and vegetables. Oddly, the York florists made an exception for gooseberries, with prizes for red, white, yellow and green plus one for the

The Window Boxes A and B gained the two First Prizes.   The centre Box C gained  the First Pupil-Teacher's Prize.
F, Fuchsia that gained a Prize.

52 Prize-winning entries in the local flower show in Leeds in 1878, illustrated in
Catherine Buckton's *Town and Window Gardening*. The fuchsia on the right, marked 'F',
had been raised by a young boy in his bedroom from a tiny cutting, which benefited from
every ray of the sun because he kept the window glass so clean.

heaviest berry, organised as a sweepstake from 1804.[25] Unfortunately
many of the records of the society are missing from 1868 to 1908, but by
the beginning of the twentieth century all kinds of classes had been added
to the three annual shows – spring, summer and autumn – which had
themselves grown into great social events, attended by large crowds entertained not only by brilliant displays but also by ventriloquist acts, parlour
songs and music played by military bands. Membership of the society had
changed: previously tradesmen and craftsmen, it was now principally
clergymen, city dignitaries, local politicians and county gentry. The chief
show flowers were dahlias and chrysanthemums, with classes for fruit,
vegetables, pot plants and 'floral art' – flower arrangements. A separate
class was made in 1869 for 'Window Gardening for the Working Classes',
with prizes offered for the best fuchsia, geranium, bulbous plant and any
other plant either in flower or not. There was no entry fee, but exhibitors
had to prove that they were 'Bona-Fide members of the working class'.[26]
How this was achieved is not recorded.

The spirit of competition was flourishing not only in cities and towns, but also in rural areas. In his paper of 1862 at the Guildhall, Samuel Hadden Parkes noted: 'Flower Shows for the poor in the country, where every cottager has a slip of garden ground, where there is plenty of warm sunlight and abundance of fresh air, are not of unfrequent occurrence. They have been held with signal success in many country villages, and neatness in the cottagers' gardens, foresight and industry among the cottagers themselves, have been some of the results.'[27] This is a somewhat rosy view of the opportunities for rural gardeners, but Parkes was trying to emphasise the disadvantages for town dwellers.

A letter from a professional gardener that appeared in *Cottage Gardener* in 1848 echoed the comments made by Robert Marnock:

> Previous to some eight or ten years since, the village alluded to [Etal in Northumberland, near the border with Scotland] was one of the most wicked places that could be found. It was no uncommon sight to see, on leaving the house of God, which was situated on a 'green', a number of the most depraved of men collected round a cock-fight, dog-fight or even man-fight, giving utterance to the most horrid imprecations and blasphemy. Now, some of the men who were once at the head of all descriptions of vice, are the principal exhibitors, and are remarkable for their Christian bearing and industrial [*sic*] habits. Pieces of ground which then bore nothing but crops of nettles and thistles are now clothed with the gayest beauties of the floral kingdom, or groaning under the loads of the finest vegetables that can possibly be grown. It is astonishing that in such a short space of time such a revolution could take place. The houses which were once dens of poverty and filth are now changed into neat white-washed cottages. The public house is giving way to the reading room, and the cock-fights to the shows. And all this, I believe, to have been caused by the establishment of a horticultural society.[28]

A detailed record of horticultural shows held in the village of Hitcham in Suffolk has been preserved. Hitcham's competitions were far from typical in that the organiser, the Revd John Stevens Henslow, had previously held the chair of botany at Cambridge. As one eyewitness reported in the *Gardeners' Chronicle* in 1857, 'a more intellectual rural fete cannot be conceived'. However, many of the conventional elements of rural shows were included and provide a picture of the kind of events that were taking place all round the country. For the show of the Hitcham Labourers' and

Mechanics' Horticultural Society held on 16 July 1851 all specimens to compete for prizes had to be taken to the rectory before 10.30 a.m. so that they might be arranged and inspected by the judges. Children competing for the nosegays were required to bring their wild flowers even earlier, by 9 a.m., and make them up under the horse chestnut tree by the house. 'At 2 o'clock any persons desirous of seeing the show may come on the lawn and amuse themselves. Those who prefer a game of cricket may adjourn to a neighbouring field.' The amusements included a marquee museum furnished with 'plates and woodcrafts, chiefly relating to the Crystal Palace . . . and a selection of natural history objects'.

Prizes were announced and distributed at 5 p.m., and an hour later 'six stewards will arrange the members of the Horticultural Society who are inclined to take a sociable cup of tea altogether and see that they are properly attended to'. The proceedings ended at 8 p.m. with the band of the local orphanage playing 'God Save the Queen' and the Revd Henslow repeating his thanks 'for the orderly behaviour and good contact which he well knows by past experience will have characterised "the proceedings" of the day'.

This summer show was focused on two groups: the nosegays of 'Village Botanists' (that is, the schoolchildren), and the vegetables grown on the village allotments. Categories for the former were wild-fruit posies and dried grass posies and, given Henslow's interests in botany and education, the species had to be named. There was also a prize for herbarium specimens, with a report from the local school. This was followed by a report on the allotments, with prizes for 'Superior Culture', 'Hatcher Sweepstakes' and specimens exhibited at the show. At a later show the distinguished botanist John Lindley distributed the prizes and recorded the judging of the allotments in his journal:

> It is the practice at Hitcham, twice in the season, to inspect the cottagers' allotments and to award some gardening implements to the owners of the best cultivated . . . year by year the inspectors find less fault, while the best are like neatly kept gardens. The first prize man had 46 crops on his allotment, yet of this variety none were neglected, as was proved by his also taking 10 prizes for different articles.[29]

Henslow's parishioners were extremely poor, and many of them could neither read nor write. Nevertheless, a principle of the Hitcham horticultural society was that every member should feel his or her independence by being a contributing subscriber, paying sixpence per annum. Practical prizes such as gardening implements would have been greatly welcomed, along with teapots and barometers, some cash prizes, and for children, 'a pinch of white snuff' – peppermint lozenges.

The autumn shows concentrated on flowers, alongside the natural history curiosities. One of Henslow's scientist friends described the October show in 1853. In one tent:

> are arranged the fuchsias, geraniums, roses, pinks, stocks, pansies, annuals and perennials, nosegays and device nosegays, and at the end the rustics are peeping with astonishment into a polyorama and a stereoscope. On the opposite side of the green is a tent devoted to general curiosities. Eggs of alligators, and eggs of ostrich, eggs of humming-birds, and eggs of some other wonderful birds incubating lilliputian cottagers in yolks of shells and moss, casts of Echini [sea urchins] in their flinty matrices and Echini in chalk, vegetable ivory, from the nut to its process of turning into pin-cushions and umbrella handles, ammonites and nautili, bright enamelled shells of all kinds, butterflies and scorpions, grasses and sedges, lace book and chocolate in the pod.[30]

In stark contrast to the bucolic, impoverished, Suffolk village of Hitcham, stood the Pennine community of Nenthead in Westmorland, replanned in around 1820 by the Quaker London Lead Company (see Chapter 5, p. 131). The lowest part of the mining village stood 1,450 feet above sea level with heavy annual rainfall of between sixty and seventy inches providing a testing challenge to gardeners, yet here was a flourishing horticultural society. To attract skilled workforces to places that were often isolated, employers had to offer allotments and gardens along with good wages, housing and schools. Indeed, local gardening societies were often established before schools or churches had been built. For the two best cultivated gardens at Nenthead prizes of 10s 6d were offered, later raised to two guineas, while the entire community, from the manager to the boys who tended the mine ponies, competed in the annual shows for fruit, flowers and vegetables.

The engineer George Stephenson began to establish a community at Clay Cross in Derbyshire in 1837 when building the North Midland Railway from Derby to Chesterfield. Rows of cottages were built to house his construction workers, but when valuable seams of coal were uncovered, these were taken over by miners and their families. Stephenson was of humble origin, and therefore was keen on educational institutes for the working classes, establishing a school and a Friendly Society before his death in 1848. The Clay Cross Company continued his work when a meeting at the Workman's Institute in 1852 drew up proposals for a Gardening Society 'to promote the cultivation of gardens, useful and ornamental, to encourage habits of industry and domestic taste, and to foster a love of home among the working classes'. Prizes for vegetables and window plants became an annual event.[31]

Bromborough Pool was another industrial community created from scratch, by the Wilson family, proprietors of Price's Patent Candle Company. The Wilsons moved from their manufactory in Battersea when fears of cholera gripped London, and in the 1850s established Bromborough in open countryside on the Cheshire side of the Mersey. Palm oil was a vital ingredient in the manufacture of candles, so it made good business sense for Price's to be close to Liverpool, the main importer of oil from West Africa. George Wilson was a keen horticulturalist, a member of the London Horticultural Society, whose special love was lilies. At Bromborough he insisted that every house should have a garden, foreshadowing Bournville and Port Sunlight, and garden cities. Allotments were also let to workers at a bargain rate of sixpence per rod. By the late 1850s, there were seventy-six houses with a population of 460, and a Horticultural Society was founded. Two shows were held each year, with prizes for vegetables, fruit and flowers, and judges touring allotments and house gardens to appraise them, and to encourage imagination. Children exhibited collections of wild flowers and leaves.

Village horticultural shows in the second half of the nineteenth century were usually organised either by the company, in the case of industrial villages; by the clergyman, as in the case of Hitcham; or by the gentry, often in association with the incumbent of the rectory. The social nuances of some of these events could be complex. A separate class for cottagers was often introduced, a move sometimes motivated by social discrimination. The possibility that an agricultural labourer might snatch the top prize for flowers from the head gardener of the lord or lady of the manor would be regarded with dismay. There were also practical reasons, for poorer gardeners, without the benefit of extensive glasshouses or such sophisticated apparatus as cucumber straighteners (said to be invented by George Stephenson, an expert on tunnels), could not compete on equal terms with the gardeners of wealthier households.

53 Florence Wilson triumphantly holding her prize-winning balsam at the flower show in Littlemore, Oxfordshire. This watercolour was painted by Miss Herschel as part of her entry to an art competition in October 1886.

Mr Evans, head gardener at Caunton Manor since the childhood of Samuel Reynolds Hole, reflected on the issue:

Now you can't do a poor man a greater kindness, in my opinion, than by giving him a garden, and encouraging him in every way to take an interest in it; and, after many years of experience, I feel convinced that the best way to do this, so far as shows are concerned, is to have separate exhibitions for cottagers in the village schoolrooms, and not to tack 'em on to those larger meetings at which they cannot possibly receive the attention and the notice which they well deserve. White and black currants don't get much praise where there's Muscat and Hamburg grapes; and nobody cares, after looking at dipladenias and allamandas and ixoras, for the poor little window-plant. That posy of Mary Smith's in the blue and white mug, with its bits of totter-grass and ferns, is as pretty in my eyes as anything in all the show; but nine out of ten whom I ask to admire it invite me, with a smile o' pity, to go and look at Lady Bigge's bouquet of orchids. Some says, let the cottagers have a tent to themselves, and they sticks 'em in a corner, like a peep-show at a fair behind Wombwell's menagerie; but I says, let 'em have a show and a holiday to themselves, and let all their neighbours go and help 'em, not only with their money, but with kind words, which is better than silver, and brotherly love, which is brighter than gold. There ain't a happier sight to be seen than the people of one place, high and low, gathered together, with goodwill to each other in their hears. And we gardeners, mind you, have much in our power, and may do our part, with our spare seeds, and our spare plants, and that better knowledge which our practice brings.[32]

The annual flower show held at Yalding in Kent provides a snapshot of late Victorian village society. At the time, Yalding's main activities were growing hops and fruit, and acting as the wharf onto the River Medway for barges to load iron ore from the Weald. The Cottage Gardeners' Mutual Improvement Society, founded in 1876, held regular fortnightly meetings where discussions were held on the cultivation of fruit, flowers and vegetables, and outstanding specimens were examined. The Society held shows every August, with their organisation charted through the years in the parish magazine.[33] The event was held initially in the grounds of the vicarage, but later in a meadow provided by one of the farm owners. A marquee would be set up, decorated with collections of plants provided by the head gardeners of local households. The competitions were divided into three categories: for cottagers, for amateurs – those who cultivated their gardens for recreation and without the services of a gardener – and for professionals.

Prize-winners in the cottager class in 1889 included Thomas Cooper with first prize for his redcurrant and third for vegetable marrows. A.G. Brooker was a versatile gardener, with a third for hand bouquets of garden flowers, first for blackcurrants, third for redcurrants, second for gooseberries, second for cherries, third for cooking apples and third for rhubarb. F. Reader, a true floriculturalist, won first prize for six marigolds, another first for twelve cut flowers, second for a 'specimen of window plant', first for three best window plants, second for hand bouquet of wild flowers, first for hand bouquet of garden flowers, first for ten-week stocks, but was no slouch with the potatoes, winning first for three kidney potatoes, and another first for two plates of round potatoes. We can get from these lists some idea of what was grown in cottage gardens in the south of England at this period in terms of flowers, fruit and vegetables.

At the show held in 1900 one of those in attendance was John Wright, the horticultural journalist and lecturer under the technical education scheme organised by the county councils of Kent and Surrey, and supported by Hole, now Dean of Rochester (see Chapter 8, p. 202). Wright had been giving educational talks to the Yalding Mutual Improvement Society, and was delighted to see the quality of the vegetables that had been grown, especially the potatoes. Indeed, the parish magazine noted that 'in several of the vegetable classes, the cottagers' exhibits were almost, if not quite, equal to those of the professional gardeners, who have for years past been the backbone of the society'. The following year new competitions were added to the flower show: handwriting for the boys in the day schools, and knitting and needlework for the girls. The flower show had grown into an important annual event, with music from the Brigade band, breadmaking competitions and baby shows. As this part of Kent was very much the hop-picking centre, these August shows must also have been attended by workers from the East End of London, who took their annual 'holiday' there helping with the harvest, and temporarily trebling the population.

* * *

Moves were made at the end of the nineteenth century to make the large society shows more democratic. Lord Calthorpe, who had provided allotments on his estate, criticised the Birmingham Horticultural and Botanical Garden Society for its exclusivity, and his was not a lone voice. The Royal Horticultural Society, perhaps embarrassed by the support given to parish enterprises by the great and the good, opened its gardens for a general show open to all London parishes in 1865, but the enterprise was not repeated as no one was prepared to take on the considerable organisation required. It was at the local level, in town and country, that flower shows became part of the social year for all classes. As Dean Hole put it, they could be effective levellers:

> Orchids, delicately reared in heat, are gathered under one tent with the hardy wild flowers of the field; the luscious grape from my lord's vinery rests upon the same table with the gooseberry, hirsute and corpulent, and the question is, not which of these is more beautiful or better than its neighbour, but which is best of its kind, which has been more care-fully and wisely cultivated.[34]

# Revolutions in Taste

Cottagers now try to fill their little plots with geraniums and calceolarias, which they are obliged to keep indoors at great inconvenience to themselves and loss of light to their rooms. Meantime my lady at the Court is hunting the nursery gardens for London Pride and gentianella to make edgings in her wilderness, and for the fair tall rockets, the cabbage roses, and the nodding columbines which her pensioners have discarded and thrown away.

So pronounced Mrs Loftie in her column 'Social Twitters', a wonderfully modern title, but dating from 1879.[1]

As Mrs Loftie noted, some working-class gardeners began in the later part of the nineteenth century to copy features from their grander neighbours, such as switching from mixed hardy planting to massed annual bedding. 'Bedding out' had become fashionable in the 1830s and 1840s, producing swathes of colour, often with plants from the hotter climes of South America, Mexico and South Africa: pelargonium, verbena, petunia, lobelia, calceolaria and salvia. These exotic plants not only provided tones that were hot and bright, but also extended the flowering season into the autumn. The season could be extended even further by including miniature versions of the very popular chrysanthemum.

The bedding-out system had been popularised by George Fleming, head gardener to the Sutherland family at Trentham in Staffordshire. In the Italianate formal gardens there he laid out ribbon borders on either side of walks, with three continuous lines of colour. The concept was taken up with enthusiasm in public gardens, where one particularly favourite colour combination was to have ribbons of red, white and blue.

A spectacular display of ribbon borders was produced for the opening of the Royal Horticultural Society's garden in Kensington, opened on 5 June 1861 by the Prince Consort in what turned out to be his last public appearance.

Yet another fashionable style, carpet bedding, was introduced in the 1860s. This was described later by Alicia Amherst as 'filling the beds to produce as great a blaze of colour as possible'.[2] The term 'carpet bedding' was in fact coined in 1868 in the *Gardeners' Chronicle* commendation of John Fleming (no relation to George but also a head gardener to the Sutherlands).[3] At Cliveden in Buckinghamshire he had created a bed arrangement of dwarf foliage and succulents that picked out the pattern of the monogram of the Countess of Sutherland. Round raised beds in this mosaic style were adopted in the gardens of the wealthy, in public parks and in suburban villas. For gardeners with very small gardens, the ribbon arrangement was possible in a modest way, but the raised carpet beds would have been difficult to fit into the narrow, rectangular sites that were the norm. Nevertheless, ambitious efforts were made by some. An account of public parks published in 1898 noted how in spring the surplus of young bedding plants from Victoria Park in east London were given to the enthusiastic amateurs for their little gardens.[4]

In order to raise annuals such as calceolaria and verbena, seeds were sewn under glass in late winter, potted on and hardened off as seedlings before being planted out in early summer. Pelargoniums would be potted up after flowering and overwintered, then propagated by tip cutting in spring. With the repeal of the tax on glass in 1845 greenhouses became much more affordable. In the January 1860 edition of the *Gardeners' Chronicle* Joseph Paxton's design for 'Glass-Houses for the Million' appeared, with the claim that 'these Buildings are of unparalleled cheapness, and being composed of simple parts can be enlarged, removed, or adapted to any Horticultural purpose by ordinary labourers. They are calculated for gardens of the highest order, or gentleman's gardens generally, for market gardens where they may be used to cover any extent and surface, and also for suburban villa and cottage gardens.'

Despite this sweeping boast, the triangular structure was beyond the pocket of most working-class gardeners. However, these were often highly practical men, adept at using their hands and their ingenuity. Samuel Broome, the head gardener at the Middle Temple in London, writing in 1860, gave details of the practical steps taken by working-class gardeners to protect their show chrysanthemums:

It is their practice to erect temporary frames, and procuring a quantity of rush-lights, stick them up all over the frames, to burn through the night; this serves well to exclude frost, as a substitute for a fire, where the party is unable to afford building a flue, or the expense of hot-water pipes. Others procure inch-bored zinc pipe, put up a one quart boiler, and heat the whole with a small oil-lamp; indeed many are the expedients and cheap inventions resorted to in order to prepare and preserve their productions for the show table, and in all cases they succeed, so much so as to surprise everyone.[5]

For those intent on keeping their plants alive through the winter rather than preparing show flowers, a homemade lean-to or a cold frame could be put to use. The *Gardeners' Chronicle* in 1891, reporting on a newly formed working men's Floricultural and Chrysanthemum Society in east London, described how the majority of the members were cabinet makers. They were able to erect in their back gardens little greenhouses, 'very homely structures, with means of artificial heating set up in a rough-and-ready fashion . . . It is during their leisure hours – generally after the day's labour is over, that time is found in which to give attention to the plants.'[6]

Seeds had also become both cheaper and easier to obtain. Gardeners outside London could purchase their flower and vegetable seeds from their local market town, or directly from seed merchants such as Suttons or Carters (see Chapter 7, pp. 192–3) by using the new postal and railway services. Henry Mayhew charts the trade in seed in the capital in his *London Labour and the London Poor*, published in 1851. In addition to the traditional suppliers of seeds, greengrocers and corn chandlers, he also describes street sellers, although their numbers were limited because of the short season in spring and the difficulty of transporting and selling on wet days. One informant told Mayhew that he cleared five shillings in one week, his principal customers being old women 'who liked to sow mignonette in boxes, or in a garden border'. The seeds would be made up into packets priced at sixpence or one shilling, or were sold by weight.[7]

Mayhew also recorded how annuals were sold by rootsellers who acquired their stock from nursery gardens on the outskirts of London, especially from Hackney and Mile End. When they did well, they were regarded as the aristocracy of the street greengrocers. He noted that although Scotsmen dominated the horticultural world of England, not a

54 George Johann Scharf's studies of London street traders, selling flowers, fruit and vegetables, made between April 1841 and May 1842. He has made notes about the vendors, including their particular cries, alongside their portraits.

single one was among this elite group. A Scot questioned about this considered that his countrymen would rather enlist in the army than undertake street selling in London.

At the end of May, and through the months of June and July, the root-sellers would set up their stalls in the main thoroughfares leading into the City. Mayhew describes how their stalls resembled the bedding schemes in gardens: 'The stall-keepers have sometimes their flowers placed in a series of shelves, one above another, so as to present a small amphitheatre of beautiful and diversified hues; the purest white, as in the lily of the valley, to the deepest crimson, as in the fuchsia; the bright or rust-blotted yellow of the wallflower, to the many hues of the stock.' Among the flowers mentioned are mignonette, pansies, calceolarias and, later, marigolds and China asters, ending with the Michaelmas daisies, 'the growth of the All-Hallow'n summer'.[8] He noted that geraniums were coming back into fashion, while balsams were going out.

For small gardens, whether in the suburbs of cities and towns, or in the country, the bedding schemes used three standard components: carpet plants, edging plants and dot plants – taller plants, especially fuchsias, to contrast with the smaller plants. The very ingenious could pick out a motto in flowers, such as 'God Save the Queen' or the name of the cottage. An economical edging for beds was oyster shells – the oyster being a food of the poor in the nineteenth century. In 1894 Henry Nevinson, who helped to organise an East End mission and taught literacy classes in Hackney, was commissioned to write short stories on working-class life in East End. One story featured Tom Briers, nicknamed Old Parky after Victoria Park because of his love of gardens:

> But far away the best thing as 'e ever done was the gardens in Thomas's Row, as turned round the corner from where 'e lived, and 'ad a square of garden almost as big as a room in front of each 'ouse. It came about through a neighbour seein' them chickins and askin' 'im to lend a 'and with clearing out the rubbish from 'is own front. And in a month's time its own mother wouldn't 'ave known that garden . . . So it got round as Parky was the man for gardens, and 'e takes 'em all on, the neighbour not begrudgin' 'im a penn'orth of seeds 'ere and there, let alone the oyster shells as 'e pick up and stuck round the borders, instead of rememberin' the grotter. And twelve month after, if yer'd passed and saw them scarlet-runners twinin' theirselves over sticks, and the jeannie's 'angin' from the winders, and the balsams and marigolds, with

55 A photograph of a London garden, taken in the late nineteenth century. The garden's dimensions are long and narrow, yet the owners have produced an ambitious border, with the fashionable low ribbon dressing at the front, marked by sempervivums.

paths and walls o' shells between, and little palin's with five-barred gates painted green with white tops, paintin' bein' Parky's work, you'd 'ave said it was a respite from the cares and troubles o' life.[9]

A close neighbour of Parky in Hackney was the Southgate family in North Street (see Chapter 6, p. 163). In his autobiography, Walter describes how his father, a pen-quill cutter, had a 'grotto' in his backyard:

a beloved Victorian garden ornament wedged between the brick WC and the coal box. He had built it of old bricks, chunks of clinker refuse, scallop shells and broken glass and chinaware ornaments. It was not a good example of garden architecture, but it was one up on old Mr Sayers down the road, who quite blatantly inserted in his 'grotto' old chamber pots in which he grew creeping jenny.[10]

Where did Mr Southgate Senior get his idea for a grotto: from a trip upstream on the Thames to Alexander Pope's grotto at Twickenham perhaps? Whatever the source, these ingenious and practical working men used what was immediately at hand.

The deployment of oyster shells as bordering material is also recorded in a cottage garden by Anne Cobbett, William's wife: 'laid with the outer side upward, and in a straight line to form an edging for the path'. Where oyster shells were not available, the shank-bones of sheep were thrust into the earth 'within an inch of the joint and packed so closely as to look like one continuous piece of carved bone'.[11] Oyster-shell edging was not approved of by Shirley Hibberd, who warned: 'Do not suffer your neighbours to laugh at an endless variety of parterres of all shapes and sizes, edged with oyster shells, and filled up with plants that would disgrace a common.'[12]

Brightly coloured borders and beds were not the only fashionable features adopted by working-class gardeners for their modest plots. Among the paintings by Helen Allingham is a depiction of a cottage garden in West Horsley in Surrey where the dominating feature is a peacock in topiary (Plate XIV). The skills required to produce such a figure suggests that it might have been made by a gardener who worked at a nearby great house. But it is not the only example of topiary work in a cottage garden – peacocks and hens were particularly fashionable, sometimes surmounted on spiral columns. Gertrude Jekyll in her account of the gardens of West Surrey reproduces a photograph of alarmingly huge clipped yews at the gate of a cottage.[13]

56 A couple outside their town garden in Bradford in Yorkshire, photographed in the late nineteenth or early twentieth century. This might be a back-to-back, or have only a backyard, so raised beds, possibly set on paving, must provide as much space as possible for flowers and vegetables. On the windowsill are shells and stones, for use as decorative features.

In her biography of her father, Joseph, Mabel Ashby describes how his aunt enjoyed a modest income from 'money in the Railways' (that is, railway bonds). She indulged herself with a front garden to her cottage in the Warwickshire village of Tysoe; the path leading up to her door was bordered deep with flowers from the opening of the snowdrops to the last tiny chrysanthemums. Her bequest to Joseph Ashby enabled him to move into Church Cottage in 1895, and also to have a little front garden with variegated maple, mountain ash, 'mock orange' and deutzia. This was thought to be rather pretentious, 'as if the curate's garden had slipped across the road'.[14] The reproach intimated by Mabel Ashby, of aping one's betters, is echoed by George Bourne in *Memoirs of a Surrey Labourer*, published in 1911. The labourer was Frederick Bettesworth, who lived at Bourne, a village just outside Farnham. The area was becoming rapidly suburbanised at the end of the nineteenth century, and Bettesworth observed with disapproval the arrival of an artisan from London. This plasterer or builder's carpenter, having bought a cottage, proceeded to destroy the natural contours of the garden with ill-devised 'improvements'.[15]

Joseph Ashby's Church Cottage also boasted a rockery, a miniature version of the monumental schemes that had become fashionable in the gardens of wealthy Victorians in the 1840s. In her book on cottage gardens, Anne Scott-James describes a garden in Berkshire that was begun in the 1880s and passed down from father to son with little alteration. It consisted of four separate rocky places made of sarsen stones, three of them planted with rock plants and, oddly, pelargoniums, while the fourth was a circle of stones enclosing a tiny pool with goldfish and a water-lily. A small gnome kept guard – whether this was a common feature in the 1880s, Miss Scott-James does not make clear.[16]

Garden gnomes are now regarded as the epitome of suburban kitsch. Their introduction to Britain, however, was made by Sir Charles Isham, who inherited the estate of Lamport Hall in Northamptonshire in 1846. Isham represented the very antithesis of the popular image of an English aristocrat: he was a teetotal vegetarian non-smoker and an opponent of all blood sports. Happily married, he devoted himself to the welfare of the employees on his estate, and to creating an immense rockery in his garden. According to the *Strand Magazine* in 1890, the rockery was thirty yards long, fourteen yards wide and eight yards high. An sheer ivy-covered wall looked south towards Lamport's lawns, while an Alpine aspect faced north, with crevices, chasms and caves. Isham here planted dwarf conifers, Japanese maples, box and ferns, purple thyme, golden saxifrage and lavender. Unlike the rockery described by Anne Scott-James, he eschewed druid stones, instead introducing a group of gnomes into the landscape. Isham was widely-read on folklore, collecting stories of gnomes and 'mine fairies' in Wales and Dovedale in the Peak District, and in Central Europe; from the latter he brought over his figures. Made from ceramic, they were tiny, just two or three inches tall, in keeping with the dwarf trees and alpine plants, and were posed around ladders and wells, as if emerging from the caverns to take refreshment after their labours. Some were even provided with banners proclaiming the need for a decent wage and a benevolent employer.[17]

Following Sir Charles's death in 1903, his daughters banished the gnomes, and only one survives, 'Lampy', fabulously precious and kept in a secure glass case in Lamport Hall. Isham had nevertheless begun a fashion in garden gnomes that was to spread. At Iffley Priory in Oxfordshire, for instance, a group was photographed by Henry Taunt, and in the same year, 1912, they made an appearance at the Royal International Horticultural Exhibition in Chelsea, where, carrying baskets of flowers, they were set at the front of the stand for Carters Seeds. This scene was not to be repeated,

57 Three gardening gnomes that inhabited the grounds of the Gothic Revival Iffley Priory in Oxfordshire, photographed by Henry Taunt in 1912. Their large size and careful detailing indicate that they are German in origin.

as gnomes were banned from Chelsea, together with 'highly coloured figures, fairies or any similar creatures, actual or mythical, as garden ornaments'.[18] In 2013, the RHS relented, and gnomes were allowed to return to celebrate the centenary of the Flower Show. Chelsea may have been made gnome-free, but these little figures represented *par excellence* a revolution in taste, for they have been populating small gardens for well over a century.

* * *

Meanwhile another revolution in taste was taking place in the opposite direction: the fashionable were turning to cottage gardening. As noted in Chapter 5, estate owners were building picturesque cottages for their tenants from the early nineteenth century, but the movement had captured the imagination right up the social ladder, and the cottage could be a substantial house, lived in by people of means. In a poem entitled 'The Devil's Walk', written collaboratively by Robert Southey and Samuel Taylor Coleridge, run the lines, 'He pass'd a cottage with a double coach-house/ A cottage of gentility'. Samuel Gilbert, the seventeenth-century florist, had written deprecatingly about 'trifles adorned amongst country women, but of no esteem to a Florist, who is taken up with things of more value'.[19] Now, however, the trifles, the flowers that had been traditionally cultivated in labourers' gardens, were set to become the height of fashion.

Not all seventeenth-century gardening writers were as dismissive as Gilbert about cottagers' flowers. John Worlidge, for instance, devoted a chapter in his *Systema Horti-culturae*, published in 1677, to what he termed 'vulgar flowers', grown by farmers' wives (see Chapter 2, p. 35). In the eighteenth century, the many gardening books produced concentrated more on the new exotic plants that were being introduced into Britain, and had comparatively little to say about the traditional flowers to be found in humbler gardens. From the beginning of the nineteenth century, however, there was a renewal of interest in the latter. John Claudius Loudon, for example, recommended cottage plants in his *Manual of Cottage Gardening and Husbandry*, published in 1830, and they made frequent appearances in his *Gardener's Magazine*.

John Clare was a keen and knowledgeable florist and gardener. In 1827 his poem, 'The Cottager', was published, including 'The Shepherd's Calendar' for June in which he talked of the flowers in the cottage gardens in his Northamptonshire village:

> . . . every farmers garden yields
> Fine cabbage roses painted like her face
> And shining pansys trimmd in golden lace
> And tall tuft larkheels featherd thick wi flowers
> And woodbines climbing oer the door in bowers
> And London tufts of many a mottld hue
> And pale pink pea and monkshood darkly blue
> And white and purple jiliflowers that stay
> Lingering in blossom summer half away
> And single blood walls of a luscious smell
> Old fashiond flowers which huswives love so well
> And columbines stone blue or deep night brown
> Their honey-comb-like blossoms hanging down
> Each cottage gardens fond adopted child
> Tho heaths still claim them were they yet grow wild
> Mong their old wild companions summer blooms
> Furze brake and mozzling ling and golden broom

Snap dragons gaping like to sleeping clowns
And 'clipping pinks' (which maidens sunday gowns
Full often wear catcht at by tozing chaps)
Pink as the ribbons round their snowy caps
'Bess in her bravery' too of glowing dyes
As deep as sunsets crimson pillowd skyes
And marjoram notts sweet briar and ribbon grass
And lavender the choice of every lass
And spr[i]gs of lads love all familiar names
Which every garden thro the village claims . . .[20]

For the names of some of the flowers he used the local dialect, and, thanks to a glossary of Northamptonshire words and phrases compiled by Anne Elizabeth Baker in 1854, we can identify these.[21] Thus 'larkheel' is larkspur, 'London tufts' is London Pride, 'blood walls' is a double, dark wallflower, 'Bess in her bravery' is a double-flowered daisy with crimson-tipped petals, and 'lads love' is southernwood. Just as Cecil Sharp collected traditional folk songs at the end of the nineteenth century, so Anne Elizabeth Baker and her contemporaries in different parts of Britain compiled glossaries of local terms, many published by the English Dialect Society, thus capturing the traditional names of flowers before they disappeared from the language.

Although Clare talks simply of the pansy, Northamptonshire names for the flower included 'Pink-eyed John'. 'Love-in-idleness' was another Northamptonshire name, shared with other Midlands counties, and was chosen by Shakespeare, a son of Warwickshire, the flower being used to enchant lovers in *A Midsummer Night's Dream*. As the flower resembles a little face, in Suffolk it was called 'kiss-at-the-garden-gate', while in Lincolnshire it was known as 'meet-her-in-the-entry-kiss-her-in-the-buttery', a tongue-twister that would not have suited Clare's verse.

It was two highly influential garden writers who made fashionable these 'vulgar' flowers: William Robinson and Gertrude Jekyll. When Robinson was put in charge of the herbaceous section of the Royal Botanic Society's gardens in London's Regent's Park in 1862, one of his responsibilities was to add to a small collection of English wild flowers, and during his travels he came to see many cottage gardens. Gradually he conceived a vision of a garden contrived as part of the natural scene, but embellished by examples of the flora of other temperate parts of the world, such as China and South America. This vision was embodied in one his most influential books, *The Wild Garden*, published in 1870.

At this period he was also developing his campaign against bedding-out (or 'pastry-work gardening', as he put it) and the clutter of statuary. Instead, he advocated wide sweeping lawns, shapely beds filled with roses, shrubs or hardy plants, and walls covered with flowery creepers. At the back of his mind was the image of the traditional English cottage garden. In 1865 he had written a series of articles on hardy plants for spring gardening for the *Gardeners' Chronicle* that elicited a huge response from readers. The leader writer reported inquiries into:

old places for Primulas, Polyanthuses, Auriculas, and other ancient favourites, which in these days of the 'bedding-out system' have been allowed to go very much out of sight and therefore out of mind . . . It is something that cultivators who have been too much engrossed with the autumnal flower garden, should become aware of the fact that there are numerous classes of hardy plants which are quite as interesting and attractive, if not so brilliant and showy as their special favourites. We trust that the interest which is awakened in spring flowers will not wear off without practical results.[22]

William Robinson concurred with this, and the next decades would be devoted to reviving interest in the humble cottage garden and its flowers. In the 1895 edition of *The English Flower Garden*, Robinson wrote:

English cottage gardens, first, are never bare and seldom ugly . . . What is the secret of the cottage garden's charms? Cottage gardeners are good to their plots, and in the course of years they make them fertile, and the shelter of the little house and hedge favours the flowers. But there is something more and it is the absence of any pretentious 'plan', which lets the flowers tell their story to the heart. They often teach lessons that 'great' gardeners should learn, and are pretty from Violet and Snowdrop time till the Fuchsia bushes bloom nearly into winter.[23]

Not only was Robinson thinking of colour and arrangement, but also of scent:

Of the many things that should be thought of in the making of a garden to live in, this of fragrance is one of the first . . . Apart from the groups of plants in which all, or nearly all, are fragrant, as in Roses, the annual and biennial flowers of our gardens are rich in fragrance –

58 A cottage garden, photographed in about 1915. Taking advantage of the fashion for such gardens, the owners have seized the opportunity to offer tea to visitors, as the sign on the fence announces.

Stocks, Mignonette, Sweet Peas, Sweet Sultan, Wallflowers, double Rockets, Sweet Scabious, and many others. These, among the most easily raised of plants, may be enjoyed by the poorest cottage gardeners.[24]

In January 1875 Robinson was visited in his office by Gertrude, sister of his friend, Herbert Jekyll, and she began to contribute to his magazine, *The Garden*. Gertrude's family was middle class and intellectual in its interests. She had ambitions to be a professional artist, made the acquaintance of John Ruskin and William Morris and acquired a well-equipped workshop where she made herself proficient in various crafts. When her father died, she created a new garden for her mother and began to design others, the first of which seems to have been for a factory worker in Rochdale who wanted it to be filled with as many plants as possible. With her own garden at Munstead Wood in Surrey, Jekyll was inspired by the idea of cottage gardens. Yet again we have to be careful about the romanticism of this genre. One garden writer has suggested, 'She simply did not see the yard-cum-garden of the average cottage, with its chicken-house, rabbit-hutches and outdoor earth-closet'.[25] Yet the photographs that Jekyll took of cottagers for her book, *Old West Surrey*, published in 1904, show the old men and women in their traditional, working clothes, a world away from the images painted by Helen Allingham. The photographs, moreover, are imbued with the dignity of the sitters. Of course Jekyll would never have considered introducing rabbit hutches and earth closets into her own garden, but she did bring in the flowers that were so carefully cherished by the cottagers.

The working-class rural gardener had become a hero. One writer on English cottage gardens included a chapter entitled 'A Museum of Plants', casting the cottager in the dual role of conservator and curator:

> Old cultivars ... lingered much longer, often much more than a century longer and occasionally for several centuries longer, in the cottage gardens than in the gardens of the prosperous burgesses or of the rich. The fact is that the cottage gardener, if only by his want of means, did a public service by preserving, for later generations who might again appreciate them, old garden plants banished from the great gardens and the gardens of the middle class.[26]

Old favourites had persisted so successfully because the cottagers had provided the same conditions for their plants as they would have enjoyed in natural surroundings: a constant supply of humus and the partial shade of other plants, which stopped the drying out of roots during the summer and the panning of ground during heavy rain in the winter. There was no need to hoe or to water, just provide an occasional mulch of decayed manure and mould. In this way the cottage garden has at times acted as a 'gene pool' for plant breeding material. Montagu Allwood, one of three Lincolnshire brothers, found an old fringed pink in a garden of his native county, which he crossed with a perpetual flowering carnation to create a new race of perpetual flowering pinks that he named Allwoodii. When he moved with his brothers to Wivelsfield in Sussex in 1910 and started a nursery, *Dianthus x allwoodii* were the stars of the show.

A similar find led to the foundation of the seed house of W.J. Unwin. Unwin was a grocer in the Cambridgeshire village of Histon who discovered growing in his cottage garden a sweet pea in a shade of shell pink with waved petals. It was close in form to a flower found in the garden of Countess Spencer at Althorp Park in Northamptonshire, which became the first of the famous Spencer peas, but was of greater importance because it was able to breed true. Unwin named it after his daughter, Gladys, and so great was the demand for this variety that the famous house was established.

The sweet pea was one of the most fashionable flowers of the Edwardian period. Another flower that became popular was the old-fashioned stock, as a result of the discovery of one of outstanding form and pronounced perfume in a cottage garden in East Lothian in 1868. The man who found it was David Thomson, head gardener to the Duke of Buccleuch, who was told that the stocks had been growing in the garden, and in others in the district, for at least three centuries. As they grew only twelve to fifteen inches in height, they were particularly suitable for window boxes and restricted bedding.[27]

Flora Thompson mentions some of the old-fashioned cottage flowers to be found in a hamlet garden at Juniper Hill:

> Sally had such flowers, and so many of them, and nearly all of them sweet-scented! Wallflowers and tulips, lavender and sweet William, and pinks and old-world roses with enchanting names – Seven Sisters, Maiden's Blush, moss rose, monthly rose, cabbage rose, blood rose, and most thrilling of all to the children, a big bush of the York and Lancaster rose, in the blooms of which the rival roses mingled in a pied white and red.[28]

Gertrude Jekyll, who devoted an entire 1902 book to roses, categorised the children's favourite, York and Lancaster, as a damask rose, associated with Cottage Maid and with Gallica Rosa Mundi, said to be named after Rosamund Clifford, 'the Fair Rosamund', mistress of Henry II, in popular legend done to death by the jealous Queen Eleanor of Aquitaine. Jekyll described Maiden's Blush as a white rose, despite its pink tinge, particularly recommended to climb up the front of a cottage. Cabbage and Moss were centifolia roses, with rich and heavy flowers.

In 1896 Gertrude Jekyll commissioned the young architect Edwin Lutyens to build her home at Munstead Wood. Lutyens used traditional materials in the Arts and Crafts style for the house, and created an architectural and geometric area to surround it, in contrast with the natural garden created by Jekyll: this was to be a formula that the two applied in their partnership over the next decades, and which exerted a great influence on many other gardens of the period. With Lutyens she explored the lanes of rural Surrey, seeking out ideal forms of old cultivars of roses and ramblers growing on walls and in cottage gardens.

There is some debate about the extent of the influence exerted by Jekyll and Lutyens and by William Robinson on Lawrence Johnson in his creation of the great garden at Hidcote Manor in Gloucestershire. There is little at Hidcote of the overt architectural style of a Lutyens garden, but Jekyll's eye for texture, form and colour is echoed in the planting, and the natural style is reminiscent of Robinson. Johnson is a deeply enigmatic figure, but he was certainly his own man as far as his plantsmanship and gardening were concerned.

When Lawrence Johnson arrived at Hidcote in 1907, the bleak farmland he found must have seemed an unpromising canvas, and he appears to have had no master plan, instead building up a sequence of terraces, lawns and flower gardens such as those in larger country house gardens, but here wrought into a chain of intimate rooms. The most intimate are the Old Garden and the White Garden, both of which were laid out by Johnson in the years running up to the First World War. An early photograph of the White Garden, then known as the phlox garden, shows little box hedges around four beds, and at the centre, a circle of grass and a sundial. Peeping above the encircling yew hedge is a thatched cottage. The Old Garden was planted mostly in shades of grey and pink, with birds cut in topiary marking its entrance. Over the years, these two gardens have been developed, and become more 'cottage-like' in their appearance. The two topiary birds in the White Garden look down on box-edged beds filled with white tulips, violas and artemesia, with acanthus and *Crambe cordifolia* providing height and form. The Old Garden is predominantly planted in blue and white, pink and mauve, with roses scrambling up the walls and luxurious flourishes of peonies, one of Johnson's favourite plants. The thatched cottage provides a rustic presiding spirit.

These two 'rooms' are Johnson's closest interpretations of a cottage garden. But in an article for the Royal Horticultural Society magazine, Vita Sackville-West queried whether the whole of Hidcote might be thus described, and in doing so examined her own concepts of what constituted a true cottager's garden:

> Would it be misleading to call Hidcote a cottage garden on the most glorified scale? . . . It resembles a cottage garden, or rather, a series of cottage gardens, in so far as the plants grow in a jumble, flowering shrubs mingle with roses, herbaceous plants with bulbous subjects, climbers scrambling over hedges, seedlings coming up wherever they have chosen to show themselves. Now in a real cottage garden, where limitations and very often the pattern – for example, the curve or the straightness of the path leading from the entrance gate to the front

door – are automatically imposed upon the gardener, this charming effect is both restrained and inevitable . . . it is very largely accidental. But in a big garden like Hidcote great skill is required to secure not only the success of the actual planting, but of the proportions which can best give the illusion of enclosure . . . At Hidcote this has been achieved by the use of hedges . . . There is just enough topiary to carry out the cottage-garden idea . . . The topiary at Hidcote is in the country tradition of smug broody hens, bumpy doves, and coy peacocks twisting a fat neck towards a fatter tail. It resembles all that our cottagers have done ever since the Romans first came to Britain and cut our native yew and box with their sharp shears.[29]

When Vita Sackville-West was making this assessment of Hidcote, in 1947, she had created with her husband Sir Harold Nicolson an ambitious garden of enclosures at Sissinghurst Castle in Kent. The setting was quite different from Hidcote: the shell of an Elizabethan castle-cum-mansion which the couple bought in 1930. In the years that followed, a series of open-air rooms were created, bounded by red-brick walls and hedges of yew, rose or hornbeam. While Nicolson, who admired Lutyens, was responsible for the structure and the architectural elements of the garden, Vita was the plants expert, taking many of her ideas from the books of William Robinson, *The English Flower Garden* and *The Wild Garden*. The South Cottage became their home, particularly loved by Nicolson as his retreat from London life, and the place where he could write. The planting in this cottage garden is based on the hues of sunset – oranges, yellows and reds. In spring there is a display of tulips teamed with wallflowers, with a spectacular centrepiece of a copper, unearthed from the former laundry, filled with lily-flowered tulips, 'Red Shine'.

Vita's idea of a cottage garden has been likened to Marie Antoinette and her attendants playing at milkmaids in the Petit Trianon at Versailles. Certainly the copper is rather superior to most containers owned by cottagers, and the surroundings of the cottage garden at Sissinghurst is more than a cut above the villages of rural labourers. However, it was through the skill and vision of gardeners such as Lawrence Johnson and Vita Sackville-West that the traditions of cottage gardeners continued into the late twentieth century. As Anne Scott-James observed: 'Sissinghurst is the last cottage garden made on a grand scale, but fortunately it does not mark the end of cottage gardening.'[30]

# CHAPTER II

# Digging for Victory in Peace and War

IT IS NOT often that gardening becomes a national political issue, but this is precisely what happened at the end of the nineteenth century. In January 1886 an amendment to an address about allotments, moved by the MP Jesse Collings, was carried by the votes of the bulk of his fellow Liberals, obliging the Conservative Prime Minister, Lord Salisbury, to resign, and returning William Gladstone to power. Ironically, Gladstone did nothing to promote the extension of the provision of allotments, preoccupied as he was with Home Rule for Ireland. Many Liberal politicians were, however, determined to carry forward legislation to increase their availability. They recognised that these plots of land were becoming ever more vital to the rural poor as the agricultural depression, that had begun in the 1870s with the competitive effect of cheaper food imports, hit British farming. Acts passed in 1819 and 1831 had lacked teeth because of Parliament's refusal to make compulsory the setting aside of land by local authorities. Instead, provision of allotments lay in the hands of philanthropic individuals and institutions, although often altruism was tempered by the desire to keep down the poor rates, and to keep the workers out of the alehouse.

The Chartists had been equivocal about allotments. In his novel *Sybil*, Disraeli has his Chartist character Field describe the factory owner Trafford as 'the most inveterate Capitalist [who] would divert the minds of the people from the Five Points by allotting them gardens and giving them baths'.[1] In other words, he was seeking to distract them from the important aim of securing political reform. The leader of the National Agricultural Labourers' Union (NALU), Joseph Arch, was not to be thus deflected. With his brilliant oratory and ability as a publicist, by 1874 he had attracted over 86,000 members, with a further 30,000 to 40,000 unionised farm workers in other organisations. This proved to be the climax of Arch's success as a union leader, for when local strikes were organised, the farmers in the eastern counties launched counter-offensives, sacking any of their employees who were union members. In his portrait of a Suffolk village, *Akenfield*, Ronald Blythe quoted a notice posted by the church-wardens at nearby Clopton: 'The Society calling itself the National Agricultural Union having ordered strikes in a portion of the county of Suffolk, all members of the same in this parish have notice to give up their allotments, and will be struck off the list of parochial and bread charities'.[2] The conflict, known as the 'Revolt of the Field' was still a bitter memory a century later. Arch, who had been attached to the Liberal cause since the late 1860s, turned to national politics, campaigning for the vote for the rural labourer.

This important watershed came with the Franchise Act of 1884. Following Disraeli's 'leap in the dark' of 1868, which had given the vote to urban working-class males, Gladstone extended the rights to the rural population. Although domestic servants, bachelors living with their families and those of no fixed abode were excluded, this act made agricultural labourers a source of interest to politicians. In *Lark Rise to Candleford*, Flora Thompson describes how in the local tavern: 'Politics was a favourite topic, for, under the recently extended franchise, every householder was a voter, and they took their new responsibility seriously. A mild Liberalism prevailed, a Liberalism that would be regarded as hide-bound Toryism now [she was writing in 1939], but daring enough in those days.' One of the number, Sam, who had met and shaken hands with Arch, would raise his pewter mug and declare 'Joseph Arch is the man for the farm labourer'.[3]

One topic discussed in the village was 'Three Acres and a Cow'. This was the slogan adopted by Jesse Collings, the MP for Ipswich, in his demand for land reform and the provision of adequate allotments. In 1887 the progressive Liberal Halley Stewart won a by-election at Spalding in Lincolnshire on the 'allotment ticket', and two years later county council elections in some areas were fought on the issue. A series of Parliamentary acts followed, but the really effective statute was the 1908 Small Holdings and Allotments Act. This consolidated previous legislation obliging local authorities to provide allotments for the 'labouring population' where they could not be obtained privately. Five acres was prescribed as the limit of land local councils might set aside for allotments without sanction of the county council. One acre was the limit any applicant might demand by right, sub-letting was forbidden and co-operative societies were eligible.

In the 1960s and early 1970s Paul Thompson and Trevor Lummis in the Department of Sociology at Essex University undertook a study, 'Family Life and Work Experience before 1918'. Oral evidence was gathered from 453 interviews with men and women born between 1870 and 1906 from various parts of England, Scotland and Wales, from different social classes, and from urban and rural areas. It is clear from the accounts given by those born into rural working-class communities in particular that allotments represented a vital part of their lives.

A good example is provided by an interview with a postman born in 1902 at Great Bentley in Essex. He was the eldest of eleven children born of an agricultural worker and his potato picker wife in a 'poor old cottage'. His father's weekly wages were a meagre 12s 6d, although the cottage did come rent free. The garden, running down one side of the cottage, was large, with an allotment for vegetables at the back. He started to work in the garden from the age of five: 'We helped in the garden all the time. If we didn't do anything in the garden, sometimes we didn't have very much to eat . . . We used to have to go home from school and do a certain amount before we had half an hour's play, and dig.' The family diet was mainly vegetables and porridge and bread, although their father, who started work before the sun was up and finished after dark in autumn and winter, was given pork for his dinner at midday two or three times a week. Rabbits were snared to provide meat for the children. Fruit from the garden was made into jam and wine.

An interview with a farm labourer born in 1896 from Woodley Arton, Gloucestershire, provides a similar picture. Again the labourer's cottage had two gardens, one adjoining, a second by the side of the road where his father grew fruit and vegetables and kept poultry. The family's diet was mostly vegetables, with bacon occasionally. The interviewee's father earned fifteen shillings per week as an agricultural labourer at the beginning of the twentieth century, and when the son started work during the First World War, his pay was the same.[4]

The responses elicited by the Thompson and Lummis project are reinforced, indeed intensified, by a study undertaken by Benjamin Seebohm Rowntree and his assistant, May Kendall. Rowntree and Kendall took a smaller number of households (forty-two), concentrating on agricultural labourers in the midland counties of England. Their findings, first published in 1913 as *How the Labourer Lives*, show vividly how grim were the lives of some rural families. The authors looked at the composition of households, their income and outgoings, their garden and allotment allocation, and their diets. Thus the Purcell family living in Leicestershire consisted of a man, his wife, two sons aged eleven and two, and a daughter aged seven. The man's income was 18s 10d per week, supplemented by 9d for his son, and extra earnings by both husband and wife at harvest time of £3. The rent of the cottage and garden was 1s 10d per week, with rates of 12s 6d per annum. The garden was fairly large, so that although potatoes had proved a failure at the time of the survey, the Purcells had many greens and could always beg a turnip. 'Then the garden contains rhubarb, from which she made part of her jam [some to sell] and gooseberry bushes and beets and cabbage to pickle. The vinegar bill for the year had amounted to 5s. She also makes mushroom ketchup, which, like the pickles, is chiefly used at home.' Rowntree and Kendall noted a 13 per cent deficiency in protein in the diet.[5]

But the Purcell household was comfortably off compared to the Leighs in Oxfordshire. This family consisted of the father, a general labourer, his wife, three sons aged five and a half, three and fifteen months, and a daughter of eight. The father's wage was 13s per week, supplemented over the year by extra earnings of £2 12s. The rent for the cottage was 1s 3d per week, while the allotment cost 4s per annum. By the end of November, the family had only three or four boilings of greens, a few turnips and parsnips and a bushel of potatoes, a diet which was causing 39 per cent deficiency in protein. Rowntree and Kendall noted grimly, 'The Leighs seem to be facing the darkness with no immediate hope of dawn.'[6] Little wonder that recruiting officers were horrified by the medical condition of labouring men signing up to fight in the First World War. Without their allotments and gardens these families would have starved.

In an article written just before the First World War, Joseph Ashby reflected on the importance of gardens for rural labourers. Although Ashby had led the fight for allotments in his native Warwickshire, and helped to push through the 1882 Allotments Extension Act, he was clear-sighted enough to recognise that allotments could be hard to cultivate if they were on difficult land, and might be sited some distance from the labourer's home.

In the future it should be almost a criminal offence to build a rural cottage without a garden . . . It has been very fairly urged in important circles that only 4 cottages should be built in an acre, and that all the surplus land should be cut up into garden ground . . . 40 cottages of 5 rooms each, with piggeries and poultry-houses, and other requisite

59 An allotment replete with cabbages, from a photograph taken in the early years of the twentieth century. Women are clearly taking part in the gardening here.

buildings scattered over a ten acre field, with all available space devoted to fruit, vegetables and flowers would be a sight worth going a long way to see.

The garden is a starting point of the land question. Its advantages are enormous. Can anyone imagine the difference between a working family without a garden at all, and a family which can place two vegetables on the table every day in the year, and have fruit enough with the addition of rhubarb used as fruit, to last them 9 months of the year, with the addition of an all-the-year-round supply of jam from home-grown fruit. And this is no overdrawn picture. The writer has in mind a particular instance in which this was done by a labourer for a family of seven persons on less than a quarter of an acre of garden, and in addition fruit enough was sold to pay the cottage rent. Besides all this, there was a bed of stuff specially grown for pig and poultry feeding, and a large quantity of offal produces to devote to the same purpose. Such instances could be many times multiplied. The advantages of a good-sized garden are incalculable.[7]

The 1908 Act obliged local authorities to provide allotments, not only in rural areas but also for the 'labouring population' in towns and cities. Up to this time, although there were allotments in urban areas, they had been predominantly for the rural working classes, but now the provision of town allotments increased significantly. In the United States a decade earlier, the first Vacant Land Cultivation Society (VLCS) had been established in Detroit supplying land for the unemployed to work. This was the idea of the Mayor of Detroit, Hazen S. Pingree, and the plots became known as 'Pingree's potato patches'. The concept was developed by a land reformer, Joseph Fels, and brought to England in 1908 and to Ireland the following year. A letter in the *Irish Times*, recognising that the rural poor had swelled the ranks of the working classes in Dublin, declared: '[A] special advantage for the work here lies in the fact that a good proportion of our unemployed men and some of women are accustomed to garden and field labour. Besides the food and money to be realized by the cultivation of these plots, the moral, physical, and intellectual advantages of such occupation for the women and their families are incalculable.'[8]

According to an article published in 1918 in the East London newspaper, the *Eastern Post*, before the war twenty-five deaths from starvation were recorded each year. The poorest boroughs lay on the eastern side of the capital, and it was here that the demand for allotments in the late nineteenth and early twentieth centuries was highest.[9] For example, the area between Bromley-by-Bow and Stratford was known by 1908 as Allotment Town. There were 290 plots in all, in what is said to have been one of the oldest sites in London, so may well have been a remnant of rural life. On Saturdays, according to the local newspaper, the whole community ventured out to their sheds, which were furnished with 'gables, porches, dormer windows and curtains'.[10]

The VLCS found it an uphill struggle to get borough councils in England to fulfil the obligations under the 1908 legislation. Gerald Butcher, the Society's superintendent and a member of the executive of the National Union of Allotment Holders, reported a lack of sympathy and the 'customary wet blanket of officialdom', so that they had only been able to secure 140 plots by the outbreak of the Great War.[11] More successful, perhaps as they were more local, were allotment societies, such as the Hackney and District Smallholders Society, founded in 1909. Nevertheless there was a dearth, with only two-thirds of all villages in England and Wales having allotments, and the situation had become particularly bad in urban areas, with demand exceeding supply.

Some interesting pre-war attitudes to allotments emerge from the Essex University survey. One theme was the social aspect of gardening for working-class men. Frederick Hanrahan, a factory store-keeper born in 1903 in Liverpool, remembered how his father's friends were the men he met on the allotment: 'an hour or two on his allotment every night during summer. In winter, he sat by the fire.' A girl in service from Gospel Oak in north London recalled her father, a ganger on the railway: 'The evening of course was always taken up because he always did his garden in the evenings and grew his vegetables up there, everything.' And Elsie Baker, a school housemaid born in 1891 in Surrey, considered that the allotment was the only hobby enjoyed by her father, a carriage-maker.[12] For many, the allotment offered escape from a cramped cottage or terraced house, and was certainly a preferable alternative to the tavern as far as their wives and children were concerned.

The idea that women might cultivate allotments was considered by some as dangerous radicalism. In a government report made in 1867, it had been claimed that working on land would 'almost unsex a woman' and create social mischief by 'unfitting or indisposing her for a woman's proper duties at home'.[13] Flora Thompson may be referring to this when she observed that women never worked in the vegetable gardens or on the allotments: 'there was a strict division of labour and that was "men's work". Victorian ideas, too, had penetrated to some extent, and any work outside the home was considered unwomanly.'[14] Were there also intimations of the garden shed phenomenon? Despite such attitudes, there are mentions of women cultivating allotments. Thomas Caswell, a car park attendant born in St Helens in Lancashire in 1895, interviewed for the Essex

University survey, recalled: 'My mother was a keen gardener. Very keen. Had a plot in Mill Lane. Yes. Down by the railway wall you know . . . it was her one delight.' From this plot she fed the family with vegetables and fruit, while her husband looked after the chickens.

A group of workers that particularly valued their allotments were miners, who must have revelled in the fresh air after days spent underground. Another man interviewed for the Essex University survey remembered how his coal miner father devoted all his time to the garden and reckoned that he grew enough to last the family about a third of the year in vegetables and fruit. Born in 1894 in Arnold in Nottinghamshire, the interviewee was one of sixteen children. Little wonder his father took up what were called club gardens, three allotments, each 300 yards in length, as well as the garden beside his home. Here he cultivated his vegetables, gooseberries and raspberries, with an apple tree or two and a plum, from which his wife made jam. The indefatigable gardener also bred pigs and ducks, so that there was meat on the table every day. When asked by the interviewer whether the family ate tinned meat, he thought it rare: in fact, the survey shows that tinned fruit and meat were not part of the diet right across working-class communities. As the son of a Cornish tin miner pointed out, there 'weren't no tin openers in they days'. This interviewee, born in 1897 in Camborne, recalled that his father 'never left anything unturned that could turn – in the vegetables, for the house . . . don't matter how small, he would utilise the land or the garden'.[15]

Although Britain declared war on Germany at the beginning of August 1914, more than two years passed before serious concerns were openly expressed about the supply of food, and no rationing was imposed. However, at Christmas 1916 the Government issued the Cultivation of Lands Orders through a regulation of the Defence of the Realm Act (DORA). Gerald Butcher described this as 'the most drastic statute of land reform', pointing out that state appropriation of land for the common good was unheard of before the war.[16] Land was acquired for smallholdings and market gardens and allotments, and private households were urged to turn their gardens over to the cultivation of vegetables. The legislation came just in time, for potato queues were growing ever longer in the poorer areas of towns and cities. On 13 March 1917 the *East London Advertiser* reported an incident in Spitalfields Market, where a crowd of 2,000 desperate people gathered around the stall of one seller who had announced that his supply of potatoes was on its way from the fields. In their anxiety to buy, they pushed over the stallholder and his rostrum and

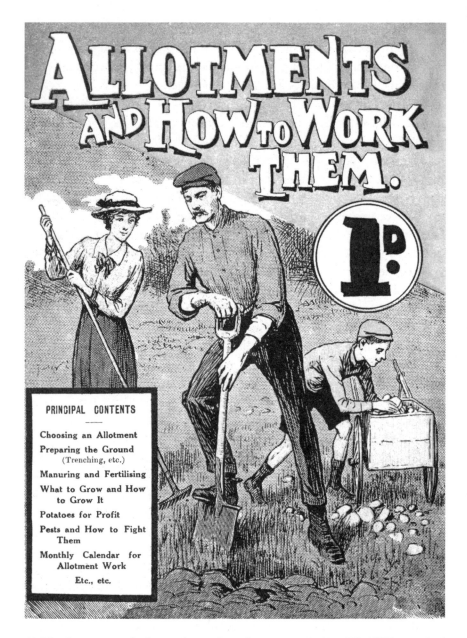

60 The drive to grow food in gardens and on allotments in the First World War involved many novice gardeners. This practical manual was produced in 1917 to guide them on their path.

the police had to be called. The previous month, Kaiser Wilhelm had threatened that German U-boats would 'frighten the British flag off the face of the waters and starve the British people until they, who have refused peace, will kneel and plead for it'. This chilling threat was prevented by a combination of naval convoys protecting British shipping and the national effort to grow as much food as possible.

A journalist who kept a diary during the First World War noted: 'It is likely that Boxing Day 1916 will be mentioned in years to come as marking the start of a movement for turning the urban classes of the community on to the vacant lands for the raising of food'.[17] By May 1917 it was estimated that the number of allotments, which had stood at around 450,000 at the beginning of the war, had more than trebled. Every bit of spare land was commandeered: undeveloped building sites, front and back gardens of empty houses, corners of parks and commons, golf courses and tennis courts. The great and the good chipped in. Prime Minister David Lloyd George made it known that he had turned his Surrey garden at Walton Heath over to the growing of King Edward potatoes. George V became a keen gardener, dividing his guests after lunch into two groups: one to serve meals to munition workers, the other to work on his allotments digging alongside Queen Mary and himself. The Archbishop of Canterbury issued a pastoral letter sanctioning Sunday labour, with ministers sent to the allotments to conduct services. Lloyd George and Sir Arthur Lee, in charge of the food production at the Board of Agriculture, did battle with what were provocatively called Britain's 'landowner Junkers' who objected to turning over their estates from pasture to agriculture. 'Was it for this that their fathers had enclosed the family lands?', they asked, as they were threatened with prison or the plough.

For rural labouring families, the war made little difference to their gardening activities, although their young menfolk left their villages, often for the first time, to sacrifice their health or their lives in the trenches. For the urban population, both working and middle class, there was inevitably a learning process when it came to the techniques of vegetable gardening. The Board of Agriculture issued a whole range of leaflets and instructors were sent out to plot-holders' meetings and to inspect allotments. The Government's Food Production department arranged for lectures to be given throughout the country on subjects such as crops, soil, manure and cultivation. Circulation of the journal of the VLCS, *Allotments and Gardens*, rose from 2,000 readers in November 1916 to 6,000 in June 1917, to 12,000 in December, and to 30,000 by March 1918. Newspapers, national and local, proffered advice. Thus in February 1917, the *East London Advertiser* launched its 'Notes for Allotment Holders', while in the following month the *Eastern Post* moved its similar advice column from the middle of the paper to page two.

Not only were many urban allotment-holders novices at growing vegetables, but they also found the sites difficult to cultivate, as they were often in industrial areas. An article in an Irish journal reported how one piece of ground in Belfast was:

> so bad that the plot holders were often to be seen (occasionally by moonlight), digging down to a depth of three to seven feet in order to bring the good soil up from below, and to bury the accumulated rubbish . . . So keen were the plot holders, that this ground, which had been regarded as impossible to cultivate, nearly won the cup for the best group of plots in Belfast in its first year of cultivation.[18]

Many of the gardeners there were shipyard workers. Another group of workers on the Isle of Dogs in London had the same experience. Even before the war the gardeners of the Millwall and Cubitt Town Horticultural Society had taken more than a year to clear their site, having 'to dig through two feet of old iron in a lumber yard, to clear away two barge-loads of burnt matches, and from the foundation of a house that was never built to remove thirty and forty tons of concrete ere they could lay down . . . their soil'.[19] Given that they were dock labourers, lightermen and boilermen, their day jobs were hard enough. Nevertheless they managed to grow cabbages, onions, carrots, beans and beetroot.

The VLCS recorded how Joseph, a brewery labourer from south-east London, had been given a site, and removed huge quantities of rubble, but found it all too much and abandoned the enterprise. His wife wrote a poignant letter to the Society:

> I am righting to ask whether you will give my husband a peace of land not to far from here. My husband is upset becas you have got no plots for him. He wants to giv up the beer but cant and if you will give him a plot i no he will give up the drink. I have fore children and a cripple and my husband to keep and so if I could have his wages instead of him paying it for drink we could be comferble. Please try and giv him an allotment as we used to have a garden when we came to London.[20]

Joseph duly got his plot and, apart from a couple of lapses, maintained it.

Sentiments about the unsexing of women were forgotten in the light of the task at hand. As Gerald Butcher pointed out, wives of soldiers proved especially good cultivators, 'demonstrating by their skilful manipulation of the gardening tools that they are worthy mates of their men across the seas'.[21] Women were enrolled into helping to measure and mark out allotment plots, so impressing one observer in Putney that he was moved to write a poem in commemoration of the 'new species of woman worker'. Titled 'Diana versus Mars', its verses included:

She passes through thy fertile land,
Nor bow, nor arrows in her hand,
Nor hunting-horn – as in the chase;
Hammer and pegs have ta'en their place.
. . .
Diana bids such wastes provide
Potatoes plump, and carrots slender,
Parsnips, succulent and tender,
Stout cauliflowers, and portly cabbage,
Gay Brussels sprouts and sombre spinach
Thus would she help thee keep each day
The German hunger-wolf at bay.[22]

Men, women and children of all classes had risen to the challenge, as one observer noted with enthusiasm: 'Allotments have now become woven into the texture of our national life . . . [The] new short-sleeved army, numbering now over 1,300,000 men and women . . . [has] held the pass with the spade while the country was in danger of semi-starvation. There is something more due to them than a notice to quit.'[23] But when war ended in November 1918 a 'notice to quit' was precisely what happened. The acres requisitioned from owners had to be returned, and a series of legal battles took place as gardeners resisted the surrender of their plots. *Allotments and Gardens* rallied the horticultural troops: 'Allotment Holders! This is the time to be up and doing. Your brothers are being evicted and others are under notice to quit. Their fight is your fight . . . The more you help the less chance of the postman knocking at your door with a pre-emptory notice to "get off the earth".'[24]

It came as an embarrassment to the government that so many wanted to carry on with their gardening, and that with the rise in price of fresh vegetables returning servicemen were also asking for plots. It has been estimated that 7,000 new applications for allotments were made in 1919, with demand hugely exceeding supply, although gradually the numbers declined. Significantly, when legislation was enacted for allotment provision in England and Wales in 1918, and in Scotland the following year, 'the labouring population' was dropped from the wording, reflecting the fact that the middle classes were now also allotment gardeners. The new Act defined an allotment as an area of land not exceeding forty poles in extent, wholly or mainly cultivated by the occupier who rented the land for the production of vegetables or fruit crops for consumption by himself and his family. Not only was allotment gardening considered a recreation for both the working and middle classes, but also an antidote to dangerous radical views, which had manifested themselves with the Russian Revolution. Neville Chamberlain wrote in 1920, that 'every spadeful of manure dug in, every fruit tree planted' converted the potential revolutionary into a citizen.[25] This is reflected in a description of Elsecar, a mining community on the estate of the Fitzwilliam family of Wentworth Woodhouse in Yorkshire: 'the first thing that strikes the eye is the number of its gardens and allotments . . . probably more than one for every householder, for some of the miners have two or three. And gardens are a fine antidote to Bolshevism.'[26]

The spectre of revolution returned just a few years later, with the General Strike in May 1926. Nearly a million workers had been locked out following a dispute with the mine owners, who were seeking to impose a reduction of 13 per cent in their wages, along with an increase of the working day from seven to eight hours. On 3 May the TUC called out in sympathy other industrial workers, including transport workers and dockers, but the strike was called off nine days later when it transpired that the TUC had been holding secret talks with the mine owners. The miners struggled on alone, but by the end of November most were back down the mines, working longer hours for less pay, while others remained unemployed for many years.

Joseph Barrie from Hetton-le-Hole in County Durham recalled in 1976 how during the General Strike his family survived thanks to their garden: 'Because my mother was a farm hand's daughter, and she always liked hens and things like that, the bottom part of the garden was hens and all the rest had to be dug. Mostly potatoes. Leeks, cabbages and we used to put a bit of lettuce in and we used to have a little flower plot at the top.'[27] Stories abound of how the miners were obliged to uproot their prized leeks, and to kill their beloved racing pigeons, their favourite sporting recreation, to eat.[28]

The importance of allotments to miners for recreation, sociability, and at times, such as during the General Strike, for survival, can still be clearly seen at Grange Villa, a small mining village near Beamish in County Durham, created when the Handen Hold Colliery was opened in the late nineteenth century. The officials' houses were built of stone in a terrace with front gardens stretching to the road, and tiny backyards. The miners, on the other hand, had brick houses, with small backyards but no gardens. Rising on the other side of the road is a virtual town of allotments, dozens of them, enclosed by fences and with numbered gates, as with the detached gardens at Hill Close in Warwick (see Chapter 6, pp. 149–50). These allotments still contain livestock, mostly concentrated in what is known as the 'poultry scheme'. Some plots are furnished with greenhouses, some with sheds, and some with crees for pigeons. The breeding of pigeons for racing and the cultivation of leeks for competition and the pot have for decades been the two pillars of Durham mining communities. Today at Grange Villa only one man still races pigeons, but the leek competition is going strong.

Rural communities in the 1920s and 1930s continued to suffer from agricultural depression, with wages reduced for labourers. In an interview given by Peggy Cole for an oral history project, she describes the difficulties for such families. Peggy, born in 1935 at Easton in Suffolk, was the daughter of a farm labourer who was dogged by bad health. During the 1930s the family had a tied cottage, with a garden allotment where vegetables were grown for the table, and chickens kept. But along with Brussels sprouts, cabbages, leeks, onions, celery and other vegetables, flowers were cultivated, such as candytuft, sweet peas, asters and pansies. A 'bumby' toilet was emptied once a year and the contents spread in a trench across the garden.[29]

When Raphael Samuel interviewed the residents of Headington Quarry, they emphasised the importance of the allotments to the impoverished community in the 1920s and 1930s. Fred Tolley's father had an allotment on Peat Moors – 'it was only 12 pole, but it seemed a hell of a lot when you started diggin' it'. The whole family was recruited to help with the potato harvest:

We used to have a couple of days off school, when we got the taters up. We used to go up, mother and us boys, and dig up all day and when

61 Market gardening was not always a large-scale enterprise. This photograph was taken in a garden in Rochdale in Lancashire in the interwar period.

the old chap came back from work, he come straight up and load them and away we come. Once we dug up the wrong plot – someone else's potatoes – and the old man came up at night; he swore, but he took them round to the fellow . . . it ended all right.[30]

For the urban allotment holders on the other hand, their plot could represent a day out. Margaret Prior's family had one of the Birmingham guinea gardens at Westbourne Road. In her memories of allotment No. 25, she recalled:

It was our day in the country, to escape city life, even if it meant a bit of weeding or hoing [sic]. We all helped. I remember Sunday teas up there and my gran and granddad and my aunts. It was good soil up there and got fed pig manure, delivered by lorry down to the allotment, and had to be shovelled and barrowed into the said garden. I remember beds of Madonna lilies, red peonies, pyrethrums, and borders of white pinks.

Another recollection of the interwar years came from Mrs E.F. Brookes: 'We had a garden at 40 Malthouse Meadows about 1936 . . . It was

62 Working on an allotment in the interwar period. Before the First World War, it was comparatively rare for women to help with allotment cultivation, but by the time this photograph was taken, it had become a family pastime.

lovely . . . We had so many visitors on Sundays for tea I would fetch the water from that nice cottage at the beginning of the lane . . . There was 13 apple trees, strawberries, currants, etc.'[31]

Ken Ausden, born in 1926 and brought up in Swindon, was part of an extended family working for the Great Western Railway Company. His family's allotment, possibly provided by the company or by the council,

> was about a mile from our house, along the canal tow-path, across the other side of the town near the railway sidings. It was a big allotment, about twenty lug, and in the spring we'd often spend all day there on a Saturday, Mum and Dad and all the kids and a great basket of jam and sandwiches, a thermos of tea and a bottle of Tizer. We all had jobs to do – Dad digging, Mum putting in the peas and beans and cabbage plants, and us kids hoeing and weeding and fetching cans of water from the brook when we weren't watching the trains go by.

This sounds like an idyllic family activity, but Ken adds, 'I hated it. It put me off gardening for life.'[32]

What the working-class gardeners thought about the invasion of their allotments by the middle classes is hinted at in an interview concerning the horticultural efforts of George Orwell, born Eric Blair, and his father, in the early 1930s. Percy Girling's father, a publican, rented an allotment in Southwold, Suffolk to the Blairs. According to Girling: 'What he grew on it, I don't know, but he and Eric knew nothing about gardening. . . . They were always coming across to borrow a rake or a shovel or ask what to do. They didn't have a clue – and owning an allotment was an odd thing for a man in his walk of life to do.' When asked what he thought their walk of life was, Girling replied: 'They were people who had missed their way somewhere, they weren't quite right, do you see? For instance, the allotment.'[33]

With the outbreak of war again in 1939, the government was determined not to be caught napping as far as food supplies were concerned. This concern was well-founded, for the nation was dependent upon a significant proportion of vegetables and fruit being imported from Europe, and thus vulnerable to blockade. Sir Arthur Lee's First World War telegraphic address had been 'Growmore', and this was initially adopted as the official slogan in October 1939. 'Growmore' bulletins, priced threepence each, were issued by the Ministry of Agriculture on what to plant and how to protect garden crops from pests and diseases.

But on 4 October the Minister of Agriculture made a rallying broadcast: 'Half a million more allotments properly worked will provide potatoes and vegetables that will feed another million adults and one and a half million children for eight months of the year, so let's get going and let "Dig for Victory" be the matter for everyone with a garden or allotment and every man and woman capable of digging an allotment in their spare time.' The catchy 'Digging for Victory' slogan caught the imagination of the media, and took over from 'Growmore', with a symbol of a foot and spade. The actual foot, his left, belonged to Mr W.H. McKie of Acton, in west London. Using the left foot was the traditional technique for those who were right-handed, in the belief that it resulted in a less twisted action when digging.

The response to this call to horticultural arms can be seen in some of the diaries kept for the Mass Observation project in the early years of the war. Mass Observation was founded by three men who met through the pages of the *New Statesman*: Charles Madge, poet and journalist; Humphrey Jennings, documentary film-maker; and Tom Harrisson, anthropologist. The project started in early 1937 with 500 volunteers from the general public as a 'national panel', who were asked to record the daily

63 The foot of Mr McKie of Acton in west London, featured on all the posters for the 'Dig for Victory' campaign. These posters were produced in their millions in various formats.

concerns of the family each month, including their dreams, hopes and fears. From time to time, they were commissioned to report on specific topics, and from the outbreak of the war in September 1939 some were asked to keep daily diaries. The diarists are predominantly, though not exclusively, middle class, but nevertheless give us a good picture of how the urban population coped with the horticultural challenges imposed upon them at this very difficult time. Thus, a thirty-seven-year-old commercial traveller, living in Wembley, records on 30 December 1940:

> Everybody busy on allotments, the food problem is now most realistic and so are the prices. It beholds everyone, with the opportunity, to grow produce in allotments and gardens, thus leaving more from the farms and market gardens for those people in the towns who have not the chance to grow any produce for themselves. I am afraid though that half the people who could grow stuff are not doing so. Some people who are able to, don't mind paying whatever price is asked, but that is, of course, not the point.[34]

Some diggers for victory found the challenges onerous. Lionel Randle, a thirty-four-year-old office worker, who lived in Bournville, probably had a garden provided by the Village Trust (see Chapter 12, pp. 290–1) as well as his allotment. His entry in his diary for 9 September 1941 reads:

> Had the day off from the office for the purpose of harvesting the potato crop from the allotment. I enjoyed the exercise, but the results were disappointing, most of the tubers being ridden with slugs. My enthusiasm waned again, and once more I decided to give up this allotment after the war. My emotions in respect to gardening fluctuate considerably. At one time I am in the clouds and at another in the depths. I have decided that the earth isn't in my blood, but no doubt I shall continue with the allotment for the duration.[35]

Neville Chamberlain's announcement of Britain's declaration of war on Germany on 3 September had represented bad timing horticulturally. This was the period of the year when plots should be dug over to allow frosts to break up the earth, and for winter greens to be firmed up. The novice allotment holders recruited in the autumn of 1939 would not realise that cottager's kale, known as 'hungry gap kale', was the ideal crop to plant over winter, and when bad weather hit right through to February 1940, winter cabbages froze and spinach wilted. Government advice to 'Plan for Winter as well as

Summer' proved too late. However, the government persisted, determined to get one allotment for every five households. The new diggers for victory were provided with information leaflets produced by the Stationery Office and the Royal Horticultural Society. Guidance was dispensed through model allotments, demonstrations in public parks and at the Botanic Gardens in Kew. The Wembley commercial traveller visited the model allotment in Hyde Park on Whit Monday, 2 June 1940, wryly recording: 'Not a weed to be seen and it seemed that every seed which had been sown had matured. It was all a bit too perfect, fine top soil a couple of feet deep, which must have been specially put there. Nevertheless the show must have inspired many people besides myself with the idea of trying to improve one's own efforts.'[36] The voice of wartime gardening on the wireless, C.H. Middleton (see Chapter 13, pp. 329–36) gave sensible hints on allotment gardening. Newspapers also provided guides on how to produce food, even if the reader had no garden. For example, the London *Evening News* published a feature headlined: 'Window-box salads. Beans on your bedroom sill. Tomatoes in tubs.'

In London every piece of spare ground was used. The Metropolitan Gardens Association, which had been founded in 1882 to provide open spaces through raising money for the purchase and layout of parks and gardens, and to encourage the conversion of disused churchyards and burial grounds, was invigorated by this new mission. By January 1940 seventy allotments had been created on a three-acre site in Wandsworth, and by April another six acres had been added, with prizes offered for the best plot. When bombs began to fall, ARP wardens' posts and fire-fighting groups asked the MGA for sites near their headquarters, so that they might grow vegetables.

The spirit of competition was yet again evoked, with certificates of merit offered by the Digging for Victory campaign for plots that 'in the opinion of judges are best cultivated to produce a continuous supply of the most suitable vegetables throughout the year. Every allotment entered for the competition will be visited twice by the judges, who will give points for cultivation, rotation, planning, compost heap, control of weeds, etc.' The response was good: 10,000 entering in one year, with 4,000 achieving the standard. For those who felt less energetic, a badge bearing the slogan 'Digging for Victory' could be bought for threepence.

Pig clubs were founded all over the country. As the Ministry of Food advised farmers to concentrate on the raising of cattle, especially dairy, so the number of pigs on farms declined. Instead, the government encouraged 'amateurs' to club together to buy, feed and look after pigs, maintaining the long tradition of gardeners and smallholders. Pig clubs were allowed to purchase small rations of corn or feed to supplement the scraps they could gather from their gardens and allotments. In London, the staff of the royal parks asked permission of their Controller, Lord Tryon, to raise pigs in Hyde Park, with the assurance that they would be secluded from public view. In February 1942 the *Daily Mirror* ran a story under the headline 'Pigging it in Mayfair', reporting that the National Fire Service had established a pig farm, along with a rabbitry, in a basement in this smart part of London. The pigs were doing so well that the firemen had started a stud book. Eventually there were 6,900 pig clubs all over the country, with hundreds of thousands of members. By 1944 domestic hen-keepers were producing about a quarter of the country's officially known supplies of fresh eggs, and by the end of the war the Domestic Poultry Keepers' Council estimated they had 1.25 million members owning 12 million birds.

The first leaflet under the Digging for Victory banner provided a cropping plan for an average garden or allotment to keep three adults and two children in fresh food for eight months, with root vegetables to the fore, and marrows suggested to bulk out jams and stews. The carrot was the great success story for the Ministry of Food. When a surplus of crops of the carrot occurred, it was suggested that the RAF's exceptional night-flying and target success was due to the vegetable's high levels of carotene. Dr Carrot, carrying a bag marked 'Vit A', was featured in recipe books and advertising campaigns, resulting in a marked rise in consumption, not only as a vegetable, but also in jam, puddings and a home-made drink, Carrolade. On the other hand, certain vegetables were not encouraged: cauliflowers were regarded as too temperamental, requiring lots of fertiliser and supplements: asparagus took up too much space; celery was thought to cause too much work for little return in nutrition, much to the disapproval of those from the north of England, who felt that the tea table was not complete without celery to accompany the cheese.

The government leaflets recommended types of vegetables that showed an interesting social mix. Varieties evocative of Victorian nurserymen and large country house gardens were represented by onions called Rousham Park Hero, Banbury Danvers Yellow and James's Long Keeping. The working-class garden was evoked by Rentpayer peas and Cottager Kale. Reminders that there was a war on came with Onward and Advance Guard, both early varieties of pea, and in 1942 the potato Home Guard, wart-resistant and an all-round heavy cropper, though often judged tasteless by the consumer. For novice gardeners bewildered by pests and diseases, the Ministry of Agriculture provided advice, from battling against rats, which they likened to Hitler as they destroyed so much food, to combating the cabbage white butterflies that invaded England from enemy-occupied France.

Fruit had to pass nutritional muster as far as the government was concerned. Gooseberries, packed with goodness, were strongly recommended, while strawberries were cast into outer darkness as they took up so much space to cultivate; market gardeners could be prosecuted for growing too many and ordered to uproot them. One victim of this purge was Douglas Gandy, who, unusually, began his market garden business on an allotment at South Kilworth in Leicestershire in the 1920s. Soon he was concentrating on growing roses, which were very popular in the interwar years, and taking over more allotments as the demand for them fell. By the 1930s, when he began to employ others beyond his own family, Gandy was growing 30,000 to 40,000 roses each year, sending them bare-rooted by rail throughout the country. This burgeoning enterprise was severely checked by the onset of war. By now based at North Kilworth, Gandy was obliged by government regulation to sell up his stock, including many unique varieties, and convert to food production. Not happy with vegetable cultivation, he was reported for growing strawberries and threatened with imprisonment if the fruit was not replaced by cabbages within a fortnight.

While wartime would seem good for the market garden trade, for nurserymen it was perilous. One Mass Observation diarist, Betty Hall, a garage assistant at Snettisham in Norfolk, reported that while she was working on her pieces of gardens, which had rose beds inter-planted with rows of vegetables, '[I] hear a big sniff from the road, look up to see our local nurseryman, who does not approve of our garden'.[37] Right at the beginning of the war, the *Gardeners' Chronicle* could see there was trouble ahead, putting in a plea from the Royal Horticultural Society for their readers to continue as normal:

> If orders are absent very much of the work that nurserymen have done during the past few years will be wasted. Moreover, it would be a calamity if, owing to the scarcity of orders, many of them were compelled to close their businesses entirely, for, unless some stock is retained during the war it will be many years after the cessation of hostilities before they will be again in a position to play their essential part in the horticultural life of the country. It is hoped that these points will be kept in mind by all amateur gardeners and that orders for trees, shrubs and other plants will not be discontinued unless this is found to be absolutely necessary.[38]

64 Anderson shelters provided a good opportunity to grow shallow-rooted sun-loving plants during the Second World War. Marrows were a favourite plant, with their scrambling habit, but gardeners could also indulge in a rare display of flowers.

However, many nurseries went under, and even those who turned to market gardening experienced difficulties with labour shortages, conscription and bombing. It was the larger seed companies, such as Webbs, Carters and Suttons, that were able to survive the war years and to expand their businesses to meet the huge demand for vegetable seeds. In early 1941, for example, Webbs were offering their 'popular collection' selected as an 'ideal assortment for the 10-pole plot', at the price of five shillings. This package was guaranteed to provide a plentiful supply of fresh vegetables throughout the year.

One new feature for wartime suburban gardeners was the Anderson shelter. Made from panels of galvanised corrugated steel, it was designed in 1938 and named after Sir John Anderson, Lord Privy Seal, who had special responsibility for air-raid precautions immediately prior to the Second World War. One and a half million shelters were distributed between February 1939 and the actual outbreak of war, with another 2 million thereafter, and were given free to those earning less than £250 a year. They were buried in the garden or allotment and covered with fifteen inches of soil, which could be planted with vegetables or flowers. On 10 August 1940 *Garden Work* ran an illustrated article, 'Turning your Dugout to Account?', in which it was suggested that marrows were particularly suitable, with their shallow roots, sprawling habit, and appreciation of the warmth of the shelter's roof slope. It also proposed that a dugout could be converted into an attractive rockery. As ever, the competitive spirit flourished, with prizes awarded for the best-planted shelter.

Margaret Prior's family were grateful for their allotment, located in the Westbourne Road site in Birmingham, where a makeshift shelter was created:

> By now my Father had taken over the allotment and being wartime we all 'grew our own' and 'did our bit' every weekend. Dad even dug an air-raid shelter. It was rather like a long trench which he lined with wood and covered with wood and soil. But when we looked at it somewhat later, it was full of water because of the heavy rains. We now had a new shed complete with a cast iron stove. It threw out a good bit of heat and we were really glad of it. Because when the bombing got bad in Birmingham, we decided to sleep in the shed every night.[39]

Even blocks of flats acquired allotments. The Peabody Estates were developed in the nineteenth century as pioneering housing for the poor in

London, the idea of the wealthy American banker, George Peabody. The estates in the central part of London, where land was at a premium, consisted of blocks of flats arranged around courtyards where the children of the resident families might play in safety, away from traffic. Pat Moriarty moved with her family into the Cleverly Estate, Shepherds Bush, aged six in 1939. She remembers the corners of the rectangular courtyards being turned into allotments during the war. With many of the men away at the front, or working long hours in reserve occupations, the allotments were cultivated by older, experienced gardeners. One of these was Jock, a Scotsman, who would watch out for manure left in the streets by the horse-drawn vans, much to the amusement of Pat and her friends, who tormented him on the subject. Little wonder that they did not benefit from the vegetables raised on his plot.[40]

By the end of the war the government had more than achieved their target of one in five households turning their gardens into allotments. But the 'we're all in it together' concept has always to be treated with caution, and not everybody was putting in equal effort. While one in every two working-class households were said to be digging for victory, the *Gardeners' Chronicle*, aimed at professional gardeners and their employers, was considering the difficulties of heating orchid houses during coal rationing. A correspondent wrote to the periodical lamenting the fact that the gardens of country houses had to be turned over to the billeting of troops: 'When one sees numbers of tents pitched and occupied by our troops, stretching almost throughout the whole length of some of our cherished herbaceous borders, one wishes that a larger number of our fighting men were plant lovers.'[41] *My Garden*, meanwhile, ran articles on snowdrops and dahlias, and deplored the necessity to cut corners and to lose staff.

When peace returned in 1945, there were probably one and a half million allotments under cultivation. Despite a post-war slogan, 'Dig for Plenty', a decline followed, as had happened after the First World War. Had the nation lost its appetite for allotment gardening and home-grown produce? The post-war period was to prove an interesting time for this particular branch of horticulture.

# CHAPTER 12

# Homes and Gardens

IN MARCH 1888 William Hesketh Lever announced: 'It is my and my brother's hope some day to build houses in which our workpeople will be able to live and be comfortable – semi-detached houses with gardens back and front in which they will be able to know more about the science of life than they can in a back-to-back slum.'[1] He was addressing his workers after his wife cut the first sod for a new model village, Port Sunlight. Lever's belief in vigorous marketing and his admiration for American branding techniques had inspired him to launch Sunlight soap, resulting in rapid expansion of his family's wholesale and retail grocery business, based in Bolton in Lancashire. In 1887, with his brother James, he moved the business to a fifty-two-acre site on the Mersey near Bebington, where he planned a self-contained colony for the workers alongside the factory.

This was one of a series of model villages provided by industrialists that was to wield a great influence on architects and planners in the early twentieth century. The cottages in Port Sunlight were designed by a series of architects in a range of picturesque styles, employing half-timbering patterned brick and white plasterwork, topped by ornate turret chimneys. The housing was sited above the roads, with much of the frontage turned over to open grass to give a landscaped unity, with the gardens placed behind the houses.

Lever became a Congregationalist, taking on their social consciousness. But he was also strongly paternalistic. As Gillian Darley explains in *Villages of Vision*, 'Like a possessive parent, Lever could not . . . leave the village which he had founded any measure of independence'.[2] Every man in the village was an employee of the factory that dominated the skyline.

Fellow industrialist George Cadbury took a rather different approach with his model village at Bournville. Cadbury had inherited his family's cocoa and chocolate manufactory in Birmingham's Bridge Street, but in 1879 moved to a site beyond the River Bourn, building a factory in a garden. Fourteen years later, he decided to forestall speculative builders by providing housing for his workers, buying up land piecemeal to create a village of cheap but good houses. Although the housing was not as stylish as at Port Sunlight, the gardens were more generous and occupancy was not tied to employment in the factory. In 1900 Cadbury established the Bournville Village Trust, giving over ownership and management of 300 acres, containing 800 houses.

Cadbury felt that a large garden around the house was almost as important as the house itself. The thinking behind the layout of the gardens was set out in a book published in 1906.[3] In all but the smallest cottages, a lawn was set nearest the house, with flower beds. Vegetables came next, with orchards at the end. To give each gardener a good start, the Village Trust made the paths, laid the lawns, rough dug the ground, planted the

65 Terraced houses, dating from the mid-nineteenth century, in Birmingham, with their tiny back gardens. Enlightened industrialists, such as the Lever brothers at Port Sunlight and George Cadbury at Bournville, set out to provide a very different environment for their workers.

hedges and fruit trees, shrubs and climbers. The paths had to be broad, at least three if not four feet wide, of six inches of ashes and three of gravel, and planned in straight lines. Where there was a lawn, the path was to run to one side of it, leaving as much space as possible for the grass. At the end of the lawn, the path should turn to allow access to vegetables and orchard, though if the plot was south-facing, it was advisable that the path continue down one side, to take the shadow of the hedge. Peas, beans, raspberry canes and so on were best planted north and south to get the sun to the length of the rows. 'The tendency is for amateur gardeners to favour winding paths, by which space is lost, besides the arrangement being inconvenient. The curved line is rarely in harmony with the setting of the cottage, and curves, if introduced, should be gained rather in the planting of trees and flowers, curves in colour being more pleasing.'

Close attention was also applied to the planting of the trees and climbers. Each Bournville garden was provided with:

> 8 apple and pear trees, assorted according to the nature of the soil, which, in addition to bearing fruit, form a desirable screen between the houses, which are back to back; 12 gooseberry, 1 Victoria plum, 6 creepers for the house, including Gloire de Dijon and William Allen Richardson rose, wisteria, honeysuckle, clematis, ivy in a number of varieties, *Ampelopsis veitchii*, white and yellow jasmine, etc, according to the aspect, as well as one or two forest trees, so placed as to frame the building. Hedges of thorn divide the houses, and form road boundaries. The choice of trees and creepers is determined not only by the suitability of soil or aspect, but also by the general effect gained.[4]

Like George Cadbury, Joseph Rowntree was a Quaker and a manufacturer of cocoa and chocolate. When he too began to create a community for his workers at New Earswick just outside York in 1902, he was in touch with Cadbury, who was flattered to be told that Bournville represented a starting point for the new village. Joseph, working with his son Benjamin Seebohm Rowntree, initially commissioned the architects Barry Parker and Raymond Unwin to build thirty houses within a community laid out on the best principles.[5] Unlike Port Sunlight or Bournville, no factory dominated the skyline. Instead there were simple terraces of houses, their bright red tiled roofs contrasting with the whitewashed walls. Footpaths led between the rows of cottages and lawns, as in ancient villages. Raymond Unwin had formed his ideas at Oxford, still dominated in the 1880s by the legacy of John Ruskin and William Morris. His brother-in-law and partner, Barry Parker, was also well versed in the Arts and Crafts movement, with its emphasis upon basics rather than ornate details. As with Bournville, Rowntree set up a village trust so that if the first community proved a financial success, then the profits could be used to provide another scheme.

Houses were built at the density of twelve per acre, compared with the fifty to seventy of inner-city slums. Many of the New Earswick houses were arranged in a planning element much used by Parker and Unwin, the cul-de-sac, angled where possible to face the sun and surrounded by gardens and common ground. Play areas for children, paths and gardens all took precedence over arterial roads, and care was taken that the backs of the houses should be quite unlike the murky rear of terraced housing that blighted so many towns and cities (Figure 65).

Parker and Unwin were also to work on the first garden city, Letchworth in Hertfordshire. This was the concept developed by Ebenezer Howard, who left his job as a City of London clerk in 1871 to travel to the United States, taking a job in Chicago, and thus witnessing the rebuilding of the city after a serious fire, involving the laying out of suburbs and extensive public parks under the label of 'garden city'. Returning to London, Howard absorbed a wide variety of ideas on land reform, including the works of the Russian anarchist Peter Kropotkin and the American Henry George. His own book, setting out his vision, was published first as *To-Morrow: A Peaceful Path to Real Reform* in 1898, and as *Garden Cities of To-Morrow* in 1902.

Howard's aim was to find a remedy for the overcrowded and unhealthy conditions in industrial cities that were growing fast, and the parallel depopulation and agricultural depression in rural areas. He felt that it was no longer acceptable for urban development to be left to the private enterprise of landowners and industrialists, and that access to the countryside was necessary for the complete physical and social development of humankind. His solution was to provide a different form of settlement, new towns created not for individual or corporate profit, but for the benefit of the whole community. These garden cities were to combine residential with industrial areas, to be well planned, and of limited size and population, surrounded by a rural belt that integrated the best aspects of town and country. The land for each garden city was to be purchased by trustees, and used as an asset against which the cost of development might be raised. His ultimate vision was an urban cluster of garden cities, with six communities of 32,000 people, and a central city of 58,000, all linked by rapid transit.

The Garden City Association was formed in 1899, and widespread interest fostered through international conferences, hosted by George Cadbury at Bournville in 1901, and in the following year by William Hesketh Lever at Port Sunlight. In July 1902 the Garden City Pioneer Company was formed, with Howard as managing director, to acquire a suitable site for the first garden city. This was achieved with the purchase of land at Letchworth and a master plan was drawn up by Parker and Unwin. The finances proved tricky, and the population remained below Howard's estimate, at just over 10,000 in 1917, 20,000 in 1951, eventually achieving his target of 32,000 in the late 1980s. More successful was his second garden city, at Welwyn, also in Hertfordshire, begun in 1919 and becoming a flourishing town of 10,000 residents by 1931.

Ebenezer Howard's friend, George Bernard Shaw, was initially sceptical of the concept of garden cities. His play *John Bull's Other Island*, written in 1904, features the following exchange:

Broadbent: Have you ever heard of Garden City?
Tim (doubtfully): D'ye mane Heav'n?
Broadbent: Heaven! No: it's near Hitchin.

But Shaw was eventually won over.

A garden suburb, as opposed to a garden city, was the brainchild of Henrietta Barnett, the wife of Canon Samuel Barnett, founder of Toynbee Hall in London's East End. She established a charitable trust to buy Wyldes Farm between Golders Green and East Finchley in north-west London, intending that 80 acres should be an extension of Hampstead Heath, while the remaining 243 acres could form a residential area. Parker and Unwin were brought in to design the first houses of Hampstead Garden Suburb in 1907, with other architects commissioned to work on individual buildings. The density was low, eight houses to an acre, with Parker and Unwin's hallmark cul-de-sacs, along with internal courts and closes. Mrs Barnett envisaged a population reflecting a mixture of all walks of life: 'the larger gardens of the rich helping to keep the air pure, and the sky view more liberal; the cottage gardens adding that cosy, generous element which ever follows the spade when affectionately and cunningly wielded as man's creation'.[6] Flats for artisans were built to the north, villas for the middle classes to the west and larger houses for the affluent to the south, adjoining Hampstead Heath. The Orchard was created for old people, and Waterlow Court for working women.

One of the architects employed by Mrs Barnett was Edwin Lutyens, who designed the central area, including two churches and an institute. He was dismissive of his patroness's ideas, describing her as 'a nice woman, but proud of being a Philistine – has no idea beyond a window box full of geraniums, calceolarias and lobelias over which you can see a goose on the green'.[7] Although in practice Hampstead Garden Suburb never really worked as a mixed community, becoming very much an enclave of the middle classes, the idea of incorporating accommodation for old people and working women did exert influence on the cottage estates built by the London County Council (LCC) in the years up to the First World War. Established in 1888, the LCC created a series of estates on the outskirts of the capital, at Totterdown Fields in Tooting, White Hart Lane in Tottenham, Norbury near Croydon, and Old Oak in Hammersmith. The number of houses per acre was higher than at Hampstead, but many of the ideas of Unwin and Parker, and Mrs Barnett, were adopted.

Raymond Unwin, a crucial influence on such developments at the beginning of the twentieth century, became Chief Planning Inspector to the Local Government Board in December 1914. He hoped to push through planning schemes for low-density garden suburban developments made possible by the Housing and Town Planning Act of 1909, but the First World War frustrated many of these projects. Instead, he was seconded as Chief Housing Architect to the wartime Ministry of Munitions, and with Benjamin Seebohm Rowntree built housing for munition workers at Gretna and Eastriggs on the Solway Firth, and at Mancot Royal near Chester, developments that prefigured the plainer manner of cottage housing adopted after the war. The Minister of Munitions was the remarkable Christopher Addison, a physician who had moved from medicine to politics, becoming MP for Hoxton – once an area of garden nurseries, but now an impoverished ward of Shoreditch in London's East End – and helping David Lloyd George with the introduction of National Insurance in 1911. In 1917 Lloyd George gave him the huge remit of health, housing, agriculture and the resettlement of the poor. Raymond Unwin was appointed to a committee chaired by the Liberal MP, Sir Tudor Walters: this body was set the task of finding a way that was both economical and swift to provide working-class dwellings across the country after the war.

Just three days before the Armistice, an article in *The Builder* observed: 'If the hundreds of thousands of cottages for the working classes, which it is expected will be built with government assistance, are to become real homes in which women are to spend contented lives, and bring up happy children, sound in mind; then the task is one worthy of the best and most sympathetic consideration of everyone concerned.' While new building projects were largely put on hold during the war years, old housing stock in inner-city areas had been deteriorating into slums. 'It is in these slums that the families of many of our brave soldiers now live, and to which they will have to return, unless a great effort is made to deal immediately with a substantial part of a housing programme.'[8]

The acute shortage of housing was highlighted by the Prime Minister, David Lloyd George, in a speech at Wolverhampton at Christmas 1918, in which he eloquently promised 'a country fit for heroes to live in'.[9] A report addressing the issue had been produced by the Tudor Walters Committee, which led to the Housing and Town Planning Act of 1919, whereby councils were required to provide new and adequate housing to meet an estimated shortfall of 600,000 and rising. The legislation, known as the Addison Act, provided generous government subsidies for local authorities to build new houses. This signalled a significant move in housing development from purely private enterprise, and in the three years from 1919 to 1922, 30,000 homes were built in this way around London, together with suburban estates on the fringes of other cities around the country. The momentum for council house building faltered as subsidies were withdrawn and then renewed by subsequent governments, but the spread of suburbia continued, with private enterprise overtaking local authorities in the rate of construction.

From 1919 to 1939, an estimated 4 million new homes were built, three-quarters by private enterprise. There was even a model industrial village in the modernist architectural style with generous gardens provided by Crittall Windows Ltd at Silver End near Witham in Essex. These developments not only changed the landscape irrevocably, most spectacularly around Glasgow, where 'the country is blotted out' according to one landowner, but also brought about a social revolution, for many of the residents of the private building developments bought their own houses, as opposed to renting, the norm for all but the wealthiest before the First World War. The revolution in housing produced a revolution in gardening too. As a contemporary noted in 1934, 'Suburbia is coming into its own. The balance of horticultural power shifts continuously from country to the "suburb". We are standing with astonished and anxious but hopeful eyes upon the threshold of a new horticultural era of new relations, new ideas, and new values.'[10]

The most ambitious local authority rehousing schemes in the interwar period were carried through by the LCC, enlarging the cottage estates begun before the First World War and developing new sites, creating a ring round London and doubling the capital's size. In 1991 some of the former residents of these cottage estates contributed to the charity Age Exchange their childhood memories, including those of their gardens.[11] May Millbank, who moved with her family from Kings Cross to Watling in Middlesex, described the shock of the new that must have been experienced by so many families. 'We looked out of the window and my brother, who was two years younger than me said "What's that over there". He couldn't make out what the green was or what the flowers in the garden were, and I was glad he asked because I wasn't sure if the flowers were also called grass.'[12]

First-time gardeners these men, women and children may have been, but they set to with determination. John Edwin Smith lived on the Downham Estate in south London, between Lewisham and Bromley. He recalled:

When we first moved in there was just a heap of clay in the garden. My father was a foreman bricklayer and I think he got one of the older bricklayers, who was a bit of a gardener, to come and mark it out. I remember him making a circular flower bed and ringing it with lumps of old stone and concrete that had been found among the building materials. I think my father took a few cuttings from the privet hedge and put them each side of the path leading to the front door, so that we had a continuous privet hedge all round.[13]

Joyce Milan's family moved to another of the estates in south London, the Page Estate at Eltham.

My parents set about developing a garden, something they had never known but had longed for. Mum was mainly in charge of the operations and it was remarkable what she achieved over the years. There was a large area of ground, so firstly a crazy paving path was laid made from broken pieces of plaster from the walls of First World War hutments being demolished. Half way along, a rustic arch was erected, which later supported huge bunches of Dorothy Perkins roses in summer. In the right hand centre was a circular rose-bed with fragrant blooms of every colour.

Every inch of the garden was used, growing flowers of every kind
... Behind the gate, we grew vegetables of all kinds, potatoes, carrots,
cabbage and Brussels sprouts. Even celery and cucumbers were given a
try. Mum planted a small apple tree which produced delicious fruit ...
Our garden was always a blaze of colour in the summer months, with
neighbours often calling at our door requesting their friends or relations could view, there not being much profusion of flora in Inner
London areas in those times.[14]

Phyllis Rhoden lived on the Downham Estate:

My mother was mad on flowers, she was a real garden lover. Her flower
garden in front of the house was a joy to behold, and I doubt if she ever
bought a plant. Different neighbours gave her cuttings and roots and
she grew a beautiful privet hedge by this method ...

We used to buy penny packets of seeds and get our bean poles from
a nursery off Burnt Ash Lane, Bromley. Mr Prior was a nurseryman
and it was really lovely going there and seeing all the plants growing.
From our seeds we grew mignonettes and little tiny black violas and we
had hundreds of flowers. Mother would gather rocks from heaven
knows where and she grew her Snow on the Mountains, London Pride
and the ice plants around them.

Our roses were the old fashioned kind, deep pink cabbage roses
with the most beautiful perfume. There were quite a few houses that
were being knocked down around our way and we used to go to their
gardens and bring an old rose tree home. We had large marguerites in
June, and the tall single sunflowers, but these were regarded as curiosities with their habit of turning their faces to the sun ... My favourites
were the hollyhocks which thrived under the plum tree and around our
windows ...

The well-tended gardens were all part of the scene and in summer
were an absolute blaze of colour. No one moaned about the grass
cutting and those were the days of non-electric garden machinery. It
was all part of having your own patch.[15]

A blaze of colour is mentioned again and again in contemporary
reports. The colourful herbaceous borders that had been a fashionable
element of country-house gardens in the late Victorian and Edwardian
periods were now favourite features for small gardens, recommended in

books and magazines. Richard Sudell, a popular garden writer of the 1930s, provided a useful key for their planning, echoing some of the advice given a generation earlier by Gertrude Jekyll:

> Colour schemes for herbaceous borders will vary according to taste, but a few suggestions might be helpful. Try a blue, mauve and white border with occasional groups of shell pink; start with pinks, whites and reds, increase to blues, yellows and orange and back to pinks and reds; for grouping try Salvia Virgata Nemerosa (purple) with Helenium July Sun (orange); Lavender with Nepata mussini; deep blue delphiniums with white Madonna lilies; Cheiranthus (deep orange) with Viola cornuta or Royal Blue Forget-me-nots.[16]

The fashion for brilliant colours is reflected by the seed packets produced by companies. In the 1930s George Russell, a York nurseryman, bred a strain of lupins in a warm range of mauves, pinks and oranges that adorned many a garden border, with the seeds marketed by Baker's.[17] Rock gardens also provided an opportunity for a colourful display, with Carters Seeds offering a specific collection, including yellow alyssum, white arabis, bright pink dianthus and aubretias in a variety of shades. As if this was not enough colour, crazy paving also came in a variety of hues, with gardening books and magazines eager to provide instructions and diagrams on how to lay the patterns once the slabs had been broken up.

Just as their Victorian forefathers had joined together in village horticultural societies, so the LCC estate residents started gardening clubs. Stanley Breeze, who lived on the Castelnau Estate at Barnes and worked as a plumber for the local council, described how such a club was set up:

> My supervisor, who liked gardening, said 'Do you think you and your Pop could set up a gardening centre on this estate?' Well, we had a meeting and my supervisor decided we needed a shed to trade from because we weren't allowed to trade from the council yard on a Sunday morning. After a couple of weeks he managed to get hold of this big shed and we had it put next to the church hall in Stillingfleet Road. We then got a notice all round the estate that the gardening club had opened . . .
>
> Naturally we used to buy in bulk and the big lorry came with the lime and pots and other things and I'd check it over . . . The things at the club would be about tuppence a pound cheaper than in the shops,

which in those days was a lot. We wasn't allowed to make a profit and we didn't want to, we were just there to help the people.

Violet Bunyan's family at Watling were also members of a club:

Everyone was new to gardening and you learnt from scratch. A little gardening club started up just for the estate and you could buy plants and anything else you needed at cost price. If you had something to sell or exchange, you could put a little note up. I had an allotment to grow vegetables, and we paid a very small rent for it, but you got your money back on it. At the club there was a shop where people could exchange vegetables and lend each other things.[18]

66 The prizes awarded annually by the LCC to estate gardens attracted stiff competition. This garden, at 7 Oldbury Road on the Watling Estate, won first prize in July 1930. Rockwork had become a popular feature, and can be seen here providing a border around the lawn.

Competitions were also organised, as noted by Stanley Breeze:

> A garden competition was started up by the LCC and each of the estates had a competition of their own. You didn't know when the judges were coming but it was sometime during the summer. Our estate was inspected and judged by the London Gardens Guild [this appears to be a branch of the National Gardens Guild at 9 Gower Street, recommended by Marion Cran in her wireless broadcasts in the 1920s and early 1930s: see Chapter 13, p. 329] and a couple of weeks before the competition, two people from the Guild, with a superintendent and perhaps a surveyor from the council, would come round. Once you knew they were on the warpath, you were out there keeping your garden up to scratch and there was great competition amongst us.
>
> Clem, a railway guard at 44 Barnes Avenue, used to take the prizes mostly. He had his garden laid out with concrete paths of diamonds, with crazy paving and all that sort of thing. He had a few bits of grass that didn't need mowing and those narrow flower beds, so he only had a small area to plant out. All he had to do was go down to the market and buy half a dozen potted plants, rather than bring them up from seeds . . . I think the first prize was ten pounds and a cup, and the other finalists got certificates. To show people who had got the prizes, copies of the certificates were put up in the estate office and as I worked for the council, I had the job of sticking them up.[19]

Wythenshawe was one of the garden suburbs created to tackle the nineteenth-century back-to-back and terraced housing that had deteriorated into slums in Manchester. In 1926 land was bought south of the city for development, much to the horror of some, concerned about the loss of the countryside. However, strong support for the acquisition came from Shena and Ernest Simon, Liberal politicians who became supporters of the Labour party. The Simons bought Wythenshawe Hall and Park and presented them to the city. The new estate was designed by Barry Parker, with cottage-type houses surrounded by gardens and open spaces. As in the LCC estates, a gardening society was established by the residents to provide advice, cheap seeds and the loan of tools. The Wythenshawe Residents' Association annual flower and vegetable show, introduced in 1934, became an important event, with prizes presented by Shena Simon. Flyers were posted around the estate well in advance, laying down the criteria for the garden competition: (1) Best cultivated and cleanest

67 A second prize was won by the owners of this garden at 45 Littlefield Road on the Watling Estate in July 1931. The gardener has used crazy paving to contrast with his central bed, with scree-loving plants between the slabs, as recommended in gardening journals of the time.

gardens, front and back; (2) The nature of the soil and situation; (3) The length of time the house had been occupied; (4) Whether any assistance had been provided by professional gardeners; and (5) The amount of money spent, with points awarded in proportion to outlay. The first year's programme for Wythenshawe's show carried its stated aim, 'to promote a healthy competitive spirit and desire for well-kept gardens on this beautiful estate'. The following year, two slogans were adopted: 'Nothing great is ever won without toil' and 'Beautiful gardens make happy homes'.[20]

There is a missionary zeal about these aims and slogans, which serve as a reminder that the brave new world of cottage estates brought difficulties as well as delights. The LCC estate at Becontree in Essex issued its residents with a handbook of regulations. For 1933, the handbook laid down the following rules about gardens:

Neglect of the garden spoils the appearance of any house.

It is of special importance that the front garden should be neat and tidy throughout the year.

A garden can be made to look attractive by the expenditure of a few shillings annually.

Strive to obtain a natural look rather than an artificial effect. Bordered edging and concrete paths do not give the restful effect of turf with neatly trimmed edges.

The residents of the LCC estates not only had local authorities watching them carefully. Where middle-class private residents found themselves cheek by jowl with working-class council tenants, there could be friction. When the LCC began to expand the Downham Estate, local private residents took the law into their own hands in 1926, building a wall across the interlinking road, which was not demolished until the Second World War when it was found to impede the emergency services. With the finely nuanced stratification of British society, working-class neighbours could also regard themselves as a cut above. Elizabeth Knight recalled how her father identified incomers as 'rag and bone people' because they did not have any roses or marguerites in their garden.[21] On the Wythenshawe Estate the council appointed an overlooker, an experienced gardener who was expected to ensure standards were maintained. These standards would seem amazingly demanding today. For example, Mr Pennington in 1932 was asked to remove a trellis he had erected next to his path to grow his sweet peas. When he ignored the directive, the council sent two men to pull it down. Charlie Hammond was likewise reprimanded for building a trellis to keep his son off his flowerpots.[22] Those who retained what were described as slum habits could face eviction, though the threat would seem to have been sufficient, for only six notices to quit for 'non-cultivation of a garden' were served in the whole of the Manchester District between 1921 and 1933.

Concerns about neglect of gardens on cottage estates are also shown to have been misguided by the statistics reported by Mass Observation in a study published in 1943.[23] The survey, which had been gathered over the previous five years (in peacetime as well as war), looked at the homes and gardens of people who lived in 'old houses' in towns ('Subtown' and 'Seatown'), in garden cities ('Modelville' and 'Gardenville') and in council cottage estates ('Oak', 'Elm' and 'Ash' – in fact, 'Oak' was Becontree, and 'Ash' was Watling). The great majority of those living on the estates wanted a garden, with only 4 per cent expressing no such desire, and another 8 per cent being doubtful. When the observers looked into the groups who neglected their gardens, they discovered that old people sometimes found them too much to maintain, while couples with children used the garden as a playground rather than for cultivation, leaving a tiny proportion that simply didn't like gardening.

Photographs of some of the winning prizes from the different LCC estates survive, showing little front gardens packed with flowers, demonstrating the ingenuity of the owners. But this abundance also brought down the criticism of writers and garden designers, who felt that too much was being created within the restricted space. One writer pronounced: 'Overcrowding is one of the evils of modern gardening and is greatly to be deplored. Trees, shrubs and flowering plants ought not to be grown for the sake of their colour display alone.'[24] Some of the cherished ornaments of these gardens were also targets for disapproval. In his tirade against the suburbanisation of one of the villages of his childhood, Little Binfield in Berkshire, George Orwell wrote of the horrors of 'the rock-gardens with concrete bird baths and red plaster elves you buy at the florists'.[25] After the First World War gnomes had lost their appeal as far as upper-class gardens were concerned. Aesthetic tastes had changed, and anything German in origin was not going to enjoy approval. Instead, the little figures had moved to suburban habitats, often accompanied by animals. Orwell talks of plaster elves, but they were often produced in concrete and then hand painted. Their future popularity was assured following the release of Walt Disney's film, *Snow White and the Seven Dwarfs*, in 1937. Gnomes were certainly present on the Downham Estate, as Edna Sevier recalled: 'I can remember seeing some gardens up at Woodbank Road . . . one was with a little bridge, gnomes and things, and that fascinated me.'[26]

In marked contrast to the regulated life of council estates, some chose to become plotlanders. Plotlands were largely a phenomenon of the interwar period, although a few date from the end of the nineteenth century, and some to the 1940s before the 1947 Town and Country Planning Act put paid to such an idea. They were the result of the agricultural depression that began in the 1870s when the competitive effect of cheaper food imports hit owner-occupier farmers, especially on marginal land, who were obliged to accept low prices for their land from speculators. The land was then divided into small plots and sold to those wanting holiday homes or smallholdings. The largest concentration of the sites was established on the south and east coasts of England and, although often

68 The proud owner of this garden dating from the 1920s was clearly impervious to the criticism levelled at small suburban gardens by writers and designers who disliked the abundance of ornaments. Animals rest on the base of his concrete bird bath, while a plaster gnome stands defiantly next to a Union Jack.

isolated and singularly lacking in facilities, appealed to working-class families as an escape, especially from the East End of London. The opportunity to own a home of their own, with a good-sized garden, meant that many in time turned their holiday home into their principal residence.

The Essex countryside proved a particular magnet for plotlanders, with a sizeable community at Langdon outside Basildon. Peter Jackson, who has co-authored a book on the Basildon plotlanders, is the descendant of two such families.[27] His maternal grandfather, Walter Firman, lived in Clapton in Hackney. It was while working in a public house in Leicester Square that he heard of the opportunity to buy land and in 1933 duly bought two plots for £20 on Hillcrest Avenue on the Dunton Hills Estate. Initially the family lived in a bell tent, spending weekends and holidays away from the noise and pollution of London. Sheds were then erected, followed by a bungalow, named 'Vera-Joan' after his two daughters. In the back garden an Anderson shelter was installed during the war, which Peter remembers as covered with cerastium, or snow-in-summer. Beyond the small lawn a central path led through an orchard of fruit trees, planted by Walter, a keen gardener like many plotlanders. Plums, damsons, apples and pears were carried back in bags to Laindon station and thence to London. The front garden, which extended along both sides of the bungalow, was set to lawn bordered by old-fashioned rose bushes, while the front gate had a climbing rose over a trellis.

Today 'Vera-Joan' and 'Wendover' (the home of Peter Jackson's paternal grandparents) have gone, and the land now belongs to the Essex

69 Walter Firman (left) with a friend in his plotland garden at Langdon in Essex in the 1930s. The garden is in its infancy, with some young fruit trees that were to become a flourishing orchard.

Wildlife Trust. Just one out of nearly 200 homes built on the site has survived as a reminder of this fascinating lifestyle. 'The Haven', now looked after by the Trust, was built in the 1930s by the Mills family and is opened as a museum. Just like Walter Firman's garden, the surrounding plot was planted with fruit trees and bushes, and vegetables and herbs were grown in the substantial garden.[28]

\* \* \*

For some council estate residents, the utopia proved too much and, turning their backs on their houses and gardens, they returned to inner-city life. The Becontree LCC estate in particular was a difficult environment for its tenants, most of whom came from the East End of London. Begun on reclaimed marshland near Dagenham in 1921, it was at the time the world's largest planned residential development, by 1934 covering 2,770 acres, with a population of 112,000 in 25,000 dwellings. In an estate with a population the size of a town such as Bath, the residents had few shops, schools, public houses or other communal amenities. Even means of transport were minimal until the District Line of the London Underground was extended in 1932. Little wonder then that one estate resident told Mass Observation she would prefer to live in 'a place where there are lots of gardens, but central and near London'.[29]

Meanwhile there were many living in inner cities who hankered after decent-sized gardens. Mass Observation noted that between 84 and 94 per cent of those living in houses in towns wanted a garden, while among flat-dwellers the figures were between 68 and 88 per cent. The lower figure was expressed by flat-dwellers who had flower-beds between the blocks.[30] Economics, however, often made it impossible for them to afford the rents charged on the council estates. Those applying for new LCC accommodation, for example, were required to provide a regular and punctual record of rent payments, monitored by a visiting inspector, who would also note whether the family was of clean and respectable appearance. Those who cleared this first hurdle had then to prove that their income was five times greater than what they would spend each week on rent, rates and fares to work. The rents were comparatively high: on Watling, between 10s and 17s 3d per week; on Becontree, 22s 6d for a six-roomed 'Cottage Parlour' type of house. On the Wythenshawe Estate the average family earned about £3 per week, while the rent was about 15s. So these gardens were only going to be available for what in earlier times might be called 'superior artisans', in regular employment and with a moderately good wage.

What is striking is the fortitude and determination of working-class urban gardeners in the years between the wars. George Cadbury's vision had been much greater than just Bournville: nothing less than the amelioration of the conditions of the working class and labouring population in and around Birmingham and elsewhere in Britain. A survey of Birmingham, produced by the Bournville Village Trust and published in 1941, described the innermost and poorest part of the city, where the typical housing was back-to-backs, mostly arranged around courtyards.

70 The Bournville Trust in their book, *When We Build Again*, published in 1941, noted how determined people were to have a garden even in the most congested urban areas. This minute garden was photographed in the central part of Birmingham.

Remarkably, a third had diminutive gardens around 100 square feet in size, some dating from the time when Birmingham was a large village, with open country less than half a mile from the Bull Ring. Copec (Conference on Politics, Economics and Citizenship House Improvement Society, specially founded in 1925 to improve Birmingham's dwellings) instituted reconditioning schemes, including transforming courts into 'gay little gardens'.[31]

Glimpses of what these might have looked like are provided by a voluntary collector for a provincial bank who went round the back-to-backs shortly after the Second World War and left an account of her memories. The industrial town is unnamed in the book, but mention of the jewellery trade and of bombing raids suggests Birmingham: 'Some of the courts . . . have patches of ground which could be gardens; and indeed, golden rod and rusty Michaelmas daisies do appear, and at the far end of one court, most astonishingly, giant dahlias.' She also tells of Mrs Butler, whose bow window was decorated with aspidistras and scented geraniums. In pots outside standing on green-painted shelves flanking her door, she sowed Virginia stock, mignonettes, candytuft and nasturtiums. On one occasion she sowed a scarlet runner bean in a box, and the shoot ran up to her window above, so that she could pick tiny beans from her window. 'Every year Mrs Butler planted a potato, and got it to flower and even to produce marbles of new potatoes. And once Edith [her greengrocer daughter] bought her a present of some parsnips, and instead of eating them, she also planted them in a pocket of earth near her drain.'[32]

Mass Observation recorded in detail a garden in 'Metrotown', apparently a cathedral city in the Midlands:

This garden measured about 25ft long by about 20ft wide. It was surrounded by brick walls 4ft high and topped by a green wooden trellis, 2½ft high covered with climbing plants. Immediately outside the back door was a small concrete yard, with a child's cycle in one corner and two bicycles under a tarpaulin in another. Opposite the door was a dustbin under a small shed, and next to it a child's sandpit with buckets and spades. In the middle of the plot was a small bit of lawn, with a greenhouse separating it from the kitchen, a concrete path separating it from a freshly dug bed on one side and a 2½ft trellis separating it from a freshly dug rose-bed on the other. At one end of the lawn was a small rockery surrounding a small ornamental pond containing irises and fish.

The investigator added:

> An exceptionally well-kept garden, and it is obvious that great pride is
> taken in it. The well-kept lawn is bordered by flowers and vegetable
> beds, and a small glasshouse grows tomatoes, etc. At the bottom of the
> garden there is an ornamental pond with irises and goldfish, edged
> with a rockery of stones and plants . . . The trellis work on the wall at
> the bottom of the garden is elaborate and decorative.[33]

This is a rare glimpse of a working-class urban garden in the interwar
period. But a record of some of the gardens in York have also survived
thanks to the investigations of Benjamin Seebohm Rowntree. As
noted earlier, he helped his father, Joseph, to create the model community
of New Earswick, just to the north-east of the city in 1902. The previous
year he published his first survey of life in York, in which he looked
at 11,560 families, almost all of whom lived in individual houses. He
defined three levels within the working classes: well-to-do artisans; families with regular incomes who usually inhabited four rooms; and the
poorest, many in slums. This was a perceptive observation, for the
tendency across the centuries and through to the present day is to lump
together the lower orders (and from the 1790s, the working class) while
blithely referring to the upper, middle and lower levels of the middle
classes.

Rowntree described the houses of artisans in 1901 as usually terraced,
with little railed-off gardens in the front, and in the back, a scullery, with
a small cemented yard 'sometimes with a narrow border of earth, a sad
apology for a garden'.[34] His middle category usually resided in terraces of
narrower houses, with the door giving straight onto the street, with a
small, and no doubt equally apologetic, garden at the back. The poorest
often lived in courts of back-to-backs, and he makes no mention of any
gardening activity, though the inhabitants probably had window boxes.

In 1941 Rowntree produced his second social survey of York, with the
aim of finding out what changes had taken place between 1899 and 1935.
This time he based his findings on 16,362 families, which covered almost
every working-class family in the city, again looking at three economic
levels. He was encouraged by what he found. The council houses that had
been built since the First World War, although not in the front rank
of layout and elevation, 'are in both respects immensely in advance of
anything which preceded them':

Up to 1920 working-class houses in York, as in most English towns, were almost without exception laid out on the monotonous and wasteful 'grid-iron pattern'. We have seen that this bad practice has too largely been followed in the lay-out of the council estates, but before 1920, none of the houses had gardens, unless a dozen square yards of border between the houses and the footpath, and found only in the best houses, could pass as such.[35]

Rowntree echoes the love of colour mentioned in relation to gardens of the interwar period:

Every house has a front and back garden, usually of from 200 to 300 square yards. In summer they are ablaze with colour. It is indeed amazing how soon families, most of whom had never had a garden before, turn the rough land surrounding their new houses into beautiful gardens. Go where you will in the different estates, everywhere care-fully tended gardens meet the eye, the death rate among weeds must be very high! Not only are the gardens beautiful but they are large enough to grow sufficient vegetables and bush fruits to make a valuable addi-tion to the family food and supply.[36]

* * *

Just as George Cadbury and Joseph Rowntree had, through their trusts, sought to improve the lives of the inner-city residents of Birmingham and York with gardens and flowers, so one borough in London wanted to enhance the lives of its residents through horticulture. Bermondsey, lying on the southern bank of the Thames between Southwark to the west and Deptford and Camberwell to the south, was one of the most over-crowded, industrialised and dreariest boroughs in London at the begin-ning of the twentieth century. In the 1920s it became a stronghold of the Independent Labour Party, with Dr Alfred Salter as its parliamentary representative from 1922 through to 1939. Like Christopher Addison, Salter was a physician who moved into politics to promote a policy of social welfare. In this he was supported by his remarkable wife, Ada, who became the first woman Labour Mayor in Britain in 1919. Ada Salter was a keen gardener, at one time serving as President of the National Gardens Guild, and became a driving force behind Bermondsey's beautification campaign.[37]

The campaign, as clarified in January 1920, set out to plant the borough's waste ground, private or public, with trees and shrubs, and to provide tubs, box gardens, rockeries, fountains and statuary. The council also offered to provide a window box to households on request. Unfortunately the town clerk, concerned with costs, cut back on these ambitious plans, though he did allow residents to be provided with free loam and plants. The campaign also sought to promote local public shows and competitions of flowers, garden produce, poultry, horses, pets and hobbies. Again the town clerk vetoed the proposals, though the department nevertheless organised two highly successful shows, one in spring and the second, a fruit and flower show, in late summer. In the years that followed, 9,000 trees were planted, and nine acres of largely derelict ground turned into model gardens and playgrounds for the enjoyment of Bermondsey's residents. A garden suburb was created, Wilson Grove, on the site of the slums of Salisbury Street, with silver birches planted and climbing roses adorning the cottage-type houses. This was intended as the first instalment of a wider programme of slum clearance, but with the drying up of housing subsidies, tenement blocks were built instead, a foretaste of what was to occur in cities all over the country in the 1950s.

By the end of 1923, Mr W.H. Johns, the borough's Superintendent of Gardens, reckoned he had under his care about 50 flowerbeds, over 15,000 square feet of borders and 168 window boxes. He was aiming for a profusion of colour, for as long a season as possible. Records show that the summer display included foxgloves, lupins, sweet william, orange lilies, irises, pansies, violas, musk, asparagus fern, snapdragons, geums, columbines and campanulas. For late autumn he planted Michaelmas daisies, dahlias and chrysanthemums to last until the first frost. Over winter, the beds were planted with pansies and polyanthus, and bulbs. The council also decorated its own buildings, including libraries and public rooms, with indoor plants and floral decorations. Mr Johns was determined to guide the residents of Bermondsey with their own gardening. In 1924 he persuaded the library service to insert leaflets with gardening tips into library books, and gave lectures to the local gardening guilds which proved so popular that he was invited to extend his circuit as far afield as Fulham, Acton, north Lambeth and Finchley. Local householders were winning competitions held by the *Daily Express*, while other newspapers sent their photographers to Bermondsey to take images of the gardens. Mr Johns's mignon dahlia seedlings were confirmed as a new strain, 'Coltness Purple', 'Yellow' and 'Salmon' by the RHS. The Society went on to grant his wish that the 'Salmon' be renamed as 'Bermondsey Gem' and the 'Yellow' as 'Rotherhithe Gem', which must have delighted Ada Salter, who was particularly keen on the dahlia.

A booklet published in 1934 declared: 'The drab sordidness of Old Bermondsey will have gone forever, and the district will be illuminated with touches of colour and beauty never known before. We shall have available to all the inhabitants many of the benefits of civilisation previously obtainable only by the favoured classes who could afford to live in the most desirable residential areas.'[38]

Bermondsey's pioneering horticultural work was not adopted by other boroughs in the interwar period, but the London Gardens Society (LGS), founded in the early 1930s, played an influential role in encouraging the capital's working-class gardeners. In 1938 Lord Snell, Chairman of the LCC, wrote:

> We take just pride in our London; but we know how mean and unworthy are some of her streets . . . Many splendidly tended gardens are, however, to be seen; and looking up at windows, or getting a glimpse of the back of houses, we find evidence that numbers of our fellow citizens who are not fortunate enough to have their own garden plots, yet manage to improve a dreary environment by flowers – it may be only a pot or two, but we get a sense of pleasant people behind, who care for things worth caring for . . . There is a real need for an organisation which can help, encourage and inspire London flower-lovers in beautifying their own surroundings and thus doing their share in ameliorating the drabness of bricks and mortar in our beloved City. This is the function which the London Gardens Society aims to perform.[39]

Competitions were held for the best-kept garden, and in 1938 an astonishing 65,000 gardeners entered as competitors, of which 1,611 were judged in a final of the All Gardens Championships. The Society had gained the patronage of Queen Mary, who made tours of inspection, and photographs show her resplendent in her toque and formal dress, flanked by proud residents in their back gardens. The society also produced a series of very modestly priced booklets. In *Hints for the Town Gardener*, issued in 1938 from the society's headquarters in Whitehall at the price of sixpence, 'First Steps in a Town Garden' were given. Two main problems were identified: pollution and the physical condition of the soil. Not much could be done about the first, a centuries-old problem, but hints on

71 The caretaker of a London Dockland club growing tulips, a photograph taken by the London Gardens Society in 1939.

trenching were provided for the second. Membership of the local Gardens Guild was also recommended, with cooperative purchase in bulk of gardening necessities, letting of lawn mowers, rollers, and even vases. Mr Ashmore from the RHS advised on suitable plants, putting in a plea for perennials in every colour, and particularly singling out heleniums, Michaelmas daisies, delphiniums, hollyhock, anthemis and lupins. Dahlias were also recommended, especially the 'Coltness' strain, the favourite of Bermondsey. Simplicity was urged: 'Cut out all affectations, such as small bridges, which with luck may support the weight of a cat, dwarf human figures, china animals, glass ornaments, model houses, windmills, etc.'[40]

The booklet also provided advice on window box gardening, with diagrams on how to construct the boxes in wood. Lists of suitable plants for sunny and shady positions were given, along with colour schemes. Old favourites appear, such as creeping jenny, nasturtiums and geraniums, with light wire trellis suggested for use with climbers. Interestingly, the great Victorian standbys of musk and balsam were not included. Hanging baskets came in two types: an ordinary flower pot with curved edges; or a bowl shaped with curved and straight edges, preferred by the author. Again lists of plants were suggested, including a variety of ferns.

72 Mrs Dyble of Blackfriars Road in London, with her tiny glass-house garden on the roof of a glass-sign factory, in 1939.

The Society's pictures of window boxes were reproduced in another book, Walter P. Wright's *Window Gardening*. Wright pointed out in his preface that window gardening 'is open to all classes, and it is gratifying to realise that the tenement-dweller in industrial districts appears to be equally able and willing, with the occupant of the most imposing set of "mansions" to perform his part'. He defined new blocks of self-contained suites of rooms as 'flats', or, when occupied by the working classes, as 'tenements'. For tenements he particularly recommended aspidistra, geraniums and hyacinth. Wright also advocated roof gardens: 'On the summit of many a flat-roofed building, whether dwelling-flat, or warehouse, or set of offices, attractive gardens can be made and the use of tubs, pots, boxes with wooden and wire frames.'[41]

Gardeners on very modest incomes could get seeds and plants from local garden guilds, as noted above. They could also buy from street markets, such as Columbia Road in Shoreditch. The flower market, which is still flourishing, appeared at the beginning of the twentieth century following the failure of an elaborate food market built by the philanthropist Angela Burdett-Coutts. Her project was based on a planned railway line to deliver fish, which never materialised, while the traders preferred to sell outdoors and their customers, many of whom were Jewish immigrants, wanted to buy on a Sunday. The flower market also began as a Saturday enterprise, but by a parliamentary act was moved to Sunday, enabling Covent Garden and Spitalfields traders to sell their leftover stock. Hard by the market is Leopold Buildings, a Victorian block of flats with spacious balconies and window boxes, attesting to the traditional love of flowers of London's East Enders.

On 10 June 1939 *Picture Post* published an illustrated spread on London gardens, noting that 'Every Londoner longs for a garden. Few can afford a big one. But thousands grow glorious flowers in backyards, and window-boxes, even on roof-tops.' The capital was growing ever bigger:

it captures the countryside; but it cannot so easily capture the countryman. It can send him to work in a factory, lodge him in a street of slum-dwellings, maroon him in a desert of tarmac and give him chimney-pots for a horizon – but it cannot deprive him of his desire to make things grow . . . In this enterprise, the Londoner has the support of the London Gardens Society . . . It pleads the working man's need for a garden, or at least a window-box, with those who are re-building the city.

73  Children planting out a garden on a new LCC estate in Hackney in 1939.

The accompanying photographs show the variety of gardens that might be cultivated by working-class gardeners not only in London but in cities throughout Britain. Caretaker Pearce digs his Dockland plot, filled with tulips. Mrs Dyble of Blackfriars Road shows her garden of boxes on the roof of a glass-sign factory. Asked how she made her dahlias, chrysanthe-mums and cowslips grow, her reply is 'I don't; they come up because they know I like them'. Mr Jobson, a tram-driver, attends to his herbaceous borders despite the chemical vapours given off by local industries in Canning Town. And Mr Clarke, unemployed, sets children to work on a new council estate in Hackney. The children are shown tending beds of flowers against a backdrop of tenement blocks.

It is a poignant spread, for within two months this world was to be changed forever by the outbreak of the Second World War.

CHAPTER 13

❦

# Ancient and Modern

'HER COTTAGE STOOD among the white mounds, with a strip of garden at the back where she grew her "yarbs". Here were horehound, tansy, pennyroyal, balm o'Gilead, all-heal, mallow and a hundred more.' This description of a healer's garden is from Mary Webb's novel, *The Golden Arrow*, published during the First World War. Webb is known for her tales of rustic life with their passionate undertones, so effectively parodied by Stella Gibbons in *Cold Comfort Farm* that the original novels are rarely quoted. However, Webb was a market gardener, selling her produce at Shrewsbury market, and she knew her plants. In *The Golden Arrow* she goes on to list the healer's 'acknowledged' patients: 'old folk with rheumatism, rickety children, field workers with a gashed hand or a whitlow, drunkards' wives with bodies covered with bruises – she prescribed with surprising efficiency; her cures were simple, often drastic, usually very sensible'.[1]

Five years earlier, the then Chancellor of the Exchequer, David Lloyd George, had introduced a scheme of National Insurance as part of his raft of measures to improve the lot of the working classes and to establish the idea of the welfare state. Although these ideas were considered by some as the end of civilisation as we know it, they seem modest today. The 1911 insurance scheme provided medical cover only for the husband, and the wife if she worked, but not the children. In times of illness a family could become 'panel patients', with a standard charge for a visit by the general practitioner of 2s 6d, on top of which medicine usually cost between sixpence and one shilling. Farm wages for agricultural labourers in the years leading up to the First World War were often as low as twelve shillings per week, so that this kind of expense was out of the question except in dire circumstances. This situation was to continue after the war. One person born in 1915 recalled: 'Working class people seldom saw a doctor because of the cost . . . Mostly it was remedies mother had learned from her mother, or something a neighbour suggested.'[2]

People living in rural areas were able to forage among the hedgerows, and many took full advantage of this, especially for concoctions that could be kept on the shelf. However, in the case of an emergency such as a burn or a cut, speed was of the essence and therefore the healer or the housewife would have grabbed a plant within easy distance, and this is when the garden came into its own. Dora Coates, in her book *Cottage Housekeeping*, underlined how the herb patch was an important corner of the cottage garden, repeating plants mentioned by Mary Webb such as balm and tansy, and adding goldenrod, comfrey, betony and camomile. Some of these were traditional garden plants, others were brought in from the wild. An Essex man speaking in the 1920s remembered: 'In our garden my father grew a clump of "Mugwort" and I think my mother used this for irregularities peculiar to women.'[3] His father had issued strict instructions that it was not to be pulled up, to assure a constant supply. Mugwort, or *Artemesia vulgaris*, was described by Nicholas Culpeper as a herb of Venus, 'most safe and excellent in female disorders' when drunk as a kind of tea with milk and sugar.[4]

This Essex household may well have had copy of Culpeper's herbal, the venerable survivor from the seventeenth century. Another, more unlikely, survivor was the herbal of John Gerard, probably as emended by Thomas Johnson and published in 1633. Agnes Arber, an authority on herbals, was told by a man who was born in 1842 that, 'during his boyhood in Bedfordshire, he was acquainted with the cottager who treated the ailments of her neighbours with the help of a copy of Gerard's herbal'.[5] Another example of Gerard being used for remedies is given by Frederick Wigby in his autobiography, *Just a Country Boy*.[6] The midwife who brought Frederick into the world in the Norfolk hamlet of Wicklewood in 1912 was Granny Davis, a practitioner of herbal remedies. She used traditional local names for many of the plants, so that the wild pansy, hearts-ease, was known as three-faces-in-one hood, a reference to the appearance of the flower, and love-in-idleness, so important to the plot of Shakespeare's *A Midsummer Night's Dream*. The stonecrop went by the wonderful name of welcome-home-though-ever-so-drunk. Gerard himself was remembered in 'herb gerard', an alternative name for goutweed.

Gabrielle Hatfield, in *Memory, Wisdom and Healing*, shows the parallels between some of the remedies of Granny Davis as described by Wigby and those of Gerard. Thus Granny Davis made a mixture of ground ivy with celandine and daisies, crushed and strained, and added to sugar and rose water to treat inflammation of the eyes. Gerard's version reads: 'Ground-Ivy, Celandine and Daisies, of each a like quantitie, stamped and strained, and a little sugar and rose water put thereto, and dropped with a feather into the eies, taketh away all manner of inflammation, spots, webs, itch, smarting, or any griefe whatsoever in the eyes.' Granny Davis chose henbane in vinegar to treat toothache. Gerard also used the herb: 'The root boiled with vinegar, & the same holden hot in the mouth, easeth the pain of the teeth.' For a cough, Granny Davis took coltsfoot. Gerard's recipe recommended a decoction of coltsfoot 'made of the green leaves and roots, or else a syrup thereof, is good for the cough that proceedeth of a thin rheume'.[7] The conclusion must be that the old lady had a copy of the seventeenth-century book with its precious illustrations of the plants. This was something that an original copy of Culpeper could not provide; it was only in the early nineteenth century that a publisher added pictures.[8]

Frederick Wigby recalled:

> When I was a boy, such things as aspirin, penicillin and other anti-biotics, were unknown. Beecham's Pills, Epsom Salts, senna pods, castor oil, lime tea and liquorice powder were in common use as laxatives. There were no injections and no sick benefit, apart from the small amount of money father received from the Foresters' Sick Club when he was ill. In most cases of minor illnesses, mother and father knew what to do and Mother Nature provided the remedy. If my parents could not cure our common ailments they sought advice of Granny Davis. The town doctor was only called in when all else had failed. In her garden, tended with loving care, were the many herbs that she used in her potions and lineaments; others she gathered from meadow, hedgerows and bank.[9]

Some of the remedies came not from a garden's herb patch but from the flower garden. In a letter to Gabrielle Hatfield in 1985 a man in West Suffolk recalled 'what my mother used to do before the [Second World] War. The White Madonna Lily she used to gather the white petals put them in a jar then cover them with Brandy, when we used to cut ourselves she put one of the petals on the cut and cover with a Bandage it used to tingle a bit. But it healed it up.'[10] This is just one record of this remedy

‡ 5 *Hyoscyamus flore rubello.*
Henbane with a reddish floure.

¶ *The Place.*

Blacke Henbane grows almost euery where by highways, in the borders of fields about dunghils and vntoiled places: the white Henbane is not found but in the gardens of those that loue physicall plants: the which groweth in my garden, and doth sow it selfe from yeare to yeare.

¶ *The Time.*
They spring out of the ground in May, bring *flouring* forth their floures in August, and the seed is ripe *ming of Iu* in October.     *1672.*

¶ *The Names.*
Henbane is called of the Grecians, *ύοσκύαμος* : of the Latines, *Apollinaris*, and *Faba suilla* : of the Arabians, as *Pliny* saith, *Altercum* : of some, *Faba Iouis*, or *Iupiters* bean : of *Pythagoras, Zoroastes*, and *Apuleius, Insana, Alterculum, Symphoniaca*, and *Calicularis*: of the Tuscanes, *Fabulonia*, and *Faba lupina* : of *Matthæus sylvaticus, Dens Caballinus, Milimandrum, Cassilago* : of *Iacobus à Manlijs, Herba pinnula* : in shops it is called *Iusquiamus*, and *Hyoscyamus*: in English, Henbane: in Italian, *Hyosquiamo* in Spanish, *Velenno* : in high-Dutch, **Bilfen kraut** : in French, *Hannebane, Endormie* : the other is called *Hyoscyamus albus*, or white Henbane.

¶ *The Nature.*
These kinds of Henbane are cold in the fourth degree.

¶ *The Vertues.*

Henbane causeth drowsinesse, and mitigateth all kinde of paine : it is good against hot & sharp A distillations of the eyes and other parts : it staieth bleeding and the disease in women : it is applied to inflammations of the stones and other secret parts.

The leaues stamped with the ointment *Populeon*, made of Poplar buds, asswageth the pain of the B gout, the swelling of the stones, and the tumors of womens brests, and are good to be put into the same ointment, but in small quantity.

To wash the feet in the decoction of Henbane causeth sleepe ; or giuen in a clyster it doth the C same, and also the often smelling to the floures.

The leaues, seed, and juice taken inwardly cause an vnquiet sleep like vnto the sleepe of drun- D kennesse, which continueth long, and is deadly to the party.

The seed of white Henbane is good against the cough, the falling of watrie humors into the eys E or brest, against the inordinat flux of womens issues, & all other issues of bloud, taken in the weight of ten graines, with water wherein hony hath bin sodden.

The root boiled with vinegre, & the same holden hot in the mouth, easeth the pain of the teeth. F The seed is vsed by Mountibank tooth-drawers which run about the country, to cause worms come forth of the teeth, by burning it in a chafing dish of coles , the party holding his mouth ouer the fume thereof : but some crafty companions to gain mony conuey small lute-strings into the water, perswading the patient, that those small creepers came out of his mouth or other parts which he intended to ease.

74 The traditional remedy to relieve toothache was henbane boiled with vinegar, as recommended in Thomas Johnson's emended version of Gerard's herbal, published in 1633, as shown here. Practitioners of herbal remedies continued to use Gerard's book right through to the twentieth century. Henbane should not be taken internally, so had to be applied with caution.

among many. The vegetable plot also yielded up ingredients for treatments. Raw onions could be rubbed on burns, while after roasting they were good for earache. Horseradish was applied to cuts and used for sore throats. Potatoes were efficacious against rheumatism, one of the banes of agricultural labourers and gardeners. In eighteenth-century Scotland, a recipe for the relief of rheumatism in the feet used water in which potatoes had been boiled, as hot as was bearable. This remedy may have played a part in the outdoor workers' habit of carrying an uncooked potato as an antidote to rheumatics and arthritis, as noted by the nineteenth-century photographer, P.H. Emerson, in his record of East Anglian life. He thought the peasants that he met were 'as wise as the Faculty'.[11]

From the roofs of outbuildings the houseleek (*Sempervivum tectorum*) could be plucked to make into a poultice for bad cuts. Cobwebs were also used as a form of bandage for wounds. An account of the latter was

75 Figwort is a signature plant, with protuberances on its roots that resemble piles and the tubercular glands of the King's Evil. It was used to cure piles (or 'figs'), ulcers and cancers. This drawing was made by James Sowerby in 1803 for *English Botany*.

76 The astringent roots of tormentil were traditionally boiled in milk and given to calves as well as children to bind their loose insides. The name derives from the Latin, *Tormina*, meaning colic – which is a torment, particularly for the young. James Sowerby made this drawing of tormentil in 1801.

recounted by a retired postman who had worked earlier as a farm labourer. When a friend was seriously cut on the arm by a billhook, he shouted for cobwebs from the barn, wrapping the wound which healed cleanly and quickly.[12] In *A Midsummer Night's Dream* Shakespeare has Bottom meeting Titania's attendant fairy, Cobweb, and saying 'if I cut my finger, I shall make bold of you', showing that this was a long-established tradition.[13] Families had not only to look after themselves, but any animals they might own. Frederick Wigby also recalled Miss Milly, eighty years of age: 'In her herb garden she kept a bush shrub, the leaves of which when plucked, cropped and mixed with the leaves of young green nettles was considered to be a remarkable cure for the "gapes" in chickens and "black head" in turkeys.'[14]

The situation in towns and cities in the early twentieth century was rather different. While the poor were not able to go out to forage in the hedgerows, and often had only small plots or backyards if they were lucky, they could avail themselves of charitable medical aid and were often members of friendly societies. But there are records of practitioners of home remedies in urban areas, relying on plants from their gardens and dried herbs acquired from the shops of chemists. One lady, born in 1920 into a mining community, recalled what she called the 'Head Consultant' who 'had a Philosophy that there was a Herb for every illness known to mankind. All mothers-to-be were prescribed an infusion of Raspberry tea, taken throughout their pregnancy, for an easy delivery. Parsley Tea for Bladder troubles: Thyme for indigestion and Stomach Acidity; Wormwood tea for a Tonic, and Depression. Sage tea for the menopause. Camomile tea for headaches.' She wryly noted 'that very often the Herb prescribed perhaps for falling hair was often the same as for some other ailment. No matter of argument, the afflicted had faith in these remedies, believed in them and found relief in their usage.' Like their rural counterparts, urban families used onions, boiled and made into a poultice, for earache, while a drink made from roasted turnip juice sweetened with sugar was used to treat coughs.[15]

During the Second World War, County Herb Committees were established and asked to collect tons of nettles, from which chlorophyll was extracted for medical use.[16] The Women's Institutes were likewise sent out to collect rose hips, foxgloves, deadly nightshade and other plants for use in medicines as stocks grew low. The Beveridge Report of 1942 recommended that with the end of the war there should be created a 'comprehensive health and rehabilitation service for the prevention and cure of disease', and when the National Health Service was set up in 1948, medical treatment was initially completely free at the point of use.

This enormously important revolution made it possible for the poorest members of society to have access to medicines, and a visit to the doctor was no longer a source of financial anxiety. This, of course, did not mean the end of gardening for herbal remedies: indeed, they remain a significant factor in medical care.

* * *

Oral traditions were applied to general gardening as well as to medicinal, with local knowledge passed down through generations in rural communities. George Ewart Evans quoted how the gardeners in Suffolk he interviewed for his book, *Where Beards Wag All*, contended: 'The books won't tell you what to do in your own particular garden. You've got to find that out for yourself.'[17] It was important to know the type of soil and what could grow in it, and traditional sayings provided pointers to these. Thus if corn spurrey – known as hungerweed – grew in a garden with the sandy soil of Hampshire, Surrey and Sussex, this was a sign that manure needed to be applied. In Lincolnshire it was said that a sixpence could be found at the bottom of a thistle's root. This might suggest that thistles indicated good soil, a belief held in Ireland, or the opposite, that every thistle plant removed a sixpence-worth of goodness from land.[18]

Timings were also important. Thomas Tusser had provided a calendar in his *Five Hundred Pointes* based on the old agricultural year and feast days, and similar sayings have survived over the centuries. Devon gardeners, for example, were told to keep tender plants indoors until the days of the local saint, St Frankan, or St Dunstan (19–21 May), had passed. This seems to have been based on a legend that the Devil made a pact with a local brewer named Frankan that he would ensure frosts on the three nights to damage apple blossom, diminish production and thus limit the production of cider, as long as the brewer adulterated his beer. The horticultural equivalent of never casting a clout until May is out is the saying 'It ain't spring until you can plant your foot upon twelve daisies'. The tradition that whatever the weather on St Swithin's Day (15 July) holds good – or bad – for forty days thereafter is well-known. However, another more unusual connection with the saint, a counsellor of the kings of Wessex, is that 'Till Swithin's Day be past, the apples be not fit to taste'.[19]

Good Friday was the date for all kinds of gardening activities, despite the fact that Easter was a moveable feast. In Wales it marked the time to plant seed potatoes; in Essex, onions; and in the North East, the all-important leek. A coalminer who worked in the Durham pits in the 1920s and 1930s described in an interview how 'Good Friday was red hot'. For these miner gardeners, the highlight of the horticultural year was the leek show in September or October. Good Friday was a rare holiday from the pits, and the chance to get the precious seeds into the ground.[20] Throughout the British Isles there was a belief that parsley should be sown on Good Friday. It was thought that the seeds visited the Devil in Hell on the day of Christ's crucifixion.

Throughout the years, the garden was planted, cultivated and harvested using these traditions, some based on observations made by one family, others more widespread. Many of the old sayings disappeared from rural communities with the Second World War, but others are with us still.

Forster's Education Act of 1870 provided almost universal, albeit rudimentary, education for boys and girls in Britain, with literacy levels rising dramatically as a result. This had a knock-on effect as far as learning about gardening was concerned. Information on gardening in national newspapers at the beginning of the twentieth century was sparse, but for the working-class readership there were the two old war-horses, *Lloyd's Weekly*, which ceased publication at the end of the First World War, and *Reynold's Weekly*, which lasted under various guises until 1967. *The Times* began a regular gardening column in 1907 but the *Daily Mail*, launched in May 1896 by Alfred Harmsworth (later Lord Northcliffe), was surprisingly slow off the mark. Although the Conservative Prime Minister, Lord Salisbury, described the *Mail* as produced by office boys for office boys, it was in fact aimed at women, and when it did start to include gardening information in 1910, the unspoken assumption was that the 'gardening lady' had some kind of professional help. In 1907 the *News of the World* claimed in its advertisements that the paper carried medical, legal and gardening correspondence, as well as enquiries for long-lost relatives and notices of missing next of kin. Advertisements for garden products were taken, but no gardening advice was offered, although a book, *Gardening for the Masses* by a practical gardener, was offered at sixpence in paper, one shilling in cloth.

The *News of the World* clearly recognised that an interest in gardening was, in the parlance of the day, 'for the millions', which makes the *Daily Mail's* sluggishness all the more remarkable, given Lord Northcliffe's attention to the market. However, in 1911, to celebrate the coronation of George V, the paper announced in February a competition for the best bunch of sweet peas with a huge first prize of £1,000. The competition was open to amateur gardeners who employed no more than one gardener. The sweet pea had become a very popular flower in Edwardian times – the colours echoed the pastel shades so favoured by fashionable ladies, accompanied by a wonderful scent. The *Daily Mail* declared grandly: 'The flower selected is at once the most decorative and most democratic, the one by every condition best suited to become the prevalent ornament of Coronation Year.' Furthermore, it described the sweet pea as the most English of flowers, and Britain as the nation of gardeners.

The vogue of the garden city, with its masses of flowers to break up the monotonous tones of our streets is one sign of this yearning for the Beauty which Nature so lavishly offers to those who cherish her . . .

the affection for the Old English flower garden is another. They are the cottager's treasure, and in the crowded town mark allotments with a little broken fragment of rainbow, the windows of the workers in whose hearts rests the covenant of peace.[21]

Good copy, though it was doubtful whether the cottager and the allotment holder would be the likeliest to win. The size of the prizes offered caused wild excitement throughout the country, and 38,000 bunches arrived at the Crystal Palace in late July. The winner was Mrs Fraser, from the manse of Sprouston, a Scottish Border village. Her minister husband won the third prize, so credit should go to their young gardener, who drew their attention to the competition in the first place and assisted with the cultivation of the blooms.[22]

It was the First World War that really encouraged the proliferation of information about gardening in the national press, supported by local and regional papers, in response to the drive to produce more home-grown food and the need to introduce novices from both the middle and working classes to this type of cultivation. With the return of peace, the information continued to be a regular spot in the Saturday issues of some newspapers, such as the *Daily Mail* and the *Daily Express*. However, even then some papers contained no gardening columns: the *Daily Mirror*, established in 1920, only started to include gardening advice in the 1930s, while the *Sunday Pictorial* ignored the subject altogether. On Easter Sunday 1930 the *Pictorial* headed one of its articles 'Come out of the Garden, Dad', pointing out that children were having a thin time when their father spent his whole weekend gardening.

The gardening journals begun in the nineteenth century, such as the *Journal of Horticulture* and the *Gardeners' Chronicle*, were aimed principally at owners of gardens who had their own staff and professional gardeners. Towards the end of the century, with the development of printing technology, new gardening magazines with illustrations in black-and-white and even colour became available. In 1898 a monthly journal, *Flowers, Fruit and Vegetables*, was launched, illustrated with photographs and priced at one penny, claiming that its language would be that of the 'Common People'. Despite these claims and its low price, even this magazine was probably beyond the means of all but the most devoted working-class gardeners.

After the First World War, magazines sought to widen their appeal to attract the gardeners from the new housing estates, both private and council. *Amateur Gardening* had simple do-it-yourself instructions to enable novice gardeners to learn about all kinds of techniques. By the 1930s, a colour cover had been added and many advertisements were carried within. *The Gardener* was retitled *Popular Gardening* in 1920, claiming to be 'Full of Bargains and Good Advice'. In 1927 William Robinson's *Garden* was absorbed into *Homes and Gardens*, and in the following year *Home Gardening* was launched as 'the gardening paper for the millions'. The latter, a weekly, ran to sixty-four pages for twopence, with a brightly coloured front cover and a special offer for the first issue of a free 'Monster Packet of Flower Seeds'. *Home Gardening* offered a free advice service, a children's column featuring the adventures of Peter, Pam and Pat, and articles without 'high falutin' language. The editor declared that it was to be: '*a real home-garden paper*, a paper which caters particularly for the needs of those who, not knowing very much – knowing, maybe, nothing at all – about gardening, would yet make their gardens beautiful. There are already thousands upon thousands of such and they are being added to every day. Are there not gardens to most of the new homes on the Council Housing Estates?'[23]

One way of putting together an illustrated reference library was to subscribe to a part-work, and this proved popular for all kinds of subjects in the interwar years. George Newnes published *The New Book of Gardening* in twenty-six fortnightly parts at 1s 3d per part in 1925–26, and seven years later the Amalgamated Press issued *The Popular Encyclopaedia of Gardening* in fifty-two weekly parts at sixpence each. These series would probably have been bought by lower-middle-class families or skilled workers, the market also targeted by many comprehensive guides and encyclopaedias.[24] Titles include *The Complete Amateur Gardener* of 1924, *Everyday Gardening* of 1931, and *The Home Gardening Encyclopaedia* of 1939.[25] Editors were very aware of the new audience of gardeners that had arrived as a result of the huge number of houses being built in the interwar years. One wrote: 'Today, especially, when countless new homes and gardens have brought into being thousands of additional gardening enthusiasts, gardening is man's chief hobby.'[26]

Learning by listening developed as a new and very potent form, through broadcasts on what was then known as the wireless. Soon after its inception in 1922, the British Broadcasting Corporation (BBC) took up gardening talks, the first going out in March 1923 and given by E.G. Evans. This was followed by C. Harding on 'Gardening in April' and L. Cook on 'Rose Gardening round London', along with a short weekly bulletin provided by the Royal Horticultural Society.

Many talks in the 1920s were delivered by Marion Cran, and on occasion by Vita Sackville-West. No original gardening scripts by Vita Sackville-West have survived, apart from garden tours of the West Country, but her talks were printed in the *Listener* and are evidently lyrical with a wonderful turn of phrase. Mrs Cran was a popular novelist who also wrote gardening books such as *The Garden of Ignorance* (subtitled *The Experiences of a Woman in a Garden*) and its sequel, *The Garden of Experience*. At the microphone she was down to earth and practical, providing regular, fortnightly talks on a variety of topics, such as 'Gardeners I Have Met', 'The Rock Garden' and 'Window Boxes'. She frequently drew her listeners' attention to the National Gardens Guild, which provided its members with advice and opened private gardens.

One of Marion Cran's last talks, broadcast on 16 April 1933 with the title 'The Small Garden', looked at town gardens. She encouraged her listeners not to be daunted by the challenge of an unpromising backyard: 'A great many people have turned their dull, ugly little cat-runs, either back or front, into charming gardens full of interest and colour; and a great many more, seeing these, would like to know *how*.' Realising that some of her audience did not have lots of money, she suggested buying a twopenny packet of seeds for annuals, and sowing some near the house. Her particular recommendation was the night-scented stock:

> It does not take much room, or make any show; indeed, there is nothing in that ragged little nobody of the day-time to tell us of the precious perfume it carries. The small slip of a thing cowers all through the bright days in a dowdy, beigey, raggedy dress, but at sunset it suddenly opens out into small starry, lilac flowers which gush out the most heavenly scent into the evening air.[27]

By this time, the pool of speakers had been joined by C.H. Middleton, whose reassuring country accent endeared him to his listeners and made him into a broadcasting phenomenon. Cecil Henry Middleton was born in 1886 in the Northamptonshire village of Weston by Weedon, the son of the head gardener to Sir George Sitwell, so that he grew up alongside the eccentric baronet's children, Edith, Osbert and Sacheverell. At the age of thirteen he began to work on the Sitwell estate, and four years later left for London with £2 10s in his pocket. In the capital he followed a traditional course for aspirational professional gardeners, working in the seed trade, studying at evening classes, and becoming a student at Kew. After

77 C.H. Middleton, the voice of gardening on radio during the Second World War.

the First World War, during which he worked on food production in the horticultural division of the Board of Agriculture and Fisheries, Middleton obtained a national diploma for horticulture, and joined Surrey County Council as an instructor, placing him in an ideal position to approach the BBC.

On 9 May 1931, Middleton began his first broadcast thus: 'Good afternoon. Well, it's not much of a day for gardening, is it?' This conversational, reassuring style guaranteed him growing popularity, and in 1934 he was given his own weekly series, *In the Garden*. Originally the talks went out at 7.10 p.m. on a Friday, but Middleton was anxious to discover the ideal time for his audience. On 25 June 1937 he sent out the following message: 'There does not seem a better way of finding out what your wishes are, whether you regard me as a stimulation for the weekend's gardening or to send you off to sleep after Sunday lunch?' Listeners were asked to send their preference by postcard. The results were 7,009 preferring Sunday, 2,950 Friday, while 62 said either way. The BBC had been caught unawares, as Middleton had included his question in a live broadcast, a situation that the Corporation has never found easy. Much angst was expended in internal communications, including concern about 'Sabbatarian feeling' in Scotland and Wales, before it was decided that Middleton should move to a regular Sunday afternoon slot at 2 p.m.[28]

In 1937 Middleton also began a series of television programmes, with a garden created specially for the purpose at Alexandra Palace. This medium, however, was so new that the audience was strictly limited, with an estimated 400 sets owned by the end of January 1937, and 2,000 by the end of the year. This was the golden age of radio gardening rather than television, with Middleton reaching a peak audience of 3.5 million. Not all these, of course, were gardening enthusiasts; the figure included people who simply appreciated his manner. Judith Hall, a garage assistant turned gardening apprentice, noted in her diary kept for Mass Observation how she had listened to Middleton for four years because she liked his voice rather than because she was interested in gardening.[29] As the writer and critic Wilfrid Rooke put it: 'It is the art of Mr Middleton to address himself to the lowest common denominator of horticultural intelligence without the faintest hint of superiority or condescension. He will assume that your soil is poor, and your pocket poor. All he asks is that your hopes are high and your Saturday afternoons at his service.'[30] Another commentator described Middleton as the most famous gardener since Adam.

At the end of 1937, Middleton was told about a series of broadcasts that were planned to go out to rural schools on Thursday afternoons, for children aged between nine and fourteen, and centred around an imaginary village of Stanwellstead, featuring its inhabitants and everyday concerns. A regular on the series was Freddy Grisewood, taking the part of an old man, 'Gaffer Brown', a great hit with his audience. It was suggested that Middleton should contribute to the summer series for 1938, in which the cottage garden would be considered. He took the part of 'Old Henry', exchanging ideas over the hedge with 'Gaffer Brown', talking about preparations for a flower show, and considering the vegetable patch. The programmes were followed by a series of questions to the children stimulating them to think about and do things in the garden. Middleton even took part in a 'Crazy Gardening Talk' for television, to be broadcast on April Fool's Day, 1938.

But it was with the outbreak of the Second World War that Middleton really came into his own. On 4 September 1939 the BBC wrote to him confirming that he would begin a weekly series, 'Your Garden in War-time', to be broadcast on a Sunday, probably between noon and 3 p.m.: 'It will, of course, be important that any advice which you give to listeners in these talks should not contradict any notices issued by the Ministry of Agriculture.' A subsequent letter from the Ministry offered to send him advance publications, as it would be helpful 'to get across the stuff we shall be putting out for the guidance of gardeners'. Middleton also wrote to the BBC with reassurance that he would largely devote himself to food growing, although he was getting letters from people like Lionel de Rothschild urging him not to neglect the flower garden, as the nursery and seed trades were both heavily stocked, and official condemnation would hit them badly. His own opinion was that where flower gardening did not interfere with food production, it should still be encouraged, and brief references were made here and there in his talks.

Middleton was requested to introduce nutritional advice, and was even approached in October 1939 by the Board of Education, asking him to persuade parents to maintain the evacuation of their children, lest they return to cities just as the air raids started. It was suggested that he might devote a few moments during his Sunday talks to the evacuees, getting them interested in making school gardens, and to encourage them to give their parents a happy picture of what they were doing.[31] He often contributed to Children's Hour programmes, ending one, 'Stick at it; keep the slugs off the green vegetables, and good luck to you all'.[32]

We can get a flavour of Middleton's style from some of his books, which were based on his talks. In *Your Garden in War-time*, first published in 1941, he naturally focused mainly on growing vegetables and fruit but, as he promised, flowers were not neglected. Thus most of the garden should be devoted to good crops, but:

> with the possible exception of a row of sweet peas. Hitler or no Hitler, war or no war, I'm going to grow a few bunches of sweet peas next summer, if at all possible. Very naughty of me, perhaps, but I had none last summer, and I missed them terribly. After all, they don't take up much room, and to me they seem to bring a breath of Heaven down to this unhallowed earth – a message of peace, of hope and a promise of better times to come.[33]

On one occasion his reassuring tone got Middleton into trouble. Such was the worry during the Second World War about security and keeping up morale that when he finished an unscripted programme with a reference to carnations, he unwisely advised: 'Some of you find them difficult subjects, but it's because they like lots of lime, so cheer up, the way things are going at the moment there will soon be plenty of mortar rubble about. Just have another go.'[34]

Apart from his publications based on radio talks, C.H. Middleton also wrote several general books, including an encyclopaedia of gardening, contributed a regular gardening column every Saturday for the *Daily Express*, and also articles for *Radio Times*, described by one of the editorial staff as '500 words in the most general, genial, Middletonian terms'.[35] This incredible activity was brought to an abrupt halt when C.H. Middleton died suddenly as he left his Surbiton home on 18 September 1945.

* * *

Although Middleton referred humorously in his broadcasts and books to working gardeners, he was very proud of the tradition represented by his father and by himself. In a talk broadcast in May 1935 he noted:

> Generally speaking, they're very much as other men are – perhaps a little better in many ways: wholesome, decent-living people who love their work – usually straight and often deeply religious people, perhaps without knowing it, and certainly without shouting about it. They

work hand in hand with Nature and they know that their work is under the direct supervision of the Great Architect.[36]

The First World War had had a profound effect on the lives of working gardeners: many were killed at the front, while others who survived were unable to resume their work through injury or disinclination ever to dig again. Nevertheless, life in large country-house gardens continued after the war, with the familiar cycle of 'learning on the job' and the same exacting standards. Norman Thomas was a bothy boy in the gardens of the Douglas-Pennant family at Penrhyn Castle in North Wales in the 1920s. This bothy was in fact a sizeable house with the facilities to accommodate eight gardeners – the foreman, Teddy Jones, six journeymen gardeners (including one studying for his RHS certificate) and the garden boy. The gardeners had to leave the bothy by seven in the morning, seven days a week, with only Saturday and Sunday afternoons off. Out of Norman's weekly wage of twenty-two shillings, he would pay around twelve to the foreman for the catering, but reckoned the rest was sufficient for clothing and entertainment.

Fruit cultivation was a speciality, often under glass. Because Lord Penrhyn, as chief official of the Jockey Club, travelled frequently around the country, grapes had to arrive at their place of destination with their bloom intact, while the packing of peaches, figs and similar fruit required special attention. 'All fruit was placed in special paper with wool and wood wool surrounding them, they were then placed in special boxes . . . Packing took place three times a week. On a Sunday this operation could take five hours to complete.' The perishable goods were sent by train, but in 1926 the General Strike obliged the gardeners to dispatch them by post. Extraordinary measures were taken in particular with the tomatoes, which were sent individually: 'One tomato was wrapped in cotton wool and put into a small cardboard box, each box with an addressed label. Scores and scores of these boxes were sent by this method. They arrived at their place of destination in perfect condition.'

Norman remembered vividly his struggles to maintain the temperature of the early vinery, his particular responsibility. In spring, the ventilators had to be opened when the sun came out, and closed when it went in. Later in the season the shading of the greenhouse was key, with constant checks as the sun continued to be awkward. If on duty at night, he had to keep careful watch lest there was an unexpected frost, with the fires banked last thing before going to bed.[37]

These recollections are remarkably similar to the experiences of John Donaldson and William Cresswell half a century earlier (Chapter 7, pp. 182–8), and not unusual for wealthy garden owners in the early part of the twentieth century. In his description of a Suffolk life, George Ewart Evans provided a portrait of Frederick Woods, who worked as second gardener at Easton Park, one of the estates of the Duke of Hamilton. Woods described to Evans the rigid apprentice system: the first year spent stoking furnaces and doing odd jobs such as mixing soil and 'crocking' (preparing the earthenware plots for plants); the second year spent working on fruit, including the careful forcing of strawberries; the third year spent in the vegetable garden; and the fourth in the orchid houses or stove houses, and pruning the vines. In addition the gardeners were expected to change the flowers in the house, strewing the table cloth with patterns of fresh leaves and flowers in the fashionable style of the time, ready for dinner.[38]

Another owner of a Suffolk country-house garden, given as Lord Covehithe, is described by Ronald Blythe in his account of a village that he calls Akenfield. One of Covehithe's gardeners was Christopher Falconer, who was thirty-nine when Blythe wrote about him in the late 1960s. He begins: 'Feudalism is a kind of game. Set and match with partners at both the serving and receiving ends knowing exactly what is expected of them and abiding unquestionably by the rules.' Falconer went to work in the garden at the age of fourteen, when the gardening staff numbered seven. He found it a frightening experience, as Lady Covehithe would shout 'swing your arms' whenever she encountered a garden boy. Wearing green baize aprons and collars and ties, whatever the weather, the gardeners were expected to make a long detour with their wheelbarrows full of weeds, lest they be seen from the terrace. As at Easton Park, the gardeners organised the flower arrangements in the house, covertly arriving before the household's breakfast. 'Lord and Ladyship must never hear or see you doing it; fresh flowers had to just be there . . . There was never a dead flower. It was as if flowers, for them, lived for ever. It was part of the magic of their lives.'[39]

Balancing these descriptions of 'feudal' garden owners, there are tales of difficult head gardeners, although C.H. Middleton in *Your Garden in War-time* noted:

I'm rather afraid that the good old days of the autocratic gardener are coming to an end. There was a time when the Duchess dare not cut a rose without first asking the gardener. I knew one who always kept the key of the vineries and peach houses and wouldn't allow his employers in unless he was there to watch over their movements. We used to have an old gardener in our village who took such a pride in his gravel paths that he was quite annoyed if anybody walked on them, and her ladyship frequently walked on the grass to avoid disturbing the peace. Another gardener I knew gave his lady notice because she insisted on having scarlet geraniums in the flower beds, he called it intolerable interference.[40]

Both kinds of behaviour were observed by a young apprentice gardener in the diary she kept for Mass Observation. Twenty-year-old Judith Hall had been employed in her family's garage in Snettisham in Norfolk at the outbreak of the war, but in April 1941 she went to Woodyates Manor in Dorset to work in the gardens.[41] 'There are 5 girls here and head lady gardener, quite young and nice . . . we live in a charming "ideal home" old cottage.' She describes Woodyates as being owned by Lady A, who one day 'sweeps into the garden and annoys the head gardener by saying everyone is to leave off what they are doing and put nets on the peaches'. The young recruit found she much preferred gardening to serving petrol or working in a factory, spending her days digging and manuring trenches and leaning on the yew hedge for support when she felt exhausted. She learned arcane practices such as pollinating peach trees by tickling them with rabbits' tails on canes. Her one bane was the temperamental boiler stove, a point of contention with the butler, who felt that it was below his dignity to act as the odd-job man and mend it. The cause of its difficult behaviour turned out to be the chimney, which badly needed sweeping. This Judith Hall did using the traditional accoutrement, a branch of holly.

After a month in Wiltshire, Miss Hall moved to Empingham in Rutland, to the garden of a retired colonel. Here she was the only girl, assisting the sixty-five-year-old gardener, Marples. She lived with Marples and his wife in 'a very clean cottage' without electricity or, more seriously, a bath, so that she was obliged to negotiate a weekly soak in the colonel's house. Marples ruled the roost in the garden, with the colonel complaining that he dominated him, and would not allow him to do what he wanted. He was only permitted to dig, but even this was checked and corrected by Marples.

This interesting relationship between employer and head gardener had been maintained for centuries, but Judith Hall was writing at a time when the profession was being revolutionised. Her apprenticeship, which lasted for only six months (this was wartime), had been arranged through the Women's Garden Association (WGA). This organisation dated back to 1899 when it was established as the Women's Agricultural and Horticultural International Union after a group of women who had attended the International Conference of Women Workers in London decided they would like to keep in touch. In 1921 it became the Women's Farm and Garden Association. During the First World War the society was responsible for the establishment of the Women's National Land Service Corps, aiming to replace the labour lost to enlistment and to counter any possible disruption of food supplies.[42]

Until the end of the nineteenth century women as working gardeners did not rise beyond the very low level described in Chapters 3 and 7, and certainly were not allowed anywhere near the bothy system. The first formal qualifications for gardeners had been instituted in 1866 by the RHS in association with the RSA with written examinations and practical tests (see Chapter 7, p. 181). Horticultural colleges were opened for men at Swanley in Kent and Studley in Warwickshire, and courses were offered at the University of Reading. In 1892 anyone interested in gardening was able to undertake the RHS examination 'for a fee of 3s payable in advance'.[43]

'Anyone' was assumed to be male, but at last the possibility of women becoming professional gardeners began to be recognised. In 1891 the Horticultural College at Swanley admitted its first female students. Initially they were in a mixed class, but as the number of women enrolling increased, a separate class was given over to them, with sixty-three students attending in 1903. Daisy, Lady Warwick, one of the mistresses of the Prince of Wales, sponsored a hostel at the University of Reading in 1898: this was to become the Studley Castle Horticultural and Agricultural College for Women. At Glynde in Sussex Frances Wolseley, daughter of the distinguished soldier, set up a gardening school, apparently after her mother hired a female gardener who had been deserted by her husband and left with children. Frances felt that artistic, well-educated, refined female head gardeners would lend intelligence, good taste and refinement to 'securing better cultivation of our great country'.[44]

Alongside these establishments was a whole series of private schools for women, including Elmwood Nurseries at Cosham in Hampshire and Aldersey Hall near Chester, founded in about 1902 by the Misses Cornelius Wheeler, and later, the famous Waterperry Horticultural School outside Oxford, established by Beatrix Havergal and Avice Sanders

78 A lesson in pruning at the Horticultural College for Women at Studley Castle in Warwickshire, about 1910.

in 1927.[45] These establishments offered to train the women to the level of the Royal Horticultural Society Examination, and after 1913 to the diploma.

Initially these newly qualified gardeners faced stiff opposition from certain areas. Female gardeners were allowed at Kew in 1895, but the Director instructed them to wear clothing 'similar to that of ordinary gardeners' – traditional brown bloomers, woollen stockings and boots, tailored jackets, waistcoats and ties, and peaked caps. Long mack-intoshes were to be worn on their journeys to and from work to hide their bloomers. A verse titled 'London Kewriosity' appeared in *Fun* magazine in 1900:

> They gardened in bloomers, the newspapers said:
> So to Kew without warning all Londoners sped:
> From the roofs of the buses they had a fine view
> Of the ladies in bloomers who gardened at Kew.
> The orchids were slighted, the lilies were scorned,
> The dahlias were flouted, till botanists mourned,
> But the Londoners shouted, 'What ho, there, Go to;
> Who wants to see blooms now you've bloomers at Kew'.

Even the Principal of Swanley Horticultural College, Mr Propert, announced that gardening work was in every way undesirable for women, who were in danger of losing their womanly shape and developing masculine muscles.

The first professional women gardeners were largely drawn from the middle classes, able to pay the fees for their training, but a few may have come from the working class. In the monthly journal of Hampstead Garden Suburb, *The Town Crier*, an advertisement appeared in November 1912 from Miss L.B. Evett and Miss H. Garlick, offering gardening work 'undertaken by day or week for long or short periods'. These jobbing gardeners lived in Waterlow Court, which had been funded by the Improved Industrial Dwellings Company and built specifically for working women.

Social attitudes towards the idea of working women gardeners were slow to change, so that Judith Hall witnessed surprise and sometimes strong disapproval, which she duly noted in her Mass Observation diary. She was being circumspect when she described Lady A: the owner of Woodyates Manor was in fact Lady Lucas, a leading light in the WGA, instrumental in launching the scheme in June 1940 for women of eighteen and over to be given free horticultural training as apprentices under head gardeners. Miss Van der Pant, Secretary of the Association, was quoted in the *Evening Standard*:

There is a serious shortage of under-gardeners now. Gardens where foodstuffs are grown are suffering from this lack of supplementary labour ... The first month of their training is probationary. During that time, if they cannot afford to contribute, they will receive 3s 6d per week pocket money and 2s a week for laundry besides their keep. The head-gardener will then report on his pupil's progress. If his report is favourable, the girl will continue for a further three months with 5s a week pocket-money plus 2s for laundry ... If the final capabilities is satisfactory, the apprentice will then be given a job as an under-gardener.[46]

The novelty of a female head gardener and five female apprentices at Woodyates excited the attentions of the press. Judith Hall's diary for 25 April 1941 records how a photographer was to take pictures of the girls posing with their tools and wheelbarrows and 'doing things we never do'. Inevitably the butler appeared in his brand new boiler suit to learn how to work the water pump from the engineer. At Empingham, Miss Hall caused even more of a stir. 'I am a great sensation in the village', she recorded on 10 May, where the idea of Land Girls had hardly been accepted, let alone women gardeners. She noted her surprise that she was regarded as an expert, having hardly done any gardening until six weeks earlier.

The men and women emerging from the horticultural colleges and private gardening schools were almost always from the middle classes. No longer was the world of working gardeners populated by lads from the labouring classes, coming up through the bothy and apprenticeship systems, who, through luck and hard work, could attain the position of head gardener. The world of large gardening establishments was also passing. Christopher Falconer described to Ronald Blythe how the supply of labour for the gardens of Lord Covehithe gushed until 1939, 'trickled dutifully' until 1950, and then dried up. Some great houses, like Chatsworth and Blenheim, were able to continue with a traditional team of gardeners, but many country-house gardens were moving, with increasing momentum, to organisations such as the National Trust and to public authorities. The amount of gardening that could be undertaken had to be reduced, often to what Graham Stuart Thomas, first Chief Gardens Adviser to the National Trust, described as 'slender staff'.

The bothy, home for so many years to working gardeners, was abandoned, often turned into a storeroom for gardening paraphernalia. Recently, however, there has been a revival of interest in how country-house gardens were run, as well as what they looked like. Just as servants' quarters and the kitchens of historic houses have been restored and recreated, so too have the bothies where gardeners like John Donaldson and William Cresswell spent their early working lives.

CHAPTER 14

❧

# A Nation of Gardeners

'WE HAVE BEEN called a nation of shopkeepers; we might with equal justice be called a nation of gardeners', proclaimed the *Nurseryman and Seedsman* on 1 June 1939, paraphrasing the oft-quoted saying made famous by Napoleon. Unfortunately the nation, whether keeping the shop or the garden, was about to be plunged into war, and when the hostilities drew to a close in 1945, Britain once more faced a huge housing crisis. As an official report from the House of Commons had noted in 1943: 'After the last war we heard a good deal about homes for heroes, and we are now hearing a good deal about the New Jerusalem which is to be built after this war. I do not think that the country is likely to stand a second disappointment.'[1]

The bomb damage was immense: London, for instance, was badly hit by V-2 rockets in 1944, wiping out 84,000 houses; Birmingham suffered 71 air-raids, with 12,000 houses destroyed and 40,000 families on the housing register; on Clydebank, only seven houses remained undamaged by the end of the war. On top of this, many surviving houses and apartment blocks had deteriorated as a result of years of neglect. One 'quick fix' to the problem was the erection of prefabricated houses (prefabs) in what was known as the Temporary Housing Programme.

Prefabs had a long tradition, including portable huts used by shepherds and timber-framed cottages clad in corrugated iron sheets that were made from the mid-nineteenth century and often exported to the colonies. Some very striking semi-detached prefabs were designed by Somerset architects John Petter and Percy Warren and can still be seen at Howell Hill, West Camel, although at £513 per home they were more expensive than standard houses. As early as 1942, when the threat of invasion had passed, thoughts turned to the reconstruction of bombed houses, and the idea that some new homes could be provided by prefabs was born. Two years later Winston Churchill announced the Ministry of Works Emergency Factory-made Programme: thirteen different types of prefab were built right across the country, and the government, wanting to reinforce the tradition of nuclear families, rented them only to families with young children. Approximately 160,000 families, the majority from the working-class areas of cities that had been badly bombed, were housed in prefabs during the war and the years that followed.

Although these homes were supposed to be temporary, they proved so popular that many survived for half a century and recent battles have been fought, for instance on the Excalibur Estate in Catford, south-east London, to prevent prefabs from being bulldozed.[2] One of the attractions was that these 'palaces for the people' had sizeable gardens surrounding them, an unprecedented luxury for most of the new residents. Kenneth

79 Prefabs had the great advantage of sizeable gardens adjoining them. This garden at 36 Downton Road in Streatham won first prize in the LCC's front garden competition in July 1952. The coronation of Elizabeth II was a year away, but the beds set into the lawn seem to have been planted in red, white and blue – a combination of allysum and lobelia with pelargoniums in the centre.

80 Formality marks the LCC prize-winning front garden of the prefab at 36 Northanger Road, Streatham, July 1952, with crazy paving hems to the topiary and stone pedestals for container displays.

Wakefield, who was brought up in an aluminium bungalow on the outskirts of Southampton, recalled: 'The space is what I remember most. We were moving from an area of mostly terraced houses with backyards and little space for a kid to run around, and going to this sea of white prefabs with gardens and trees on large greens. As far as I was concerned I was moving to the countryside.'[3] Some models even re-created the country cottage look that had been adopted in the pre-war council estates, with roses pinned to a pergola around the door.

Sheds were provided for most of the gardens, sometimes Anderson air-raid shelters with bricked-up rear wall and door to the front. During the 1940s, the gardens would be dedicated to the growing of vegetables and fruit, with perhaps one bed of decorative flowers. Getting the garden into cultivation could be hard work. Some of the estates in South Wales were built on slag heaps, so that the men were obliged to go off into the mountains with wheelbarrows to bring back topsoil.

By the 1950s, many prefab tenants found they could give over part of the garden for their children, or for decorative planting. Bright colour was the order of the day, so begonias, lobelias and alyssums were popular, along with roses, often tea roses planted against the 'Peerless' mesh fencing. Margaret Sinnott, remembering her childhood in Hackney Wick in the early 1950s, noted: 'My father, a Pool of London dockworker, was a very keen gardener, who grew vegetables, flowers and fruit trees. He also built a summerhouse, a greenhouse, garden swings, a hammock and a seesaw. During the coronation year he followed the trend and planted our front garden in red, white and blue flowers.'[4]

Meanwhile new housing estates were being built around the cities that had been devastated by the war. In London it was the eastern parts around the docks that had been particularly hit, an area largely populated by the working classes. Back in 1943 the architect Patrick Abercrombie had published the County of London Plan, covering the inner section of the capital with the exception of the City. The key problems addressed by the plan were traffic congestion, poor housing, and inadequate and haphazardly distributed open space. The following year, the Greater London Plan was published, covering the capital's outer area and parts of the Home Counties. Abercrombie drew four rings, beginning with the consolidation of the urban core, through a suburban ring, to a green belt and an outer, country ring. The green belt was intended to curb further spread of suburbs. Beyond it, in the fourth ring, it was intended that there should be new towns, such as Harlow New Town in Essex and Crawley in Surrey. In addition, there were 'out-county estates', such as Debden and Harold Hill in Essex, to house large sections of the population from the poorest parts of London. Abercrombie also helped to plan new estates for other parts of Britain, such as Hull, Plymouth and Edinburgh.

As a result of the extensive building programme that followed the New Towns Act of 1946 and the Town and Country Planning Act of 1947, thousands of city dwellers found themselves for the first time with a garden (as opposed to a backyard) to cultivate. These new gardeners must have been among the crowds that flocked to the Festival of Britain in the summer of 1951. The idea for the festival had first been mooted by the Royal Society of the Arts in 1943 to celebrate the centenary of the 1851 Great Exhibition. Rejecting the idea of an international exhibition at a time of intense austerity, the government chose to mount a series of displays about the arts, architecture, science, technology and industrial design. The festival also proved a vital morale booster for the nation, pointing to a better future. In central London there were two main sites, on the South Bank, and further upstream at Battersea Park. The former was placed in the hands of a group of landscape architects who provided a riverside setting for the Festival's Pavilion of Homes and Gardens, with a 'moated' garden, murals and sculpture. The area was landscaped using boldly shaped plants such as polygonum and bamboo. Bedding plants in cone-shaped plant-holders gave some colour amid the prevailing green of the shrubs and the grey of the concrete paving. Far more colourful, however, were the Pleasure Gardens in Battersea Park. The approach here was more traditional and informal, with restaurants and other eating areas named after the old London pleasure gardens of Vauxhall, Ranelagh and Cremorne. There was also a funfair, a grotto and the Far Tottering and Oyster Creek Railway designed by Ronald Emmett. Many among the crowds found these gardens more to their taste, with just over 8 million visitors compared to the 8,456,000 who went to the South Bank.

The Festival organised exhibitions all over the country, including a 'live architecture' exhibition in Poplar in east London. This was the idea of the architect Frederick Gibberd, as part of the development of the public housing estate named after the Labour MP for Poplar, George Lansbury, in an area badly damaged by wartime bombing. Gibberd was given the responsibility for the market square and precinct that provided the focus for the whole of the new estate. As a keen gardener, he promoted the idea of considered planting and green spaces penetrating the housing areas, something he was to carry through with considerable success in the development of Harlow New Town, one of the satellites from the Abercrombie Act.

However, as the need for more housing grew ever greater, and the amount of room available grew ever less, so high-rise buildings became the order of the day in many of the council developments of the 1950s and 1960s, and the gardening available to the residents was limited to window boxes and balconies. One resident of a flat reflected sadly some years later, 'I was between two thorns, I didn't want a flat, but I didn't want to leave Bethnal Green'.[5] Moreover, not everybody was rehoused following the war. Hilda Kean has written of her grandparents, both from London East End families. In the 1950s, they rented the bottom floors of a nineteenth-century house in south Hackney, with a garden full of flowers: roses, marigolds, lily of the valley and Solomon's seal, which particularly flourished in the sour soil. Her grandmother considered the flowers were not for picking, as they were provided by God, which Kean attributes to her Huguenot ancestry.[6]

81 In the 1950s pressure on space meant that many councils adopted a policy of building high-rise apartments. This did not preclude horticultural ingenuity, as shown in this prize-winning balcony garden at Newburn House in Vauxhall in 1960.

Whatever the size of the plot or the window box, gardeners were united in their love of and desire for colour. At the end of the Second World War, government regulations had permitted only a 10 per cent fringe of colour from flowers in gardens: the rest was to concentrate on the cultivation of fruit and vegetables. Now the colour needed to seep back into people's lives. *Housing Estate Garden*, a book published in 1953, was written by S.J. Poole, a resident on a Nottingham housing estate and the winner of many local gardening competitions. He concentrated on gardens of about 250 square yards, and suggested schemes for annual bedding which reflect the popularity of colour. Thus one scheme was for yellow calceolaria and *Salvia patens*, edged with viola 'Bridal Morn', giving a mix of yellow, blue and mauve. In coronation year, his patriotic mix was antirrhinum 'White Wonder' with *Lobelia cardinalis* 'Queen Victoria' as dot planting, with an edge of blue lobelia. For a round bed, he suggested a central feature of *Zea japonica* 'Quadricolor', with red zonal pelargoniums, yellow calceolaria, and an edging of blue lobelia, *Chrysanthemum parthenium* and *Pyrethrum aureum selaginoides*, producing a vivid combination of red, yellow and blue.

But flowers were not the only ingredient of Poole's garden. The years after the war were marked by austerity and rationing, so he also recommended growing vegetables and fruit. For those thinking of entering competitions, he counselled: 'A good vegetable patch may earn more points than any other part of the garden. The trim, well-kept lawn and lovely flowers in the garden at the front of the house may attract the most attention from passers-by, but, alone, it cannot win a competition design to encourage gardening in all its aspects.'[7]

Poole warned against a tendency to over-elaboration and ornamentation: 'One sees it in scalloped, concrete kerbs; elaborate ponds, sunken gardens, artificial-looking rock gardens, badly proportioned pergolas.' He reported how Shrewsbury Housing Committee had ordered 300 of its tenants to clear their front gardens of any fences, kerbs and ornaments they had built. While criticising the committee for issuing peremptory orders of this kind, he commended them for recognising vulgarity in the gardens on the estate: 'Council house gardens are too small for a lot of fussiness and fancy confectionery. Simplicity is the key to beauty and charm in a small garden.'[8] One can only imagine what he must have made of gnomes.

* * *

From the end of the Second World War a plethora of reports and surveys began to appear concerning the British and their gardening. Some claimed to be in the tradition of Charles Booth and Benjamin Seebohm Rowntree, looking at the proportion of garden owners from different levels of society; others were more concerned with studying the nation's leisure activities. The number of statistics can be bewildering and sometimes confusing, especially as some sociologists would not appear to be familiar with what gardening actually involves. As the nineteenth-century agricultural labourers were only too aware, after a day spent working in the fields, tending their gardens could be wearisome, particularly tackling certain types of soil. In cities soil was often poor and sour, a result of centuries of pollution, only halted by the passing of the Clean Air Act of 1956. Gardeners in council houses often fared better, as they were sometimes supplied with topsoil to improve fertility.

In 1948–49 a survey carried out by the government estimated that 72 per cent of households in England, Scotland and Wales had a garden, allotment, or window boxes and indoor plants. This figure accorded with a Mass Observation report made ten years later, which reckoned that about two-thirds of the population did some kind of gardening. Not surprisingly those without gardens were in the lowest income bracket, and upper-class men spent less time in the garden than their working-class counterparts. J.A.R. Pimlott, in an article entitled 'A Nation of Gardeners?' published in 1964, expressed surprise that so many women should prove to be gardeners, as he had accepted the long-held view that gardens were a male domain. Tusser would have contradicted this with his cry of 'Wife into thy garden', and the notion had certainly become outdated from the First World War onwards, except in the most traditional of communities. According to Pimlott, 5,650,000 male householders (just under half the total) and 2,840,000 housewives gardened regularly.[9]

The immense proliferation in suburban housing estates both before and after the Second World War had given many working-class and middle-class households a sizeable plot for the first time. These were found in surveys to provide an extension of the house, an extra room in which the family's life could be played out, and one that did not always involve actual gardening. Thus the sociologists Peter Willmott and Michael Young in their study of the LCC estate at Dagenham in Essex noted that people with young children used their gardens to hang out the washing, as a play area, and for storing vehicles, and were keen that there should be adequate fencing to ensure privacy. Elderly gardens owners might find the garden too much to cope with, although other surveys noted that interest in horticulture was one of the leisure activities that did not decline with age.[10]

Although Pimlott somewhat disappointingly concluded in 1964 that, rather than a nation of gardeners, the British were 'even more a nation of dish washers, cooks and darners of socks', the interest in gardening continued and flourished. By the end of the 1960s, 80 per cent of house-holds had gardens, and an estimated £10 million was being spent annually on plants and other garden items.[11] These figures, of course, cover both the working and middle classes, and the distinction between the two was becoming increasingly blurred. Indeed, when Willmott and Young under-took their study of families moving from Bethnal Green to Greenleigh, the LCC estate in Essex, they suggested that a semi-detached house with a garden was a sign of a shift from working-class to middle-class status, although this seems a questionable conclusion given that the working men of the household retained their former occupations in London.[12]

To balance the fact that increasing numbers of people were spending time travelling from their suburban homes to their places of work, they were working shorter hours. In 1900, according to Benjamin Seebohm Rowntree, a fifty-four-hour week prevailed in factories, from 6 a.m. to 5 p.m., with an hour and a half for meals.[13] By 1939 the average working week had been reduced to forty-four or forty-eight hours per week, with the working day starting at 7.30 a.m. Shops also decreased their working hours, with early-closing day introduced in 1912. One change that particularly helped gardeners was the introduction in 1916 of British Summer Time, enabling work to continue later into the evenings during the summer months. Further reductions in working hours came after the Second World War, and in the 1950s the half-day on Saturday was phased out for many, at last allowing employees to enjoy the concept of the weekend.

Gardening advice and inspiration were increasingly available right across the social spectrum. Following the sudden death of C.H. Middleton in 1945, the BBC was concerned about the future of the garden talks, *In Your Garden*. However, Fred Streeter, who had broadcast alongside Middleton from the mid-1930s, proved a successful and very popular presenter. A BBC memo from 1946 commends his rich Sussex accent as well worth listening to, and lauds the content of his talks.[14] The series therefore continued, to be amalgamated in 1950 with *Backs to the Land*, which had concentrated on husbandry subjects during the war. The new programme, *Home Grown*, covered a very wide range of gardening topics, including flower and vegetable growing in small gardens and allotments, plant collecting and botanical exploration, landscape designing and design, livestock breeding and pigeon racing. One feature was unusual horticultural personalities, such as market-gardening soldiers and railwaymen orchid-growers. Although it was noted that 'The merging of gardening and backyard interests is probably a timely reflection of social change in the post-war world', the ambitious coverage evoked in the minds of the BBC producers the publishing of John Lindley's *Gardeners' Chronicle* at the time of the Great Exhibition, the Irish potato famine and the imminent discoveries of Pasteur and Mendel.

The compères for *Home Grown* were Roy Hay and Fred Streeter. The backgrounds of these two men were rather different, and reflected the changing times. Fred Streeter was the son of a farmworker, born in the late 1870s at the time of the agricultural depression. He worked first as a garden boy, then for a number of nurseries including Veitch, before becoming head gardener in the 1920s to Lord Leconfield at Petworth

House in Sussex. Charles Quest-Ritson relates the nice, and telling, story of how Streeter, travelling around the country to learn from other gardens and gardeners, had his pronunciation of Latin names corrected by a London banker, Vicary Gibbs, owner of a famous garden at Aldenham in Surrey. Gibbs averred that it was only gentlemen who could pronounce these names, and that even his own head gardener, Edwin Beckett, a distinguished exhibitor and writer, made an awful muddle of them – almost as bad as Streeter.[15] Social attitudes do indeed die hard.

Roy Hay had a rather different *curriculum vitae*. He was a generation younger than Streeter, born in 1910, the son of the head gardener at Hopetoun Gardens at Linlithgow. Hay was brought up amid distinguished horticulturalists as his father went on to become superintendent of various parks before taking charge of the royal gardens in London. He began his own career working for a wholesale seed merchant before turning to journalism. He first worked on the *Gardeners' Chronicle* and later edited the publications of the RHS, as well as acting as gardening correspondent of *The Times*. Soon after joining *Home Grown* Hay found himself enmeshed in discussions about when the programme should go out – after lunch on Sundays, the slot that *In Your Garden* had filled for so many years, or moving back to Friday evening. Once more the arguments considered a decade earlier by Middleton and the BBC were rehearsed, with Hay worrying about shift workers, housewives washing up, and gardeners either sleeping off their lunch or wanting to get into their gardens. Gardening on the radio still enjoyed a major position.

Another radio programme had also established itself as a national favourite, *Gardeners' Question Time*. This was the idea of Robert Stead, a BBC Radio talks producer based in Manchester. He later explained that he wanted to get away from the lecture format, instead adopting the style of *The Brains Trust*, with experts answering questions posed by members of a local gardening society. The first programme, *How Does Your Garden Grow?* was broadcast on 9 April 1947 from the Broadoak Hotel in Ashton-under-Lyne in Lancashire, with Bob Stead in the chair, and the expert team consisting of Bill Sowerbutts from Ashton, Fred Loads from Burnley, T.E. Clark, Parks Superintendent from Bolton, and Dr W.E. Sensome from Manchester University. The questions were posed by members of the Smallshaw and District Garden and Allotments Society. Unfortunately no record was kept of the questions or answers aired that night, although Bill Sowerbutts not surprisingly remembered that the meeting was attended by an eighty-one-year-old man under the impression that he was taking part

82 One of the most popular radio broadcasters on gardening was Fred Streeter. 'Labour saving' was very much the theme of the 1950s, a decade of austerity.

in Wilfred Pickles' popular show, *Have A Go*, who insisted on playing his cornet.[16]

Details do survive for the broadcast of *How Does Your Garden Grow?* that went out six months later, on 21 November 1947, from the Elephant and Castle Hotel in Knaresborough, Yorkshire. Maurice Jackson, chairman of the Knaresborough Garden and Allotment Society, had sought questions from his members, sending these through to Bob Stead, along with notes about those putting the questions. Bill Heslop, relief signalman on the LNER, was noted as winning first prizes at local shows for his scarlet runners grown from seed. It was suggested that he might be asked the secret of getting the beans so long. Jackson also recommended that he could tell a good tale about his second question, 'Has the moon any influence on sowing of seeds? A very old-fashioned saying was that you should not sow seeds on a rising moon. Why?' This question was chosen, and presumably Bill Heslop told his good tale, while the answer from the scientists was that there was no influence. The local hairdresser, A. Rogers, was described as a comic who gave a turn at concerts, and who used his customers' hair as manure. He submitted several questions, but the one chosen was 'Why is it that a tomato sometimes remains hard, green or yellow, near the stalk, this part refusing to ripen? Is it a fault of the feeding, or is it the soil mixture?' The notes plotting out the recording, probably made by Bob Stead, show that he was interested in local questions, and felt humour was important, although backchat, showing off and meandering were not to be encouraged from either the experts or the audience. One question came from a twelve year old concerning his leeks, and this too was chosen. *Gardeners' Question Time* (*GQT*) still welcomes contributions from budding gardeners.

After the broadcast, Maurice Jackson wrote to Stead to report that he had been receiving questions about gardening not only from locals, but from as far afield as Westmorland, Cumberland, Staffordshire and Shrewsbury, and that Knaresborough was now on the map. *How Does Your Garden Grow?*, which became *Gardeners' Question Time* in 1951, was also clearly appealed to the north of England. In December 1947, the host was the Humshaugh and District Gardens and Produce Association, with the meeting held in Hexham, County Durham. The questions, collected by the stationmaster, came from all walks of life and were sought on a range of subjects. The vicar, 'keen gardener and very anxious to do everything right', wanted to know about liming local soil to balance the alkaline content. The treasurer of the Women's Institute, 'wife of a keen sweet pea grower, and always helping anyone in trouble', was worried about wire-worms. The local postmaster, 'great grower of flowers, but not greatly interested in vegetables', needed advice on the best method and time of year to strike cuttings of camellia, magnolia and clematis. A waterworks labourer from the Newcastle & Gateshead Water Company, 'good keen man, very quiet, says very little, but always interested', wanted to know the cause of club root in cabbages.

This was a formula that has endured. Although *GQT* is still produced in Manchester, it became part of the national network in 1957, moving to the popular 2 p.m. slot on a Sunday. Over the years the backgrounds of the team has inevitably changed, reflecting the developments in the world of professional horticulture. In 1987, for instance, the team consisted of Dr Stefan Buczacki of Stratford-upon-Avon, Geoffrey Smith of Harrogate, Daphne Ledward of Spalding and Fred Downham of Lancaster, with Clay Jones of Chepstow in the chair. Stefan Buczacki had an academic background: plant pathology at Southampton University, and forestry at Linacre College, Oxford, and had worked at the National Vegetable Research Station at Wellesbourne. Geoffrey Smith had qualified at Askham Bryan College of Horticulture at York, and had practised gardening around the country before becoming Superintendent of the RHS garden at Harlow Car. Daphne Ledward had trained as a quantity surveyor and social worker before turning to horticulture, working in a garden centre and as a jobbing gardener. Fred Downham in some ways represented the old tradition: self-taught, with one market-gardening grandfather and the other a cottage gardener. He worked in the family nursery until it closed in the 1950s, then ran a seed and florist stall in Lancaster market. Although their backgrounds were varied, all took part in regional broadcasting programmes, and wrote for newspapers. *GQT* remains one of the most popular gardening programmes, with the team retaining a similar make-up, and questions coming from local gardening clubs and societies that are not so different from those posed back in the late 1940s.[17]

In the 1930s, when C.H. Middleton broadcast television programmes on gardening from Alexandra Palace, the audience was extremely limited, and probably almost entirely middle class in social make-up. When TV started broadcasting again in June 1946, sets were still prohibitively expensive, but sales were given a huge boost by the decision to televise the coronation of Queen Elizabeth II in June 1953. The man who became the presenter of the first regular gardening programme, *Gardening Club*, was Percy Thrower, who came from the same tradition as C.H. Middleton.

Just as Middleton's father had been head gardener on a country house estate, Percy Thrower's father was head gardener at Horwood House in Buckinghamshire. The fourteen-year-old Percy joined his father's staff as the pot-and-crock boy, moving to the royal gardens at Windsor Castle as an improver, and living in the bothy with a weekly wage of £1. From private he moved into municipal gardening, becoming deputy parks super-intendent at the arboretum in Derby that had been created by Loudon. In 1939 he began to organise the local 'dig for victory' effort, and spent the war helping novice gardeners with their vegetable cultivation.

In 1947 Percy Thrower started his broadcasting career, first for BBC radio, then moving to television in 1951 to talk about a garden that he had designed in Germany. Four years later he began to present *Gardening Club*. The earliest programmes were created in a former wrestling arena on the outskirts of Birmingham, with the greenhouse and potting shed dismantled and the soil removed after each episode. Later, when colour television was introduced, a real garden site became necessary. In 1968 the programme's title changed to *Gardeners' World*, with the programme coming first from some of the venerable guinea gardens in Birmingham, and then from Thrower's own garden at The Magnolias in Shropshire.

Thrower, with his experience in municipal gardening, was at ease with the cultivation of flowers and shrubs, but for vegetables he turned to his friend, Arthur Billitt, travelling to Clack's Farm in Worcestershire. The presentation of the programme was hands-on, practical and proved very popular with audiences nationwide, with millions tuning in. However, Thrower was dropped from *Gardeners' World* in 1975: not only had he fronted commercials for garden chemicals, but they were screened by the rival channel. His was the generation that advocated the use of chemicals to keep down pests and encourage growth. Moreover, his experience of the hard graft of gardening of his youth made him an equally keen advocate of labour-saving machines and tools. The great success of the programme continued, however, first with his friend Arthur Billitt, to be followed by Geoff Hamilton. After Hamilton's untimely death in 1996, the programme was ushered into the twenty-first century by Alan Titchmarsh and Monty Don, making household names of them all.

When Percy Thrower presented the early programmes, ostensibly from his greenhouse – he gave the game away once when he put his hand through what should have been glass – television technology was in its infancy. But as the decades developed, so it was possible for programmes to focus on broader topics than the basic techniques and jobs needed in the

83 Percy Thrower presenting an edition of *Gardeners' World* at Nymans in West Sussex.

garden. Histories of gardens were made, along with programmes on gardens abroad, appreciated by a public which was increasingly able to travel. The beauty of flowers and shrubs could be appreciated by viewers from their armchairs, watching the television coverage of the

Chelsea Flower Show. More horticulturally suspect, but aiming for fun and excitement, were the instant garden makeovers introduced in 1997 with *Ground Force*. Excitement was certainly provided by the sight of the presenter Charlie Dimmock, working without a bra. Only a century before, women gardeners had been directed to wear all-enveloping mackintoshes to hide their bloomers.

Book publishing, like every other business, was profoundly affected by the Second World War, particularly hit by restrictions on paper. With the coming of peace, the industry gradually recovered, and colour began to seep back into printing, especially with the boost provided by the coronation of Elizabeth II and the surrounding heraldic pomp. Colour photographs would seem to be a natural accompaniment to gardening books, and indeed the late 1950s and 1960s saw a gradual rise in the number of illustrated publications both as individual titles and as partworks. However, the really successful gardening book of the late 1950s relied principally on diagrams and tables. In 1958 David Hessayon, the son of a Cypriot landowner who grew up in Salford, published *Be Your Own Gardening Expert*. Dr Hessayon got the idea of producing a down-to-earth practical manual when he was the chief scientist of Pan Britannica Industries (PBI). As the author explained on the front cover, 'This invaluable book tells you in plain language all you need to know about improving your soil, understanding the needs of your plants, and recognising and dealing with the pests and diseases that attack them. It is full of answers to questions you have so often asked and never been able to find answered in ordinary gardening books.'

*Be Your Own Gardening Expert* was priced at a very affordable 1s 6d, and included a soil tester so that novice gardeners could identify whether their soil was stony, peaty or chalky. It proved a winner, and more 'Expert' titles followed. To date there are twenty in twenty-two languages, and in 2008, the fiftieth anniversary of the initial title, the 50-millionth copy was printed. As Dr Brent Elliott, the distinguished garden historian and librarian of the RHS, wrote, 'I would say that the Expert Books have been the biggest innovation in gardening publications since the death of William Robinson in 1938'.[18]

The planting in public parks had long provided a source of ideas for working-class gardeners, but now many more private gardens were being opened to the public. The National Gardens Scheme began in 1927, when 609 private gardens opened to raise funds for the Queen's Nursing Institute for District Nurses. Within four years, the number had risen to 1,000 and a book was produced to list them all. This is now known as the

84 Dr Hessayon's *Be Your Own Gardening Expert*, with its clear instructions and low retail price, revolutionised practical manuals from its first appearance in 1958.

'Yellow Book', but until the 1950s it came in a range of pastel colours. Vita Sackville-West first opened Sissinghurst Castle to the public on May Day 1938, charging one shilling per person, with children admitted free. In 1950, with the Festival of Britain coming up, Harold Nicolson predicted an influx of visitors, and so the White Garden was devised, featuring flowers that flourished in the summer months. Sackville-West was apparently much happier with her ordinary visitors, whom she called her 'shillings's', than with 'clever people'. One visitor recalled how she was making a list of the flowers when Vita, who was famously shy, introduced herself.[19]

When the National Trust for Places of Historic Interest or Natural Beauty was founded in 1895, gardens were not part of the original brief.[20] Most of the great gardens were in the hands of families or institutions with the staff to maintain them. The first country-house garden to arrive in the Trust's portfolio was at Montacute in Somerset, which came with the Jacobean mansion acquired in 1931. However, in 1947 the first major garden was acquired in its own right, Lawrence Johnson's Hidcote Manor, and more followed fast on its heels, including Bodnant in North Wales, Mount Stewart in Northern Ireland and Nymans in Sussex. Gardens have always been the most popular properties as far as visitor figures are concerned, reflecting the national love of gardening and the changes in their appearance over the seasons. Hidcote and Sissinghurst, given to the Trust by Nigel Nicolson in 1967, are two that have consistently topped the visitor lists, and a reason for this may lie in the fact that they are made up of a series of small gardens, and are thus closer to the experience of 'ordinary' gardeners. The National Trust is regarded as a staunchly middle-class institution, but the large numbers enjoying its gardens have always included working-class visitors, arriving first in charabanc parties, and later, with the fast-growing vehicle ownership that took place in the 1960s, in individual cars. Garden tourists not only had the National Trust's gardens to admire and learn from, but also those of its sister organisation north of the border, the National Trust for Scotland; privately owned gardens, such as Hatfield House and Chatsworth; the RHS garden at Wisley; and, more recently, gardens looked after by English Heritage.

The Second World War had not been kind to nurseries, but the mail order seed companies did well, with demand outstripping supply for vegetable seeds, although their catalogues and packets lost their colourful look with the restrictions on paper and printing. With the end of the war, colour reappeared in full measure. One of the old established companies was Cuthbert's, founded as part of a trading store by James Cuthbert in 1797. Originally from Scotland, he set up a landscaping and general supplies service just outside London in Southgate. The seeds part of the company really took off in 1937 when a deal was struck between Cuthbert's and F.W. Woolworth and with the return of peace the business boomed. Clay Jones, with his melodious Welsh accent, was one of the regular panellists on *Gardeners' Question Time,* and presenter of a gardening programme in Welsh, *Garddio,* and was employed by Cuthbert's to tour the Woolworth counters to check on stock and give crash courses in horti-culture to the staff, whom he called 'horticgirls'.

The idea of the garden centre came from the United States. In 1953 the managing director of Waterers Nurseries in Bagshot, Surrey, returned to England from a business trip, inspired by the idea of selling ready-potted plants and gardening accessories in a form of self-service store. At the Chelsea Flower Show that year, the Waterers stand showed plants in containers, with labels about how to grow them and indication of the flowering season. The idea took off, and was copied by the Suffolk firm of nurserymen, Notcutts. In 1958, a garden centre was built by the side of the existing nursery in Woodbridge, including a 'planteria'. Instead of having to buy bare root plants out of season and waiting six months before finding out whether the correct order had been received from the nursery cata-logue of Latin names, the inexperienced gardener could visit his or her local garden centre and buy on the spot. With the growing number of privately owned cars, visiting garden centres became a popular day out, and the first on-site café was opened at Stewart's at Christchurch in Dorset in 1961.

In 1988 the market research company Mintel conducted a national survey looking at two areas of leisure, gardening and DIY. A group of 1,444 adults were posed the question 'which of these [list of] interests and activities have you spent one hour or more doing in the past week?' The response was that 28 per cent had done some weeding and tidying; 26 per cent cutting grass; 14 per cent digging and preparing for planting; 11 per cent gathering fruit and vegetables; 10 per cent pruning shrubs, roses and trees; and 9 per cent planting seeds and shrubs. The figures for DIY were consistently smaller. The survey also looked at patterns of shopping for plants, and gardening accessories. Garden centres proved the most popular retail outlets, followed by large DIY warehouses, although the former were considered more expensive than other outlets. They were regarded as good places to find horticultural advice, and as interesting places for a trip out by a significant proportion of those questioned. Mintel's general comment on gardens at that time was that many had been 'upgraded from a grassed area bordered by flower beds, where the children play and the washing is hung, to a well-planned, sometimes landscaped area of patios, built-in barbecues, conservatories, well-stocked flower beds, barrels, hanging baskets and neat lawns – a place to entertain guests and to dine'.[21]

# WATERERS FLORAL MILE

**over 200 acres of Nursery Stock—embracing Herbaceous Plants, Irises, Alpines, Fruit Trees—and over 250,000 Roses**

## DISPLAY GARDEN

We have established at our Floral Mile Nursery an attractive Display Garden covering an area of more than 2 acres.

Numerous beds of Floribunda and Hybrd Tea Roses, Bearded Irises, Phlox, Lupins, Michaelmas Daisies, Chrysanthemums, Dahlias, etc. have been planted to give flower throughout the season.

These beds are interspersed with wide grass paths leading to a Rock Garden and well planned Shrub and Herbaceous Borders.

This feature gives a wonderful opportunity for our customers to see a wide range of plants flowering in their natural setting and will prove of great assistance in choosing desirable subjects for garden culture.

*EVERY PLANT IS DISTINCTLY LABELLED—THERE IS PLENTY OF ROOM TO WALK ROUND*

## GARDEN CENTRES

At both the Floral Mile, Twyford and at our Tree & Shrub Nursery at Bagshot, Surrey, we have a special department well-stocked with a large selection of Shrubs, Roses, Fruit, Climbing Plants, Conifers, Bedding Plants, Alpines, etc.—in season—available for "CASH & CARRY" sale.

85  Waterers Garden Centre at Twyford in Surrey, the first of its kind in Britain.

In his book on Victorian gardens, Brent Elliott, commenting on style in gardening, declared 'It would be no exaggeration to say that since the beginning of the nineteenth century we have lived in an aesthetic anarchy'.[22] Gardeners in the late twentieth century could choose any style they wanted, furnish their gardens with a wide range of plants and shrubs available from garden centres as well as nurseries, inspired by a plethora of books offering ideas and advice. One of the popular writers on garden style was the designer John Brookes, whose first book, *Room Outside: A Plan for the Garden*, was published in 1968. Nine years later he followed this up with *The Small Garden*, offering ideas for a series of small spaces including gardens on roofs, on balconies, and in conservatories. People from all levels of society were now able to travel abroad, a recreation previously only possible for the privileged. They could return with ideas of Mediterranean gardens, water features from Spanish courtyards and wildflower meadows on the mountainsides of Switzerland. The venerable English cottage garden style was championed by Marjory Fish, who had moved from London with her husband to a cottage in Somerset in 1937, aware of the imminence of war. At East Lambrook Manor she not only produced the archetypal cottage garden, but also a nursery in response to requests for the plants that she mentioned in her books, including the famous *We Made a Garden*, published in 1956.

If no garden was available, then hanging baskets and tubs could decorate a yard or patio. Hanging baskets, like gnomes, have their detractors, but are in the fine tradition of container gardening, having adorned the greyest of Victorian and Edwardian courts and alleys. In other words, 'anything goes' for gardeners today, whatever their status, although experience and care have always been an important factor in horticultural success.

* * *

Allotment gardening enjoyed a rollercoaster history following the end of the Second World War. The government was keen that the drive for home grown fruit and vegetables should continue, promoting the concept of 'Dig for Plenty', but the number of allotments in cultivation, which stood at about one and a half million in 1945, began to decline. The reasons were similar to those pertaining at the end of the First World War: a return of emergency sites to peacetime uses and wholesale redevelopment of city centres. It is reckoned that one-fifth of the allotments provided by councils were lost in the 1950s, while private losses rose from one-fifth in the 1950s to one-half in the 1960s. In Leeds, for example, the number of private plots declined from 5,000 to 500, while in Birmingham, a city with a tradition of allotment cultivation, the number declined from 4,000 in 1948 to 2,000 in 1970.

Matters were made worse with the implementation of Dr Beeching's report on the reshaping of British Railways in 1963. Beeching, the Chairman of British Railways, was commissioned in the early 1960s to

reduce the network's costs and make the system more efficient. As a result
of his report, 4,000 route miles were cut by 1966, leaving 13,721 miles,
with a further reduction of 2,000 by the end of the decade. Ever since the
railway system was developed in the nineteenth century, the companies
had provided allotments for their own workers, and for rent to local residents. In the 1950s, however, railway land for plots had been cut by a
quarter, and then along came Beeching, and the number of plots was
reduced even further, especially in rural areas, where the branch lines had
been particularly affected by his axe.[23]

Many of the figures quoted above come from the Thorpe Report. As
both the pressure on urban land and the market price increased in the
1960s, Frederick Willey was appointed by the Wilson government as
Minister of Land and Natural Resources. Willey commissioned a report
on the general policy on allotments in England and Wales, chaired by
Harry Thorpe, professor of geography at the University of Birmingham.
In 1969 Thorpe duly delivered a 460-page report, looking at the history of
allotments and providing forty-four major recommendations. As David
Crouch and Colin Ward, in their study of allotments, point out, Thorpe's
committee took its task more seriously than the government did, and none
of their recommendations was acted upon. Nevertheless, the Thorpe
Report represents a landmark in the history of allotments.[24]

In an article published after the report, Thorpe painted a grim picture
of the state of allotments in Britain:

> A monotonous grid of rectangular plots, devoted mainly to vegetables
> and bush fruit, and tended by an older stratum of society, particularly
> men over forty and old age pensioners. Prominent over the site were
> assemblages of ramshackle huts, redolent of 'do it yourself' from the
> corrugated roofs of which sagging down-spouting carried rainwater
> into a motley collection of receptacles, long since rejected elsewhere,
> but again pressed into service here and ranging from antiquated baths
> to old zinc tanks and rusting oil drums. Where plots had been vacated,
> weeds in summer grew waist-high, almost reaching the tops of aban-
> doned bean-poles from which tattered pennants of polythene still flut-
> tered noisily to scare birds from non-existent crops.[25]

Oddly, considering he was writing a report for a Labour government,
Thorpe was rather dismissive of the working-class gardener, at one stage
remarking 'a prize onion or leek never looks quite as attractive as a prize

86 'Jake Arkle at the Pigeons', one of a series of paintings of pit life by James
MacKenzie. The artist was born at Bedlington Station in 1927, the son of a coalminer
and a brickworker. He worked in the pit and became a member of the Ashington School
of Painters in the 1970s. In this picture he shows Jake feeding his pigeons in front of
their cree in Alexandra Road, Barrington. Cabbages are cultivated in rows on the left, but
on the right is one all-important leek. (See also Plates XX and XXI.)

chrysanthemum'.[26] Instead, he looked to Europe for the way ahead.
Gardens sites were visited by the committee in the Netherlands, Denmark,
West Germany and Sweden. Equivalents of British allotments existed,
devoted almost solely to the production of vegetables and fruit, but there
was also a second type of garden, tended by the tenants according to their
individual taste, with an emphasis on flowers, shrubs and lawns, and often
furnished with a summerhouse. In Sweden, almost all the gardens were
like this, while in Denmark they were predominant in urban areas, and in
Holland the demand for them was growing. Since the mid-nineteenth
century the Germans had developed *Schrebergärten*. These were named
after Daniel Schreber, a physician from Leipzig, who advocated exercise
and outdoor recreation for the young, although he actually had no connection with allotments. Parallel with this was the growth in Germany of
*Laubenkolonien*, summerhouse colonies, much appreciated by families

living in overcrowded cities. Ironically these types of gardens were very much like the detached garden grounds on the outskirts of Birmingham, Nottingham and Warwick described in Chapter 6.

Thorpe's recommendations were based on two propositions. First, that the existing legislation was vague, obsolete and incomprehensible, and in need of revision under a single Act. Secondly, that the word allotment carried with it a stigma of charity, and needed to be replaced by the concept of the leisure garden, with sites improved to become a recreational facility for the entire family, on the lines of examples that the committee had seen in other European countries. In the event, a whole range of factors anticipated neither by Thorpe nor by the government caused a demand for allotments that has never ceased to this day. In 1970, when there were just over half a million plots available, 21 per cent were vacant, and the waiting list was just under 6,000. Within just three years the figures had changed radically, with vacancy falling to 7.7 per cent and the waiting list had shot up to over 27,000. Two years on again, in 1975, and the vacancy level was 5.5 per cent, but the waiting list had reached a startling 83,298. A social as well as a horticultural revolution was taking place: the middle classes were discovering the joys of allotments.

In 1975 a BBC television sitcom series, *The Good Life*, began its three-year run. Set in Surbiton in south-west London, it featured Tom and Barbara Good, played by Richard Briers and Felicity Kendal, and their neighbours, Jerry and Margo Leadbetter, played by Paul Eddington and Penelope Keith. On his fortieth birthday, Tom threw in his job as a draughtsman, and with Barbara turned the back and front gardens of their home into allotments growing soft fruit and vegetables, and keeping livestock, to the horror of the conventional Leadbetters. The series played on the incongruity of self-sufficiency in Surbiton, and the differing attitudes of two middle-class families, but it captured the mood of the times, and the growing interest in cultivation of food and allotment gardening.

Behind this revolution were some influential books. In 1962 *Silent Spring* was published in the America by Rachel Carson, a well-known writer on natural history. Her concerns in particular about the widespread harm being wrought by pesticides led a decade later to the ban of DDT for agricultural purposes in the United States, and also raised the world's awareness to the pollution of the environment. In 1972 the British economist E.F. Schumacher published *Small is Beautiful: A Study of Economics as if People Mattered*, a collection of essays advocating appropriate technologies that could empower people. This message, that bigger was not necessarily better, coincided with the growth of the ecological movement, and of environmentalism.

In between the appearance of these two books came the fashion for alternative lifestyles. One pioneer who had embraced the idea of a different lifestyle back in the 1950s was John Seymour. Having studied at agricultural college and worked on a farm, in 1956 he acquired a five-acre smallholding in Suffolk with his wife Sally. Eight years later they moved on to a sixty-two-acre farm in Pembrokeshire and together wrote their first self-sufficiency title in 1973. In 1976 came Seymour's most famous title, *The Complete Book of Self-Sufficiency*, with a foreword written by Dr Schumacher. Seymour is direct in his preface, explaining that 'self-sufficiency is not "going back" to an idealised past where people grubbed for food with primitive implements and burned each other for witchcraft'. Rather 'it is going *forward* to a new and better sort of life, a life which is more fun than the over-specialized round of office or factory':

> Self-sufficiency does not mean 'going back' to the acceptance of a lower standard of living. On the contrary it is a striving for a higher standard of living, for food which is fresh and organically-grown and good, for the good life in pleasant surroundings, the health of body and peace of mind which come with hard varied work in the open air, and for the satisfaction that comes from doing difficult and intricate jobs well and successfully.

Seymour was not only talking to those who had taken five acres, but also to the suburban gardener, who can 'dig up some of the useless lawn and put some of those dreary hardy perennials on the compost heap and grow his own cabbages'. He maintained that a good-sized suburban garden might practically keep a family, while a woman of his acquaintance grew the best outdoor tomatoes in a window box twelve floors up in a tower-block, as the height made it impossible for them to be afflicted by blight.[27] The book proved an enormous success, being translated into eight languages, including Japanese and Serbo-Croat.

Not only had Professor Thorpe miscalculated the future of the allotment, but also the social make-up of the allotment gardener, declaring: 'There is certainly no evidence to suggest that many immigrants from Africa, Asia or the West Indies have taken to allotment gardening; it remains essentially a British pursuit'.[28] That he and his committee should have come to this conclusion seems extraordinary. Although the number of immigrants arriving in Britain by the end of the 1960s was much less than today, there had been a long tradition of immigrant cultivation of plots of land, dating far back to the end of the sixteenth century with the arrival of the Huguenots. Crouch and Ward described two long-established Italian allotments at opposite ends of the country: one belonging to a family with an ice-cream parlour business opened in north Scotland in 1918, and the other in a south London suburb in 1929. The latter was still flourishing in 1988 with a productive vegetable plot, a vineyard and green-houses. Their summerhouse was decorated with coloured calendars, plaster cherubs and Chianti flasks. The political upheavals of the 1930s sent another Italian, Sebastiano Spada, to England after fighting on the losing side in the Spanish Civil War. Finding it easier to be accepted as a Spaniard (and going by the name Sebastien Espada), he rented a plot from the Ealing Pitshanger Allotment Society and won the mayor's prize for the best allotment year after year. After the war, he was able to acquire seeds and cuttings from all over the world, astonishing his fellow plot-holders with his Spanish beans, peppers and artichokes.

These immigrants were from Europe, but another group began to arrive from the British Empire. The first of these, nearly 500 from Jamaica, aboard the *Empire Windrush* docked at Tilbury on 22 June 1948. Naturally these newcomers wanted to grow the plants for their own cuisine, and found Britain's temperate climate made this possible. It is difficult now to realise just how limited was the range of vegetables and fruit available in shops. When Elizabeth David's first cookery book, *Mediterranean Food*, was published in 1950, she introduced all kinds of ingredients unfamiliar to the British palate, such as aubergines, peppers, courgettes and garlic, if not the more exotic callaloo and red peas that were a staple part of West Indian cuisine.[29]

Four years after the publication of the Thorpe Report, a survey was made of allotment holders in Swindon in Wiltshire, formerly a railway town but now with half its labour force employed in manufacturing. The statistics showed that 86 per cent were indigenous British, 6 per cent Italian, 6 per cent Polish, and 2 per cent were from India and Pakistan. Even these figures were considered questionable: the proportion of gardeners from overseas was probably larger, but it was thought that diffi-culties with language had excluded some questionnaire returns.[30] The survey published the following observations about the social profile of the allotment gardeners: Indians and Pakistanis grew a preponderance of beet-root, carrots, peas, beans and potatoes; the Poles always had greenhouses; the Italian favoured aesthetic greenhouses, where they grew tomatoes, peperoncini and basil, and in their vegetable beds, haricot beans and garlic. The one observation that did tie in with Thorpe's findings was that there was a preponderance of old age pensioners.

A more recent example of a group of London allotment holders shows that today, in urban areas, the proportions of immigrants can often be markedly higher. The Leyes Road Allotments in the Docklands occupy a site that was probably set aside for the dockworkers in the period following the completion of the Victoria Dock in 1854. Now part of the borough of Newham, in 2001 the site contained fifty-six plots, each 100 by 30 feet. The council rented them out annually at £40 for the waged, £5 for unwaged, and provided a small shed and running water for each plot. A small shop was run by the gardeners, providing seeds, cuttings and fertilisers.[31]

The gardening activities of four men were featured in the survey. John Costello, ex-RAF from County Limerick, grew traditional vegetables: potatoes, carrots, peas and onions, but surrounded them with alliums, crocuses, oxalis and anemones. Like the working gardeners of the nineteenth century, he kept charts and records of his successes and failures, including triple grafted pears, a combination of Conference, Williams' Bon Chrétien and Doyenne du Commice, and apples, Tydeman's Early Worcester, Cox's Orange Pippin and Ellison's Orange. Sid Graham's father came to London from Barbados in 1912, married a local girl, and was a dockworker all his life. His vegetables were conventional: peas, lettuces, onions, and the one exotic, garlic. Sid married the daughter of Mr Shaw, who came to England from Jamaica in 1958, and focused on cultivating Caribbean plants: 'I grow pumpkin, sweet-corn, French bean and callaloo for my swordfish. I've tried sweet-potato, but no luck with it yet.' Dave Thurtle had political interests, having served on the executive committee of NALGO and been a member of the Communist Party. An avid orchid lover, he was the Display Manager of the London Orchid Society. He reckoned that his interest in orchids came about as a result of the war:

It was a bloody grey, miserable existence in London at the time, every-thing was covered in soot and that, and I think I was searching for a bit of colour . . . I used to send away for seeds . . . I remember I got a Bird of Paradise (strelitzia regina) and I used to grow ferns from spores . . .

And then I bought a flask of seedling orchids (odontioda) and that was it.[32]

Other plot-holders were former dockers, carpenters, boxing trainers, chemists, housewives, chartered surveyors, a teacher and a freeman of the City of London, who all described themselves as working class. As with so many allotments in recent times, there was a waiting list for plots.

It is interesting, and significant, that the gardeners of Leyes Road Allotments all said that they were working class, though some of their professions would suggest otherwise. A survey carried out in 2013 found that over 70 per cent of the British population thought that they were part of the middle class, while another survey had 60 per cent of people considering themselves working class. This confused picture, inflamed by the national obsession with the subject, does not mean that Britain is classless. The upper class has achieved a remarkable feat in remaining little changed, with a significant proportion of land held by the same small number of families when a 'domesday' survey was held comparing 1970 with 1870. The distinctions between the middle and working classes have increasingly disappeared, with Margaret Thatcher's decision to sell off council houses to their owners in 1979 eliminating one yardstick, and the decline of industry another.

Grayson Perry, the ceramic artist, recently produced a series of television programmes in which he concluded that class is no longer a matter of economics and education, but rather of tribes. Individuals may decide through their tribal loyalties to what social class they belong. This has been reinforced by the complex table produced by the BBC following a study, the Great British Class Survey, in which it is claimed more than 161,000 people took part. Rather than the traditional categories of working, middle and upper classes, fitting only 39 per cent of the population, this new system lists seven categories, ranging from the 'elite' at the top to the 'precariat' at the bottom. Those wishing to work out where they stand in the social table find themselves plunging down the order, or rising spectacularly, depending on their answers about their social capital (income, savings, house value) and cultural capital (their spare-time interests and activities). What is clear in these difficult financial times is that there are two main groups, the 'haves' and the 'have-nots' – often grimly labelled 'the underclass'.

This history opened in 1577 with William Harrison getting himself in a muddle when trying to discuss the status of various members of the 'lower orders', and it ends on yet another confused note. By the end of the twentieth century, those factors that in earlier times had been particularly 'working class' – cottage gardening, plants in a small town backyard, and the cultivation of allotments – are all recreations shared by the middle class. Even gardening for a living has become an occupation for which formal qualifications are required, rather than on-the-job experience. So, what is the future of gardening by ordinary people?

# Epilogue

As I GATHERED my research for this book, persistent themes began to emerge. The time frame is long, encompassing five centuries, but the threads weave through them all.

One theme is that gardening has been regarded as 'A Good Thing', as the authors of *1066 and All That* would put it. For ordinary people it has provided a source of nutrition, and sometimes the only source. In the eighteenth century, and probably earlier, it provided a passionate hobby for florists. It has also been perceived by those who considered themselves superior as having a civilising effect on the lower orders, especially in the nineteenth century, when it kept men out of the alehouse or, in cities, the gin palace. In the twentieth century, horticulture was commended as a useful antidote to bolshevism. In times of war, gardening not only proved vital for supplying food, but with the 'Dig for Victory' campaign gave a sense of moral purpose to all levels of society.

In the seventeenth century, when the concept of the commonwealth was much discussed by writers and became for a brief period a political reality, John Worlidge emphasised the sense of community that horticulture could bring (see Introduction, p. 5). Now, more than ever, it plays an important role, especially in Britain's cities, where many do not have gardens; there is heavy competition for allotments, and people seek communal activities. So, to end this book, I will look briefly at just a few of the many schemes that have appeared in recent years.

The Incredible Edible Project was launched in 2008 by Pamela Warhurst, Mary Clear and a group of like-minded people in Todmorden in West Yorkshire. The scheme encourages local people to come together in their own time to turn neglected pieces of land into community gardens, growing food to share. The idea has now been taken up by communities all over the world.[1]

London has particular pressure on land, and many who would love to garden find themselves without the opportunities to do so. The first Chelsea Fringe Festival was held from 19 May to 10 June 2012, an event intended to complement the Chelsea Flower Show. In an earlier article in the *Daily Telegraph*, the founder-director, Tim Richardson, described how a new breed of guerrilla gardeners was set to break down social barriers through various projects.[2] One was the Edible Bus Stop, an unfenced strip of land next to a real bus stop in Brixton, south London, which was turned into a communal vegetable patch. A volunteer behind the scheme explained: 'Our garden functions like the old garden fence idea: you can lean on your fence and share knowledge, make friends and break down social and economic barriers. Whether or not we get a bumper crop is neither here nor there.'[3] In west London, the disused kitchen garden of Chiswick House, once the home of Paxton's 6th Duke of Devonshire, has been turned into a communal garden by Karen Liebreich. In addition, she

87 Brixton's Edible Bus Stop, 2013.

has set up Abundance London, to harvest some of the fruit that goes unpicked on the capital's trees each year. Karen too emphasised the social aspects of gardening in a city where people can be so isolated.

In Islington, north London, a beautiful little communal garden, run by volunteers, has been created and named after the radical apothecary, Nicholas Culpeper, who did so much to provide information on healing herbs to the poorest members of society. The organic garden comprises a lawn, ponds, rose pergolas, ornamental beds, vegetable plots and an area given over to wildlife. There are fifty plots, including two raised beds for disabled gardeners: these small gardens are for community groups, children, and for people living nearby who do not have gardens.

Allotments are now a sought-after commodity. When Tony Carroll applied for an allotment in Sheffield Council, he was told that it would be about seven years until he got one; eighteen months later he was told he would have the same span to wait. Instead, he began growing fruit and vegetables wherever he could, and in 2010 started the group Garden Gorilla to create instant allotments in schools, on vacant land such as rooftops and along the sides of roads.[4]

The therapeutic effects of gardening have long been recognised. At Elder Stubbs in Cowley, just outside Oxford, allotments were awarded to the poor after their common land was lost through an enclosure act in 1852. A century and a half later, the charity still provides over a hundred allotments for local residents, but has diversified by letting tenancies to other charities. One of these is a horticultural therapy project run by the mental health charity Restore from the local psychiatric hospital, which now holds workshops and has an onsite kitchen. A second development is provided by the Porch Steppin' Stone Centre, a project to provide opportunities for the cultivation of vegetables for the long-term homeless and unemployed.[5]

Despite all the interest in gardening in Britain, there is, surprisingly, a lack of people with horticultural training. One charity that is tackling this shortage is the Walworth City Garden Farm in Southwark, south London. Here unemployed residents of Southwark are offered QCF training in work-based horticulture, and given practical help to find sustainable employment thereafter.[6] Likewise, the Growing Communities project based in east London has an apprenticeship scheme, giving training one day each week in the principles of organic gardening and market gardening to a wide cross-section of the community.[7] One of Growing Communities' sites occupies part of Allens Gardens in Stoke Newington, where the

Victorian philanthropist Matthew Allen provided model flats with a communal garden for the residents' use (see Chapter 6, p. 166).

These are just a few examples of how gardening and the community can work together, many of them with echoes of a long tradition. Although some popular television shows may beg to differ, as one historian has noted, gardening is the 'true popular art of the country – we do not sing, or dance, we garden'.[8]

# Appendix

Table I Gardening work, 11–16 October 1690, Arbury Hall, Warwickshire.

| Name | Sat | Mon | Tues | Wed | Thurs | Fri | Wages |
|---|---|---|---|---|---|---|---|
| Joseph Bagley (head gardener) | Lay sick | Same | Same | Same | Same | Same | |
| Jeofry Paul | Howing weeds from amongst the early choaks | Rolling great garden and paving alleys in ye Kitchen Garden | Looking to ye Greens & gather apples | Same through oaks in ye Middle Barn | Same & cutting of ye Corron [currant] & Gooseberry Trees | Same & Gathering Apples in ye Dove Coat orchards | 3s 6d per week |
| William Warmingham | Wheeling earth off ye Mellon Ridges | Same | Same & help gather apples | Rolling in ye Great Garden and through Oaks | Went to Crabb Mill with 12 striks of Crabbs | Help gather Apples in Dove Coat Orchard | 3s 6d per week |
| Goody Bass | Cleansing of rooms over stables | Same | Same & picking of Apples | Absent | At ye Crabb Mill with Warmingham | Sweeping Gardeners Causway by order | 5 days, 1s 8d |
| Goody Wagster | Absent | Cleansing rooms over ye Stables | Same & picking of Apples | Absent | Rakeing up Leaves in Kitchen Garden | Sweeping up leaves in Kitchen Garden | 4 days, 1s 4d |
| Ann Suffolk | Cleansing rooms over ye Stables | Same | Same & picking of Apples | Absent | At ye Crabb Mill with Warmingham | Sweep Gardners Causway by order | 5 days, 1s 8d |

Table II Gardening work, 20–25 April 1703, Arbury Hall, Warwickshire.

| Name | Sat | Mon | Tues | Wed | Thu | Fri |
|---|---|---|---|---|---|---|
| John Risdall | Making hot bed [. . .?] turfing at garden | Mowing Dairy Court, watering greens and raddling earth | Turfing the Island, sowing kidney beans and arack | Sowing lettuce, radish and spinach seeds, watering and grinding scythe | Mowing flower garden, digging to find pipes in great garden | Mowing in greenhouse garden, watering greens, planting tuberoses in pots |
| William Sargent | Working with above | Working with above | Working with above | Digging in kitchen garden | | |
| J. Jacomb | Working with above | Working with above | Working with above | Working with above | Working with above | Working with above |
| P. Smith | Digging in kitchen garden | Same | Same | Digging for pipes in kitchen garden | Same | With plumber James Moris |
| Christopher Lonton | With above | With above and hoeing in Dairy Court | Digging in kitchen garden | Same and carrying clay to Square house moat | With Jacomb | Digging drains in great garden, laying trough by Square house |
| Ann Suffolk + Elizabeth ? | Weeding in flower garden | Weeding in kitchen garden | Watering in kitchen and flower gardens | Same | Weeding in flower garden | Sweeping grass, weeding kitchen garden |

Table III Gardening work, 8–15 June 1821, Arbury Hall, Warwickshire.

| Name | Sat | Mon | Tues | Wed | Thurs | Fri | Wages |
|---|---|---|---|---|---|---|---|
| Henry Twigg (foreman) | Shifting succession pines, 3d per time | Shifting succession & part of fruiting plants | Washing leaves of orange trees | Preparing cuttings of hard-wooded plants | Making up hot-bed for salading | Removing peach trees from ice-room to pinery | |
| J. Green (gardener) | Digging in the parterre | Transplanting China asters to shrubbery | Removing ivy from magnolia wall | Shifting plants in Lady Almeria's glass closet | Attending the young Lord in Idles Wood | Went to see the new plants at Froghall | 3s per day |
| C. Fisher (gardener) | Nailing the creepers in Drystove Dome | Removing the apples from cellar to fruit-room | Pruning with Lord Madottle in Torwood | Potting hydra-angeas in sinarium | Arranging sinarium and frames | Repairing box edgings in east shrubbery | 2s 6d per day |
| R. Fraser (labourer) | Digging a drain in Crooked copse at 2d per rod | Same | Same | Trenching quarter No.1 at 1s 6d per perch | Same | Absent | £1 6s 6d for job |
| J. Gott (apprentice) | In the house with H. Twigg | Same | At B with some cuttings of struthiola | With master pruning | With Henry Twigg and also C. Fisher | Sweeping all the sheds and gathering mushrooms | |
| A. Teisel (female worker) | Searching for insects and worms | Searching for snails and slugs &c | Weeding turnips | Gathering goose-berries for wine | Same | Weeding the walks | 1s per day |

# Notes

## Introduction

1. Mary Russell Mitford, *Our Village*, Oxford University Press, 1988, pp. 4–5.
2. *The Poems of Thomas Hood*, introduction by Walter Jerrold, London, 1880, p. 15.
3. Charles Dickens, *Bleak House*, Oxford University Press, 1953, p. 106.
4. Charles Dickens, *Little Dorrit*, Oxford University Press, 1953, p. 296.
5. John Pechey, *The Compleat Herbal of Physical Plants*, London, 1694, p. 145.
6. Stephen Constantine, 'Amateur Gardening and Popular Recreation in the 19th and 20th Centuries', *Journal of Social History*, 14(3) 1981, p. 387.
7. John Worlidge, *Systema Horti-culturae or The Art of Gardening*, London, 1677, pp. 4–5.

## Chapter 1 Finer Points of Husbandry

1. The bubonic plague arrived with black rats on ships, affecting English ports, and particularly London. It spread to country villages when the fleas transferred from these rats to their brown British cousins. Following the outbreak of plague in London in 1603, the disease spread out across much of the Midlands counties, including Nottinghamshire. See Paul Slack, *The Impact of Plague upon Tudor and Stuart England*, Routledge and Kegan Paul, 1985, pp. 12, 212.
2. F.H. West, *Rude Forefathers: The Story of an English Village 1600–1666*, Bannisdale Press, 1949.
3. Wiltshire and Swindon Archives, 2057/S3: Survey of Lord Pembroke's Estate, Roll 2.
4. William Harrison, *The Description of England*, ed. Georges Edelen, Dover Publications, 1994, pp. 94, 117–18.
5. Ibid, p. 271.
6. Ibid, p. 264.
7. Thomas Tusser, *Five Hundred Pointes of Good Husbandrie*, p. 34. Edition of 1580 collated with 1573 and 1577, plus the 1557 edition (unique copy) of *A Hundreth Good Pointes of Husbandrie*, ed. with notes and glossary by W. Payne and S.J. Herrtage for the English Dialect Society, 1878.
8. Ibid, p. 229.
9. Ibid, p. 41.
10. Ibid, p. 40.
11. Harrison, *The Description of England*, p. 139.
12. Tusser, *Five Hundred Pointes*, p. 40.
13. Ibid, p. 129.

14. In addition to Tusser, the sources used are a list of herbs compiled by the Surrey land-owner Thomas Fromond, reproduced in an early Tudor cookery manuscript book, and the late medieval text of John Gardiner's *Feate of Gardening*.
15. Thomas Hill, *Proffitable Arte of Gardening*, 1568, sig. dd3r.
16. *John Stow's Survey of London*, ed. Charles Lethbridge Kingsford, Oxford University Press, 1971, vol. I, p. 179.
17. These include the 'Copperplate' made in 1555, which is largely lost, but formed the basis for a copy by Ralph Agas, and the Braun and Hogenberg map of 1572. For the plant lovers of Lime Street, see the first chapter of Deborah Harkness, *Jewel House: Elizabethan London and the Scientific Revolution*, Yale University Press, 2007.
18. Alicia Amherst, *London Parks and Gardens*, A. Constable and Co., 1907, pp. 14–15.
19. *John Stow's Survey of London*, vol. I, pp. 80, 126.
20. Ibid, vol. II, p. 77.
21. Philip Stubbes, *Anatomy of Abuses*, London, 1583, pp. 48–9.
22. John Parkinson, *Paradisi in Sole*, London, 1629, p. 6.
23. *A Relation of a Short Survey of the Western Counties made by a Lieutenant of the Military Company of Norwich*, ed. L.G. Wickham Legg, *Camden Misc*, xvi (1936), p. 43.
24. Figures taken from Penelope Corfield, 'Urban Development in England and Wales in the Sixteenth and Seventeenth Centuries' in D.C. Coleman and A.H. John (eds), *Trade, Government and Economy in Pre-Industrial England: Essays Presented to F.J. Fisher*, Weidenfeld and Nicolson, 1976.
25. Thomas Hill, *The Gardeners Labyrinth*, London, 1577, p. 7.
26. Ibid, p. 22.
27. Ibid, p. 50.
28. Tusser, *Five Hundred Pointes*, p. 35.
29. Sir John Fitzherbert, *Boke of Husbandry*, London, 1568, fol. coii.
30. A.P. Appleby, *Famine in Tudor and Stuart England*, Liverpool University Press, 1978, pp. 138–9.
31. 'England in the reign of King Henry the Eighth, Part I, Starkey's Life and Letters' with an appendix, giving an extract from Sir William Forrest's *Pleasuant Poesye of Princelie Practise*, 1854, ed. S.J. Herrtage, Early English Text Society, London, 1878, p. 71.
32. Richard Gardiner, *Instructions for Manuring, Sowing and Planting of Kitchin Gardens*, printed by Edward Allde for Edward White in London, with second edition in 1603. Facsimile edition, Da Capo Press, 1973, sig. D3.
33. Samuel Hartlib, *His Legacy of Husbandry*, London, 1655, p. 9.
34. T. Cromwell, *History and Description of the Ancient Town and Boro of Colchester*, vol. II, p. 299, London 1825. Quoted in Nigel Goose and Lien Luu (eds), *Immigrants in Tudor and Early Stuart England*, Sussex Academic Press, 2005, p. 149.
35. Revd George Ormsby, 'Selections from the Household Books of the Lord William Howard of Naworth Castle', Surtees Society, 1877, pp. 29–32.
36. Canterbury Cathedral Archives, Sir Arthur Throckmorton's Diary, vol. II, fol. 118.
37. Ann Robey, 'The Village of Stock, Essex, 1550–1610: A Social and Economic Survey', unpublished thesis for the London School of Economics, 1991, p. 199.
38. Hartlib, *His Legacy*, p. 35: 'Ashes of any kind, sea-cole ashes with horse dung, the gardiners of London much commend for divers uses.'
39. Exchequer accounts: PRO E36/237/454. See J. Musty, 'Pots for the Hot-houses of Hampton Court and Hanworth', *Post Medieval Archaeology*, vol. 10, 1976, pp. 102–3.
40. Essex Record Office D/DP A10; ERO D/DP A1.
41. Goose and Luu, *Immigrants in Tudor and Early Stuart England*, p. 1.
42. Malcolm Thick, 'Root Crops and the feeding of London's poor in the late 16th and early 17th centuries', in *English Rural Society 1500–1800: Essays in Honour of Joan Thirsk*, ed. John Chartres and David Hey, Cambridge University Press, 1990.

43. Norfolk Record Office INV/14 no. 42, INV/12 no. 232.
44. Joan Thirsk and J.P. Cooper, *Seventeenth-Century Economic Documents*, Clarendon Press, 1972, p. 109.
45. Now in the Folger Library, Ms V.a.318.
46. Ian Archer, Caroline Barron, Vanessa Harding (eds), *The Markets of London in 1598*, London Topographical Society, 1988, p. 32.
47. British Library, Landsdowne Ms 74, ff. 75–6.
48. Quoted in Ronald Webber, 'London Market Gardens', *History Today*, 23, 1973, p. 874.
49. Rowland Parker, *The Common Stream*, Collins, 1975, p. 108.
50. Sir Thomas Overbury, *The Overburian Characters*, ed. W.J. Paylor, Basil Blackwell, 1936, p. 59.
51. Ben Jonson, *Epigrammes*, 133, London, 1616.
52. Parkinson, *Paradisi in Sole*, p. 509.

## Chapter 2  Vital Remedies

1. Thomas Tusser, *Five Hundred Pointes of Good Husbandrie*, p. 97. Edition of 1580 collated with 1573 and 1577, ed. with notes and glossary by W. Payne and S.J. Herrtage for the English Dialect Society, 1878.
2. See Linda A. Pollock, *With Faith and Physick: The Life of a Tudor Gentlewoman, Lady Grace Mildmay, 1552–1620*, St Martin's Press, 1993, pp. 127ff.
3. A.S. Harvey, *Ballads, Songs and Rhymes of East Anglia*, Jarrold, Norwich, 1936, pp. 129–30.
4. John Aubrey, *The Natural History of Wiltshire*, ed. J. Britton, London, 1847, p. 51.
5. Blanche Henrey, *British Botanical and Horticultural Literature Before 1800*, Oxford University Press, 1975, vol. I, p. 206; John Worlidge, *Systema Horti-culturae*, London, 1677, sig. A3v.
6. Ibid, p. 156. The full list is as follows: aconite, apple of love, bachelor's buttons, balsam apple, bellflowers, blew-bottles, candytufts, champions, cranesbill, crowfoot, dame's violet or queen's gilliflowers, double chamomile, double daisies, double featherfew, double lady-smocks, double pellitory, flower of the sun, foxgloves, grove-thistles, hollow-root, marsh marigold, monkshood, moth-mulleins, nigella or fennel-flower, non such or flower of Bristol, pilewort, amaranthus, satten-flower, scabious, thorny-apple, toadflax.
7. Goodwife Cantrey's social status and gardening activities are mentioned, without sources, in Bea Howe's introduction to her book on Jane Loudon, *Lady with Green Fingers*, Country Life, 1961. The receipt for the plants she supplied to the Hattons is included in the Finch Hatton papers, 2455, in the Northamptonshire Record Office.
8. Mrs B., Age Concern essay quoted in Gabrielle Hatfield, *Memory, Wisdom and Healing: The History of Domestic Plant Medicine*, Sutton Publishing, 1999, p. 163.
9. The origin of the term 'simpling' was that the medicine was made from one constituent part.
10. William Coles, *Art of Simpling*, London, 1656, p. 4.
11. The College took on royal status during the reign of Charles II.
12. See Margaret Pelling, *Medical Conflicts in Early Modern London*, Oxford University Press, 2003.
13. Margaret Pelling, 'Medical Practice in Early Modern England: Trade or Profession?' in Wilfrid Prest (ed.), *The Professions in Early Modern England*, Croom Helm, 1987, p. 109.
14. Ann Windsor, Nottingham Record Office, Saville Ms 221/97/7, quoted in Pollock, *With Faith and Physick*, p. 94.
15. 'Of Blind Buzzards and Cracking Combatters', in *A brief and necessarie Treatise*, London, 1585, in F.N.L. Poynter, *Selected Writings of William Clowes*, Harvey & Blythe, 1948, p. 77.

16. Quoted in Trea Martyn, *Elizabeth in the Garden: A Story of Love, Rivalry, and Spectacular Design*, Faber & Faber, 2008, pp. 54–5.

17. St Thomas's Hospital at this period was located just off Borough High Street in Southwark, and the herb garret above the church of St Thomas may still be visited: see www.thegarret.org.uk.

18. The plants featured in the pharmocopaiea of 1618 are featured in the medicinal garden of the Royal College of Physicians next to Regents Park in London.

19. W. Ryves, *The Life of the Admired Physician and Astrologer of our Times, Mr Nicolas Culpeper . . .*, London, 1659, sig. C3r.

20. *Culpeper's school of physick*, London, 1696, sig. C6r.

21. Nicholas Culpeper, *The English Physitian*, London, 1662 edition, p. 127.

22. See C. Paul Christianson, 'Herbwomen in London 1660–1836' in *The London Gardener*, 6, 2000–01. The material concerning the women and the London markets is taken from the Corporation of London Records Office, Misc Mss Boxes 332 and 333.

23. Greater London Records Office, MS AM/FW Archdiocese of Middlesex Probate Wills 1758/27.

24. *The Diary of Samuel Pepys*, ed. R.C. Latham and W. Matthews, HarperCollins, 1976, vol. V, p. 268; vol. VII, p. 235.

25. Hartlib, *A Designe for Plentie*, 1652, pp. 4, 11.

26. Hartlib, *His Legacy of Husbandry*, 1655 edition, p. 9.

27. William Harrison, *The Description of England*, ed. Georges Edelen, Dover Publications, 1994, pp. 350–1.

28. Essex Record Office Q/SR 76/22, quoted by Ann Robey in 'The Village of Stock, Essex, 1550–1610: A Social and Economic Survey', unpublished thesis, London School of Economics, 1991, p. 106.

29. Mrs Turner, who was hanged at Tyburn in 1615 for her part in the notorious Overbury murder, is said to have invented the process of dyeing ruffs yellow with saffron. I am grateful to Clare Browne for this information.

30. John Parkinson, *Paradisi in Sole*, London, 1629, p. 533; Culpeper, *English Physitian*, London, 1662, p. 144.

31. Pehr Kalm, *Account of his Visit to England, 1748*, trans. Joseph Lucas, London, 1892, pp. 8–9, 35.

32. *Letters of John Cockburn of Ormistoun to his Gardener, 1727–1744*, ed. James Colville, Scottish History Society, 1904, Letter VI, 27 December 1734, pp. 17–26.

33. Malcolm Thick, 'Market Gardening in England and Wales, 1640–1750', in Joan Thirsk (ed.), *Agrarian History of England and Wales*, vol. III, Cambridge University Press, 1990, pp. 249–52.

34. Emily Cockayne, *Hubbub: Filth, Noise and Stench in England*, Yale University Press, 2007, pp. 84–104.

35. Zachary Clark, *An Account of the Charities Belonging to the Poor of the County of Norfolk*. See 'The FACHRs Allotment Project: summary and conclusions' in Jeremy Burchardt and Jacqueline Cooper (eds), *Breaking New Ground: Nineteenth-Century Allotments from Local Sources*, Family and Community Historical Research Society, 2010, pp. 9 and ff.

36. Ibid, p. 11.

37. Worlidge, *Systema Horti-culturae*, pp. 172–3.

38. Thomas Tryon, *The Way to Health*, London, 1683, pp. 209, 212–13.

39. John Gerard, *The Herball of General Historie of Plants*, London, 1597, p. 782.

40. Richard Caulfield (ed.), *Council Book of the Corporation of Youghal*, Guilford, 1878, p. 546.

41. Royal Society, 1662, Misc Papers of the Council, 20 March.

42. Quoted in Edward MacLysaght, *Irish Life in the Seventeenth Century*, Basil Blackwell, 1950, p. 367.

43. See 'The Potato and Irish America' in Henry Hobhouse, *Seeds of Change: Five Plants that Transformed Mankind*, Sidgwick & Jackson, 1985, pp. 191–232.

44. Quoted in Redcliffe Salaman, *The History and Social Influence of the Potato*, Cambridge University Press, 1949, p. 450.
45. E. Austen Leigh, *Memoir of Jane Austen*, Constable, 1978, p. 5.
46. Gilbert White, *Natural History of Selborne*, John Lane, The Bodley Head, 1900, vol. II, p. 122.
47. William Alexander, *Notes and Sketches Illustrative of Northern Rural Life in the Eighteenth Century*, Edinburgh, 1877, p. 12.
48. Sir Thomas Bernard, *Account of a Cottage near Tadcaster*, printed for T. Becket, Bookseller, Pall Mall, 1797, p. 4.
49. Ibid, pp. 4, 1.
50. Ibid, p. 9.

## Chapter 3  Working Gardeners

1. John Harvey, *Early Nurserymen*, Phillimore, 1974, p. 1.
2. Ibid, p. 33.
3. Letters and Papers Foreign and Domestic of the Reign of Henry VIII, cited in C. Paul Christianson, *The Riverside Gardens of Thomas More's London*, Yale University Press, 2005, pp. 110–11.
4. British Library, Add. Ms 39831. For a transcript see Andrew Eburne and Katz Fetuś (eds), *Lyveden New Bield Conservation Management Plan*, The National Trust, 2008, p. 208.
5. See Richard Altick, *The English Common Reader*, University of Chicago Press, 1957, p. 22.
6. Statute of Artificers, 1562, 5 Eliz. C4, Section XI.
7. W.G. Hoskins, 'The Rebuilding of Rural England, 1570–1640', *Past and Present* 4, p. 44.
8. Guildhall Library, Ms 3396, Appendix I, letters patent.
9. Hatfield House, Bills 58/2, 58/3, Gen. 11/25 and 58/31.
10. William Lawson, *A New Orchard*, London, 1619, Chapter 1, 'Of the Gardner and his Wages'.
11. Gladys Scott Thomson (ed.), *Life in a Noble Household, 1641–1700*, Jonathan Cape, 1950, p. 245.
12. *John Evelyn: Directions for the Gardiner and other Horticultural Advice*, ed. Maggie Campbell-Culver, Oxford University Press, 2009, pp. 122, 123, 129.
13. Bristol Record Society, XXXV, 1982, pp. 70, 176–7.
14. J.T. Cliffe, *The World of the Country House in Seventeenth-Century England*, Yale University Press, 1999, p. 101.
15. West Yorkshire Archive Services, Leeds, Mss of the Earl of Mexborough, MX/R1/93 and R42/52.
16. 'It is never difficult to distinguish between a Scotsman with a sense of grievance, and a ray of sunshine', from 'The Custody of the Pumpkin,' in *Blandings Castle*, first published London, 1935, Penguin edition, 1954, p. 25.
17. *The Diary of Sir Henry Slingsby of Scriven, Bart*, ed. D. Parson, 1838, p. 64.
18. Jane Helena Ellis, 'A Warwickshire baronet, Sir Richard Newdigate: Politics, Influence and Estates Management, 1678–1710', MA thesis, Warwick University, November 1985. I am grateful to Sally O'Halloran for alerting me to the Newdigate garden books.
19. Warwick Record Office, CR136V17.
20. Warwick Record Office, Garden Book, 1689–92, CR1841/58.
21. Warwick Record Office, Garden Labour Book, 1701–03, CR1841/28.
22. I am grateful to Adam Nicolson for introducing me to this fascinating character. See 'The Autobiography of Leonard Wheatcroft of Ashover, 1627–1706', ed. Dorothy Riden, in *A Seventeenth-century Scarsdale Miscellany*, Derbyshire Record Society, Chesterfield, 1993, pp. 71–117.

23. Ibid, p. 84.
24. Ibid, p. 95. Wheatcroft notes this visit as taking place in February 1685, but the Duke only made these changes in the 1690s.
25. Stephen Switzer, *The Nobleman, Gentleman, and Gardener's Recreation*, London, 1715, pp. vii–viii.
26. Stephen Switzer, *Ichnographia Rustica*, London, 1718, vol. I, preface, pp. xxiv–xxv.
27. *Autobiography of Dr. A. Carlyle of Inveresk, 1722–1805*, ed. John Hill Burton, Thoemmes Press, 1990, pp. 379–80.
28. Minute Book, Guildhall Library.
29. Philip Miller, *The Gardeners Dictionary*, London, 1731, p. xi.
30. Miller to Charles Alston, 1 October 1737, Edinburgh University Library, Laing III, 375, fol. 24av.
31. John Amman to Linnaeus, 15 November 1737, in James Smith (ed.), *A Selection of the Correspondence of Linnaeus and other Naturalists*, London, 1821, vol. II, p. 195.
32. Alexander Garden to Linnaeus, 15 March 1755, in Smith, *A Selection*, vol. I, pp. 284–5.
33. Northampton Record Office, Finch Hatton Papers, 2452.
34. John Worlidge, *Systema Horti-culturae*, London, 1677, pp. 271–8.
35. For further details, see Malcolm Thick, 'Market Gardening in England and Wales, 1640–1750', in Joan Thirsk (ed.), *Agrarian History of England and Wales*, vol. III, Cambridge University Press, 1990, pp. 257 and ff.
36. Pehr Kalm, *Account of his Visit to England, 1748*, trans. Joseph Lucas, London, 1892, pp. 24–5.
37. See Malcolm Thick, *The Neat House Gardens*, Prospect Books, 1998, Chapter VI.
38. *Illustrated London News*, 27 June 1846, p. 421.
39. In one of his books, *A Year's Residence in the United States of America*, Cobbett condemned 'Ireland's lazy root' with its tendency 'to debase the common people as everything does which brings their mode of living to be nearer that of cattle. The man and his pig, in the potato system live pretty much upon the same diet'. As so often Cobbett's argument was casuistical, for in another book, *The English Gardener*, he gave detailed instructions for growing potatoes. His concern was that politicians were trying to turn the potato into a staple food, and the terrible results in Ireland in the 1840s vindicated his argument.
40. *Gardening Magazine*, vol. III, p. 363.

## Chapter 4  A Passion for Flowers

1. Cited in the *Oxford English Dictionary* as from Isaac Walton, *Reliquiae Wottonianae*, p. 407.
2. Visit to Paris, 23 May 1651, *The Diary of John Evelyn*, 6 vols, ed. E.S. de Beer, Oxford University Press, 2002, vol. III, p. 33.
3. Ralph Knevet, *Rhodon and Iris*, Bodleian Library, Mal. 174(4).
4. Bodleian Library, E.325, fol. 129.
5. Bodleian Library, Douce S7.
6. Samuel Gilbert, *Florists Vade-Mecum*, London, 1682, p. 116.
7. William Jolly, *The Life of John Duncan: Scotch Weaver and Botanist*, London, 1883, pp. 304–5.
8. Quoted by Robert Thornton in his *Temple of Flora*, London, 1799, in 'A group of carnations', fn. 2.
9. Quoted in Ruth Duthie, *Florists' Flowers and Societies*, Shire Publications, 1988, p. 15.
10. From the newspaper cuttings collection in Hackney Archives.
11. The early records of the Society are now in the Borthwick Institute in York. The first minute book, running from 1768 to 1803, is AYSF 1/2/1.
12. See Ruth Duthie, 'The Ancient Society of York Florists', *York Historian*, 3, 1980.

13. William Hanbury, *The Whole Body of Planting and Gardening*, London, 1770–71, p. 286.
14. Minute Book 1 in the Heritage Library, Paisley Central Library.
15. Quoted by John Claudius Loudon in his *Encyclopaedia of Gardening*, London, 1822, pp. 1252–3.
16. Minute Book 2, p. 26.
17. John Claudius Loudon, *An Encylopaedia of Gardening*, London, 1822, pp. 1252–3.
18. A copy of the book is in the RHS Lindley Library.
19. J. Beck (ed.), *Florist, Fruitist and Garden Miscellany*, quoted in Miles Hadfield, *A History of British Gardening*, revised edition, John Murray, 1979, p. 263.
20. Thomas Hogg, *Concise and Practical Treatise on the Growth and Culture of the Carnation*, London, 1822, pp. 261–72.
21. William Howitt, *Rural Life in England*, London, 1844, p. 548.
22. Quoted by Jenny Uglow in *A Little History of British Gardening*, Chatto & Windus, 2004, p. 199.
23. Mary Russell Mitford, *Our Village*, first published London, 1832; paperback edition, Oxford University Press, 1982, p. 114.
24. *Floricultural Cabinet*, vol. I, March 1833, p. 3.
25. Ibid, vol. I, June 1833, pp. 75–6.
26. Introduction to James Douglas, *Hardy Florists' Flowers*, London, 1880.
27. *Horticultural Magazine*, 1846, quoted in Roy Genders, *Collecting Antique Plants*, Pelham, 1971, p. 35.
28. Genders, *Collecting Antique Plants*, p. 187.
29. *Journal of Horticulture*, 18, 1870, p. 221.

**Chapter 5  Two Nations**

1. William Howitt, *The Rural Life of England*, London, 1838, vol. I, p. 173.
2. Walter Rose, *Good Neighbours*, Cambridge University Press, 1942.
3. Flora Thompson, *Lark Rise to Candleford*, Oxford University Press, 1945, p. 79.
4. Quoted by J.L. and Barbara Hammond, *The Village Labourer*, Nonsuch, 2005, Appendix A(i), p. 273.
5. SBCP Report, i, p. 100.
6. Arthur Young, *Annals of Agriculture and other Useful Arts*, vol. XXV, 1796, p. 530.
7. Rose, *Good Neighbours*, p. 75; David Crouch and Colin Ward, *The Allotment: Its Landscape and Culture*, Faber & Faber, 1988, p. 167.
8. Letter of 19 September 1836, written 'at Mr Emery's cottage in the middle of the hundred acre garden', to the *Farmer's Magazine*, and reprinted in the *Labourer's Friend Magazine*, LXX, 1837, pp. 8–9.
9. *Facts and Illustrations*, 1832, p. 176, quoted by Jeremy Burchardt, *The Allotment Movement, 1793–1873*, Royal Historical Society, 2002, p. 79.
10. 'Cottage Husbandry', *The Irish Farmers' and Gardeners' Magazine*, I, Dublin, 1834, p. 335.
11. 'On Cottage Husbandry', *The Irish Farmers' and Gardeners' Magazine*, III, Dublin, 1836, p. 334.
12. The Young Englanders were a group of radical, socially conscious aristocrats appalled by the dispiriting effects of industrialisation, and attributing many of the injustices of society to the utilitarian philosophy of Jeremy Bentham. The debate was known as the 'Condition of England Question'.
13. No Young Englander he: Dryden presided over his Northamptonshire estates for sixty-two years and became known as 'the Antiquary'.
14. L. Jenyns, *Memoir of the Rev. John Stevens Henslow*, London, 1862, p. 51.
15. John Glyde, *Suffolk in the 19th Century*, Ipswich, 1856, p. 357.
16. Select Committee on the Labouring Poor, 1843, VII, p. 93.

17. The Six Points were: universal manhood suffrage, a secret ballot, abolition of the property qualification for MPs, payment for MPs, equal electoral districts and annual parliamentary elections.
18. *Labourer's Friend Magazine*, CXXXIII, 1842, p. 54.
19. Jeremy Burchardt and Jacqueline Cooper (eds), *Breaking New Ground: Nineteenth-Century Allotments from Local Sources*, Family and Community Historical Research Society, 2010, pp. 199ff.
20. Royal Commission on the Framework Knitters, 1844–45, pp. 818, 958.
21. 'A Union Meeting', *The Land Magazine*, 1899.
22. Thomas Hardy, *Tess of the d'Urbervilles*, Wessex edition, Macmillan, 1974, p. 395.
23. Burchardt and Cooper, *Breaking New Ground*, Table 5, p. 63.
24. Thompson, *Lark Rise to Candleford*, p. 63.
25. *Leamington Chronicle*, 6 May 1893, p. 55; 21 January 1893, p. 17.
26. Gertrude Jekyll, *Old West Surrey: Some Notes and Memories*, Longmans, Green & Co., 1904, pp. 273, 219.
27. William Howitt, *The Rural Life of England*, London, 1838, vol. I, p. 302.
28. George Borrow, *Romany Rye*, J.M. Dent, 1907, p. 120.
29. Thompson, *Lark Rise to Candleford*, p. 117.
30. Rose, *Good Neighbours*, p.73.
31. Ibid, pp. 9, 60.
32. Jekyll, *Old West Surrey*, pp. 269, 268.
33. Quoted in Gillian Darley, *Villages of Vision*, Architectural Press, 1975, p. 28.
34. *Country Life*, 23 December 1899, pp. 814–17.
35. It is thought that Leadhills provided the prototype for Robert Owen to found his enlightened community at New Lanark. See Margaret Willes, *Reading Matters: Five Centuries of Discovering Books*, Yale University Press, 2008, pp. 214–17.
36. Arthur Raistrick, *Two Centuries of Industrial Welfare: The London (Quaker) Lead Company, 1692–1900*, Kelsall & Davis, 1987, pp. 20, 27–8.
37. Gardens cultivated by the Pennines leadminers have been recreated at nearby Killhope Lead Mining Museum in County Durham.
38. S.D. Chapman, *Stanton and Staveley: A Business History*, Woodhead-Faulkner, 1981, p. 161. See also Clive Lievers, 'The Provision of Allotments in Derbyshire Industrial Communities' in Burchardt and Cooper, *Breaking New Ground*.
39. Interview by Cliff Johnson, 1976, in the Beamish Archives.
40. P. Searby, 'Great Dodford and the later history of the Chartist Land Scheme', *Agricultural Historical Review*, 1968, p. 44.
41. Nellie Shaw, *History of Whiteway*, 1935, quoted in Gillian Darley, *Villages of Vision*, Architectural Press, 1975, p. 88.
42. Quoted in Martin Hoyles, *The Story of Gardening*, Journeyman Press, 1991, p. 285.
43. Raphael Samuel (ed.), *Village Life and Labour*, Routledge & Kegan Paul, 1975, Part 4: '"Quarry Roughs": Life and Labour in Headington Quarry, 1860–1920: An Essay in Oral History'; Raphael Samuel, 'Headington Quarry: Recording a Labouring Community', *Oral History*, 1(4) 1972, pp. 107–22.
44. Oxfordshire History Centre, Headington Quarry Tape, Morris and Coppock, 5.
45. Ibid, Coppock, fol. b.10.
46. Ibid, Tolley, fol. c.1.
47. Oxfordshire History Centre, Acc. 4043.
48. William Cobbett, *Rural Rides*, Peter Davies, 1930, vol. II, p. 407; vol. I, p. 23.

**Chapter 6 Hard Times**

1. 'The Diary of John Ward of Clitheroe, Weaver, 1860–64', *Transactions of the Historic Society of Lancashire and Cheshire*, vol. 115, 1964, p. 138.
2. John Parkinson, *Paradisi in Sole*, London, 1629, p. 2.

3. John Evelyn, *Fumifugium*, facsimile edition, University of Exeter, 1976, p. 14.
4. Thomas Fairchild, *City Gardener*, London, 1722, p. 1.
5. Shirley Hibberd, *The Town Gardener*, London, 1855, p. 5. Hibberd wrote with great verve. Here he is referring to the dandy, Beau Brummel, who drove his valet to despair as he rejected cloth after cloth in an effort to create the perfect cravat.
6. William Cowper, 'The Task', in *Poetical Works*, ed. H.S. Mitford, Book IV, *The Winter Evening*, Oxford University Press, 1934.
7. Dickens, *Little Dorrit*, Oxford University Press edition, 1953, p. 574.
8. Whitmore, 'Respite Hours', *Firstlings*, Chapman, London, 1852.
9. John Clay, *Report on the Sanitary Condition of the Borough of Preston*, 1844, p. 180.
10. 'Hand-loom versus power-loom' in John Harland, *Songs of Lancashire*, London, 1865, p. 189.
11. See Neville Flavell, 'Urban Allotment Gardens in the Eighteenth Century: The Case of Sheffield' in *The Agricultural History Review*, 51, 2003, Part I.
12. These agreements are now in the city archives and in the archives of the Duke of Norfolk at Arundel Castle.
13. William Buchan, *Domestic Medicine*, London, 1769, pp. 143, 144.
14. Sheffield Archives TC 1045, fols. 50, 51, 58, 59, 114.
15. Camden, *Britain, or a Chorographical Description*, London, 1637, p. 567.
16. See Phillida Ballard, 'The Guinea Gardens in Birmingham: Early Urban Allotments', in Jeremy Burchardt and Jacqueline Cooper (eds), *Breaking New Ground*, Family and Community Historical Research Society, 2010. The editors note that guinea gardens do not conform to the widely used definition of allotments.
17. Jane Rowton, 'Rented Gardens in Birmingham, 1823-37', unpublished thesis, Birmingham University, 1975.
18. Quoted in Sheila Hughes, 'Guinea Gardens, with particular reference to the only remaining site', in Peter Leather (ed.), *Rewriting the History of Birmingham*, 1992, Birmingham Central Library, LF71.
19. William Hutton, *History of Birmingham*, 2nd edition, 1793, pp. 202–3.
20. J.A. Langford, *A Century of Birmingham Life*, 2nd edition, 1870, vol. I, pp. 296, 109.
21. Samuel Jackson Pratt, writing as The Gleaner in his *Harvest-Home: consisting of supplementary gleanings, original dramas and poems, contributions of literary friends*, vol. I, 1805, p. 311.
22. Calthorpe Estate papers, Birmingham City Archives, MS2126/Estate Box 11/18.
23. R. Dent, *Old and New Birmingham*, vol. III, 1878–80, reprinted 1973, W/1878A in Birmingham Central Library.
24. The other three cited are Coventry, Birmingham (Westbourne Road Leisure Gardens) and Nottingham (St Ann's Close). The information on the Hill Close Gardens is taken from their guidebook.
25. Birmingham City Archives, Ms 3782/12/59, Letters 210 and 211.
26. Most of the Birmingham back-to-backs have been demolished, but the National Trust looks after the last surviving court on Hurst Street.
27. *Horticultural Register*, 9 June 1831.
28. William Howitt, *Rural Life in England*, 1844 edition, pp. 550–1.
29. Samuel Reynolds Hole, *A Book about Roses*, Edward Arnold, 1905, p. 18.
30. Harry Wheatcroft, *My Life in Roses*, Odhams Press, 1959, p. 18.
31. *Labourer's Friend Magazine*, CXLIII, February 1843, pp. 29–31, based on original material from the *Leeds Intelligencer*. I am grateful to Jeremy Burchardt for these details.
32. Catherine Buckton, *Town and Window Gardening*, London, 1879, p. ix.
33. Ibid, p. 142.
34. Pehr Kalm, *Account of his Visit to England*, 1748, trans. Joseph Lucas, London, 1892, p. 85.
35. Charles Dickens, *The Old Curiosity Shop*, Penguin edition, 1985, pp. 171–3.

36. Samuel Hadden Parkes, *Window Gardens for the People and Clean and Tidy Rooms, being an experiment to improve the homes of the London poor*, London 1864, pp. 48–50. The story about little gardens being turned into drying yards and the stubbornness of the horseradish was in fact lifted from Henry Mayhew's *London Labour and the London Poor*, London, 1851, vol. I, p. 140. Mayhew was making a general statement about the cottages and their gardens in Lisson Grove, Islington, Hackney, Hoxton and Stepney.

37. Hector Gavin, *Sanitary Ramblings*, 1848, p. 9.

38. Ibid, pp. 11–12.

39. Millicent Rose, *The East End of London*, Cresset Press, 1951, p. 171.

40. J. Mitchell, 'Reports from the Assistant Hand-loom Weavers Commissioners', Parliamentary Papers, 1840, vol. XXIII, 49, p. 218.

41. Dickens, *Great Expectations*, J.M. Dent, 1907, pp. 192–3.

42. Old Bailey sessions, Eades, John Mortimer, 19 September 1810, Reference: t18100919-141.

43. Report and Minutes of Evidence, OP-RC/108 and 109, 2000, p. 81.

44. Walter Southgate, *That's the Way It Was: A Working-class Autobiography, 1890–1950*, Oxted in association with the History Workshop, Centre for London History, 1982, pp. 18–19.

45. Fairchild, *City Gardener*, 1722, p. 57.

46. Dickens, *Our Mutual Friend*, Chapman & Hall, 1907, p. 264.

47. Published in *All the Year Round*, NS, no. 285, Chapter 1, p. 115.

48. *Floral World*, June 1871, p. 229.

49. Samuel Hadden Parkes, *Window Gardens for the People*, London, 1864, pp. 3, 27.

50. Ibid, pp. 54–5.

51. Parkes, *Flower Shows of Window Plants for the Working Classes of London*, London, 1862, p. 7.

52. Parkes, *Window Gardens*, pp. 38–9.

53. *The Day of Rest*, September 1865, p. 458.

54. The gardens are now accessible to the public, and include an urban market garden run by Growing Communities (see pp. 372–3).

55. The information on the Shaftesbury Park estate was given to me by Philip Temple from the Survey of London. I am very grateful to him. See Colin Thom (ed.), *Survey of London*, vol. 50: *Battersea*, Yale University Press, 2013.

56. *Clarke's History of Walthamstow*, originally published in 1861, reprinted 1980 by the Walthamstow Antiquarian Society.

57. A Society for the Diffusion of Beauty had been proposed by Octavia's sister Miranda. This became the Kyrle Society, named after Alexander Pope's philanthropist, the Man of Ross. Among its objectives was the preservation of open spaces in cities, which Octavia Hill memorably described as 'out-door sitting rooms for the people'.

## Chapter 7 Climbing the Wall

1. Written many years later for the Duke of Devonshire's *Handbook of Chatsworth*, which he had printed privately for his sisters.

2. Violet Markham, *Paxton and the Bachelor Duke*, Hodder & Stoughton, 1935, p. 5.

3. Quoted in Kate Colquhoun, *A Thing in Disguise: The Visionary Life of Joseph Paxton*, Fourth Estate, 2003, p. 23.

4. Preface to *Self-Instruction for Young Gardeners*, London, 1845.

5. J.C. Loudon, *An Encyclopaedia of Gardening*, London, 1822, pp. 1322–3; see also Chapter 5, p. 13 for the miners of Leadhills.

6. *Gardener's Magazine*, vol. I, April 1826, p. 8.

7. Ibid, p. 1328.

8. Ibid, p. 482.

9. Ibid, pp. 1199–2000.

10. Ibid, vol. II, 1827, pp. 109–10.
11. Ibid, vol. I, 1826, pp. 141–2.
12. Preface, *Self-Instruction for Young Gardeners*.
13. *Gardeners' Chronicle*, 21 July 1860, pp. 672–3.
14. Toby Musgrave provides passages from some of these articles in *The Head Gardeners*, Aurum Press, 2007, pp. 72ff.
15. Jonathan Bate, *John Clare: A Biography*, Picador, 2003, p. 71.
16. The diary was taken to America when Donaldson emigrated there. In 1984 his grandson, Thomas Cureton, presented a copy to Duff House, which is now looked after by Historic Scotland, and a transcription has been made. The extracts are courtesy of Historic Scotland.
17. Donaldson's diary, 24 September 1874, p. 66.
18. Ibid, 12 November 1873, p. 5.
19. Ibid, 11 September 1874, p. 63.
20. 9 September 1873 in *William Cresswell: Diary of a Victorian Gardener*, English Heritage, 2006, p. 56.
21. Musgrave, *The Head Gardeners*, p. 84.
22. *William Cresswell*, pp. 62–3.
23. Ibid, pp. 69, 79, 82.
24. H. Rider Haggard, *A Gardener's Year*, Longmans, Green, 1905, pp. 195, 290.
25. Thomas Fairchild, *The City Gardener*, London, 1722, p. 68.
26. Shirley Hibberd, *The Amateur's Flower Garden*, London, 1871, p. 102.
27. *Gardener's Magazine*, 1826, vol. I, pp. 24–6.
28. Shirley Hibberd, *The Town Garden*, London, 1859, p. 99.
29. *Gardener's Magazine*, 31 January 1874, p. 51; 8 January 1876, p. 15; 3 June 1876, pp. 285–6.
30. *An Oxfordshire Market Gardener: The Diary of Joseph Turrill of Garsington, 1863–7*, ed. E. Dawson and S.R. Royal, Alan Sutton, 1993, p. 122.
31. Ibid, p. 96.
32. Ibid, p. 41.
33. Notes to Plate XXIX in P.H. Emerson, *Pictures of East Anglian Life*, London, 1888, pp. 134–5.

### Chapter 8  Sources of Inspiration

1. N. Cole, head gardener to Mrs Silver of St John's Wood, in the *Gardeners' Chronicle*, 21 January 1860, pp. 49–50.
2. William Jolly, *The Life of John Duncan*, London, 1883, pp. 482, 488, 315.
3. Jane Loudon, *Botany for Ladies*, London, 1842, p. vi.
4. Samuel Reynolds Hole, *The Six of Spades: A Book About the Garden and the Gardener*, London, 1872, pp. 136–7.
5. Quoted in Martin Hoyles, *The Story of Gardening*, Journeyman Press, 1991, p. 242.
6. The portraits, with their poems, hang in the Servants' Hall at Erddig.
7. Jolly, *The Life of John Duncan*, p. 265.
8. *East London Observer*, 31 March 1866, p. 2.
9. Samuel Reynolds Hole, *Our Garden*, London, 1899, pp. 242, 244–5.
10. Report of the committee for 1906–07, *Irish Gardening*, 3, Dublin, 1908, p. 34.
11. From Abercrombie's *Practical Gardener*, revised by Mr James Mean, 1817, pp. x–xi.
12. I am very grateful to Malcolm Thick for this.
13. A full list of these periodicals is given by Anne Wilkinson in *The Victorian Gardener*, Sutton, 2006.
14. Ibid, p. 36. The citation is to Elisabeth B. MacDougall (ed.), *John Claudius Loudon and the Early 19th Century in Great Britain*, Dumbarton Oaks, 1980.
15. *Horticultural Journal*, 1833, vol. I, p. 31.

16. Hole, *A Book of Roses*, London, 1870, p. 100.
17. Will Tjaden, 'George Glenny, Horticultural Hornet', *The Garden*, 1986, p. 318; *Horticultural Journal*, vol. III, 1835, pp. 6, 8.
18. *Gardeners' Chronicle*, 2 January 1841, p. 1.
19. G.A. Sala, *The Life and Adventures of George Augustus Sala*, London, 1875, vol. I, p. 209.
20. Such was the paper's appeal that Matilda Alice Victoria Wood called herself Marie Lloyd when she sought a memorable stage name.
21. *Lloyds Weekly*, 1 February 1852, p. 8.
22. Ibid, 14 March 1852, p. 8.
23. Ibid, 2 May 1852, p. 8.
24. *The Memories of Dean Hole*, London, 1892, p. 240.
25. Charles Lawrence, *Practical Directions and General Management of Cottage Gardens*, London, 1831, pp. 3, 25.
26. *Gardener's Magazine*, January 1827, pp. 19, 271.
27. *Cottage Gardener*, 3 March 1857, p. 388.
28. Samuel Reynolds Hole, *Our Gardens*, London, 1899, p. 242.
29. Basil and Jessie Hartley, *Gardener at Chatsworth*, Hanley Swan, 1992, p. 154.
30. Quoted in Hoyles, *The Story of Gardening*, p. 185.
31. Quoted by Ann Robey, in Margaret Willes (ed.), *Hackney: An Uncommon History*, Hackney Society, 2012, p. 46.
32. Notices from the *Exeter Flying Post*: 7.8.1834; 6.6.1850 and 1.8.1850, quoted by Clare Greener in 'The Rise of the Professional Gardener in Nineteenth-century Devon: A Social and Economic History', unpublished thesis, University of Exeter, 2009, p. 20.
33. *Morning Herald*, 18 August 1852.
34. *The Times*, 25 June 1852.
35. *Gardeners' Chronicle*, 1866, pp. 879–80.
36. Quoted in Charles Poulsen, *Victoria Park*, Journeyman Press, 1976, p. 16.
37. Letter in the *Morning Advertiser*, 20 August 1872, in which Mr Stanley, MP, recalled the circumstances surrounding the creation of the park.
38. Quoted in Poulsen, *Victoria Park*, p. 18.
39. I am grateful to Julia Matheson for the horticultural details of the park.
40. *Illustrated London News*, 18 July 1846.
41. Revd George Alston, letter to *The Times*, 7 September 1847; George Glenny, *Lloyd's Weekly*, 14 June 1863.
42. Quoted in Philip Mernick and Doreen Kendall, *A Pictorial History of Victoria Park, London E5*, East London Historical Society, 1996, p. 11.
43. Quoted in ibid, p. 12.
44. Robert Thompson, *The Gardener's Assistant*, 1881 edition, Plates 9 and 10.
45. *Daily News*, 30 November 1863, p. 5.
46. Lt-Col J.J. Sexby, *The Municipal Parks, Gardens and Open Spaces of London*, London 1898, pp. 552–3.
47. Walter Wright, 'Gardening London', in George R. Sims (ed.), *Living London*, Cassell, 1901, vol. I, p. 308.
48. Given in *London Gardener*, vol. X, 2005.
49. *Gardener's Magazine*, 12 August 1865.

## Chapter 9 The Spirit of Competition

1. *Floricultural Magazine*, 2, 1838, pp. 297–8.
2. *Gardener's Magazine*, 12, 1836, p. 380.
3. This was an accusation levelled by the gardening journalist, Donald Beaton, blaming shows for encouraging 'purse gardening' which gave an unfair advantage to the wealthy

who could afford large-scale greenhouse cultivation. He made this point in *Cottage Gardener*, vol. VIII, 1852, pp. 189–91.

4. See Anne Wilkinson, 'Stoke Newington and the Golden Flower', *Hackney History*, 5, 1999.
5. *Illustrated London News*, 24 October 1863, p. 423.
6. *East London Observer*, 10 December 1859, p. 3.
7. *Gardener's Magazine*, 26 October 1889, p. 673.
8. Samuel Broome, *Penny Illustrated Paper*, 8 November 1861, pp. 67–8.
9. *Gardener's Magazine*, 11 April 1868, p. 155.
10. Glenny's *Gardening Gazette and Midland Florist*, June 1864, p. 67.
11. This point is well made by Julia Matheson in 'Common Ground: Horticulture and the Cultivation of Open Space in the East End of London, 1840–1900', unpublished PhD thesis, Open University, 2011, p. 34.
12. *Day of Rest*, November 1865, p. 28.
13. Gertrude Jekyll, *Wood and Garden*, Longmans, Green, 1989, pp. 185–7.
14. Samuel Reynolds Hole, *A Book About Roses*, Edward Arnold, 1905, pp. 12–22.
15. Samuel Hadden Parkes, *Flower Shows of Window Plants for the Working Classes of London*, London, 1862, p. 3. See also Julia Matheson, 'A New Gleam of Social Sunshine', *The London Gardener*, vol. IX, 2003/4.
16. Samuel Hadden Parkes, *Window Gardens for the People and Clean and Tidy Rooms, being an experiment to improve the homes of the London poor*, London, 1864, pp. 27, 33.
17. Parkes, *Flower Shows*, p. 3.
18. Ibid, p. 4.
19. *Penny Illustrated Paper*, 5 July 1862, p. 3.
20. *City Press*, quoted in *Gardener's Magazine*, 30 May 1863, p. 175.
21. Parkes, *Window Gardens*, p. 47.
22. *All the Year Round*, 20 August 1864, pp. 33–4.
23. *Holborn and Bloomsbury Journal*, 16 July 1864, p. 2.
24. Catherine Buckton, *Town and Window Gardening*, London, 1879, p. viii.
25. Borthwick Institute, University of York, Ancient Society of York Florists (ASYF) 3/1/3.
26. ASYF 3/1/2 Minute Book, 1864–80.
27. Parkes, *Flower Shows*, p. 3.
28. *Cottage Gardener*, letter from J.L. Middlemiss, gardener to A. Pott Esq. of Tunbridge Wells, 25 October 1848.
29. Jean Russell-Gebbett, *Henslow of Hitcham*, T. Dalton, 1977, pp. 77–82.
30. Ibid, p. 79.
31. See S.D. Chapman, *Clay Cross, 1837–1987*, 1987, pp. 9–16. The Gardening Society Minute Book survives at the Clay Cross Company.
32. Samuel Reynolds Hole, *The Six of Spades*, London, 1872, pp. 197–8. The cottager class is still maintained in many village flower shows today. For example, for the Annual Fete and Flower Show in August 2011 at Rackham near Pulborough, West Sussex, the cottager division was defined as for those who receive wages, are bona fide occupiers of a cottage and who garden without hired assistance.
33. My thanks to Anthony Kremer for providing me with this information from copies of the *Yalding Church Monthly*.
34. Hole, *A Book About the Garden and the Gardener*, Nelson, 1909, p. 130.

## Chapter 10 Revolutions in Taste

1. Mrs M.J. Loftie, *Social Twitters: Essays Reprinted from 'The Saturday Review'*, London, 1879.
2. Alicia Amherst, *A History of Gardening in England*, London, 1895, p. 295.
3. See Brett Elliott's entry for John Fleming in the *Oxford Dictionary of National Biography*.

4. J.J. Sexby, *The Municipal Parks, Gardens, and Open Spaces of London*, London, 1898, p. 552.
5. 'Chrysanthemum Culture', *Gardener's Magazine*, 2 January 1860, p. 3.
6. *Gardeners' Chronicle*, 29 August 1891, pp. 22–3.
7. Henry Mayhew, *London Labour and the London Poor*, London, 1851, vol. I, pp. 138ff.
8. Ibid, p. 138.
9. Henry W. Nevinson, *Neighbours of Ours*, J.W. Arrowsmith, 1895, pp. 4–5.
10. Walter Southgate, *That's the Way It Was: A Working-class Autobiography, 1890–1950*, Oxted, 1982, in association with the History Workshop, Centre for London History, p. 19.
11. Quoted in Elizabeth Drury and Philippa Lewis, *The Victorian Flower Album*, Collins & Brown, 1993, p. 59.
12. Shirley Hibberd, *The Town Garden*, London, 1855, p. 29.
13. Gertrude Jekyll, *Old West Surrey*, Longmans, Green, 1904, p. 276.
14. M.K. Ashby, *Joseph Ashby of Tysoe: A Study of English Village Life*, Merlin Press, 1974, p. 174.
15. George Bourne, *Memoirs of a Surrey Labourer*, Duckworth, 1911, p. 131.
16. Anne Scott-James, *The Cottage Garden*, Allen Lane, 1981, p. 107.
17. H. Pratt, 'A Wonderful Rock Garden', *Strand Magazine*, 1890, pp. 225–30. See also Twigs Way, *Garden Gnomes: A History*, Shire, 2009.
18. Quoted in Twigs Way, *Garden Gnomes*, p. 35. Confusingly, the Royal International Horticultural Show in 1912 was not organised by the RHS, though they did back it, having cancelled their own Great Spring Show. In 1913, the RHS show moved to Chelsea from the Inner Temple garden.
19. See Chapter 4, note 6.
20. *Major Works of John Clare*, Oxford World Classics, 2004, pp. 138–9.
21. See Dialect and Nature at www.ryenats.org.uk/dialect.htm: it provides 2,000 terms from Anne Elizabeth Baker's *Glossary of Northamptonshire Words and Phrases*, 2 vols, London, 1854; facsimile edition by Lark Publications, 1995.
22. *Gardeners' Chronicle*, 29 July 1865, p. 697.
23. William Robinson, *The English Flower Garden*, London, 1895, p. 34.
24. Ibid, p. 232.
25. Ronald King, *The Quest for Paradise*, Whittet Books, 1979, pp. 235–6.
26. Edward Hyams, *English Cottage Gardens*, Nelson, 1970, p. 65.
27. These and more examples are taken from Roy Genders, *The English Cottage Garden and the Old Fashioned Flowers*, Pelham Books, 1969, pp. 14–17.
28. Flora Thompson, *Lark Rise to Candleford*, Oxford University Press, 1945, p. 79.
29. Vita Sackville-West, 'Hidcote Manor', *Journal of the Royal Horticultural Society*, 74, 1947, pp. 476–81.
30. Scott-James, *The Cottage Garden*, p. 119.

## Chapter 11  Digging for Victory in Peace and War

1. Benjamin Disraeli, *Sybil*, London, 1871, p. 457. In fact, the Chartists had six points: see p. 384, n. 17.
2. Ronald Blythe, *Akenfield*, Penguin, 1972, p. 21.
3. Flora Thompson, *Lark Rise to Candleford*, Penguin, 1973, pp. 65–6.
4. Economic and Social Data Service, SN 2000, 'Family Life and Work Experience before 1918', 1870–1973, Interviews 001 and 002.
5. Benjamin Seebohm Rowntree and May Kendall, *How the Labourer Lives*, T. Nelson, 1913, Study XXIX, pp. 209ff.
6. Ibid, Study IV, pp. 59ff.
7. *Warwick Advertiser*, 10 January 1914.
8. *Irish Times*, 22 June 1909.

9. *Eastern Post*, 5 May 1918. See also Elizabeth Anne Scott, 'Cockney Plots: Working Class Politics and Garden Allotments in London's East End, 1890–1918', thesis for the Department of History, University of Saskatchewan, 2005.

10. *East End News*, 28 August 1908, Tower Hamlets Library, Allotments File, no. 630–1.

11. Gerald W. Butcher, *Allotments for All: The Story of a Great Movement*, Allen & Unwin, 1918, p. 15.

12. Economic and Social Data Service, SN 2000, Interviews 121, 133, 057.

13. Quoted by Twigs Way in *A Nation of Gardeners*, Carlton Publishing, 2010, p. 115. The decrease in the number of women employed in agriculture since the mid-eighteenth century is noted in the first chapter in K.D.M. Snell, *Annals of the Labouring Poor: Social Change and Agrarian England, 1660–1900*, Cambridge University Press, 1985. This reduction is attributed to economic and technological changes, reinforced in the nineteenth century by shifts in social attitudes. Anecdotal evidence suggests that this decline was not so great in horticulture, with many women employed seasonally in market gardening (see Chapter 3, pp. 77, 88) and some in country-house estate gardens (see Chapter 7, p. 185).

14. Thompson, *Lark Rise to Candleford*, p. 114.

15. Economic and Social Data Service, SN 2000, Interviews 098, 278, 422.

16. Butcher, *Allotments for All*, Preface.

17. Michael Macdonagh, *In London During the Great War*, Eyre and Spottiswoode, 1935, p. 164.

18. Johns, 'Allotment Gardens in Belfast', Department of Agriculture and Technical Instruction, *Journal*, 1916, pp. 317–19.

19. *East London Observer*, 3 September 1910, Tower Hamlets Library, Allotments File, no. 630–1.

20. Butcher, *Allotments for All*, p. 39.

21. Ibid, p. 35.

22. Ibid, p. 26.

23. F.E. Green, 'The Allotment Movement', *Contemporary Review*, July 1918, quoted in David Crouch and Colin Ward, *The Allotment: Its Landscape and Culture*, Faber & Faber, 1988, p. 71.

24. VLCS, *Allotments and Gardens*, May 1919.

25. Chamberlain was writing in *The Times*'s housing supplement. See Keith Feiling, *The Life of Neville Chamberlain*, Macmillan, 1970, p. 86.

26. Quoted in Catherine Bailey, *Black Diamonds: The Rise and Fall of a Great English Dynasty*, Penguin, 2007, p. 192.

27. Beamish Archives, Oral Histories, 1976–123.

28. This was to be repeated in the miners' strike of 1984–85.

29. British Library, 'Down to Earth: An Oral History of British Horticulture', F12666–F12672.

30. Oxfordshire Record Office, Raphael Samuel interviews, Tolley, fols. a.1 and b.1.

31. David Lambert, 'Westbourne Road Leisure Gardens Report', W1992c and W1992.

32. Ken Ausden, *Up the Crossing*, BBC Books, 1981, p. 166.

33. Percy Girling in an interview with Audrey Coppard, Southwold, 27 December 1974, quoted by Bernard Crick in *George Orwell: A Life*, Penguin, 1980, pp. 243–4.

34. Mass Observation Diary 5150. The Mass Observation diaries and other material are stored in the library of the University of Sussex, but are available online through certain libraries. The project was originally Mass-Observation, but recently the hyphen has been dropped.

35. Diary 5176.

36. Diary 5150.

37. Diary 5323.

38. *Gardeners' Chronicle*, 23 September 1939, p. 212.

39. Lambert, 'Westbourne Road Leisure Gardens Report', W1992c.

40. Personal communication to author.
41. Quoted in Twigs Way, *A Nation of Gardeners*, p. 140.

**Chapter 12  Homes and Gardens**

1. Quoted in Gillian Darley, *Villages of Vision*, Architectural Press, 1975, p. 74.
2. Ibid, p. 74.
3. Alexander Harvey, *The Model Village*, Batsford, 1906. A copy is in the Birmingham Central Library.
4. Ibid, p. 24.
5. Benjamin Seebohm Rowntree was a pioneering sociologist who carried out a survey of housing and provision of gardens in York in 1901, and of agricultural labourers in the Midlands counties, published in 1913. See Chapter 11, pp. 266–7.
6. Quoted in Mireille Galinou (ed.), *London's Pride*, Anaya, 1990, p. 183.
7. Quoted in Standish Meacham, *Regaining Paradise: Englishness and the Early Garden City Movements*, Yale University Press, 1999, p. 162.
8. *The Builder*, 8 November 1918.
9. Reported in *The Times*, 24 December 1918.
10. Preface by E. Percy Schofield in F. Henslow and W. Geoffrey (eds), *Suburban Gardens*, Rich & Cowan, 1934.
11. Antonia Rubinstein, Andy Andrews and Pam Schweitzer (eds), *Just Like the Country: Memories of London families who settled the new cottage estates, 1919–39*, Age Exchange, 1991.
12. Ibid, p. 28.
13. Ibid, p. 36.
14. Ibid, pp. 36, 39.
15. Ibid, pp. 38–9.
16. Richard Sudell, *The New Illustrated Gardening Encyclopaedia*, Odhams Press, 1937, p. 195.
17. Russell (1857–1951) was a leading member of the Ancient Society of York Florists.
18. Rubenstein et al, *Just Like the Country*, p. 38.
19. Ibid, pp. 36–7.
20. Tape 63 in Manchester Archives Dept, M14/1/26 and 14/1/11; see also Chapter 4 by Ann Hughes and Karen Hunt in Andrew Davies and Stephen Fielding (eds), *Workers' Worlds: Cultures and Communities in Manchester and Salford, 1880–1939*, Manchester University Press, 1992.
21. Rubenstein et al, *Just Like the Country*, p. 52.
22. Tapes 56 and 116, Manchester Archives Dept.
23. *An Enquiry into People's Homes: A Report Prepared by Mass-Observation*, John Murray, 1943.
24. H.H. Thomas, *The Complete Amateur Gardener*, Cassell, 1924, p. 3.
25. George Orwell, *Coming up for Air*, Secker & Warburg, 1948, p. 263.
26. Alistair Black, 'Building of the Downham Estate', pp. 68–9, unpublished master's thesis, Birkbeck College, 1981, quoted by Matthew Hollow in 'Suburban Ideals on England's Interwar Council Estates', *Garden History*, 39(2) 2011.
27. Deanna Walker and Peter Jackson, *A Portrait of Basildon Plotlands: The Enduring Spirit*, Phillimore, 2010.
28. The 1930s layout has been retained, but at the time of writing, there is no gardener, so it is overgrown. See www.essexwt.org.uk/haven-plotlands-museum.
29. *An Enquiry into People's Homes*, p. 219.
30. Ibid, p. 163.
31. Bournville Village Trust, *When We Build Again*, Allen & Unwin, 1941.
32. Gwendolen Freeman, *The Houses Behind*, Allen & Unwin, 1947, pp. 10, 173–4.
33. *An Enquiry into People's Homes*, p. 160.

34. Benjamin Seebohm Rowntree, *Poverty, a Study of Town Life*, Macmillan, 1901, p. 148.
35. Benjamin Seebohm Rowntree, *Poverty and Progress: A Social Survey of York*, Longmans, Green, 1941, p. 234.
36. Ibid, pp. 234–5.
37. Elizabeth Lebas, 'The Making of a Socialist Arcadia: Arboriculture and Horticulture in the London Borough of Bermondsey after the Great War', *Garden History*, 27(2) 1999, pp. 219–37.
38. *Twelve Years of Labour Rule on the Bermondsey Borough Council, 1922–24*, published by the Labour Institute, 1934.
39. Preface to *Hints for the Town Gardener*, London Gardens Society, 1938.
40. Ibid, p. 10.
41. Walter P. Wright, *Window Gardening*, J.M. Dent, 1937, p. 26.

## Chapter 13 Ancient and Modern

1. Mary Webb, *The Golden Arrow*, Constable, 1916, p. 176.
2. E.L.A, unpublished Age Concern essay, 1990. This and the quotations that follow were included in Gabrielle Hatfield's *Memory, Wisdom and Healing*, Sutton Publishing, 1999. Unfortunately Age UK have been unable to trace the originals.
3. Hatfield, *Memory, Wisdom and Healing*, p. 77.
4. *Culpeper's Complete Herbal*, W. Foulsham & Co., nd, p. 241.
5. Agnes Arber, *Herbals: Their Origin and Evolution*, 2nd edn, Cambridge University Press, 1953, p. 270.
6. Frederick Wigby, *Just a Country Boy*, Geo. R. Reeve, 1976.
7. John Gerard, *The Herball of General Historie of Plants*, amended by Thomas Johnson, London, 1636, pp. 856, 355, 813.
8. Ebenezer Sibly added illustrations in his edition published in London in 1805.
9. Wigby, *Just a Country Boy*, p. 65.
10. Hatfield, *Memory, Wisdom and Healing*, p. 72.
11. P.H. Emerson, *Pictures of East Anglian Life*, London, 1888, p. 16.
12. Mr J. in personal communication to Gabrielle Hatfield, Witton, Norfolk, 1988, quoted in *Memory, Wisdom and Healing*, p. 80.
13. Act III, Scene I.
14. Wigby, *Just a Country Boy*, p. 22.
15. Mrs M.W. of Saffron Walden, Age Concern essay, quoted in Hatfield, *Memory, Wisdom and Healing*, pp. 102–3.
16. F. Ranson, *British Herbs*, Penguin, 1949, p. 84.
17. George Ewart Evans, *Where Beards Wag All*, Faber & Faber, 1970, p. 59. The curious title is a quote from Thomas Tusser.
18. These traditions and the ones that follow are taken from Roy Vickery's first chapter, 'A Time for Every Purpose', in *Garlands, Conkers and Mother Die*, Continuum, 2010. Others appear on www.plant-lore.com.
19. Quoted in Jill Shearer, *The Poor Man's Best Friend: The Story of the Great Somerford Allotments, 1809–2009*, Somerford Press, 2009, p. 31.
20. Interview with Mr Cawson from Kibblesworth, Beamish Archives, 1993–5.
21. *Daily Mail*, 20 February 1911, p. 6.
22. The story is told in Henry Donald, *A Bunch of Sweet Peas*, Canongate, 1988.
23. *Home Gardening*, 1, no. 1, 1928.
24. See Stephen Constantine, 'Amateur Gardening and Popular Recreation in the 19th and 20th Centuries', *Journal of Social History*, 14(3) 1981, p. 398.
25. *The Home Gardening Encyclopaedia*, edited by Walter Brett and published by Pearson in 1939, was the reference book owned by my grandfather, a printer's compositor who worked in the City of London and was a keen amateur gardener.
26. John Coutts, Preface to *All About Gardening*, revised edition, Ward, Lock, 1931.

27. BBC Written Archives, transcripts on microfilm.

28. Note to A.B. Ryan, the Middleton Poll, 7 July 1937, quoted by Asa Briggs, *The History of Broadcasting in the UK*, vol. II, Oxford University Press, 1995, p. 254, and BBC Written Archives, R.Cont.1, C.H. Middleton Talks File, 1, 1937.

29. Mass Observation Diary 5324, 23 May 1941.

30. *Catholic Herald*, 27 September 1935.

31. BBC Written Archives, R.Cont.1, C.H. Middleton Talks File, 1939, 24 October 1939.

32. BBC Written Archives, Children's Hour File, 1933–40, memo 20 March 1940.

33. C.H. Middleton, *Your Garden in War-time*, Allen & Unwin, 1941, p. 5.

34. Information from J. Green, February 1969, quoted in Briggs, *The History of Broadcasting in the UK*, vol. III, p. 41.

35. BBC Written Archives, letter from Guy Fletcher, R.Cont.1, 910MIS, File II, 1937–41.

36. BBC Written Archives, transcript, 24 May 1935.

37. Norman Thomas's recollections have been recorded by the National Trust as part of their oral history project. The quotations are courtesy of the Trust.

38. Evans, *Where Beards Wag All*, pp. 60ff.

39. Ronald Blythe, *Akenfield*, Penguin, 1972, pp. 116, 119.

40. Middleton, *Your Garden in War-time*, p. 162.

41. Mass Observation Diary 5324. She was probably the younger sister or cousin of Betty Hall, Diary 5323 (Chapter 11, p. 285).

42. The archives of the Women's Farm and Garden Association are held at the University of Reading, Museum of Rural Life, ref GB 007 SR WFGA.

43. J.H.C, *The Garden*, LXI, 1 March 1902. See also Clare Greener, 'The Rise of the Professional Gardener in Nineteenth-century Devon: A Social and Economic History', unpublished thesis, University of Exeter, 2009, pp. 77ff.

44. Quoted by Twigs Way, *A Nation of Gardeners*, Carlton Publishing, 2010, p. 84.

45. See Anne Meredith, 'Horticultural Education in England, 1900–40: Middle Class Women and Private Gardening Schools', *Garden History*, 31(1) 2003, pp. 67–79.

46. *Evening Standard*, 17 June 1940.

## Chapter 14  A Nation of Gardeners

1. Official Report from the House of Commons, 4 May 1943, vol. 389, col. 81–2.

2. Six of the Uni-Seco prefabs on the estate have been preserved under the protection of English Heritage.

3. Quoted in Greg Stevenson, *Palaces for the People: Pre-fabs in Post-war Britain*, Batsford, 2003, p. 137.

4. Ibid, p. 169.

5. Michael Young and Peter Willmott, *Family and Kinship in East London*, Routledge & Kegan Paul, 1957, p. 127.

6. Hilda Kean, *London Stories: Personal Lives, Public Histories*, Rivers Oram Press, 2004.

7. S.J. Poole, *Housing Estate Garden*, W.H. & L. Collingridge, 1953, p. 25.

8. Ibid, p. 105.

9. *New Society*, 3(82), 23 April 1964, pp. 18–19.

10. Peter Willmott and Michael Young, *The Symmetrical Family: A Study of Work and Leisure in the London Region*, Routledge & Kegan Paul, 1973, p. 47.

11. *Woman*, 66, 1970, p. 33.

12. Young and Willmott, *Family and Kinship in East London*, p. 155.

13. Benjamin Seebohm Rowntree, *Poverty and Progress*, Longmans Green, 1941, p. 331. Charles Booth had noted even longer hours for workers such as market porters (seventy-two) and railway carmen (eighty-four).

14. BBC Written Archives, 19 March 1946.

15. Charles Quest-Ritson, *The English Garden: A Social History*, Viking, 2001, p. 231.
16. From the press pack in the BBC Written Archives, produced in 1987 for the celebration of forty years of the programme.
17. Details from BBC Written Archives, File N8/14/1.
18. 'You're Booked!,' *Independent*, 16 June 1997.
19. Letter from Charlotte Osborne, quoted in Jane Brown, *Sissinghurst: Portrait of a Garden*, Weidenfeld and Nicolson, 1990, p. 32.
20. This National Trust now looks after properties in England, Wales and Northern Ireland. The National Trust for Scotland was founded as a separate organisation in 1931.
21. Mintel, *Leisure Intelligence*, vol. IV, 1989, 2.3.
22. Brent Elliott, *Victorian Gardens*, Batsford, 1990, p. 10.
23. The number fell from 75,306 plots on 4,321 acres in 1948, to 38,094 on 2,128 acres in 1963.
24. David Crouch and Colin Ward, *The Allotment: Its Landscape and Culture*, Faber & Faber, 1988, p. 7.
25. Harry Thorpe, 'The Homely Allotment: From Rural Dole to Urban Amenity: A Neglected Aspect of Urban Land Use', *Geography*, 60(3), July 1975, pp. 169–83.
26. Report, para. 455.
27. John Seymour, *The Complete Book of Self-Sufficiency*, Faber & Faber, 1976, p. 7.
28. Thorpe Report, Cmnd 4166, 1969, 142.
29. A recent cookery book shows how times have changed. *Moro East*, by the restauranteurs Sam and Sam Clarke (Ebury Press, 2007) featured recipes from produce grown in the Manor Garden Allotments in Hackney Wick. These were bequeathed in 1900 by the Hon. Arthur Villiers 'in perpetuity' to East End families. Eighty-one plots, located by the River Lea, were until 2007 cultivated by a multinational community of all ages, consisting of born-and-bred East Enders and more recent incomers from the Mediterranean and the West Indies. Crops included wild plums, figs, rhubarb, herbs of every kind, carrots, beans and potatoes, artichokes, chillis, rocket and kohlrabi. All were lost in 2007 when, despite a campaign by the Manor Gardens Allotments Society to have the allotments incorporated in the Olympic site, they were bulldozed and buried under the Olympic Park. See www.lifeisland.org.
30. Denis Moran, *The Allotment Movement in Britain*, Peter Lang, 1990, p. 130.
31. Kevin Ducker, 'Growing Pains: Allotment Gardening and the East End', *Rising East: The Journal of East London Studies*, 4(3) 2001.
32. Ibid, pp. 81, 82.

## Epilogue

1. www.incredible-edible-todmorden.co.uk.
2. *Daily Telegraph*, 17 March 2012.
3. www.theediblebusstop.org.
4. www.gardengorilla.co.uk. Article in the *Telegraph* Magazine, 18 July 2011.
5. www.restore.org.uk/our-services/recovery-groups/elder-stubbs; www.theporch.org.uk/allotments.html.
6. www.walworthgardenfarm.org.uk.
7. www.growingcommunities.org.
8. Gillian Darley, 'Cottage and Suburban Gardens' in *The Garden: A Celebration of One Thousand Years of British Gardening*, ed. John Harris, Mitchell Beazley, 1979.

# Select Bibliography

### Primary Manuscript Sources

Ancient Society of Florists (ASYF), Borthwick Institute, York.
Joseph Ashby, in 'Rural Vignettes' by J.A. Benson, *The Land Magazine*, 1899, Warwickshire Record Office, CR 2500/14/6.
BBC Written Archives, www.bbc.co.uk/archive/tv_archive.shtml.
John Donaldson diary, Duff House, Banff.
Newdigate Papers, Warwickshire Record Office.
Paisley Florist Society Minute Books, Local Studies Library, Paisley.
Charles Snow diaries, Oxfordshire History Centre, Acc 4043.
Papers of the Women's Farm and Garden Association, 1899–1991, University of Reading, Museum of English Rural Life, GB 007 SR WFGA.

### Primary Printed Sources

(Dates refer to first publication, unless subsequent editions are significant)

Bernard, Thomas, *An Account of a Cottage and Garden*, London, 1797.
Buckton, Catherine, *Town and Window Gardening*, London, 1879.
Cobbett, William, *Cottage Economy*, Peter Davies, 1926 edition.
—— *Rural Rides during the Years 1821 to 1826*, Peter Davies, 1930 edition.
Colville, James (ed.), *Letters of John Cockburn of Ormistoun to his Gardener, 1727–1744*, Scottish History Society, 1904.
Culpeper, Nicholas, *The English Physitian or An Astrological-physical Discourse of the Vulgar Herbs of this Nation*, London, 1652.
Fairchild, Thomas, *The City Gardener*, London, 1722.
Freeman, Gwendolen, *The Houses Behind*, Allen & Unwin, 1947.
Gardiner, Richard, *Instructions for Manuring, Sowing and Planting of Kitchin Gardens (1603)*, facsimile edition, Da Capo Press, 1973.
Gavin, Hector, *Sanitary Ramblings*, London, 1848.
Harrison, William, *The Description of England*, ed. Georges Edelen, Dover Publications, 1994.
Hibberd, James Shirley, *The Town Garden: A Manual for the Management of City and Suburban Gardens*, London, 1855.
Hill, Thomas, *The Gardeners Labyrinth*, London, 1608 edition.
Hogg, Thomas, *A Concise and Practical Treatise on the Growth and Culture of the Carnation, Pink, Auricula, Polyanthus, Ranunculus, Tulip, Hyacinth, Rose and other Flowers*, London, 1822.

Hole, Samuel Reynolds, *A Book About Roses*, Edward Arnold, 1905.
—— *A Book About the Garden and the Gardener*, Nelson, 1909.
—— *Our Gardens*, J.M. Dent, 1899.
Howitt, William, *The Rural Life of England*, 2 vols, London, 1838.
Jekyll, Gertrude, *Old West Surrey: Some Notes and Memories*, Longmans Green, 1904.
Jolly, William, *The Life of John Duncan: Scotch Weaver and Botanist*, London, 1883.
Kalm, Pehr, *Account of his Visit to England, 1748*, trans. Joseph Lucas, London, 1892.
King, Gregory, *National and Political Observations and Conclusions upon the State and Condition of England, 1696*, appended to 'Estimate of the Comparative Strength of Great Britain', London, 1802.
Loudon, John Claudius, *An Encyclopaedia of Gardening*, London, 1822.
—— *Self-Instruction for Young Gardeners*, London, 1847.
Mayhew, Henry, *London Labour and the London Poor*, 3 vols, London, 1851.
Parkes, Samuel Hadden, *Flower Shows of Window Plants for the Working Classes of London*, a paper read before the Social Economy Section of the National Association for the Promotion of Social Science, Guildhall, London, 1862.
—— *Window Gardens for the People and Clean and Tidy Rooms, being an experiment to improve the homes of the London poor*, London, 1864.
Riden, Dorothy (ed.), 'The Autobiography of Leonard Wheatcroft of Ashover, 1627–1706', Derbyshire Record Society, Chesterfield, 1993.
Royal Commission on the Housing of the Working Classes, 1884, Reports and Minutes of Evidence, OP-RC/108 & 9.
Stow, John, *A Survey of London*, Oxford University Press, 1971.
Thompson, Flora, *Lark Rise to Candleford*, Oxford University Press, 1945.
Tusser, Thomas, *Five Hundred Pointes of Good Husbandrie* (edition of 1580 collated with 1573 and 1577, and unique 1557 edition of *A Hundreth Good Pointes of Husbandrie*), W.Payne and S.J. Herrtage (eds), English Dialect Society, London, 1878.
Worlidge, John, *Systema Horti-culturae or The Art of Gardening*, London, 1677.

**Secondary Material**

Ashby, M.K., *Joseph Ashby of Tysoe: A Study of English Village Life*, Merlin Press, 1974.
Bell, Jonathan and Mervyn Watson, *Rooted in the Soil: A History of Cottage Gardens and Allotments in Ireland since 1750*, Four Courts Press, 2012.
Bourne, George, *Memoirs of a Surrey Labourer: A Record of the Last Years of Frederick Bettesworth*, Duckworth, 1911.
Bournville Village Trust, *When We Build Again*, Allen & Unwin, 1941.
Briggs, Asa, *The History of Broadcasting in the UK*, 5 vols, Oxford University Press, 1995.
Burchardt, Jeremy, *The Allotment Movement in England, 1793–1873*, Royal Historical Society, 2002.
Burchardt, Jeremy and Jacqueline Cooper (eds), *Breaking New Ground: Nineteenth-Century Allotments from Local Sources*, Family and Community Historical Research Society, 2010.
Butcher, Gerald W., *Allotments for All: The Story of a Great Movement*, Allen & Unwin, 1918.
Cadbury, Peter, *Fifty Years On*, Bournville Village Trust, 1952.
Chapman, S.D., *The Clay Cross Company, 1837–1987*, Clay Cross, 1987.
—— *Stanton and Staveley: A Business History*, Woodhead-Faulkner, 1981.
Christianson, C. Paul, 'Herbwomen in London, 1660–1836', *The London Gardener*, 6, 2000–01.
—— *The Riverside Gardens of Sir Thomas More's London*, Yale University Press, 2005.
Cliffe, J.T., *The World of the Country House in Seventeenth-Century England*, Yale University Press, 1999.
Cockayne, Emily, *Hubbub: Filth, Noise and Stench in England*, Yale University Press, 2007.

Colquhoun, Kate, *A Thing in Disguise: The Visionary Life of Joseph Paxton*, Fourth Estate, 2003.

Constantine, Stephen, 'Amateur Gardening and Popular Recreation in the 19th and 20th Centuries', *Journal of Social History*, 14(3) 1981, pp. 387–406.

Corfield, Penelope, 'Urban Development in England and Wales in the Sixteenth and Seventeenth Centuries', in D.C. Coleman and A.H. John (eds), *Trade, Government and Economy in Pre-Industrial England: Essays Presented to F.J. Fisher*, Weidenfeld and Nicolson, 1976.

Cresswell, William, *Diary of a Victorian: William Cresswell and Audley End*, English Heritage, 2006.

Crouch, David and Colin Ward, *The Allotment: Its Landscape and Culture*, Faber & Faber, 1988.

Darley, Gillian, *Villages of Vision*, Architectural Press, 1975.

Dawson, E. and S.R. Royal (eds), *An Oxfordshire Market Gardener: The Diary of Joseph Turrill of Garsington, 1863–67*, Sutton, 1993.

Ducker, Kevin, 'Growing Pains: Allotment Gardening and the East End', *Rising East: The Journal of East London Studies*, 4(3) 2001.

Duthie, Ruth, 'The Ancient Society of York Florists', *York Historian*, 3, 1980.

—— 'English Florists' Societies and Feasts in the Seventeenth and First Half of the Eighteenth Centuries', *Garden History*, 10(1) 1982, pp. 17–35.

—— *Florists' Flowers and Societies*, Shire Publications, 1988.

—— 'Florists' Societies and Feasts after 1750', *Garden History*, 12(1) 1984, pp. 8–38.

Elliott, Brent, 'Flower Shows in Nineteenth-century England', *Garden History*, 29(2) 2001, pp. 171–84.

—— *Victorian Gardens*, Batsford, 1986.

Ellis, Jane Helena, 'A Warwickshire Baronet, Sir Richard Newdigate: Politics, Influence and Estates Management, 1678–1710', unpublished M.Phil thesis, Warwick University, 1985.

Evans, George Ewart, *Where Beards Wag All*, Faber & Faber, 1970.

Flavell, N., 'Urban Allotment Gardens in the Eighteenth Century: The Case of Sheffield', *The Agricultural History Review*, 51(1) 2003.

Galinou, Mireille (ed.), *London's Pride: The Glorious History of the Capital's Gardens*, Anaya, 1990.

Gardiner, Juliet, *The Thirties: An Intimate History*, Harper Press, 2010.

Genders, Roy, *Collecting Antique Plants: The History and Culture of the Old Florists' Flowers*, Pelham, 1971.

—— *The English Cottage Garden and the Old Fashioned Flowers*, Pelham, 1969.

Goose, Nigel and Lien Luu (eds), *Immigrants in Tudor and Early Stuart England*, Sussex Academic Press, 2005.

Greener, Clare, 'The Rise of the Professional Gardener in Nineteenth-century Devon: A Social and Economic History', unpublished thesis, University of Exeter, 2009.

Hadfield, Miles, *A History of British Gardening*, revised edition, John Murray, 1979.

Hammond, J.L. and Barbara Hammond, *The Village Labourer*, Nonsuch, 2005.

Harding, Jane and Anthea Taigel, 'An Air of Detachment: Town Gardens in the Eighteenth and Nineteenth Centuries', *Garden History*, 24(2) 1996, pp. 237–54.

Harris, John (ed.), *The Garden: A Celebration of One Thousand Years of British Gardening*, Mitchell Beazley, 1979.

Harvey, John, *Early Nurserymen*, Phillimore, 1974.

Hatfield, Gabrielle, *Memory, Wisdom and Healing*, Sutton, 1999.

Henrey, Blanche, *British Botanical and Horticultural Literature Before 1800*, Oxford University Press, 1975.

Hollow, Matthew, 'Suburban Ideals on England's Interwar Council Estates', *Garden History*, 39(2) 2011, pp. 203–17.

Horn, Pamela, *The Changing Countryside in Victorian and Edwardian England and Wales*, Athlone Press, 1984.
—— *Life and Labour in Rural England 1760–1850*, Macmillan, 1987.
Horwood, Catherine, *Potted Histories*, Frances Lincoln, 2007.
Hoyles, Martin, *Gardeners' Books*, vol. 1, *Gardeners Delight*, Pluto Press, 1994; vol. 2, *Bread and Roses*, Pluto Press, 1995.
—— *The Story of Gardening*, Journeyman Press, 1991.
Hughes, Sheila, 'Guinea Gardens, with Particular Reference to the Only Remaining Site', in Peter Leather (ed.), *Rewriting the History of Birmingham*, 1992, Birmingham Central Library, LF71.
Hyams, Edward, *English Cottage Gardens*, Nelson, 1970.
Langley, Anne (ed.), *Joseph Ashby's Victorian Warwickshire*, Brewin Books, 2007.
Lebas, Elizabeth, 'The Making of a Socialist Arcadia: Arboriculture and Horticulture in the London Borough of Bermondsey after the Great War', *Garden History*, 27(2) 1999, pp. 219–37.
Leith-Ross, Prudence, *The John Tradescants and the Rose and Lily Queen*, Peter Owen, revised edition, 2006.
London Gardens Society, *Hints for the Town Gardener*, London Gardens Society, 1938.
Longstaffe-Gowan, Todd, *The London Square*, Yale University Press, 2012.
Mass Observation, *An Enquiry into People's Homes*, John Murray, 1943.
Matheson, Julia, 'Common Ground: Horticulture and the Cultivation of Open Space in the East End of London, 1840–1900', unpublished PhD thesis, Open University, 2011.
—— '"A New Gleam of Sunshine": Window Garden Flower Shows for the Working Classes, 1860–75', *The London Gardener*, 9, 2003–04.
Mernick, Philip and Doreen Kendall, *A Pictorial History of Victoria Park*, East London History Society, 1996.
Moran, Denis, *The Allotment Movement in Britain*, Peter Lang, 1990.
Moreton, C. Oscar, *The Auricula: Its History and Character*, Ariel, 1964.
Musgrave, Toby, *The Head Gardeners*, Aurum Press, 2007.
O'Halloran, Sally, 'The Serviceable Ghost: The Forgotten Role of the Gardener in England, 1600–1730', unpublished thesis, University of Sheffield.
Parker, Rowland, *The Common Stream*, Collins, 1975.
Pelling, Margaret, *Medical Conflicts in Early Modern London*, Oxford University Press, 2003.
Potter, Jennifer, *Strange Blooms: The Curious Lives and Adventures of the John Tradescants*, Atlantic, 2006.
Poulsen, Charles, *Victoria Park*, Journeyman Press, 1976.
Quest-Ritson, Charles, *The English Garden: A Social History*, Viking, 2001.
Raistrick, Arthur, *Two Centuries of Industrial Welfare: The London (Quaker) Lead Company, 1692–1900*, Kelsall & Davis, 1977.
Rider Haggard, Henry, *A Gardener's Year*, Longmans, Green, 1905.
Robey, Ann, 'The Village of Stock, Essex, 1550–1610: A Social and Economic Survey', unpublished PhD thesis, London School of Economics, 1991.
Rose, Walter, *Good Neighbours*, Green Books, 1988.
Rowntree, Benjamin Seebohm, *Poverty, a Study of Town Life*, Macmillan, 1901.
—— *Poverty and Progress: A Second Social Survey of York*, Longmans, Green, 1941.
Rowntree, Benjamin Seebohm and May Kendall, *How the Labourer Lives*, Nelson, 1913.
Rowton, Jane, 'Rented Gardens in Birmingham, 1823–37', unpublished thesis, Birmingham University, 1975.
Rubinstein, Antonia, Andy Andrews and Pam Schweitzer (eds), *Just Like the Country: Memories of London Families Who Settled the New Cottage Estates, 1919–39*, Age Exchange, 1991.

Russell-Gebbett, Jean, *Henslow of Hitcham: Botanist, Educationalist and Clergyman*, T. Dalton, 1977.

Salaman, Redcliffe N., *The History and Social Influence of the Potato*, Cambridge University Press, 1949.

Samuel, Raphael, 'Headington Quarry: Recording a Labouring Community', Oral History Society, 1(4), 1972.

—— (ed.), 'Quarry Roughs: Life and Labour in Headington Quarry, 1860–1920', in *Village Life and Labour*, Routledge & Kegan Paul, 1975.

Scott, Elizabeth Anne, 'Cockney Plots: Working Class Politics and Garden Allotments in London's East End, 1890–1918', unpublished thesis, Department of History, University of Saskatchewan, 2005.

Scott Thomson, Gladys (ed.), *Life in a Noble Household 1641–1700*, Cape, 1950.

Shephard, Sue, *Seeds of Fortune: A Gardening Dynasty*, Bloomsbury, 2003.

Sitwell, Sacheverell, *Old Fashioned Flowers*, Country Life, 1948.

Southgate, Walter, *That's the Way It Was: A Working-class Autobiography 1890–1950*, in association with History Workshop, Centre for London History, Oxted, 1982.

Stevenson, Greg, *Palaces for the People: Prefabs in Post-war Britain*, Batsford, 2003.

Taylor, Geoffrey, *The Victorian Flower Garden*, Skeffington, 1952.

Thick, Malcolm, 'Market Gardening in England and Wales, 1640–1750', in Joan Thirsk (ed.), *Agrarian History of England and Wales*, vol. 3, Cambridge University Press, 1990.

—— *The Neat House Gardens: Early Market Gardening Around London*, Prospect Books, 1998.

—— 'Root Crops and the Feeding of London's Poor in the Late Sixteenth and Early Seventeenth Centuries', in *English Rural Society 1500–1800: Essays in Honour of Joan Thirsk*, ed. John Chartres and David Hey, Cambridge University Press, 1990.

Thomas, Keith, *Man and the Natural World: Changing Attitudes In England, 1500–1800*, Allen Lane, 1983.

Turner, E.S., *Dear Old Blighty*, Michael Joseph, 1980.

Vickery, Roy, *Garlands, Conkers and Mother-Die: British and Irish Plant-Lore*, Continuum, 2010.

Walker, Deanna and Peter Jackson, *A Portrait of Basildon Plotlands: The Enduring Spirit*, Phillimore, 2010.

Walker, Penelope and Eva Crane, 'The History of Beekeeping in English Gardens', *Garden History* 28(2) 2001, pp. 231–61.

Ward, Colin, *Cotters and Squatters: Housing's Hidden History*, Five Leaves, 2009.

Waters, Michael, *The Garden in Victorian Literature*, Scolar Press, 1988.

Watson, Alan, *Price's Village: A Study of Victorian Industrial and Social Experiment*, Price's (Bromborough) Ltd, 1966.

Way, Twigs, *A Nation of Gardeners: How the British Fell in Love with Gardening*, Carlton Publishing, 2010.

—— *Virgins, Weeders and Queens: A History of Women in the Garden*, Sutton, 2006.

Webber, Ronald, 'London Market Gardens', *History Today*, 23, 1973, pp. 871–8.

West, F.H., *Rude Forefathers: The Story of an English Village, 1600–1666*, Bannisdale Press, 1949.

Wheatcroft, Harry, *My Life with Roses*, Odhams Press, 1959.

Wigby, Frederick, *Just a Country Boy*, Geo. R. Reeve, 1976.

Wilkinson, Anne, *The Victorian Gardener: The Growth of Gardening and the Floral World*, Sutton, 2006.

Williams, John, *The Home Fronts: Britain, France and Germany, 1914–1918*, Constable, 1972.

Wright, Walter P., *Window Gardening*, J.M. Dent, 1937.

Wulf, Andrea, *The Brother Gardeners: Botany, Empire and the Birth of an Obsession*, Heinemann, 2008.

**Electronic and Archival Sources**

'Down to Earth: An Oral History of British Horticulture', British Library, C1029.
'Family Life and Work Experience before 1918, 1870–1973', P. Thompson and Trevor Lummis, University of Essex, SN2000, Economic and Social Data Service, http://uk dataservice.ac.uk/use-data/guides/dataset/family-life.aspx.
'Mass Observation Online', www.massobs.org.uk/accessing_material_online.htm.

# List of Illustrations

**Figures**

1 Anthony Gross, 'South London', 1930s. Garden Museum, by kind permission of Mary West.
2 Bird's-eye view of Wilton, Wiltshire, c. 1565. Wiltshire and Swindon Archives (2057/S3).
3 Alfred Watkins, photograph of Upton Mill, 1880s. Herefordshire Libraries (no. 1654).
4 Ralph Agas, detail of *Civitas Londinium* (the 'Copperplate' map), c. 1559. London Metropolitan Archives, City of London / The Bridgeman Art Library.
5 Gardeners, from Thomas Hill's *The Gardeners Labyrinth*, 1577.
6 Gardeners at rest, from the part title of Thomas Hill's *The Gardeners Labyrinth*, 1577.
7 Cheapside Market, London, 1598. By permission of the Folger Shakespeare Library (Ms V.a.318, fol. 15).
8 Alembics and herbs, from William Bullein's *Bulwarke of Defence Against all Sicknesse, Soareness and Woundes*, 1562. Wellcome Library, London.
9 Herbs, from Bullein's *Bulwarke of Defence*, 1562. Wellcome Library, London.
10 Simplers, from John Thomas Smith's *The Cries of London*, 1839. London Metropolitan Archives.
11 Saffron crocuses, from Crispin de Passe's *Hortus Floridus*, 1614. Wellcome Library, London.
12 Coates Farm, Bethnal Green, 1773. © Victoria and Albert Museum, London.
13 Virginian potato, from John Gerard's *Herball of General Historie of Plants*, 1597. Wellcome Library, London.
14 A potato garden, County Roscommon, *Illustrated London News*, 15 May 1880.
15 Title page of *An Account of a Cottage and Garden near Tadcaster*, 1797. © British Library Board (1608/5725).
16 Title page of William Lawson's *New Orchard and Garden*, 1618.
17 Kitchen garden, from John Evelyn's *French Gardiner*, 1658.
18 Arbury Hall, Warwickshire, from Aylesford's *Country Seats*, 1708. Birmingham City Archives, vol. 1/16.
19 Pieter Brueghel the Elder, 'Spring', 1570. © The Trustees of the British Museum.
20 Frontispiece to Thomas Fairchild's *City Gardener*, 1721.
21 'September', from *Twelve Months of Flowers*, 1730. © The Trustees of the British Museum.
22 Carnations, from John Parkinson's *Paradisi in Sole*, 1629. Wellcome Library, London.
23 Carnations, from James Maddock's *Florist's Directory*, 1792. © The British Library Board (968.i.14).
24 Tulip and fuchsias, from Joseph Harrison's *Floricultural Cabinet*, c. 1843. Wellcome Library, London.
25 Spitalfields handloom weaver, from the *Queen*, 21 September 1861.
26 Frontispiece to the *Labourer's Friend Magazine*, 1835. © The British Library Board (PP1090).
27 Gertrude Jekyll, photograph of an old labourer, from *Old West Surrey*, 1904.
28 Gertrude Jekyll, photograph of a cottager in her garden, from *Old West Surrey*, 1904.
29 Elderly couple in their cottage garden, early twentieth century. Rebecca Preston Picture Library.
30 Henry Taunt, photograph of Headington Quarry, 1906. Oxfordshire County Council – Oxfordshire History Centre (HT9815).
31 Nathaniel Buck, detail of a prospect of Preston, Lancashire, 1774. © The British Library Board (Map C.2.e.6).
32 Nathaniel Buck, detail of a prospect of Durham, 1774. © The British Library Board (Map C.2.e.6).
33 & 34 Coram Place, Bloomsbury, from Samuel Hadden Parkes's *Window Gardens for the People*, 1864. © The British Library Board (7055 b.58).
35 George Johann Scharf, sketch of Woolwich, 1825. © The Trustees of the British Museum.

# Acknowledgements

There are many people to thank for their help in producing this book, but first I must express my gratitude to the Marc Fitch Fund for giving me the wherewithal to travel around Britain and to undertake original research. The support of Christopher Catling and his colleagues gave me confidence in my project as well as practical assistance. I would also like to thank Sir Keith Thomas and Dr Stephen Harris in this context.

I have visited many libraries and archives, and would particularly like to express my appreciation to the following: Bob Holman and Christine Dicks at the Weald and Downland Open Air Museum, Sussex; Jonathan Kindleysides at Beamish, County Durham; David Weir at Renfrewshire Local Studies Library in Paisley; Karen at the Herb Garret in Southwark; Trish Hayes at the BBC Written Archives; and Elizabeth Gilbert at the RHS Lindley Library. When I began to seek out pictures, Rebecca Preston was very helpful, Jeremy Smith at the London Metropolitan Archives came to my rescue, and Philip Norman at the Garden History Museum coped brilliantly with my final demands.

Serendipity has played an invaluable role: a lecture given by Sandra Cummings about something completely different led me to the diary of the apprentice gardener at Duff House; a request to the Central Library in Birmingham introduced me to Richard Abbott, Chairman of the Westbourne Road Leisure Gardens; a meeting with Sally O'Halloran led me to the Arbury Hall garden record books; and an even more chance meeting with Anne Langley provided me with the journalistic articles of Joseph Ashby. A reference to a mutual cottage garden society introduced me to Antony Kremer and the records of the Yalding horticultural shows, and a conversation with Sue Adams of the Plotland Museum to Peter Jackson and his gardener grandfather.

I have been struck by the generosity of those experts who shared information, answered questions and provided direction: Jeremy Burchardt, Malcolm Thick, Anne Wilkinson, Pippa Lewis, Imogen Magnus, Hannah Parham, Colin Fletcher and David Marsh. Ann Robey's doctoral thesis introduced me to the Tudor community of market gardeners-cum-potters at Stock in Essex, and Julia Matheson's hugely helpful thesis on the Victorian horticulturalists of east London confirmed that working-class gardeners may have been poor and found books expensive to buy, but were fervent in their determination to cultivate their tiny plots. A whole team helped me with the Durham miners and their gardens, including Hugh Dixon, John and Rosemary Gall, Ian and Barbara Harrison, Jo Tudor, Pauline Moger and Judith Hurst.

Generosity has also been shown by my hosts and hostesses during my research forays: Anne Carter, Bettina and David Harden, Sue and Alan Warner, Ros and Bruce Alexander, Ennis and Liz Brown, and Elizabeth Archibald.

I would also like to thank Sue Lockett at Age Exchange for permission to reproduce some of the interviews with residents of LCC estates in the interwar period, and Economic and Social Data for the reproduction of material from the oral history survey made by Paul Thompson and Trevor Lummis at Essex University. The extracts from Mass Observation diaries are copyright of The Trustees of the Mass Observation Archive, and reproduced with permission of the Curtis Brown Group Ltd on behalf of the Trustees.

Last, but not least, I am grateful to my publisher, Yale University Press: to Robert Baldock for providing me with such a wonderful subject to tackle, and to my editor, Rachael Lonsdale, for coping with a whole array of tasks from wise advice to holding my hand when dealing with daunting technology.

# Index